P9-DDZ-674

The
Process of
Research in
PSYCHOLOGY

3rd Edition

To my family: Jeff, Connor, Daphne, and Cleo

⑤SAGE | 50 YEARS

SAGE was founded in 1965 by Sara Miller McCune to support the dissemination of usable knowledge by publishing innovative and high-quality research and teaching content. Today, we publish more than 850 journals, including those of more than 300 learned societies, more than 800 new books per year, and a growing range of library products including archives, data, case studies, reports, and video. SAGE remains majority-owned by our founder, and after Sara's lifetime will become owned by a charitable trust that secures our continued independence.

Los Angeles | London | New Delhi | Singapore | Washington DC

Dawn M. McBride

Illinois State University

3rd Edition

The
Process of
Research in
PSYCHOLOGY

Los Angeles | London | New Delhi
Singapore | Washington DC

Los Angeles | London | New Delhi
Singapore | Washington DC

FOR INFORMATION:

SAGE Publications, Inc.
2455 Teller Road
Thousand Oaks, California 91320
E-mail: order@sagepub.com

SAGE Publications Ltd.
1 Oliver's Yard
55 City Road
London EC1Y 1SP
United Kingdom

SAGE Publications India Pvt. Ltd.
B 1/I 1 Mohan Cooperative Industrial Area
Mathura Road, New Delhi 110 044
India

SAGE Publications Asia-Pacific Pte. Ltd.
3 Church Street
#10-04 Samsung Hub
Singapore 049483

Acquisitions Editor: Reid Hester
Associate Editor: Nathan Davidson
e-Learning Editor: Lucy Berbeo
Editorial Assistant: Morgan McCardell
Production Editor: Jane Haenel
Copy Editor: Kristin Bergstad
Typesetter: C&M Digitals (P) Ltd.
Proofreader: Tricia Currie-Knight
Indexer: Terri Corry
Cover Designer: Candice Harman
Marketing Manager: Shari Countryman

Copyright © 2016 by SAGE Publications, Inc.

All rights reserved. No part of this book may be reproduced or utilized in any form or by any means, electronic or mechanical, including photocopying, recording, or by any information storage and retrieval system, without permission in writing from the publisher.

All trademarks depicted within this book, including trademarks appearing as part of a screenshot, figure, or other image are included solely for the purpose of illustration and are the property of their respective holders. The use of the trademarks in no way indicates any relationship with, or endorsement by, the holders of said trademarks. SPSS is a registered trademark of International Business Machines Corporation.

Printed in the United States of America

Library of Congress Cataloging-in-Publication Data

McBride, Dawn M.

The process of research in psychology / Dawn M. McBride. — 3rd edition.

pages cm
Includes bibliographical references and index.

ISBN 978-1-4833-4760-8 (pbk. : alk. paper) 1. Psychology—Research—Methodology. 2. Psychology, Experimental. I. Title.

BF76.5.M376 2016
150.72'1—dc23   2015022640

This book is printed on acid-free paper.

SUSTAINABLE FORESTRY INITIATIVE
Certified Chain of Custody
Promoting Sustainable Forestry
www.sfiprogram.org
SFI-01268
SFI label applies to text stock

15 16 17 18 19 10 9 8 7 6 5 4 3 2 1

Brief Contents

Detailed Contents

3 Ethical Guidelines for Psychological Research 43

PART II. THE NUTS AND BOLTS OF RESEARCH METHODS AND ANALYSIS

9 The Nuts and Bolts of Survey Research

10 The Nuts and Bolts of Correlational Studies

Preface

My goal in writing this text is to provide a clearly written, student-friendly introduction to conducting research in psychology. In organizing the text, I have drawn on my experiences over the past 17 years teaching methods courses and the hands-on approach I take with this topic in the classroom. The text covers topics with a step-by-step approach to help students understand the full process of developing, conducting, and presenting a research study. To this end, concepts important for developing research ideas, subject sampling, and ethics are covered in early chapters of the text along with a brief overview of data collection techniques and research designs presented in Chapter 4. More detailed coverage of these topics is included in the Nuts and Bolts chapters, which are designed to be inserted in any order according to instructor preference and given the level of coverage an instructor chooses for the course. In addition, concepts and skills relevant to more than one stage of the research process are covered in multiple contexts. This approach allows students repeated exposure to the topics that are most important in learning research skills and to the topics in a methods course that I have found students have the most difficulty learning. For example, internal validity is covered in multiple chapters and discussed as it relates to different designs such as experiments and correlational studies. Thus, important and difficult concepts are repeated in different scenarios to aid students' learning with spaced repetition of concepts so that knowledge and skills are more easily gained. Using findings from memory research, I present material in ways that will optimize student learning. Most research in memory shows that spaced repetition of information leads to better long-term memory. In this text, I use this approach with different research design types such as in experiments and correlational studies. These designs are covered briefly in an early chapter of the text, as well as in separate chapters near the end of the text to allow instructors flexibility to choose the amount of coverage and timing of coverage for each design type that is right for their course. I also include opportunities for the student to practice recalling the information both within the text of the chapters and in the end-of-chapter quizzes to strengthen their retention of the material.

The text also includes numerous research examples from published studies and activities in each chapter that come from a wide range of psychological settings, giving students a useful overview of real research. Additional exercises with research examples are available online at edge.sagepub.com/mcbride3e.

This book mirrors the steps in the research process and creates logical scaffolding upon which students can build their knowledge. I hope students will find this text to be a readable and practical guide to conducting psychological research.

With J. Cooper Cutting, I have also written *Lab Manual for Psychological Research, Revised Third Edition,* which can serve as a hands-on supplement to this book by providing students with additional practice of research methods skills and activities related to conducting their own research project.

NEW TO THIS EDITION

I have retained the original text's hallmark readability and conciseness, but based on feedback from instructors and students I have updated this edition to more effectively meet their needs in the following ways:

- Moved Ethics material earlier (now Chapter 3) to aid in early focus on ethics
- Divided Experiments coverage into two chapters, one that focuses on simple one-factor experiments and one that focuses on more complex multi-factor experiments and inter-actions to provide more coverage of interactions and factorial designs
- Updated the research examples throughout the text and most of the end-of-chapter Thinking About Research sections
- Added short "Stop and Think" sections throughout the text chapters to help students gauge their understanding of the material as they read and to help them strengthen their retention of the material

SUPPLEMENTAL MATERIALS

Several sets of supplementary materials are also available on the SAGE edge website for both students and instructors. Go to edge.sagepub.com/mcbride3e to access the companion site.

SAGE edge for Students provides a personalized approach to help students accomplish their coursework goals in an easy-to-use learning environment. The open-access study site includes the following:

- A customized online action plan with mobile-friendly practice quizzes, eFlashcards, multimedia resources, and more.
- Answers to all of the *Test Yourself* sections that appear at the end of each chapter. Students are encouraged to use these sections as a tool for checking understanding and comprehension of the material presented in the chapter.
- SPSS* data files for the data examples in Chapter 15, *The Nuts and Bolts of Using Statistics,* with some additional SPSS data examples for each statistical test covered in the chapter.
- Thinking About Research sections from the second edition of *The Process of Research Methods in Psychology* that were replaced in this edition, now available online for instructors and students who wish to continue using the original research examples and to provide additional examples of this useful feature.

SAGE edge for Instructors, a password-protected instructor resource site, supports teaching by making it easy to integrate quality content and create a rich learning environment for students. The following chapter-specific assets are available on the teaching site:

- Course cartridges that provide easy LMS integration.
- PowerPoint presentations that follow the chapter structures with figures from the text.

---

*SPSS is a registered trademark of International Business Machines Corporation (IBM® SPSS® (PASW) 18.0).

- A test bank, written by Dawn McBride, available in Word and Respondus formats.
- An instructor's manual with chapter-specific discussion questions, class assignments, and more.
- Sample syllabi that you can use in setting up your semester or quarter class syllabus around *The Process of Research in Psychology*.
- A Lab Exercise Matrix, which serves as a guide for using this text in conjunction with the *Lab Manual for Psychological Research, Third Edition*, along with an Answer Key to the manual.

Acknowledgments

I'd like to acknowledge a number of important people who helped in many ways in the writing of this text and helped to improve it from its initial drafts. First is Jeff Wagman, who read every chapter, offered feedback, and provided essential support during the writing of the text. In addition, my family, friends, and colleagues provided support and helpful feedback during the writing process. In particular, Cooper Cutting, Jennifer Coane, Nicole Gage, Derek Herrmann, Jef Kahn, John Williams, and Corinne Zimmerman provided useful feedback on individual chapters. Several reviewers also provided valuable suggestions that greatly improved the quality of the text. Lauren Saternus, Bruce Stoffel, Jackie Cavallo, and Geoff Anthony all contributed their time or expertise to the text. The helpful folks at SAGE provided much appreciated support during the production of the current edition: Reid Hester, Lucy Berbeo, Nathan Davidson, and Morgan McCardell. I would also like to thank the Illinois State University College of Arts and Sciences and Psychology Department for providing a sabbatical leave during which much of the writing of the first edition of this text took place, and my thanks to the students at Illinois State University who have taken my PSY 231 course and influenced my teaching of this material. Finally, I wish to thank Jim Nairne, who encouraged me to begin this project and connected me with the folks at SAGE, and Barbara Dosher, who mentored me as I learned how to put the material in this text into practice in my own research. All the individuals named here contributed in important ways to the production of this text and have my sincere thanks and gratitude.

The author and SAGE gratefully acknowledge the contributions of the following reviewers:

Elizabeth Arnott-Hill, Chicago State University

Deborah Baldwin, University of Tennessee

Tamara Bond, Bradley Hospital, Chronobiology and Sleep Research Lab

Birgit Bryant, Le Moyne College

Marcie Desrochers, State University of New York, Brockport

Kimberley Duff, Cerritos College

Carrie E. Hall, Miami University of Ohio

Heather Hill, University of Texas, San Antonio

Erika Hoff, Florida Atlantic University

Stephanie Keller, University of Texas, San Antonio

Katharine Kelly, Carleton University

Brenda Kirby, Le Moyne College

Sarah Kulkofsky, Texas Tech University

Kathryn LaFontana, Sacred Heart University

Sharolyn Lane, North Carolina State University

Charlotte Markey, Rutgers University

Stuart McKelvie, Bishop's University

Joe Morrissey, State University of New York, Binghamton

Carlotta Ocampo, Trinity University

Scott Peterson, Southwest Minnesota State University

Michael Rader, Northern Arizona University

Bob Ryan, Kutztown University

Royce Simpson, Spring Hill College

Harold Stanislaw, California State University, Stanislaus

Pamela Trotter, Virginia State University

John Wallace, Ball State University

Shannon Whitten, University of Central Florida

2nd Edition Reviewers:

Michele C. Baranczyk, Kutztown University

Stephen L. Crites, Jr., University of Texas at El Paso

Iris Firstenberg, University of California, Los Angeles

Ashley E. Maynard, University of Hawai'i

Kim O'Neill, Carleton University

Shawn Powell, Casper College

L. James Smart, Miami University of Ohio

3rd Edition Reviewers:

William Ajayi, Kent State University

Cynthia R. Davis, Judge Baker Children's Center/Harvard Medical School

Amber DeBono, Winston-Salem State University

Bridget V. Dever, Georgia State University/Lehigh University

Sheila J. Foley, Bay Path College

Jamie Hughes, University of Texas of the Permian Basin

Tina L. Jameson, Bridgewater State University

Linda Juang, University of California at Santa Barbara

Maria Maust-Mohl, Manhattan College

April Phillips, Northeastern State University

Christina Sinisi, Charleston Southern University

Maxwell Twum-Asante, Fayetteville State University

About the Author

Dawn M. McBride is a professor of psychology at Illinois State University, where she has taught research methods since 1998. Her research interests include automatic forms of memory, false memory, prospective memory, and forgetting. In addition to research methods, she teaches courses in introductory psychology, cognition and learning, and human memory, and a graduate course in experimental design. She is a recipient of the Illinois State University Teaching Initiative Award and the Illinois State University SPA/Psi Chi Jim Johnson Award for commitment to undergraduate mentorship, involvement, and achievement. Her nonacademic interests include spending time with her family, traveling, watching Philadelphia sports teams (her place of birth), and reading British murder mysteries. She earned her PhD in cognitive psychology from the University of California, Irvine, and her BA from the University of California, Los Angeles.

PART I

Overview of the Research Process From Start to Finish

Psychological Research

The Whys and Hows of the Scientific Method

Consider the following questions as you read Chapter 1

- Why do psychologists use the scientific method?
- How do psychologists use the scientific method?
- What are the canons of the scientific method?
- What is the difference between basic and applied research?
- How do basic and applied research interact to increase our knowledge about behavior?

As an instructor of an introductory psychology course for psychology majors, I ask my first-semester freshman students the question, "What is a psychologist?" At the beginning of the semester, students typically say that a psychologist listens to other people's problems to help them live happier lives. By the end of the semester and their first college course in psychology, these same students will respond that a psychologist studies behavior through research. These students have learned that psychology is a science that investigates behaviors, mental processes, and their causes. That is what this book is about: how psychologists use the scientific method to observe and understand behaviors and mental processes.

The goal of this text is to give you a step-by-step approach to designing research in psychology, from the purpose of research (discussed in this chapter) and the types of questions psychologists ask about behavior, to the methods used by psychologists to observe and understand behavior and, finally, how psychologists describe their findings to others in the field.

WHY PSYCHOLOGISTS CONDUCT RESEARCH

Think about how you know the things you know. How do you know the earth is round? How do you know it is September? How do you know that terrorist threats are increasing around the world? There are probably many ways that you know these things. In some cases, you may know things because you used your intuition or previous knowledge to deduce these facts. For example, you may know from past experience that where you live, in the month of September, days tend to be warm but start to get cooler, especially at night. Therefore, remembering the characteristics of the weather you are experiencing, and knowing you are still living in the same location as past years, you can deduce that the month is September from your knowledge base. You may have first learned that the earth is round from an authority figure like your parents, teachers, or text authors. You may have also observed that the earth is round by viewing photographs of the earth taken from space. You may know that terrorist threats are increasing from authority figures as well (e.g., magazine and newspaper reporters, your country's leaders' statements). These are the primary ways that we learn new facts: intuition, deduction, authority, and observation.

Intuition: relying on common sense as a means of knowing about the world

Deduction: using logical reasoning and current knowledge as a means of knowing about the world

Authority: relying on a knowledgeable person or group as a means of knowing about the world

Observation: relying on what one observes as a means of knowing about the world

Suppose something occurred that caused you to suspect that the authority figures you have learned these facts from are not reliable sources of information. Perhaps they have been caught lying about other facts. You might also consider a situation where you do not have enough previous experience with a topic to use your intuition to determine the information for yourself. In these situations, what is the best way for you to find the facts? The answer is observation. If you had reason to believe, for example, that an increase in terrorist threat is not being represented accurately, you could examine the incidence of terrorist attacks (e.g., from public records) over a period of time to find out if people are representing the true conditions.

This is why psychologists conduct behavioral research; it is the best way to make certain that the information they have about behavior is accurate. By conducting careful and systematic observations, they can be certain that they are getting the most accurate knowledge they can about behavior. This does not mean that every study conducted will yield accurate results. There are many cases where the observations collected by different researchers conflict, but this is an important part of the process. Different ways of observing a behavior may yield different observations and these different observations help us to better understand how behaviors occur. See Table 1.1 for some examples of the different ways of knowing information.

Using Science to Understand and Explain Behavior

Observation is really what sets scientific fields apart from other fields of study. Someone who wants to know about the political situation during the Civil War may read historical documents and use his or her intuition to describe the situation based on these documents. He or she might also read books by experts (authority figures) on the Civil War period or books on important figures who lived during that time. However, historians typically cannot observe the historical event they are studying. Psychologists have an advantage in that the behavior they want to learn about is happening in humans and other animals in the world around them. The best way to learn about it is to just observe it.

Table 1.1   Examples of Ways of Knowing Information

Way of Knowing	Example
Intuition	I want to know if my phone is on. I decide that it is because my phone is always on.
Deduction	I want to know which direction I am facing. The sun is setting to my right, and I know the sun sets in the west so I know that west is the direction where the sun is setting.
Authority	I want to know what my pancreas does. I know that my pancreas produces hormones important for digestion because that is what my high school biology teacher told me.
Observation	I want to know how much sleep on average Americans get per night. I determine this by conducting a survey of Americans to learn that most Americans get an average of 6 to 8 hours of sleep per night (e.g., Moore, 2004).

Some behaviors, such as mental processes, cannot be directly observed (e.g., thoughts or memories). Thus, psychologists have developed techniques for inferring information about mental processes through observation of specific behaviors that are affected by the mental processes. Psychologists then attempt to understand mental processes through observation of these behaviors and the investigation of the factors that influence those behaviors. That is what this book (and the course you are taking) is all about—understanding the methods psychologists use to observe, measure, and study behavior and mental processes (Figure 1.1).

Research is the foundation of the field of psychology. Many people think of the *helping* professions when they think about what psychologists do. This is because most people with a graduate degree in psychology work in these helping (or related) professions (American Psychological Association, 2003). However, to do their jobs well, helping professionals, such as clinicians and counselors, need to understand the findings from research about behavior so that they know what types of treatments and therapies can best help their clients. The research studies conducted in psychology also help clinicians and counselors understand what constitutes "normal" behavior and what behaviors might be considered "abnormal."

Thinking about the field of biology may help you understand how influential research is in the field of psychology. In the biological field, there are researchers who investigate the way our bodies react physically to the world around us (e.g., after being exposed to a virus). This knowledge helps other researchers determine which drugs may be effective in helping us improve these physical reactions (e.g., reduce our symptoms as we fight the virus). Finally, the knowledge gained in biological research helps doctors correctly diagnose and treat their patients (e.g., what symptoms indicate the presence of a particular virus and which drugs are most effective in treating these symptoms). The field of psychology works a lot like the field of biology (although the term *psychologist* applies to both scientists and practitioners in psychology, sometimes causing confusion). Some researchers investigate what causes certain types of behaviors (e.g., distraction in people with attention-deficit/hyperactivity disorder, or ADHD). Other researchers investigate what treatments are effective in reducing these behaviors

Figure 1.1   Psychologists May Study Communication Differences Between Men and Women by Observing Their Behavior While They Talk to Each Other

SOURCE: Copyright by Cartoon Stock, http://www.cartoonstock.com.

(e.g., rewarding someone for staying on task). Finally, some psychologists work with clients to help them deal with problem behaviors. For example, school psychologists work with teachers and parents to develop a reward system for students with ADHD who have difficulty completing work in class because they become easily distracted. The research that investigated the behaviors associated with ADHD and the factors that can reduce those behaviors was necessary for the school psychologist to be able to develop an effective treatment plan for the student.

Stop and Think

(1.1)   Think about some things you know are true about the world. For each of these facts, try to determine the way you know that information (intuition, deduction, authority, or observation).

(1.2)   Suppose you wanted to know about the factors that cause college students to become anxious. Describe how you might learn about these factors using the observation way of knowing.

(1.3)   Explain how the fields of psychology and biology are similar.

HOW PSYCHOLOGISTS USE THE SCIENTIFIC METHOD

Our starting place for conducting research studies in psychology is an understanding of the assumptions that come along with the methods of science. We need to keep some concepts in mind when we use the scientific method to understand behavior. As discussed earlier, scientific study requires observations. It is the primary aspect of the scientific method. However, there are actually four primary facets or *canons* (i.e., rules or principles that guide a field of study) that define the scientific method. They are empiricism, determinism, parsimony, and testability.

Empiricism

The first canon is empiricism and this is just what we discussed above—that the scientific method relies on observations. We have several important people to thank for the empirical nature of science. Galileo, for example, was an influential scientist who used observations to understand the world (Sharratt, 1996). Much of the learning up to Galileo's time (1564–1642) had relied on authority figures, such as Aristotle and Plato, and their ideas about the world to understand how the world worked. However, Galileo (Figure 1.2) and his contemporaries (e.g., Copernicus, Newton) claimed that to learn how the world works, one should observe it. When Galileo wanted to understand how our solar system worked, he *observed* the movement of the planets around the sun through a telescope, instead of simply accepting the authoritative position held by Aristotle that the earth was the center of the solar system and everything revolved around it. He made careful, systematic observations of the phenomena of interest to better understand those phenomena. What we do in psychology is not very different from what Galileo did. If developmental psychologists want to know about bullying behaviors in elementary school children, they go out and carefully observe specific playground behaviors among these children or systematically observe the behaviors of children who have been identified as bullies.

> **Empiricism:** gaining knowledge through systematic observation of the world

Why do psychologists observe behavior? Observing behavior gives researchers a more accurate understanding of the causes of behaviors than other methods of gaining knowledge. Relying on an authority to learn about behavior, for example, greatly limits our understanding of behaviors across large groups of individuals, because not all authority figures are equally reliable and some may have faulty information.

How do we use empiricism to learn about behavior? There are many different ways to do this. We can simply observe people in their normal environment (e.g., children on a playground at recess). We can ask them to complete a survey (e.g., have the subjects respond to items that help us measure their mood). We can ask them to come into a lab and complete a task on a computer (e.g., test their memory for different types of information). Each of these methods allows us to gather empirical measurements of behavior (observation techniques are discussed further in Chapter 4).

One thing to keep in mind is that one observation (either from one individual or from one study) is never enough for us to be sure that the knowledge we are gaining is real. Chance factors can cause us to observe a particular behavior when we observe it only once. Therefore, it is important to replicate our observations, both across multiple individuals within a study and/or across multiple studies using different sets of subjects and, oftentimes, different procedures.

This replication of results assures researchers that the behaviors they observe are not just due to chance and can be used to make more confident conclusions about how behavior works. We will discuss the importance of replication across individuals further in our discussion of sampling in Chapter 6.

Determinism

Another important aspect of the scientific method is the adherence to determinism. This is the concept that phenomena in the world (and human behaviors) occur naturally and have identifiable causes (in extreme cases, determinism can indicate a denial of free will). In other words, by conducting studies to observe behavior, we can understand the factors that *cause* those behaviors to occur. One goal of psychological research is to be able to explain behavior by understanding the causes of different types of behavior. For example, why do people get depressed? What causes false memories? Does sleeplessness cause anxiety? Does anxiety cause sleeplessness? The assumption of determinism in psychological research is that each of these behaviors (depression, false memories, anxiety, and insomnia) has a specific cause or set of causes and we can understand these causes through observation of behavior in different circumstances. For many behaviors studied by psychologists, multiple causes may affect the behaviors. However, not all research is conducted to directly test causes of behavior. In some cases, the behavior first must be described and related factors identified. Although these types of studies do not directly test a cause of behavior, they do contribute to our knowledge of the behavior, which is one step in the scientific process of understanding its causes. We will discuss the different ways we conduct psychological studies and the different goals researchers may have in their studies in Chapter 4.

Figure 1.2   Galileo

SOURCE: https://geolocation.ws/v/W/File:Galilée%20 Offices.jpg/-/en (public domain).

Determinism: the assumption that phenomena have identifiable causes

---

How is determinism used in psychological research? Because the overall goal of research is typically to gain a better understanding of behavior and its causes, researchers design their studies to contribute to this goal through the description of behaviors (e.g., How common is anxiety among college freshmen?), through the identification of factors related to the behaviors (e.g., Are students who are younger in age more anxious their freshmen year in college than older students?), and through the testing of specific causes of the behaviors (e.g., Does technology use in coursework reduce anxiety in college freshmen?).

Parsimony

In the 1997 film *Contact,* Jodie Foster's character, Dr. Ellie Arroway, attempts to explain her beliefs as a scientist to Matthew McConaughey's character, Palmer Joss. She tells him that simpler explanations of the world are preferred over more complex explanations, particularly if there is no scientific evidence that a complex explanation is correct. She calls this concept "Occam's Razor" (after the Franciscan friar who suggested it as an important part of the scientific method). Parsimony is what Arroway is speaking of when she talks about the preference for more simple explanations. In psychological research, we develop explanations of behavior starting with the simplest descriptions and expanding those descriptions only when it becomes clear that the behavior is more complex than our original description of it. In other words, simple explanations are preferred. It is assumed that the simpler explanation is more likely to be correct. More complex explanations should be developed only after simpler explanations have failed to be supported by research studies.

Why is parsimony useful in psychological research? Parsimony helps scientists test their ideas because it is easier to develop a study that might falsify a simple explanation than to develop a study that might falsify a more complex explanation. Falsification is an important part of the research process. This idea is relevant to the concept of testability as well and will be discussed further in the next section.

Testability

The fourth canon of science is testability. The scientific method can only be used to examine ideas that can be tested through observation. The only explanations of behavior that can be tested with the scientific method are those that can be contradicted with observations of behavior. *Why* is falsifiability important? It is important because a test of an explanation of a behavior that allows that explanation to be falsified provides a stronger test of that explanation. If we look only for evidence to support our explanations of behavior, we are likely to find that evidence and hold on to those explanations longer even if they are wrong. Seeking only confirmatory evidence and ignoring contradictory evidence is known as the confirmation bias. If, instead, we design research studies that can show us behaviors inconsistent with our explanations, we are more likely to find evidence against them, if such evidence exists. It takes only a few studies with results inconsistent with an explanation of behavior to falsify it. However, it takes many studies conducted in many different contexts to produce results consistent with an explanation of behavior to support it.

Testability is one of the reasons that many of Sigmund Freud's ideas have not had more influence in current clinical and personality psychology theories—they are difficult to test using the scientific method. For example, Freud proposed that many of our personality traits are a product of a struggle between constructs of our minds (id, ego, and superego) that we do not have full conscious access to (Nairne, 2009). It is difficult to test this theory, because the constructs Freud proposed are difficult to connect to observable behaviors. Thus, it is difficult to systematically observe behaviors in a research study that would contradict the theory. We can, however, answer questions about other types of mental

---

Parsimony: the assumption that the simplest explanation of a phenomenon is most likely to be correct

Testability: the assumption that explanations of behavior can be tested and falsified through observation

Confirmation Bias: seeking only evidence that supports our beliefs and ignoring evidence that contradicts those beliefs

processes that are indicated by observable behaviors. For example, we can test the idea that anxiety causes sleeplessness. We can observe behaviors of sleeplessness in situations where people are placed in anxiety-provoking situations with anxiety verified by self-report. If anxious people are sleeping well, this contradicts our explanation of sleeplessness (i.e., anxiety) and provides us with a good test of our explanation (although this particular result is unlikely to be found). As psychologists using the scientific method, it is important that we ask questions and test explanations about behavior that can be falsified by observations of those behaviors.

How is falsifiability used in psychological science? As indicated above, falsification of explanations of behavior advances psychological science much more than supporting explanations (Platt, 1964). Whenever researchers can show that an accepted explanation is not supported, it changes the direction of investigation in an area of research and moves psychological science forward in gaining new knowledge about behavior. Making predictions about the results they will find in their studies helps researchers contribute to the testability of their observations. With clear predictions made before a study is conducted, researchers can design good tests of their ideas about behavior and help them avoid falling prey to the confirmation bias in believing the results are consistent with their ideas regardless of how they turn out.

The canons of science provide a general "how to" guide for psychologists designing research studies, because they help us conduct good tests of our explanations of the causes of behaviors and further our understanding of why certain behaviors occur. The rest of this text describes more of the details of how psychologists apply these canons in designing and conducting research and walks you through the process of developing research studies of your own.

Stop and Think

(1.4) Which assumption of the scientific method suggests that simple explanations are most likely to be correct? Which assumption of the scientific method suggests that observation is the best means of learning about the world?

(1.5) Explain how confirmation bias could affect your decision making.

(1.6) Explain why replication of results is an important part of the scientific process.

BASIC AND APPLIED RESEARCH

As you begin to consider the types of questions that can be answered in psychological research studies (a topic that will be covered more in Chapter 2), it is important to keep in mind the goals of two major categories of research: basic research and applied research.

The goal of basic research is to understand the most fundamental processes of behavior and how they operate. Research questions in

Basic Research: research conducted with the goal of understanding fundamental processes of phenomena

Applied Research: research conducted with the goal of solving everyday problems

basic research are typically about how a behavior works. How much information can we store in short-term memory? Who exhibits more symptoms of depression: men or women? Do we have implicit stereotypes that affect our social behavior?

Figure 1.3   Both Basic and Applied Research Studies Contribute Important Knowledge About Behavior

SOURCES: © iStockphoto.com/annedde (*left*); © iStockphoto.com/Squaredpixels (*right*).

Applied research is generally focused on answering questions related to solving real-world problems. What type of automated teller machine (ATM) is the easiest to use? Which treatments are best in helping people who are depressed? What type of work environment increases productivity of employees?

Typically, basic research provides fundamental knowledge of how behaviors operate that is useful to researchers conducting applied studies. For example, suppose that a researcher finds that people who report having insomnia also report symptoms of anxiety (a similar result was reported by Morphy, Dunn, Lewis, Boardman, & Croft, 2007). A conclusion from this study might be that anxiety and sleeplessness are related in some way (note that this does not mean that anxiety *causes* sleeplessness, only that they are related). This conclusion represents basic knowledge about the connection between emotional state and sleeplessness or insomnia. Researchers interested in the more applied question of how we help people with sleep problems may use this basic knowledge to test treatments for sleeplessness that focus on reducing anxiety to determine whether the relationship found in the above study is causal or not. The basic research in this case is vital for the development of applied studies that address a real-world problem (i.e., insomnia). Table 1.2 provides some additional examples of basic and applied research studies.

It is also important to remember that the applications of basic research may not be obvious when it is initially conducted. The utility of such research to real-world problems may not be revealed until much later when enough is known about an issue to apply the knowledge gained in the basic research studies. For example, early neuroscientists (e.g., Santiago Ramón y Cajal, as cited in Meyers, 2007) conducted basic research studies to understand how neurons function. The applications of this knowledge were not clear until much later when neuroscientists better understood how this neural functioning affected behavior. For example, we now know that some types of disorders (e.g., depression) are linked to neuron functioning that is abnormal (e.g., higher levels of serotonin than are typical; Barlow & Durand, 2008), and drugs have been developed to alter neuron functioning to help individuals with such disorders. The understanding

Table 1.2   Examples of Basic and Applied Research Studies

Basic research

- Researchers investigated participants' awareness of the effects of handheld objects on their ability to pass through an opening (such as a doorway). Participants held objects while viewing an opening and reported whether they could pass through the opening holding the objects (Wagman & Taylor, 2005).
- To investigate possible spatial-ability differences in male and female infants, a group of 5-month-olds completed a task to determine if they recognized objects that had been rotated from their original orientation (Moore & Johnson, 2008).
- Participants were randomly assigned to mixed-race groups, while their brain activity was recorded to investigate brain areas involved in in-group biases (Van Bavel, Packer, & Cunningham, 2008).

Applied research

- Researchers investigated how to increase volunteers for charitable organizations by presenting participants with information about the organizations to determine what type of information affects whether someone will volunteer (Boezeman & Ellemers, 2008).
- Two experiments were conducted to determine which emotional states contribute to people being willing to accept advice from others (Gino & Schweitzer, 2008).
- From self, peer, and supervisor ratings, researchers determined whether managers with better work-life balances were less likely to advance in their careers (Lyness & Judiesch, 2008).

of the basic knowledge of neural functioning became useful in helping individuals with disorders long after this research had been completed. Thus, basic research is important to conduct, even if an application is not immediately clear.

Because applied research investigates realistic problems, applied researchers are often concerned with the external validity of their studies. This means that they attempt to observe behaviors that can be applied to real-life situations. This is important because these researchers want to be able to apply their results to a problem that generalizes to individuals who are not participants in their study

External Validity: the degree to which the results of a study apply to individuals and realistic behaviors outside the study

(as well as to those individuals who were observed in the study). External validity is also a consideration in basic research but in some cases can be less important than it is in applied research.

In turn, knowledge gained in applied studies can also help basic researchers refine their theories about how behavior works. Suppose in the above example regarding anxiety and insomnia, the applied studies showed that treatments reducing anxiety did not reduce the symptoms of insomnia (similar results were reported by Morin, Belanger, & Fortier-Brochu, 2006). In this case, the basic researchers may use this knowledge to hypothesize that the link between anxiety and insomnia may not be a simple causal relationship and conduct further studies to better understand the causes of insomnia and how it is related to anxiety. In this way, the two types of research, basic and applied, interact with each other, showing that both types of research are critical to the field of psychology.

As you encounter descriptions of psychological research, you may find that not all research fits neatly into basic or applied categories. Some research can both answer fundamental questions about behavior and help solve a realistic problem. It may be better to think about research as primarily basic or applied. In other words, basic and applied descriptors may be end points in a continuum of types of research studies with each research study falling somewhere between these end points.

WHY SHOULD I CARE ABOUT RESEARCH IF I DON'T WANT TO DO RESEARCH IN MY CAREER?

Through my years of teaching psychology methods courses, this question is often asked by students taking courses who don't think they want to conduct research in their careers. Many students majoring in psychology are interested in working as a practitioner of psychology or may be completing a psychology minor that is related to another career they want to pursue (e.g., education, social work, etc.) and do not understand why research methods courses are part of their curriculum. In fact, the majority of individuals who hold a degree in psychology do not conduct research in their jobs. As mentioned earlier, the majority of individuals working in psychological areas are in the helping professions. However, much of what we know about effective treatments and counseling techniques comes from research in these areas. When a new treatment technique is tested, its effectiveness is determined by the research conducted on it. Thus, just as medical doctors do, clinicians and counselors must evaluate the latest research in psychology to determine whether a new treatment is one they should adopt. Knowledge of how research is conducted can help them evaluate this research more effectively to aid their practice. In addition, it is important that we as individuals understand how to interpret the vast amounts of information we take in each day through media sources.

To give you a recent example, in debates about global warming and the seriousness of the problem, many opponents of global warming solutions point out that there is disagreement among scientists about the subject. As voters and consumers, it is important that we understand how research is conducted and that there will almost always be disagreement among researchers in an area, because no single study can fully answer a research question. In order to fully understand what answers the research provides on a question, we must consider the accumulation of data in many research studies. We must also understand that new knowledge is always gained and we must be flexible in our conclusions about an issue when new data suggest a different answer. Remember, there was a time when most humans believed the sun revolved around the earth. Scientific study revealed this idea to be false and over time humans adapted their beliefs to the new knowledge.

Understanding research methods can also help you better interpret research study results that are reported in the media. In almost all cases, media sources present concise and simplified reports of a research study and its results, leaving many questions about the quality of the study still to be answered. When one encounters reports of research in the media, some important questions should come to mind. Who were the research subjects? Was an appropriate sample tested? Was an appropriate method used to investigate the question? Were the results published in a high-quality source where other researchers were able to critique the work? How do the results correspond to past studies on this topic? The topics covered in this text and in your methods course will help you ask and answer these questions as you evaluate the reports you receive in the media to make decisions about your life.

Finally, the new knowledge you gain from your study of research methods may help you decide how to evaluate claims made by others in general. When you see an ad on television for a new miracle diet pill that the ad claims has helped people lose weight in studies, should you buy the pill? When your friends tell you that drinking energy drinks helps you study better and do better on exams, should you follow their advice? Hopefully, one of the things you will consider as you learn about research is to be skeptical about claims that seem too good to be true. As described earlier, a good researcher uses the data to decide what the best thing to do is rather than using unsubstantiated advice from others who just sound knowledgeable about a topic. Examples of how to evaluate claims and research reported in the media are given in the *Using Research* sections found at the end of some of the chapters in the text.

Stop and Think

(1.7) Explain how external validity differs for basic and applied research studies.

(1.8) In what way(s) can knowledge of the scientific process help you in your daily life?

CHAPTER SUMMARY

Reconsider the questions from the beginning of the chapter:

- Why do psychologists use the scientific method? Psychologists use the scientific method because it provides the best way to gain new knowledge about behavior.
- How do psychologists use the scientific method? Psychologists use the scientific method to observe behaviors as they occur in everyday life and in situations researchers are interested in learning about.
- What are the canons of the scientific method? The canons are empiricism, determinism, parsimony, and testability.
- What is the difference between basic and applied research? Basic research is designed to answer fundamental questions about behavior. Applied research is designed to gain solutions to everyday problems.
- How do basic and applied research interact to increase our knowledge about behavior? Basic research advances our understanding of the causes of behavior. In applied research, these explanations are tested in everyday situations to inform researchers about the best solutions for everyday problems. Knowledge gained about these problems in applied research can then inform basic researchers about how explanations of behavior may need to be revised to explain behaviors that occur in everyday life.

THINKING ABOUT RESEARCH

A summary of a research study in psychology is given below. As you read the summary, think about the following questions:

1. What behaviors are the researchers observing?

2. How are the observations being recorded by the researchers?

3. Were the researchers able to identify a cause of behavior from this study?

4. Were the researchers able to answer their research questions with the observations they collected? How?

5. What results would have falsified the explanation of behavior the authors were testing?

6. Do you think this study qualifies as primarily basic or applied research? Why?

7. What are some examples of real-world behaviors that the results of this study might apply to?

Research Study. Strayer, D. L., & Johnston, W. A. (2001). Driven to distraction: Dual-task studies of simulated driving and conversing on a cellular phone. *Psychological Science, 12,* 462–466. [Note: Only Experiment 1 of this study is described.]

Purpose of the Study. The researchers were interested in how use of a cell phone while driving influences driving performance. They describe previous studies that have shown that devices that require one's hands while driving (e.g., the radio, temperature controls, etc.) can reduce driving performance. In this study, they predicted that cell phone use would reduce driving performance. They tested two ideas about how cell phone use could decrease driving: (1) that the hand use of the phone would interfere with driving and (2) that the attention requirements of a phone conversation would interfere with driving.

Method of the Study. Forty-eight undergraduates (half male, half female) participated in the experiment. Each of the students was randomly assigned to one of three cell phone conditions: hand-held phone, hands-free phone, and no phone (radio control only). The participants performed a computer-simulated driving task where they moved the cursor on the screen to match a moving target as closely as possible, using a joystick. Red and green lights flashed periodically during the task and subjects were instructed to press the "brake" button as quickly as possible when the red light flashed. They performed this task on its own in a practice segment and two test segments, with a dual-task segment placed between the two test segments. In the dual-task segment, they were given an additional task that included one of the following to match the conditions listed above: hand-held phone conversation with another person (who was part of the research team) about a current news story, hands-free phone conversation with another person about a current news story, or controlling a radio to listen to a broadcast of their choice. The frequency of missing red lights and the reaction time to hit the "brake" button when a red light appeared were measured and compared for the three phone conditions.

Results of the Study. The two cell phone use conditions did not differ in their results, suggesting that driving performance in response to red lights is similar for hand-held and hands-free phone use. Figure 1.4 shows a graph for each of the measures according to the phone (combined for hand-held and hands-free conditions) and no-phone conditions. The data are shown in each graph separately for driving performance in the driving only segments (single task) and for the phone/radio task while driving (dual task) segment. The graphs show that more red lights were missed and time to press the "brake" button was longer when subjects were talking on the phone (compared with when only driving), but there was no difference in driving performance when subjects listened to the radio while driving and when they just performed the driving task on its own.

Conclusions of the Study. The authors concluded that phone use, regardless of whether it requires one's hands, interferes with driving performance more than just listening to the radio. This suggests that the attention component of phone use is the key factor in the driving performance interference.

Figure 1.4 Driving Performance as Measured by Responses to Red Lights in the Driving Task While Performing the Driving Task on Its Own (Single Task) or While Also Performing the Phone or Radio Task (Dual Task)

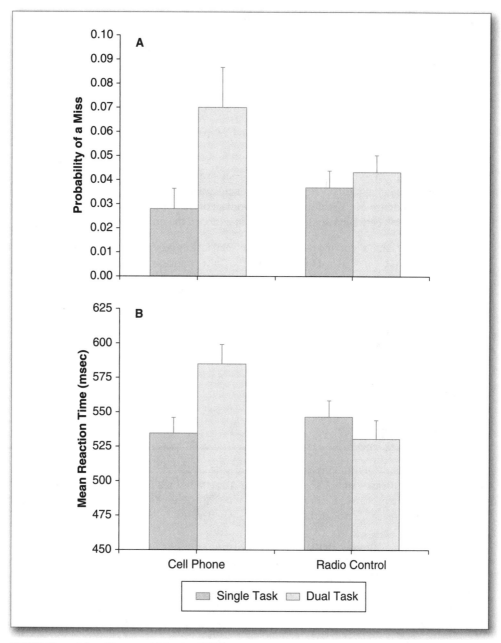

SOURCE: Figure 1 from Strayer and Johnston (2001).

COMMON PITFALLS AND HOW TO AVOID THEM

Problem: Assuming that psychology equals practice in a *helping* profession, ignoring or dismissing the scientific aspect of psychology.

Solution: Understand that science and practice are both important aspects of the field of psychology. In addition, although there is debate about this issue, many psychologists find it important that practitioners of psychology stay abreast of current research findings to ensure that they are using the most effective treatments.

Problem: Positive test bias—designing studies that provide supportive evidence of an explanation of behavior without including the possibility for contradictory evidence.

Solution: Carefully design studies to allow collection of data that can support or contradict explanations of behavior.

Problem: Misinterpretation of causation—study of cause and effect relationships requires manipulation (e.g., randomly assigning participants to different situations), but many people confuse reports of relationships with evidence of causation. In other words, correlation does not equal causation, but many people assume a link between two things means one caused the other.

Solution: Do not assume a reported relationship between factors is evidence that one factor causes another unless the study has been designed in such a way that other noncausal relationships can be ruled out.

Problem: Dismissing basic research—some people dismiss basic research as unimportant because it is not designed to solve a real-world problem.

Solution: View the "big picture" of knowledge in psychology to see how basic research informs applied research by providing fundamental knowledge of behavior that guides research questions and interpretation of results in applied studies. In addition, for a basic research study do not assume that because an application is not immediately evident the study is not valuable. Applications of basic research findings are often not clear until long after the basic research has been conducted.

USING RESEARCH

The number one cause of death in Americans today is heart disease, which can be caused by high cholesterol (Centers for Disease Control and Prevention, 2011). Many ads for fish oil supplements suggest that taking the supplements can reduce the risk of heart disease. Should you start taking fish oil supplements to prevent heart disease? Consider the following as you decide:

- The ads also indicate that the U.S. Food and Drug Administration (FDA) has not evaluated those claims. That means that there may not be research showing benefits for the supplements or the research may have been conducted only by the companies selling the supplements. Why should we be skeptical of research conducted only by the company selling the product?
- A recent study indicated that for men who had suffered a heart attack, taking fish oil supplements was associated with their chance of having another heart attack and/or dying suddenly. Should this result affect your decision to take fish oil supplements? Why or why not?

• The National Institutes for Health (2011) suggest that fish oil is effective for lowering triglycerides, an element of maintaining good cholesterol. What other questions are important to ask before using this information to decide about taking fish oil supplements?

TEST YOURSELF

Match each canon of science below with its correct definition.

1. Determinism
2. Empiricism
3. Testability
4. Parsimony

(a) The scientific method can be used to test descriptions and explanations of the world that can be contradicted by observations.

(b) The scientific method is used to examine phenomena that have an identifiable cause.

(c) An assumption of science is that simpler explanations are more likely than complex explanations to be correct.

(d) Knowledge is gained in science by systematically observing the phenomenon being studied.

5. Freud hypothesized that many of our personality traits are controlled by an unconscious conflict between aspects of ourselves—the id, ego, and superego—that we are not consciously aware of (Nairne, 2009). Using what you know about the scientific method, explain why this hypothesis is difficult to support with observations of behavior.

6. Explain how parsimony is helpful in psychological studies.

7. For each reference listed below, decide whether the study is primarily basic or applied.

(a) Drews, F., Pasupathu, M., & Strayer, D. (2008). Passenger and cell phone conversations in simulated driving. *Journal of Experimental Psychology: Applied, 14,* 392–400.

(b) Roediger, H. L., III, & Geraci, L. (2007). Aging and the misinformation effect: A neuropsychological analysis. *Journal of Experimental Psychology: Learning, Memory, and Cognition, 33,* 321–334.

(c) Bratcher, N. A., Farmer-Dougan, V., Dougan, J. D., Heidenreich, B. A., & Garris, P. A. (2005). The role of dopamine in reinforcement: Changes in reinforcement sensitivity induced by D-sub-1-type, D-sub-2-type, and nonselective dopamine receptor agonists. *Journal of the Experimental Analysis of Behavior, 84,* 371–399.

(d) Declercq, F., Vanheule, S., Markey, S., & Willemsen, J. (2007). Posttraumatic distress in security guards and the various effects of social support. *Journal of Clinical Psychology, 63,* 1239–1246.

(e) West, R. (2007). The influence of strategic monitoring on the neural correlates of prospective memory. *Memory & Cognition, 35,* 1034–1046.

(f) McClernon, C. K., McCauley, M. E., O'Connor, P. E., & Warm, J. S. (2011). Stress training improves performance during a stressful flight. *Human Factors, 53,* 207–218.

(g) Weaver, J. R., & Bosson, J. K. (2011). I feel like I know you: Sharing negative attitudes of others promotes feelings of familiarity. *Personality and Social Psychology Bulletin, 37,* 481–491.

(h) Blanchette, I., & Leese, J. (2011). The effect of negative emotion on deductive reasoning: Examining the contribution of physiological arousal. *Experimental Psychology, 58,* 235–246.

8. I believe that the best way to study for exams is to reread my notes three times from start to finish, because last semester I did that and I got an A on my psychology exam. I believe this despite the fact that I have tried this method before and did not receive an A on an exam. I am falling prey to the _____.

9. The scientific method relies on which way of knowing information about the world?

10. If I am concerned about whether the behavior exhibited in my research study maps on to the everyday behaviors of individuals, I am considering the _____ of my study.

Answers can be found at edge.sagepub/mcbride3e.

STOP AND THINK ANSWERS

(1.1) Answers will vary—should use some of the ways of knowing: intuition, deduction, authority, and observation.

(1.2) Answers will vary, but should include a measure that will indicate anxiety based on some type of observation.

(1.3) Psychology and biology both have research and practice areas, where the two areas inform each other.

(1.4) Parsimony, empiricism

(1.5) Confirmation bias can hinder decision making in keeping you from considering all evidence for something because you are focused on finding evidence to support your own beliefs.

(1.6) Replication is important because each individual study is based on just a small subset of subjects, and chance factors could be causing the results obtained.

(1.7) External validity is typically higher in applied studies than basic studies, because applied studies are designed to solve a real-world problem, whereas basic studies are designed to understand a fundamental process of behavior with control over extraneous factors.

(1.8) Answers will vary, but will be focused on considering evidence for something before deciding on things relevant for your life.

$SAGE edge™

Visit edge.sagepub.com/mcbride3e for the tools you need to sharpen your study skills:

- Web Quizzes
- eFlashcards
- Thinking About Research
- SAGE Journal Articles
- Web and Multimedia Resources

Chapter 2

Hypothesis Development

Where Research Questions Come From

Consider the following questions as you read Chapter 2

- How do researchers develop a research question?
- How do researchers conduct a literature review?
- What are some useful resources for a literature review?
- What will you find in a literature review?
- What are the different types of research articles, and how are they organized?
- How do we use a literature review to make hypotheses?
- What are the different types of hypotheses that a researcher can make?

A few years ago, I was playing the game Catchphrase with some friends. In this game, a handheld device displays a target phrase (e.g., a name or object) while ticking down a timer. The players with the device must provide clues to the target phrase (without saying it) to get their teammates to say the phrase. Meanwhile, the timer ticks faster and faster until it runs out and buzzes. When the time runs out, the player who ends up with the device loses a point for their team. The game moves swiftly, with teammates constantly calling out phrases to guess the target phrase.

After the game ended, we discussed the sequence of guessing of a particularly difficult phrase. Two players, Joel and Renée, claimed to have guessed the phrase, but only one had actually done so. Everyone agreed that Renée had actually guessed the phrase, but Joel claimed to have a clear memory of guessing it. It was determined that although Joel believed that he had guessed the correct phrase, he actually did not accurately recall (had an inaccurate memory) the events of the game. He had a *false memory* in remembering who had actually guessed correctly. Perplexed by his error, Joel suggested that "someone should study this." As a memory researcher, I became interested in this phenomenon and conducted experiments to investigate false memories like the one that Joel had during the game (e.g., Coane & McBride, 2006; McBride, Coane, & Raulerson, 2006). This story illustrates how everyday events such as these can spark psychological research questions (e.g., Why do false memories occur?).

DEVELOPING A RESEARCH QUESTION

Choosing a research question is the first step in the research process (see Figure 2.1). Answering a research question is the researcher's primary motivation for designing and conducting a study. These questions come from many sources. Primarily, they come from what the researcher is interested in learning about. Think about what topics in psychology interest you the most. Can you think of questions about behavior that you would like to have answered? Have you ever asked yourself a "What if . . . " question about a behavior? That is often where research questions begin—from the questions a researcher is interested in. In the situation described above, a research question was sparked by an everyday event (e.g., Why do false memories occur?). In other cases, research questions are developed to solve a real-world problem (e.g., How does the use of a cellular phone affect driving performance?). Finally, explanations of behavior that need to be tested (theories) can guide research questions (e.g., Do negative thoughts cause depression?).

Research questions can be descriptive, such as whether a specific behavior occurs (Are college students anxious?), what the nature of the behavior is (How does anxiety manifest itself in college students?), or whether behaviors occur together (Do college students who smoke also tend to be anxious?). Questions can also be causal—about causes of behavior (What types of events cause college students to become anxious?). Many causal research questions are also designed to test a theory about the cause of a behavior (Is anxiety in college students caused by a lack of confidence in their abilities?) or to compare theories about behavior to see which theory has more support (Is anxiety in college students caused by a lack of confidence in their abilities or a lack of social support?). As described in Chapter 1, research questions can answer fundamental questions about behavior (What are the causes of anxiety among college students?) or questions about how to solve real-world problems (What kinds of student-oriented programs can a college or university initiate that will reduce anxiety in college students?). This is the difference between basic research questions and applied research questions. The type of question a researcher pursues is based on whether the researcher is interested in basic questions about a behavior or applications of the behavior in daily life. However, even though researcher interest is often a starting place for choosing a question to study, researchers should consider how appropriate their question is for both scientific methods and the specific field of study before moving on to designing a study.

One important issue in choosing a research question is whether the question can be answered with the scientific methods described in Chapter 1. Can observations of behavior provide an answer to the question? Some questions that would be difficult to test with

---

Theory: an explanation of behavior that can be tested through research studies

Descriptive Research Question: a research question that asks about the presence of behavior, how frequently it is exhibited, or whether there is a relationship between different behaviors

Causal Research Question: a research question that asks what causes specific behaviors to occur

Figure 2.1   Steps in the Research Process: Choosing a Research Question

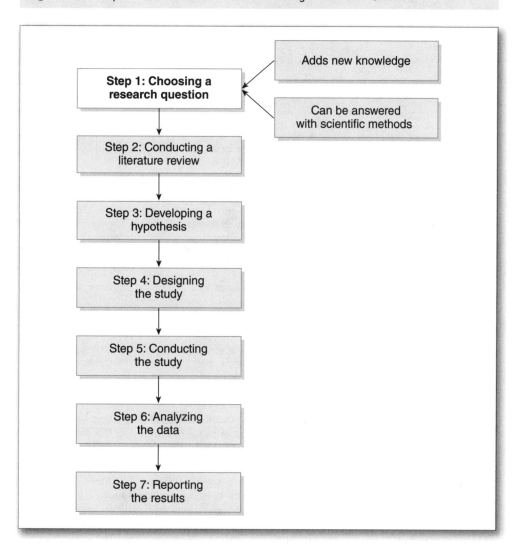

scientific methods are "Does God exist?" and "Was the Iraq War a moral war?" If specific observations of behavior can be made to help answer the question, then it might be an appropriate question for psychological research. Table 2.1 provides some examples of research questions that have been examined in different areas of psychological research to give you some examples of questions that can be answered by observing behavior. In addition, Chapter 4 describes some specific ways to observe behaviors and how they help answer a research question.

Another important consideration in choosing a research question is how much is already known about the question. In other words, what has been learned from previous studies about

Table 2.1   Examples of Research Questions in Different Areas of Psychology

Area of Psychological Research	Examples of Research Questions
Social psychology	How does an authority figure influence behavior? (Milgram, 1963)
	What types of faces are considered attractive? (Corneille, Monin, & Pleyers, 2005)
Cognitive psychology	What types of memory decline as people age? (Lipman & Caplan, 1992)
	How does our knowledge of the world influence our perception? (Ban, Lee, & Yang, 2004)
Industrial-organizational psychology	How does work environment affect job stress? (Pal & Saksvik, 2008)
	How does perception of power in the workplace affect perceptions of sexual harassment? (DeSouza & Fansler, 2003)
Clinical psychology	What types of people benefit most from cognitive behavioral therapy? (Green, Hadjistavropoulos, & Sharpe, 2008)
	What are the causes of schizophrenia? (Compton, Goulding, & Walker, 2007)
Biological psychology	What are the effects of amphetamine on the brain? (Heidenreich, 1993)
	What are the neurological causes of Parkinson's disease? (Olzmann, 2007)

the question? To investigate what is known about a research question from previous studies, a thorough literature review should be conducted. A literature review involves searching research databases or other sources to find relevant research that has been done in an area of the field. By reading about what other researchers have done, the literature review helps a researcher to determine what is already known about a research question, determine what methods have been used to investigate the question, and find information that can help him or her make a prediction about what the answer to the research question will be. (Making predictions will be discussed in detail later.) Conducting a literature review ensures that a new study will add to the knowledge in an area without duplicating what is already known. However, it can take many studies with the same research question before the answer to the research question is supported by enough evidence to allow for confidence in the answer. Thus, replication of results is an important part of the scientific process. Just because a study had been done before on a specific research question does not mean more studies are not needed to fully answer the question. A research question does not need to be wholly original to contribute to psychological science (Figure 2.2).

Literature Review: a process of searching for and reviewing previous studies related to a study being developed to add to the knowledge in an area and make appropriate predictions about the data

Figure 2.2   A Literature Review Can Help a Researcher Determine What Is Already Known About a Topic

SOURCE: Copyright by S. Harris, http://www.sciencecartoonsplus.com/scimags.html.

Stop and Think

(2.1)   For each of the research questions below, identify whether they are descriptive or causal questions:

- How often does operant conditioning occur in daily life?
- Does jet lag affect one's mood?
- Can cognitive training decrease dementia?

(2.2)   Explain why a researcher should conduct a literature review before conducting a study.

HOW TO CONDUCT A LITERATURE REVIEW

There are many sources researchers use to conduct a literature review. Searching through databases helps identify studies relevant to a research question. Databases may also hold references to helpful reviews of research in an area. However, if you want to learn about the most recent studies in an area, databases may not be the best source because these databases typically reference published works, and the publication process can take a year or more from the time an article or a book chapter is written to when it is published and cataloged in the database. Therefore, to conduct the most up-to-date literature review, it can be helpful to attend a psychological conference in an area where researchers often present studies that have not yet been published. More information about the sources for conducting a literature review is provided in the rest of this chapter (Figure 2.3).

PsycINFO

A very useful database for a literature review of psychological research is PsycINFO. PsycINFO is a searchable database that contains records of articles, books, and book chapters written by researchers about research studies in an area of psychology. Although each version may have a

Figure 2.3   Steps in the Research Process: Conducting a Literature Review

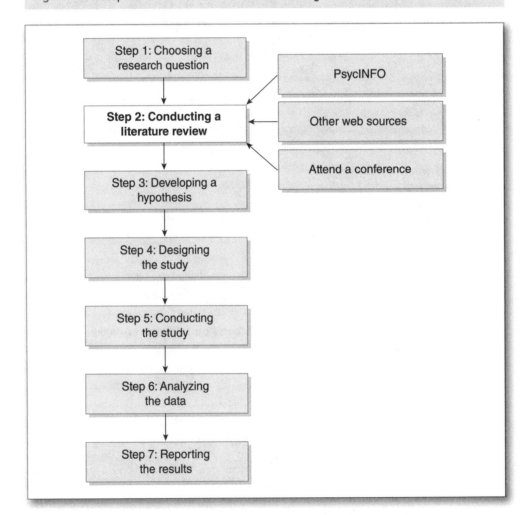

different appearance, all versions of PsycINFO can be searched by topic words, words that appear in the citation information for the article (this includes the title, authors, abstract, and topic words), author names, journal in which the article was published, and so on. In other words, there are many ways to find articles and book chapters about a research question using PsycINFO. Searching by topic words (called key words in PsycINFO) is a good way to start a search for a literature review.

There are two primary ways to search for articles and chapters by key words. One is to map the term to a subject heading. The American Psychological Association (APA) has designated specific subject headings as general topics of study in psychology. Each article or chapter has been coded by the subject headings that best describe the topic of the article. In PsycINFO, you click a box or a button to turn on the mapping to subject headings, and various subject headings appear that correspond to the key words you have typed in (you do not have to know the exact subject heading—PsycINFO searches for subject headings similar to what you type in). You can choose to focus on a specific heading or "auto explode" the search to include all the subheadings that might be contained in the more general heading. You can also choose to search just the key words you entered, which allows PsycINFO to search for articles and chapters that contain those words in the title or abstract. You can also combine searches that focus on different key words.

An example helps explain how this works (you can follow along by trying this out in PsycINFO if it is available at your college or university—if you have a different database available to you, such as PsycARTICLES, you may be able to follow this process, as most databases allow you to search in similar ways—see also http://www.apa.org/pubs/databases/training/search-guides.aspx for information on searching different databases). Suppose that you are interested in conducting a literature search for the relationship between depression and bullying behaviors in children. A good place to start is a key word search in PsycINFO. You can start by typing *depression* into the key word window and mapping it onto the subject headings if such an option is shown. A window such as the one shown in Table 2.2 may appear where you see several different forms of depression listed as well as the general heading of depression. Different versions of PsycINFO have different appearances, so your version may not show the window as it appears in Table 2.2, or it may display different subject terms. Continue to execute a search of articles that have *depression* anywhere in the full reference of the article (e.g., title, abstract, topic words). You should find that PsycINFO yields a large number of records that fit these key words. Depending on which subject terms you choose, different sets of articles are found. Obviously, there are far too many for us to search through one by one, so we need to narrow the search further and include the bullying portion of our topic.

We can conduct a second key word search for *bullying* using the same search procedure described above for depression. This search should find a large number of records as well but fewer records than the search for *depression* as there have been fewer studies conducted on the topic of bullying. Finally, to narrow our search to the specific topic we started with (depression and bullying), we can combine our two searches. Your version of PsycINFO may have a Combine function for this purpose. If not, you can type "1 and 2" into the search window and PsycINFO will combine the searches for you. If you combine your searches, you should find a more reasonable number of records to look at (when I conducted this search in June 2011, I found 192 records, but you may find more if your search terms include more choices or if additional articles have been published on these topics since that time).

Before we look at the results of the search, consider a possible outcome of our *bullying* search. Suppose that *bullying* was not the proper term, and we find no subject headings that

Table 2.2   An Example of a Key Word Search in PsycINFO for *Depression*: Each Version of PsycINFO May Have a Different Appearance

Select	Subject Heading	Auto Explode	Focus
○	Anaclitic depression	○	○
○	Atypical depression	○	○
○	Beck Depression Inventory (BDI)	○	○
○	"Depression (emotion)"	○	○
○	Endogenous depression	○	○
○	Major depression	○	○
	. . .		
○	depression.mp search as key word		

are relevant. One thing we can do to be certain that we get the right subject headings is to use a shorter form of our term and search for truncations. We can do this by shortening our term to *bully* and adding a "*" or "$" to the end of it in the search window. This addition searches for all words that begin with bully and finds any variations that might get us closer to our search objective. Be sure to use the truncation symbols if you are not certain that you have the right term or if you do not find appropriate subject headings with a given search term.

What will the PsycINFO search give you? If you view the results of the search we conducted above, you will see a list of articles (probably the most recently published articles first) that indicates the names of the authors, the title of the article, the type of article (journal article, book chapter, dissertation, etc.), and where and when the article was published. For each article, you can choose to view the *abstract* of the article. The abstract is a short paragraph that summarizes the content of the article (abstracts are discussed in detail later when the structure of journal articles is presented). You can then read through the abstracts of articles that might be relevant to your topic. You might also see a link to the article available online in PDF format or a link to search your library for the journal or book in which the article was published to assist you in locating any articles you find relevant to your literature review. Finally, the reference sections of the articles you find may also lead you to other relevant articles on your topic.

Suppose that you find an article that is especially relevant to your topic and that you would like to know if the same author has published other articles relevant to your topic. You can find articles by a particular author by conducting an author search in PsycINFO (you could also just click on the reference for the article and the author name will appear as a link that will give you a list of all articles in the database by that author). Simply type the author's last name and first initial into PsycINFO and you will see choices, in alphabetical order, that match what you typed. You can choose any that seem relevant (sometimes the same author will be listed in a few different ways—with or without middle initial) and PsycINFO will list the publications by that author. You can also limit key word and author searches by year if you are just interested in the most recent articles that have been published. Finally, articles in a particular psychology journal can be searched in PsycINFO (see below for a description of psychology journals). For more information on PsycINFO searches go to http://www.apa.org/pubs/databases/training/search-guides.aspx for APA guides on how to use PsycINFO.

PubMed and ERIC

Although most articles published in psychology journals can be found in PsycINFO or similar databases, some journals publish articles in other topic areas that overlap with psychology, and you will find them only in other databases. For example, journals that publish research in biological and medical areas can be found by searching the PubMed database. If you are interested in conducting a literature review on topics in biological psychology or about psychological disorders or specific conditions such as autism, you may want to search PubMed in addition to PsycINFO to complete a thorough literature review. Articles in areas related to education can be found in the ERIC (Education Resources Information Center) database. Thus, if you are conducting a literature review on topics such as standardized testing, you may also want to search for articles in ERIC. Like PsycINFO, PubMed and ERIC can be searched by topic, author, and journal with advanced search capabilities that can include year of publication, language of publication, and so on. The search screen will have a different layout, depending on the version of the database that you are viewing, but many versions of both PubMed and ERIC have drop-down menus for choosing a search by these features of an article. A database dealing with more general topics, called Web of Science, is also available for searching for journal articles in different areas of research.

Other Sources

In addition to PsycINFO and similar databases, there are search engines that can be accessed to obtain articles relevant to your topic. The first is a subengine of Google called *Google Scholar*. You can access Google Scholar at http://scholar.google.com/. Google Scholar searches the web for academic journals and books to find articles relevant to a defined topic or specific author. As with PsycINFO, you may not always find links to copies of the articles on Google Scholar, but you may find articles that were not found in a search of PsycINFO. Because Google Scholar will search for articles on many different topics, you are not limited to what is categorized in a particular database (e.g., you can find articles that are in both PsycINFO and PubMed in Google Scholar). With search engines, though, you are also more likely to come across articles that have not been peer reviewed (see below for more discussion of peer review). Articles that have not been peer reviewed are typically less reliable sources of information, because they have not been evaluated by experts in the field who verify the quality of the study.

Other search engines may yield information on a topic, but the veracity of that information may vary. Whereas PsycINFO and Google Scholar yield peer-reviewed articles on a topic, most search engines produce other types of information, such as popular press articles that may or may not report research findings accurately. Thus, a search of a database such as PsycINFO or Google Scholar is a necessary step in any literature review. Simply typing your topic into Google or Wikipedia will not provide an adequate search for a literature review. The sources that are represented in such searches are not reliable enough to use to design a study or to write a research report of a study (more on writing research reports is presented in Chapter 8).

Wikipedia provides unverified information on a topic that is too general for use in a literature review and a normal Google search of the web will not provide a thorough search of the articles on your topic, as many are not freely available on the web. You will also likely find sources that are not reliable with a Google search. In other words, Google web searches and Wikipedia searches are how *not* to do a literature review.

Finally, psychology conferences can provide a way to get the most up-to-date information about research conducted in an area (often so new that it has not been published yet). If you are unable to attend such a conference yourself, you can often search the program of these conferences online to view titles, authors, and abstracts or research studies that will be or have been presented at the conference. Some of the larger conferences that cover many areas of psychology are the American Psychological Association (APA) Convention (typically held in August each year) and the Association for Psychological Science Convention (typically held in May each year). In addition, there are many area-wide psychological association conferences for all areas of psychology (the Midwestern Psychological Association, the Southeastern Psychological Association, the Western Psychological Association, etc.) that can be found on the APA web page (www.apa.org) under News & Events. Many areas of psychology also hold annual conventions (a quick web search will yield some of these meetings and sites).

WHAT YOU FIND IN A LITERATURE REVIEW

As described above, a PsycINFO search (or a search with one of the other sources) provides you with a list of journal articles and/or book chapters that are relevant to your topic. How can these sources help you as you attempt to make a prediction about your research question? As you read the articles, you may find important information for your literature review in different sections of the articles. Before you complete your literature review, becoming familiar with the structure of different types of articles and what type of information you can expect to get from the different sections helps you complete your literature review more easily. Thus, we discuss here the structure of some of the different article types. We begin by describing journal articles.

What Is a Journal Article?

An empirical journal article is written by a researcher (or multiple researchers in many cases) to describe a research study to others who might be interested in knowing what the researcher did (someone like you if you are conducting a literature review on the researcher's topic). The researcher's article may describe a single study (e.g., one experiment) or it may describe multiple studies, all of which relate to the same research question. After the researcher has written the article, the researcher submits it to a psychological journal to attempt to get it published. If the article is published, it will be cataloged in PsycINFO, PsycARTICLES, or another database if the journal topic is primarily outside of psychology. The article is typically sent out to several reviewers who are experts on the general topic of the article (i.e., they are researchers who have done studies on the topic in the past). This is a process known as peer review. These reviewers make

---

Peer Review: a process that takes place prior to publication of an article in many journals where experts make suggestions for improving an article and make a recommendation about whether an article should be published in the journal

recommendations about revisions to the article to improve it and indicate whether or not they feel the journal should publish the article. The editor of the journal uses these reviews to decide if the article can be published in the journal and which revisions are most important. The author of the article then revises the article or may attempt to submit it to a different journal (if the editor has decided not to publish the article in that particular journal). If the revised article is submitted to the same journal, it may then be reviewed again, or it may be accepted by the editor for publication. The review process can be lengthy (sometimes taking many months or even a year), but it is important in verifying the quality of the study before it is published. Thus, articles that are not peer reviewed may describe studies of lower quality. If you conduct only a simple Google search of the web for your literature review, you may find only some of these unpublished articles. After the article is accepted for publication, it can then take a few more months before the article appears in the journal. Consequently, articles are rarely published very soon after they are written, which means that research is already a year or more old before it is published.

Empirical journal articles are considered primary sources for research information because they are written by the researchers who conducted the research and details of the study are provided. Journal articles differ from popular magazine articles. Popular magazine articles often contain short summaries of the study written by an author other than the primary source (i.e., they are secondary sources) and may not provide an accurate account of the study in all cases. Thus, popular magazine articles are considered secondary sources. An accurate and thorough literature review requires review of primary sources (i.e., journal articles).

Many areas of psychology have journals devoted to research on a particular topic, but there are also journals that publish research in all areas of psychology. Table 2.3 provides a list of some general psychology journals, as well as journals that specialize in a particular area. In most cases, you can figure out what types of studies are published in the journal from the title of the journal.

Table 2.3   A List of Psychological Journals by Type of Article Published

General psychology journals—these journals publish studies from various areas of psychology

Psychological Science

Journal of Experimental Psychology: General

Journal of Experimental Psychology: Applied

American Psychologist

Canadian Journal of Experimental Psychology

Experimental Psychology

Personality and social psychology

Journal of Personality and Social Psychology

Journal of Experimental Social Psychology

Personality and Social Psychology Bulletin

Personality and Individual Differences

Journal of Research in Personality

(Continued)

Table 2.3   (Continued)

Cognitive psychology

Journal of Experimental Psychology: Learning, Memory, and Cognition

Journal of Experimental Psychology: Human Perception and Performance

Cognition

Journal of Memory and Language

Memory and Cognition

Applied Cognitive Psychology

Developmental psychology

Journal of Experimental Child Psychology

Child Development

Psychology and Aging

Developmental Psychology

British Journal of Developmental Psychology

Biological psychology

Neuropsychology

Neuropsychologia

Applied Neuropsychology

Review and theoretical journals—these journals publish review articles and/or articles describing new or revised theories about behavior (some of these journals publish empirical studies as well)

Psychological Review

Psychological Bulletin

Psychonomic Bulletin & Review

Developmental Review

Best Practices in School Psychology

Behavioral and Brain Sciences

Structure of an Empirical Journal Article

Journal articles are organized into sections. Each section provides specific information about a study. Each major section of a journal article is described in this section.

---❧---

Abstract: a summary of an article that appears at the beginning of the article and in searchable databases of journal articles

Abstract. As described earlier, an abstract is a short summary of the study that allows readers to decide if the article is relevant to their literature review without their reading the entire article. Abstracts of articles are cataloged in PsycINFO. They are typically 120 to 150 words long (strict APA style allows a maximum of 120 words—see Chapter 8 for more information about APA style) and include a sentence or two summarizing each of the major sections of the article. Thus, the abstract usually includes (a) the general topic of the study, (b) a brief description of the methodology, (c) the major results of the study, and (d) what was learned from the study.

Introduction. As the title implies, the Introduction section of the article introduces the topic, research question, and other relevant information for the study. If an introduction is written well, it should contain the following information:

- Introduction to the general topic of the study (e.g., the bystander effect)
- General problem that the study addresses (e.g., factors that affect the bystander effect)
- Discussion of relevant background studies that inform the researchers about what is known about the problem and how these studies are related to the present study the researchers are describing in their article (e.g., studies that were found in a literature review of factors that affect the bystander effect)
- Justification of the present study (i.e., what aspect of the research question the present study will answer that has not been determined from past studies)
- Brief description of how the current study addresses the relevant aspect of the research question (may include variables that are being studied and a short outline of the method of the study)
- Predictions (i.e., hypotheses) that the researchers made about the outcome of the present study

The introduction should essentially make an argument about what the present study will contribute to knowledge in the selected area of psychology and why the researchers made their hypotheses. If you can identify the points of support for the authors' argument, then you probably have a reasonable understanding of the important information in the introduction.

Introduction: a section of an APA-style article that introduces the topic of the study, reviews relevant background studies, and presents predictions for the data

Method: section of an APA-style article that describes the participants, design, stimuli, apparatus, and procedure used in the study

Method. The purpose of the Method section is to provide enough information about how a study was conducted so that others can evaluate and (if they wish) reproduce the study to see if the results replicate. There are four subsections of the Method: Participants (also called *Subjects* in non-APA-style journals or if animal subjects are used), Design, Materials, and Procedure. The Participants subsection describes who the participants in the study were (How many were there? Were they college students? How many males and females participated? If they were animal subjects, what species were they?). How the participants for the study are obtained is also described (Did they volunteer from a participant pool? Were they recruited on a website? If they were animal subjects, were they bred by the researcher?). The Design subsection describes the design of the study (What were the variables studied? How were they studied?). The Materials subsection describes the various materials and apparatus that were used in the study (If there were stimuli shown to the participants, what were the stimuli? If a survey was used, what kinds of items did it include?).

The Procedure subsection provides a chronological description of what the participants did in the study (What were their tasks? What instructions were they given? How many trials did the participants complete?). Sometimes authors will combine some of these subsections (e.g., Design and Materials) as the information in these sections can overlap. In very short empirical articles (e.g., *Psychological Science* short reports), the subsections will all be combined into one large Method section.

Results: section of an APA-style article that presents a summary of the results and the statistical tests of the predictions

Discussion: section of an APA-style article that compares the results of a study to the predictions and the results of previous studies

---

Results. The Results section provides a summary of the data (often in tables or figures) and information about the statistical tests that were performed to analyze the data. The findings are described in the text with statistical values given as support for the findings described. The specific types of values given depend on the type of tests the researchers conducted. Thus, if the tests themselves are not familiar to you, focus on the description the authors provide of the findings. Were there group differences? Was there a relationship between the behaviors measured? Look back at what the authors expected to find to see if you can match their findings to their predictions.

Discussion. The last section of the article is the Discussion section. The authors go back to their predictions and discuss their findings in reference to their predictions. If the findings support their predictions, the authors indicate what they learned about the research question and perhaps where researchers should go next in this area. If the findings do not support their predictions, they should describe some possible explanations for why they did not support the predictions. A discussion of the results in the context of previous findings is also included. Finally, a summary of what was learned from the study should be included in the Discussion section, including possible limitations of these conclusions based on strengths and weaknesses of the study conducted. Researchers may also suggest a direction for future research in that area.

Multiple Experiment/Study Articles. Many articles that are published include more than one study that addresses the same research question. In this case, the article includes one Introduction that provides the background and motivation for all the studies. It may also include short introductions to each study/experiment to describe the motivation for each study separately. The article also includes separate Method and Results sections for each study. The Results section for each study also includes a short Discussion section for that study, but a General Discussion section concludes the article that then ties all the studies together.

Review Articles and Book Chapters

Most of the articles you come across in a literature review are empirical journal articles as described above. However, a smaller set of articles may be found that fit into the categories of review article or book chapter. The purpose of these articles is to organize and summarize research in a particular area of psychology to give researchers a review of the research to date. Accordingly, these sorts of articles can be very useful in a literature review because they allow a researcher to find a lot of information about a topic in a single article. These reviews also provide a list of references that can be helpful in searching for empirical articles about specific studies that may be important for developing a prediction for the researcher's study. The main difference between review articles and book chapters is where they are published. Some psychological journals are devoted entirely to review articles (see Table 2.3 for some examples). There are also journals that reserve a small portion of space for review articles (e.g., *Psychonomic Bulletin & Review*). Review articles go through the same rigorous review process as that for empirical journal articles (described above). Book chapters are typically published in a book that is either entirely written by a set of authors (i.e., every chapter is written by the authors) or in an edited book where editors compile chapters on a similar topic from multiple authors. The review process for book chapters is variable and may not be as rigorous as that for journal articles.

Stop and Think

(2.3)   What is the purpose of a journal article?

(2.4)   How can reading journal articles aid in a literature review?

(2.5)   In what way(s) can peer review affect the quality of a journal article?

(2.6)   Briefly describe the major sections of a journal article.

USING THE LITERATURE TO MAKE HYPOTHESES

The primary goals of a literature review are to (a) determine what research has been done on a research question to avoid duplicating previous research and (b) review previous findings and theories to allow a hypothesis to be made about the outcome of a study. A hypothesis is the prediction for the findings of the study. For example, a researcher might hypothesize that a relationship exists between two measures of behavior. For a different type of study, a researcher might predict that one group of participants will have average scores that are higher than the average scores of another group. There are two primary types of information that researchers use to make hypotheses from a literature review: theories and previous results. These types of information result in theory-driven hypotheses and data-driven hypotheses. However, regardless of the types of hypotheses that are developed, hypotheses should be stated as specifically as possible in terms of how behaviors and conditions are related (Figure 2.4).

Hypothesis: prediction regarding the results of a research study

Theory-Driven Hypothesis: hypothesis for a study that is based on a theory about the behavior of interest

Data-Driven Hypothesis: hypothesis for a study that is based on the results of previous, related studies

Figure 2.4   Steps in the Research Process: Developing a Hypothesis

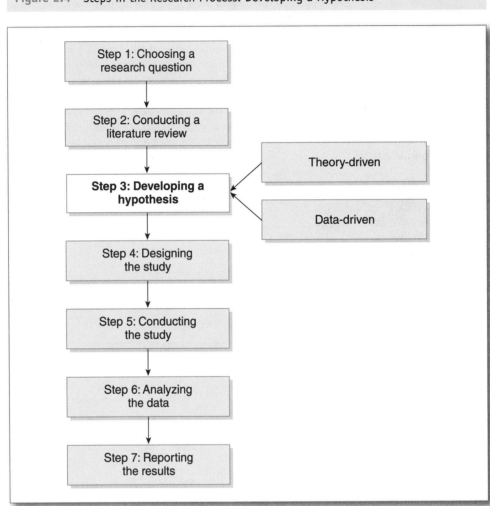

Theory-Driven Hypotheses

Theory-driven hypotheses are made from the predictions of a theory. These are typically made for studies designed to test a theory (i.e., look for data that support or falsify a theory—see the Testability section in Chapter 1). For example, suppose a theory has been proposed that anxiety causes insomnia. A researcher conducting a study to test this theory might then predict that if two groups of participants are compared, one that is put in an anxiety-provoking situation and one that is put in a relaxing situation, the anxious group will report more problems sleeping than the relaxed group. In other words, the researcher might predict that the anxious group, on average, will report fewer hours of sleep per night than the relaxed group. This hypothesis would be consistent with the theory that anxiety causes insomnia and is therefore a theory-driven hypothesis. A theory-driven hypothesis involves deductive reasoning in that a researcher is taking a general statement about behavior (the theory) and making a specific prediction (the hypothesis) about the study from this general statement.

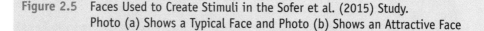

Deductive Reasoning: using general information to make a specific prediction

Another example of a theory-driven hypothesis can be seen in a recent study on face perception. Sofer, Dotsch, Wigboldus, and Todorov (2015, Experiment 1) tested a theory that the typicality of a face is important in social evaluations of a person. From this theory, the researchers hypothesized that more typical faces would be judged as more trustworthy, because trustworthiness is an important part of social interaction. To test the hypothesis, they conducted a study where female students were presented with female faces created from composites of two faces: an attractive female face and a typical female face (see Figure 2.5). Thus, the faces ranged from highly typical to highly attractive depending on the amount of each of the two original faces present in the composite. Subjects in the study were asked to judge both the attractiveness and the trustworthiness of each face. The results were consistent with their hypothesis: The more typical the face was, the higher the ratings of trustworthiness from the participants. The attractiveness ratings supported their prediction as well, as the less typical faces were judged as more attractive and less trustworthy than the more typical faces. Thus, their study supported the hypothesis that typical faces are judged as more trustworthy, which provided support for the theory that the typicality of a face is important in social evaluations.

Figure 2.5 Faces Used to Create Stimuli in the Sofer et al. (2015) Study. Photo (a) Shows a Typical Face and Photo (b) Shows an Attractive Face

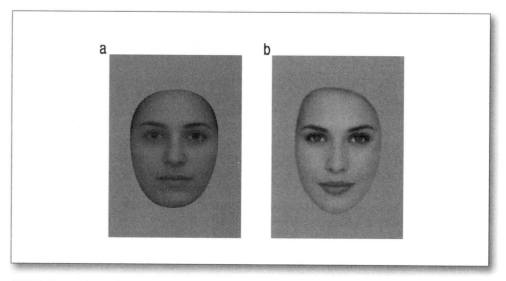

SOURCE: Figure 1 from Sofer et al. (2015).

Now, consider how the process of a literature review can aid you in developing research questions and hypotheses for your studies. Suppose you are interested in the origin of math abilities and you are conducting a literature review on the development of mathematical concepts and you found that a researcher had suggested the theory that understanding of mathematical operations (e.g., addition, subtraction) is innate (something children are born with). Can you think of a way to make a theory-driven hypothesis for a study that tests this theory? Think about how the study would be conducted and then use the theory to make a hypothesis about the outcome of the study (an example of how this could be done is presented after the Test Yourself section at the end of this chapter).

Data-Driven Hypotheses

Another way in which researchers can make hypotheses about a study is by examining the specific findings of previous studies that are similar and generalizing the findings to their study. Hypotheses made in this way are considered data-driven hypotheses because they are made based on data from previous studies. This type of hypothesis involves inductive reasoning because the researcher is taking a specific result from another study and using it to make a more general prediction for the research question of interest. For example, suppose researchers are interested in causes of insomnia. In their literature review, they come across a study that found that people who report high levels of anxiety also report getting less sleep per night. From this study's results, they may conclude that anxiety is related to insomnia and make the hypothesis for their study that a relationship between level of anxiety and number of hours of sleep will be found.

Inductive Reasoning: using specific information to make a more general prediction

A study by Schnall, Benton, and Harvey (2008) provides an example of a hypothesis based on data from previous studies. These researchers were interested in the connection between emotions and moral judgments. Previous studies had shown that when participants were induced to feel disgust (e.g., exposed to a bad smell), they judged an action as more immoral than control participants who did not experience the disgusting situation (Schnall, Haidt, Clore, & Jordan, 2008). Schnall, Benton, and Harvey (2008) hypothesized from these results that, if feelings of cleanliness were induced, the opposite effect should occur: Participants should judge actions less harshly. They conducted two experiments to test this data-driven hypothesis. In both experiments, one group of participants was primed with the concept of cleanliness, while another group was not primed with this concept. Participants then judged the actions of others in a set of moral dilemmas (e.g., keeping money in a found wallet). Results indicated that participants who experienced the concept of cleanliness in the study rated the actions in the dilemmas less harshly than participants who were not primed with the concept. Thus, Schnall et al. supported their data-driven hypothesis with the results of their study.

Descriptive and Causal Hypotheses

Regardless of where the information comes from, hypotheses will either attempt to describe behavior or make a causal prediction about behavior. This distinction maps on to the different types of research questions described above: descriptive and causal. Which type of research question is being asked will also dictate which type of hypothesis is made: a descriptive hypothesis or a causal hypothesis. If researchers are interested in the causes of behavior, they state a prediction about a particular cause of behavior, typically as a difference in groups or conditions that differ based on the cause being studied. For example, if researchers have the research question "Does drinking caffeine on the day of an exam cause an improvement in test performance in college students?" then their hypothesis may be that a group of students who are asked to drink caffeine the day of an

---

Descriptive Hypothesis: a prediction about the results of a study that describes the behavior or the relationship between behaviors

Causal Hypothesis: a prediction about the results of a study that includes the causes of a behavior

---

exam will have higher test performance than a group of students who are asked not to drink caffeine. If, however, the researchers are interested only in whether certain behaviors occur together or wish to document the occurrence of a particular behavior, they are likely to have a descriptive research question and a descriptive hypothesis. For example, if researchers have the research question "Do students who score low on an exam also have high levels of anxiety?" then their hypothesis may be descriptive, such that a relationship between these behaviors is predicted (i.e., when these behaviors are measured together, students with lower test performance will have higher anxiety scores). As you will see in Chapter 4, descriptive and causal hypotheses are also tested with different types of research designs.

One important thing to note about testing hypotheses and theories: We can never *prove* a hypothesis or theory is correct in our research studies. The best we can do is to support or not support the hypothesis/theory from the data we observe in our study. This is due to the limitations of the research process (e.g., we are testing a small sample, our statistical tests are based on the probabilities of outcomes, etc.). We will discuss these limitations throughout the text, but know that they are part of any scientific process. The goal is not to prove facts, but to support predictions and explanations of the phenomena through the observations we make in our studies.

Stop and Think

(2.7)   Explain the difference between a theory-driven and a data-driven hypothesis.

(2.8)   How does a literature review help researchers make hypotheses about their study?

(2.9)   Describe the difference between a theory and a hypothesis.

CHAPTER SUMMARY

Reconsider the questions from the beginning of the chapter:

• How do researchers develop a research question? Research questions come from many sources, including researchers' curiosity. However, research questions should be relevant to current knowledge in the field of study and answerable using scientific methods. A literature review helps researchers know if their research question fulfills these criteria.

- How do researchers conduct a literature review? A literature review is a thorough review of research done in an area of study. Searchable databases, such as PsycINFO and PsycARTICLES, are useful for conducting a literature review. Conducting a Google web search or using Wikipedia is *not* a good way to conduct a literature review.
- What are some useful resources for a literature review? Searchable databases that provide researchers access to empirical and review journal articles include PsycINFO, PsycARTICLES, PubMed, and ERIC. Google Scholar may also be useful in locating some of these sources.
- What will you find in a literature review? A thorough literature review produces journal articles that researchers can use to understand what types of research questions add to knowledge in a field of study, what methods researchers are currently using to answer those research questions, and the theories or past results in an area that help researchers develop hypotheses for their studies.
- What are the different types of research articles and how are they organized? Research articles are either empirical, review, or theoretical. Empirical articles describe a study conducted by the authors of the article. Review articles summarize results and methods from a particular area of study. Theoretical articles discuss new or revised theories of behavior in an area of study.
- How do we use a literature review to make hypotheses? Researchers can use theories described in journal articles to develop hypotheses, or researchers can use past studies' results to develop a hypothesis about the outcome of their study.
- What are the different types of hypotheses that a researcher can make? A researcher can make theory-driven and data-driven hypotheses.

THINKING ABOUT RESEARCH

A summary of a research study in psychology is given below. As you read the summary, think about the following questions:

1. What type of hypothesis (theory-driven or data-driven) did the authors make?

2. Do you think this is a causal or a descriptive hypothesis? How do you know?

3. Can you state the authors' research question? From the description of the study, where did this research question seem to come from?

4. If you were to conduct a literature review for their research question on PsycINFO, how would you proceed? Describe the steps you would take.

5. Write an abstract for the study in your own words that adheres to APA guidelines.

6. If you were to read an APA-style article describing this study (which you can do by finding the reference below), in which section would you find information about the paragraphs the participants read during the study? In which section would the authors report what statistical test they conducted? In which section would they indicate if their hypothesis was supported?

Research Study. Vohs, K. D., & Schooler, J. W. (2008). The value of believing in free will: Encouraging a belief in determinism increases cheating. *Psychological Science, 19,* 49–54.

Purpose of the Study. Vohs and Schooler (2008) were interested in the effects of a belief in determinism (i.e., believing that events in a person's life are not under their control) on moral behaviors. Their interest stemmed from recent findings from neuroscientists that our behaviors may be caused by factors out of our control (e.g., our genes, the functioning of our brain, our environments, etc.). They reported that a previous study (Mueller & Dweck, 1998) had found that children exert less effort in a task if they are told that their failure, in a difficult task they had previously completed, was due to their intelligence level rather than their level of effort. From this finding, Vohs and Schooler reasoned that a belief in determinism may negatively affect behavior. Thus, in their study they predicted that exposure to a deterministic argument would result in more cheating behaviors than if this belief was not promoted.

Method of the Study. Thirty college students participated in the study. Participants were randomly assigned to read one of two paragraphs taken from the same book. One of the paragraphs suggested that scientists believe that free will is an illusion. The other paragraph discussed consciousness and did not mention the topic of free will. All participants were then asked to complete a set of math problems, presented one at a time on a computer screen. Participants were asked to complete each problem. They were also told that the computer program had an error such that the answers to some of the problems may appear with the problem and that they should try to solve the problems on their own (they could make the answer disappear by pressing the space bar when the problem appeared). The researchers measured the number of times the participants pressed the space bar as a measure of cheating behavior (more presses means less cheating).

Results of the Study. The results indicated that the group that read the determinism paragraph pressed the space bar less often (about 5 times during the study) than the control group (about 10 times during the study) that read the consciousness paragraph. Figure 2.6 displays the mean space bar presses for each group.

Conclusions of the Study. From their results, Vohs and Schooler (2008) concluded that a belief in determinism (i.e., free will is an illusion) causes more immoral behavior (e.g., cheating) to be exhibited by individuals.

Figure 2.6 Mean Number of Space Bar Presses for Each Group

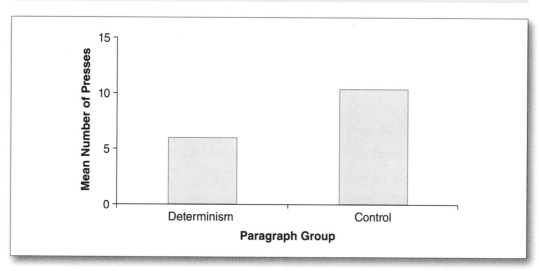

SOURCE: Results from Vohs and Schooler's (2008) study.

COMMON PITFALLS AND HOW TO AVOID THEM

Problem: Using inappropriate search engines—students often use common search engines such as Google, Yahoo, and Wikipedia to search for information about psychological research, which is unreliable and incomplete.

Solution: Use databases such as PsycINFO, PsycARTICLES, ERIC, and PubMed to search for primary source journal articles about psychological research.

Problem: Use of inappropriate sources—sometimes students include sources in literature reviews that are either not peer reviewed or are not the most relevant sources for the research question of interest.

Solution: Check the type of publication for sources (this information is provided by PsycINFO) to ensure that sources included in a literature review are the most appropriate for the research question.

Problem: Hypotheses stated too generally—students often state hypotheses for studies too generally without addressing specific aspects of the study.

Solution: Attempt to state hypotheses as specifically as possible, including variables of the study when appropriate (see Chapter 4 for more information on variables).

Problem: Focus on full-text articles—oftentimes students will focus a literature review too heavily on articles with full text access online, missing important studies for their topic.

Solution: Be sure to conduct a thorough literature review, even if that means walking over to the library to pick up a hard copy of an article that does not have full text available online.

Problem: Reading only the abstract—because the abstract contains a summary of the article, students sometimes believe that they can fully understand the article by reading just the abstract.

Solution: Abstracts are written to provide a short summary of the article and may not fully represent the method or results of a study. Thus, it is important to read through the entire article when conducting a literature review. In addition, you should never cite a source that you have not fully read.

TEST YOURSELF

1. For the information listed below, indicate in which section(s) of a journal article it should be found.

    (a)   Average scores for different groups in a study

    (b)   Number of participants in the study

    (c)   Researchers' hypotheses

    (d)   Comparison of results of present study with results of previous studies

    (e)   Summary of the instructions given to the participants

2. Describe how theory-driven and data-driven hypotheses are made.

3. Explain why the research question below is not an appropriate research question for psychological research:

   Does every human being have a soul?

4. What is a *peer-reviewed journal article*, and how does it differ from an article you might find in a popular magazine?

5. What is a literature review, and why is it an important part of the research process?

6. Explain the differences between a database such as PsycINFO and a search engine such as Google.

7. A short summary of a journal article that appears at the beginning of the article and in databases such as PsycINFO is called a(n) _____.

8. Creating a theory-driven hypothesis involves _____ reasoning.

9. A hypothesis that proposes a link between exercise and memory would be classified as a _____ hypothesis.

10. What is the difference between an empirical journal article and a book chapter or review article?

Answers can be found at edge.sagepub/mcbride3e.

Example of Theory-Driven Hypothesis for Innateness of Mathematical Operations (From the section "Theory-Driven Hypotheses"): To determine that something is innate, you would need to test infants who are very young and have not had enough experience with objects to develop an understanding of mathematical operations such as addition and subtraction. You could then test these infants in a study where you show them objects of a set number that they are habituated to (no longer show interest in), occlude the objects with a screen, and then either add an object or remove an object behind the screen so that the infant can see the object being added or subtracted. You then remove the screen and show them the objects, but show them an incorrect number of objects based on the operation. If the infants show interest (indicating something that was not expected by the infants) in what they are shown, this can be seen as evidence that the infants understand what they should have seen after the operation was performed. Thus, the theory-driven hypothesis for this study is that infants will look longer when the number of objects does not match the operation than when the number of objects does match the operation.

A study like this was performed by Wynn (1992), where her findings indicated that infants as young as 5 months looked longer when the number of objects did not match the operation than when the number of objects shown was correct based on the operation. Wynn argued that these results support the theory that understanding of addition and subtraction operations is innate.

STOP AND THINK ANSWERS

(2.1) (a) descriptive

   (b) causal

   (c) causal

(2.2) A literature review helps researchers determine what the open questions still are in a field, what hypotheses they should make and what methodologies work best in that area.

(2.3) The purpose of a journal article is to report to others what was found in a research study.

(2.4) Reading journal articles can help researchers determine what research questions they should ask, what hypotheses they should make, and what methodologies work best in that area.

(2.5) Peer review is conducted to improve the quality of a journal article by having experts in an area provide suggestions to improve the writing, research, or conclusions of the authors. It also helps determine whether a study gets published or not.

(2.6) Abstract—short summary; Introduction—provides research questions, hypotheses, and relevant background and purpose for a study; Method—provides details of the methodology such that other researchers could replicate the study if they wish; Results—summarizes data collected in a study and provides tests of the hypotheses from the data; Discussion—describes conclusions from the results of the study; References—provides full references for all sources cited in a paper

(2.7) Theory-driven hypotheses are ones based on a theory or description of how behavior works. Data-driven hypotheses are based on results from similar, past studies. Some hypotheses are based on both theory and past results.

(2.8) Reading journal articles can help a researcher make both theory-driven and data-driven hypotheses.

(2.9) A theory is a description of how behavior operates. A hypothesis is a prediction about how results will turn out in a study that might provide a test of a theory.

Visit **edge.sagepub.com/mcbride3e** for the tools you need to sharpen your study skills:

- Web Quizzes
- eFlashcards
- Thinking About Research

- SAGE Journal Articles
- Web and Multimedia Resources

Chapter 3

Ethical Guidelines for Psychological Research

Consider the following questions as you read Chapter 3

- Why do we need ethical guidelines for research?
- How were ethical guidelines for psychological research developed?
- Were the Milgram (1963) and Zimbardo (1974) studies ethical? Why or why not?
- What are the current ethical guidelines for human participants?
- What is an institutional review board (IRB), and what purpose does it serve?
- What are the current ethical guidelines for animal subjects?
- How do ethics influence the way we report research?

In 1932, in Tuskegee, Alabama, the U.S. Public Health Service began a research study to investigate the course of syphilis in the human male. The researchers recruited 399 African American men who had previously contracted syphilis. The men were told that they had "bad blood" and that they could receive free health care by coming to the clinic where they were studied. None of the men were informed that they had syphilis by the researchers, and none of the men were treated for the disease (Brandt, 2000).

At the time the study started, the treatment for syphilis was dangerous and was not always effective. Thus, the researchers of the Tuskegee syphilis study were interested in better understanding the damage that the disease did to the men as it progressed to help determine if treating the disease was better than not treating it. By 1947, however, penicillin had become available as a safe and effective treatment for syphilis. Yet the researchers of the Tuskegee syphilis study did not end their study until 1972 and did not make penicillin available to the participants to treat the disease.

Through this study, the researchers learned a good deal about the progression of the syphilis disease. They learned about the different stages of the disease and about the many symptoms that accompany the disease. These symptoms include rashes, warts on the genitalia, and pus-filled skin pox. Later stages involve damage to the internal organs, including dementia when the brain deteriorates in some patients.

The researchers who were responsible for the Tuskegee syphilis study believed for the most part that their study was ethical (Brandt, 2000). They thought the medical knowledge about syphilis that would be gained was an important contribution to science. In addition, they argued that the men in the study were not being harmed by the study. The participants had already contracted syphilis, so the researchers believed that they were not doing anything to worsen the disease. The participants were also receiving free medical examinations that they could not have afforded on their own. In addition, in 1969, the Centers for Disease Control (CDC) reaffirmed the need for the study after concerns about the ethics of the study were raised. They also won the approval of the American Medical Association (AMA) for the study.

Do you agree with the attitudes of the researchers of the Tuskegee syphilis study that their study was not harmful to the participants in the study? If you answered "no" and believe it was harmful, *why* do you think it was harmful? In what way did the study harm the research participants? The answers to these questions have been a major point of discussion among psychologists and medical researchers for the past 50 years or so, as changes in the way society views the ethics of research on human participants have taken place. These changes in ethical guidelines for research have been motivated in large part by the discussion of studies such as the Tuskegee syphilis study, where it is clear to many people that the researchers did not meet their ethical obligations. In this chapter, we discuss the historical context for ethical guidelines that provides the motivation for current ethical standards, the current guidelines for research with humans and animals, and the role of an institutional review board in the research process. See Figure 3.1 for an indication of the steps in the research process to which ethics are relevant.

HISTORICAL CONTEXT FOR ETHICAL GUIDELINES

Why do we need ethical guidelines for research in psychology? There are several reasons that researchers are held to ethical standards, but the most important one is that researchers are not always able to be objective about the effects of a study on the participants and whether or not a study will be harmful to the participants. In addition to the Tuskegee syphilis study, there are a few other important examples of studies that were conducted to advance scientific knowledge but also may have harmed the research participants in the process. Some particularly heinous examples are the experiments conducted by the Nazis on World War II concentration camp prisoners.

Nuremberg Code

At the end of World War II, the world learned of the atrocities the Nazis had committed during the war. Among their horrific acts were experiments conducted on concentration camp inmates. These experiments were conducted by scientists interested in learning about the limits of the human body and mind. Many of the experiments were designed to better under-stand the conditions soldiers are able to endure in war and involved participant exposure to

Figure 3.1   Steps in the Research Process: Ethical Guidelines

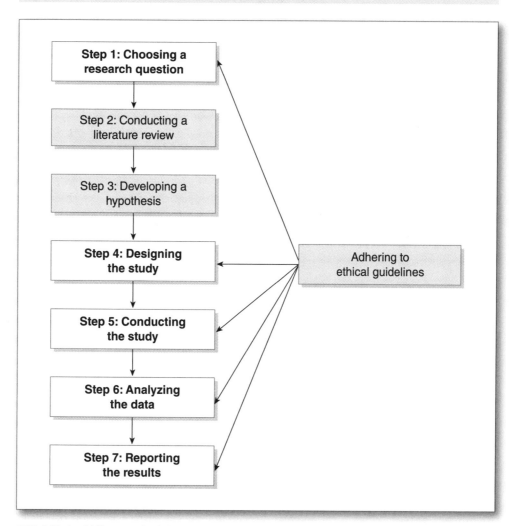

NOTE: Ethical guidelines must be followed at several steps in the research process.

extreme temperatures, infections, and noxious chemicals (Schuler, 1982). The subjects of these experiments were forced to participate as prisoners in the Nazi concentration camps. The details of the experiments became public during the Nuremberg trials held between 1945 and 1949, where Nazi officers and officials were tried for war crimes (see Figure 3.2). The Nuremberg Code was developed by officials involved in the trials (judges, medical experts) as a result of what was learned about the Nazi experiments and was an early attempt

Figure 3.2   Experiments Conducted on Nazi Concentration Camp Prisoners During World War II Prompted the Development of the Nuremberg Code of Ethics

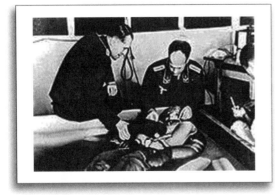

SOURCE: http://wikipedia.org/wiki/File:Dachau_cold_water_immersion.jpg.

to specify ethical standards for any research involving human participants.

The Nuremberg Code focuses on the issues of informed consent, which is informing participants about the study and then gaining their consent for participation, and coercion, where the participants' right to refuse or end participation in a study is taken away. The code also includes other important ethical guidelines that remain part of the current ethical guidelines for psychologists. The Nuremberg Code states the following (Schuler, 1982):

1. Participation in research is voluntary, and participants must be given information about the risks involved in the research (i.e., informed consent and freedom from coercion).

2. The research must contribute to scientific knowledge and be conducted by qualified researchers.

3. The researchers must avoid unnecessary harm, take precautions against risk, ensure that benefits outweigh the risks of the study, and terminate the study if unforeseen harm comes to the participants.

4. The participants have the right to discontinue their participation in the study (i.e., freedom from coercion).

Nuremberg Code: set of ethical guidelines developed for research with human participants based on information gained during the Nuremberg trials after World War II

Informed Consent: consent obtained from participants for participation in research after the participants have been informed about the purpose, procedure, and risks of the research

Coercion: forcing participants to participate in research without their consent

Deception: misleading participants about the purpose or procedures of a research study

APA Code

In 1953, the American Psychological Association (APA) codified its own ethical standards for the field of psychology, including psychological research (Schuler, 1982). (The European Federation of Psychologists' Association, www.efpa.eu, and several other international psychologists' associations have developed similar ethics codes that have been adopted by other countries.) Many of the elements in the APA code overlapped with the main elements of the Nuremberg Code described above. Two additional elements were included in the guidelines for research: (1) the researchers must reduce harm due to deception, which is misleading the participants about the study's purpose or procedures, and (2) the researchers must ensure the confidentiality of participant data. However, the original APA code left the responsibility for overseeing research studies to the researchers, and several researchers used the element of weighing of benefits against risk to justify harmful studies by claiming that the studies were highly beneficial. In some psychological studies, the researchers have argued that the important knowledge gained in the study justified the risk to the participants. Two well-known examples of research conducted by psychologists that many have argued stretched the APA ethical standards are described below: the Milgram (1963) obedience study and the Zimbardo (1973) prison study.

Milgram (1963) Obedience Study. During the Nuremberg trials, several defendants argued that they were not responsible for their wartime actions because their actions were carried out to follow orders of their superiors. This defense led social psychologists to some interesting research questions. How strong is the power of authority? Does a person need to have sadistic tendencies in order to harm another person, or is an order from an authority figure enough to cause someone to commit these actions? Stanley Milgram became interested in these questions and wondered how many people would harm another person simply because an authority figure told them to do so. Milgram designed a study to investigate these research questions that examined the effect of an authority figure on participants' behavior. In his study, participants were recruited to administer a memory task to a second participant. The second participant was actually a confederate in the study. In other words, the second participant was not an actual participant; instead, the confederate acted a part in the study to make the participants believe that he or she was just another participant in the study.

> **Confederate:** a person who is part of a research study but acts as though he or she is not, to deceive the participant about the study's purpose

The confederate was placed behind a screen and attached to electrodes in the participants' presence. After that point, the participants could hear the confederate but could not see him during the study. The participants were then asked to read word pairs to the confederate for a later memory test. The participants administered the memory test by reading a word and asking the confederate to choose from four choices of the word it was paired with in the study list. Each time the confederate answered incorrectly, the participants were instructed to deliver an electric shock to the confederate by pressing a button on a console placed in front of them. For each wrong answer, the participants were told to increase the level of shock delivered. Shocks were not actually delivered to the confederate, but participants were led to believe that they were actually shocking the confederate. The confederate cried out after some of the shocks as if in pain and was silent for the more severe shock levels. The buttons on the participants' console were labeled such that the shocks appeared to increase in intensity with each incorrect answer. If participants resisted (verbally or nonverbally), an experimenter in a white lab coat (i.e., an authority figure) encouraged them to continue, with statements increasing in strength as more resistance was displayed (see Figure 3.3).

At the start of the study, Milgram asked other social psychologists how many participants they thought would continue the experiment to the end, where the shocks were labeled "danger" and "XXX." Most predicted that only the very cruelest participants (less than 2%) would administer all the shocks. However, the results of Milgram's study showed that almost two thirds of the participants administered all the shocks, and none of the participants

Figure 3.3   An Experimenter and Participant in the Milgram (1963) Study

SOURCE: http://thechart.blogs.cnn.com/2011/12/09/my-summer-with-stanley-milgram/.

NOTE: The photograph shows that an experimenter in a lab coat served as the authority figure and encouraged the participants to continue the study if they were hesitant to administer electric shocks to the "learner" confederate.

checked on the confederate without asking permission first. This study showed that the presence of an authority figure greatly influences people's behavior, to the point where people may harm another person when ordered to do so.

Milgram justified his study by arguing that although the participants were deceived in the study, they did not experience long-term harm from the study. The participants were fully debriefed after the study to show that no harm had been done to the confederate. In addition, vital knowledge about human behavior was learned. The social psychologists Milgram had surveyed at the start of the study had been unable to predict the results of the study. Thus, new knowledge was gained about the effect of authority figures on behavior. However, critics of the study argued that the stress of the situation and deception of the participants were too great and were psychologically harmful (Schuler, 1982). Furthermore, it is unclear whether the participants felt they could withdraw from the study if they wished, given that every time they protested the experimenter told them that they were required to continue.

Imagine how you would feel if you were a participant in the Milgram study and learned that you were willing to shock another person simply because a stranger in a lab coat told you to. How would that knowledge change the way you felt about yourself? Milgram countered the criticisms with a survey of the participants after the study that showed that a large majority of them were "glad" or "very glad" to have participated, despite the stressful situation they experienced in the study. Despite Milgram's arguments, an exact replication of the Milgram study is unlikely to meet the ethical standards for research currently in use in psychology (but see Burger, 2009, for a description of a recent modified replication that was also covered on the ABC News show *Primetime*).

Zimbardo (1973) Prison Experiment. Another famous study that was criticized for stretching ethical standards for research was conducted by Phillip Zimbardo at Stanford University in the early 1970s. Zimbardo was interested in how the roles we are given in a society affect our behavior toward others. He created a mock prison in the basement of the psychology building at Stanford and randomly assigned students to play the role of prisoner or guard in the mock prison. He carefully screened the participants to ensure that they were all similar in terms of intelligence and personality characteristics. Thus, the only difference between the prisoner and guard groups was the role they were assigned to play in the prison experiment.

Zimbardo created conditions for the prison that were as realistic as possible. He had the participants assigned as prisoners publicly arrested by campus police before they were placed in the prison. They were given prison clothes to wear and assigned a number. They remained in the prison 24 hours a day for the length of the experiment. Small cells were built in the prison area to confine the prisoners for much of their time. The guards were given uniforms and worked set shifts at the prison, returning to their student lives during their off hours.

Zimbardo had planned for the prison experiment to take place over 2 weeks but stopped the study after only a few days, when he realized that the study had become harmful to the participants. Some of the prisoners had extreme stress reactions and had to be released. Several of the guards became cruel and forced the prisoners to engage in embarrassing behaviors. However, none of the participants ever asked to stop the experiment. Both groups of participants, prisoners and guards, had lost the reality that they were participants in an experiment and were greatly affected by the situation they were placed in during the experiment.

Zimbardo followed ethical guidelines in designing the experiment. He considered alternate ways of studying the effects of the prisoner/guard roles, received informed consent from all the participants before beginning the study, and discussed the purpose of the study and its benefits (a process called debriefing) with the participants after the study ended (Zimbardo, 1973). He also stopped the experiment earlier than planned to avoid further harming the participants (see www.prisonexp.org for more information on this study provided by Zimbardo). However, critics of the study claimed that the participants should not have been placed in such a stressful situation in the study. Furthermore, given the powerful influence of the prison context, it was difficult for those involved in the study to be objective about the effects of the study. Zimbardo himself admitted to being influenced by the context of the prison study, feeling like a prison warden at times when the study was taking place (Reiniger, 2001).

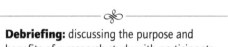

Debriefing: discussing the purpose and benefits of a research study with participants, often done at the end of the study

---

Stop and Think

(3.1) Describe the elements of the Nuremberg Code that are still present in ethical guidelines for researchers.

(3.2) Explain what is involved in obtaining informed consent.

(3.3) Which ethical guidelines (if any) do you think the Milgram and Zimbardo studies may have violated?

CURRENT ETHICAL GUIDELINES FOR HUMAN PARTICIPANTS RESEARCH

Due to the criticism leveled at studies such as Milgram's and Zimbardo's, the APA Ethics Code has been revised several times to ensure that researchers include a thorough debriefing of the participants, more clearly define the conditions under which deception may be used, and include specific guidelines for research with animal subjects. See Table 3.1 for a summary of the current APA Ethics Code guidelines for research.

Table 3.1   Summary of the APA Ethics Code for Research

APA Code	Ethics Issues Addressed
1. Research should be approved by the researcher's IRB, where applicable.	IRB approval
2. Research must include an informed consent process, including the following:	Informed consent
(a) purpose of the research	
(b) expected duration of the participants' participation	
(c) procedures used in the research	
(d) participants' right to decline to participate and withdraw participation at any time and the consequences of withdrawal	
(e) foreseeable risks of the research to the participants	
(f) benefits of the research	
(g) confidentiality rights of the participants	
(h) incentives for participation	
(i) whom to contact for questions or concerns	
3. In addition to (2), if the research involves an experimental treatment, the participants must be informed that it is experimental, how participants will be assigned to groups, the available alternative treatments, and the compensation they will receive for participation.	Informed consent; Reduce harm
4. In addition to (2), if the research involves video or audio recording of the participants, they must be informed ahead of time if it does not compromise the research to do so.	Informed consent; Confidentiality
5. Incentives for participation must be reasonable so as not to be coercive.	Coercion
6. If the research involves deception, the researchers must determine that the deception is necessary and justified and explain any use of deception to participants as soon as possible at the completion of the study. Researchers may not use deception that is expected to cause physical pain or severe distress.	Deception; Reduce harm
7. Thorough debriefing must be given for the study. If it is not possible to give debriefing immediately, researchers must protect against participants' harm.	Reduce harm
8. If researchers become aware of unexpected harm to participants, they must take reasonable measures to reduce harm, including termination of the study if necessary.	Reduce harm

APA Code	Ethics Issues Addressed
9. The following are rules to be remembered while doing research with animals:	Animal research ethics
(a) adhere to federal and local guidelines for care and treatment of animals	
(b) involve trained personnel	
(c) minimize discomfort to the animals	
(d) painful or stressful procedures must be justified and only used when alternative procedures cannot be used	
(e) use anesthesia and prevent infection when surgical procedures are used	
(f) terminate animals quickly with minimal pain if termination is necessary	
10. Researchers must report data accurately and correct errors if they are discovered.	Ethics in reporting research
11. Researchers must properly cite others' ideas and work when reporting research.	Ethics in reporting research
12. Publication credit can be taken only for work the authors have performed, and credit order should be determined according to the contribution of each author.	Ethics in reporting research
13. Data should be shared with other researchers to allow verification of results.	Ethics in reporting research

SOURCE: American Psychological Association (2002).

In addition to the APA Ethics Code, federal ethical guidelines exist that must be adhered to by all institutions that receive public funds. After the Tuskegee syphilis study became public, the U.S. Government formed a committee to discuss appropriate ethical guidelines for medical and psychological research. The committee produced the Belmont Report (National Commission for the Protection of Human Subjects of Biomedical and Behavioral Research, 1979, p. 200), which lists the responsibilities of researchers as they conduct research with human participants and the rights of those participants before, during, and after a study (a copy of the full report can be viewed at www.nihtraining.com/ohsrsite/guidelines/belmont.html). The Belmont Report provides the set of ethical guidelines that researchers in psychology must adhere to. Three major principles described in the report outline the responsibilities of researchers: (1) *respect for persons*, (2) *beneficence*, and (3) *justice*. We will consider how these principles translate to ethical guidelines for psychological research in the section below. Table 3.2 also provides an overview of the application of these principles to psychological research.

Respect for Persons

The first principle of the Belmont Report, respect for persons, refers to the treatment of participants in research studies. Informed consent is an important element of this principle, and it includes informing the participants about the nature of their participation in a study, including

Table 3.2   Applications of the Belmont Report Principles

Principle	Application
Respect for persons	Provide information about the study before it begins (nature of participation, purpose, risks, benefits)
	Obtain voluntary consent from participants after they are informed (i.e., informed consent)
	Give participants opportunity to ask questions
	Inform participants of right to withdraw
Beneficence	Reduce risk of harm to participants
	Potential benefits of the study must outweigh risks
	Inhumane treatment of participants is never justified
Justice	Selection of participants must be fair
	All participant groups must have opportunity to receive benefits of research
	No participant groups may be unfairly selected for harmful research

———— ✠ ————

Consent Form: a form provided to the participants at the beginning of a research study to obtain their consent for the study and to explain the study's purpose and risks, and the participants' rights as participants

what the participants will do in the study, the purpose of the study, any risks associated with the study, benefits of the study, information about alternative treatments (if applicable), and the participants' rights during the study (especially their right to withdraw from the study and their right to ask questions about the study). It is the researchers' responsibility to ensure that the participants have the ability to understand the information they are given during the informed consent process. Often, researchers provide a consent form that includes the information listed above about the study that the participants need to read and sign before their participation in the study. Special protections must be provided for participants who may not have the ability to fully comprehend the information (e.g., children, persons with certain types of disabilities or illnesses). The amount of protection needed depends on the risk of harm to those individuals and the benefits of their participation.

As part of the informed consent process, research participants must volunteer to participate in the study after they are informed about the study as described above. This creates a dilemma for participants who may feel coerced to participate in the study. For example, the rights of participants who are prisoners must be carefully considered to reduce any implied coercion the participants may feel to participate. This may also be an issue when students are included in a research study where the instructor is a researcher for the study. In this case, the instructor needs to make it clear in the informed consent process that the participants have the right to refuse to participate without it affecting their evaluation in the course. If non-English-speaking participants are included, a translated version of the informed consent information must be provided. If children or other individuals with legal guardianship are included as participants, informed consent must be obtained from the legal guardian and assent for their participation must be obtained from the participants. The assent process must explain what the participation will entail and must be explained in a way that the participants can understand what they are being asked to do.

Beneficence

Beneficence refers to the reduction of risk of harm to the participants as compared with the benefit of the study. In other words, a risk-benefit analysis should be conducted to ensure that the benefits of a study outweigh the risks to the participants. In addition, the risk of harm to the participants should be reduced as much as possible when designing a study. There are many types of risks that must be considered in psychological research. Physical risk is an obvious factor but is an issue in only a small number of studies. More common are risks to a participant's psychological health, reputation, and social standing. Some studies can be emotionally upsetting to partici-pants or cause them stress (as the 1963 Milgram study did). If they are asked to consider difficult or traumatic experiences during an interview or in answering a questionnaire, participants can experience psychological harm in a study. In some studies, negative mood induction may occur to compare mood states. Thus, altering participants' moods may also psychologically harm them. Risk to participants' social standing may occur if their confidentiality is breached in dis-seminating a research study. Consequently, it is the researcher's responsibility to maintain the participants' confidentiality at all times during the research process.

Risk-Benefit Analysis: weighing the risks against the benefits of a research study to ensure that the benefits outweigh the risks

Confidentiality: it is the researcher's responsibility to protect the participants' identity and right to privacy (including participant responses) during and after the research study

The risks described above are weighed by the researcher against the benefits of the study to society to ensure that the benefits outweigh the risks. The researcher must determine what the likely benefit of the study is, determine the likely risks to the participants—often by reviewing past studies conducted in a similar manner to determine their impact on the participants—and describe the study in terms of its potential benefits to justify whatever risks might befall the participants during the study. Hence, studies with the potential to gain important knowledge may have increased risks as compared with studies with lesser potential benefits. However, inhumane treatment of participants is never justified, and the researcher is responsible for determining what conditions may be too harmful to participants to include in a study.

Justice

Fair selection of participants is covered by the justice principle. Researchers are responsible for ensuring that all participants have a fair chance of receiving potentially beneficial treatments in research (e.g., treatments for specific mental illnesses or conditions), as well as ensuring that potentially harmful conditions are not exclusively administered to a specific group (as it was when treatment was withheld from African American men with syphilis in the Tuskegee study). Special considerations must be provided for groups that may be easier to manipulate (e.g., individuals with illnesses, low-income individuals). For example, suppose that you are a researcher conducting a study in a geographical area where there are many economically disadvantaged individuals (e.g., a low-income area of a large city, a developing country). As compensation, you plan to offer the participants $50 to participate in your extensive study (e.g., you plan to interview the participants extensively and observe them for a period of time). Compensation of $50 is a reasonable amount to offer U.S. students for this type of participation, so you offer the same amount to the low-income participants in your study. However, $50 has a different value to low-income individuals than it has to middle-class individuals. Even if the participants did not want to participate in your study, they may feel compelled to participate to earn the $50, which may feed their family for a period of time. Thus, many would consider this type of compensation coercive to the low-income participants. These individuals may feel that they have less choice in participating because they are in greater need of the compensation than higher income individuals. These issues must be considered by researchers to ensure that the selection of their participants is fair. If a participant group is to be excluded from a research study, there must be a scientific justification for the exclusion.

An Example

Consider a study by Mihai et al. (2006). These researchers were interested in testing a possible treatment for alcohol abuse. After long-term alcohol abuse, individuals may experience delirium tremens. These episodes can include hallucinations, disorientation, motor tremors, and severe anxiety. In the Mihai et al. study, the treatment involved videotaping patients with severe alcohol dependence while they were experiencing a delirium tremens episode.

Patients who were hospitalized with delirium tremens were recruited for inclusion in the study. To be eligible, patients had to have severe alcohol dependence for at least 3 years and consume a large quantity of alcohol per day. Consent to videotape the patients was obtained from the patients' families. Patients were videotaped during their delirium tremens episode with a psychiatrist and a medical assistant present. Consent for the study was obtained from the patients themselves at some point after videotaping. After the patients had recovered from their delirium tremens episode (9 to 27 days later), they were randomly assigned to one of two groups. One group of patients (the experimental group—see Chapter 4) was shown the videotapes of their episodes with a psychiatrist explaining the symptoms and their connection to the alcohol abuse. The other group (the control group—see Chapter 4) was given the choice to erase their tapes or to view them after 6 months had passed. None of the patients in the second group elected to view their videotapes before a 6-month follow-up occurred.

Each month for 6 months after the beginning of the study, the patients were tested for relapse rates, number of days per week they drank, and number of drinks they had on each day they drank. Results indicated that the group that viewed their videotapes showed lower relapse rates, fewer drinking days per week, and fewer drinks per drinking day than the group that did not view their videotapes. Mihai et al. concluded that the videotape treatment was effective in reducing relapse in patients with alcohol dependency.

Based on the ethical guidelines described above (see Tables 3.1 and 3.2), what are the ethical issues involved in this study? What issues should the researchers consider before they conduct this study? One issue you may consider is the coercion of the participants. Initial consent for the study was obtained from the patients' families instead of from the patients themselves. Consent was not obtained from the patients before videotaping took place. However, the researchers may have felt that the patients were not in a position to provide consent during their delirium tremens episode. Instead, they destroyed the videos of any patient who refused to consent after the videotaping took place. Another issue is the participants' confidentiality. The videotapes of the participants' delirium tremens episodes provide a lasting record of a difficult and potentially defaming episode in the participants' lives (see Broyles, Tate, & Happ, 2008, for a more thorough discussion of ethical issues involved in videotaped records collected in research). Where the videotapes are stored, who is allowed access to them, and what happens to them when the study is concluded are all important issues in this study. In fact, the researchers reported destroying the videotapes at the conclusion of the study (if they had not already been destroyed prior to this time at the participants' request) to protect the confidentiality of the participants. A third issue is the harm the study procedures may bring to the participant and whether the risk of harm out-weighs the benefit of the study. The participants in the study may have experienced stress, anxiety, or other negative emotions while viewing the videotapes of their delirium tremens episodes. However, the researchers may have argued that the possible benefit of finding an effective treatment for alcohol abuse may outweigh the negative emotions experienced by the participants in the study. This is a difficult question best answered by society at large: When is the discomfort of a few worth knowledge that may aid many? We will return to this question later in the discussion of animal research ethics.

INSTITUTIONAL REVIEW BOARDS

In response to reported abuses of research ethics, the U.S. Department of Health and Human Services (DHHS) currently requires that all institutions where research is con-ducted (universities and colleges, hospitals, companies, etc.) have an institutional review board (IRB) to oversee the research conducted

Institutional Review Board (IRB): a committee of knowledgeable individuals who oversee the ethics of research with human participants conducted at an institution

at that site or the research done by researchers affiliated with that institution in order to ensure that ethical guidelines are adhered to in research with human participants (U.S. DHHS, 2005). This policy applies to all institutions that are subject to federal regulations. The IRB reviews all research proposed at the institution to provide a more objective evaluation of the ethics of a study. The IRB is made up of at least five members with backgrounds sufficient to ensure qualified review of the research proposals. If the IRB finds ethical problems with a proposed study, the board can instruct the researcher to revise the study or simply disapprove the study. In other words, before researchers can conduct a study, they must first receive approval from their IRB.

There are three categories of review by IRBs. The category for a study is determined by the amount of risk there is to the participants in the study. Riskier studies require more care-ful and thorough review. The three categories of IRB review are (1) *exempt*, (2) *expedited*, and (3) *full review*.

Exempt Studies

Exempt studies are those studies that have the smallest amount of risk involved. They are typically studies that involve educational or cognitive testing of participants, where there is no physical or psychological risk and little or no risk of loss of social standing if confidentiality were to be breached. Archival studies where the individuals cannot be identified in the data also fall into the exempt category. Research conducted in educational settings for educational purposes also qualifies for exempt review. Studies that fit into this category are typically given a brief review and then assigned exempt status, which means that they are exempt from further review as long as the procedures of the study do not change in the future.

Expedited Studies

The DHHS identified a category of expedited review for studies that involve minimal risk (U.S. DHHS, 2005). Expedited studies need to be reviewed by only one member of the IRB, which speeds the process of review. Expedited studies may involve a small amount of physical or psychological risk. For example, studies involving noninvasive medical procedures (measurements of heart rate, galvanic skin response, brain-wave activity, etc.), collection of blood by normal means (finger stick, venipuncture, etc.), video- or audiotaping of observations, and survey or questionnaire studies with minimal emotional impact are typically given expedited review.

Full-Review Studies

Studies with the highest amount of risk receive full review by the IRB, meaning that each member of the IRB reviews the research proposal. Studies requiring full review are often studies where a special population has a risk of harm, such as studies with particular risk to children or other individuals who may not be capable of providing informed consent on their own. Studies involving invasive medical procedures or high psychological risk, as with deception that could cause stress or questionnaires about behaviors that could cause emotional distress, typically require full IRB review.

Criteria for IRB Approval

IRB members use a set of criteria to evaluate research proposals and ensure that the research meets the ethical guidelines described in the Belmont Report (U.S. DHHS, 2005). The criteria are as follows:

1. The researcher minimizes unnecessary risk to the participants.

2. The risk in the study is justified by the potential benefits of the study.

3. The selection of the participants is fair and appropriate for the study.

4. An informed consent process is included in the study and can be documented by the researcher.

5. The researcher monitors collection of the data to ensure the safety of the participants during the course of the study.

6. The privacy and confidentiality of the participants is protected by the researcher.

7. If a special participant group is included in the study, procedures must be included to protect the rights of these participants.

A research proposal sent to the IRB for review must address each of these elements. Individual IRBs may have their own proposal form that researchers must complete to allow all elements of the criteria to be addressed clearly in the proposal.

Deception and Debriefing

In addition to the criteria listed above, the APA Ethics Code (APA, 2002) requires sufficient justification for studies involving deception and a debriefing process in all studies. If a study makes use of deception, the researcher must justify why the deception is necessary and why alternative procedures that do not use deception cannot be employed. The deception cannot be used if it will cause physical or severe psychological harm. Note, however, that there is a difference between deception and not fully disclosing the study's purpose. In many cases, researchers do not fully disclose the purpose of the study to reduce demand characteristics, where the participants may alter their behavior based on their perception of the study's purpose or hypothesis (see Chapter 4 for more discussion of demand characteristics). For example, in research testing a type of memory called *indirect memory*, researchers may not call the test a memory test, because they do not want the participants to intentionally retrieve studied items during this test. In other words, indirect memory tests involve a form of memory that is used unintentionally. In studies of indirect memory (e.g., Roediger & McDermott, 1993), participants are given a study session and then a task that they are to complete as quickly as possible (e.g., identify a word flashed very quickly on the computer screen) with studied items included in the task. No mention is made of the study episode when the indirect memory test is given, and participants are often told that it is an unrelated task. This is done to discourage participants from using direct memory in the test (i.e., intentionally retrieving studied items). Indirect memory can be measured in these tests by the faster speed with which participants identify words they have studied versus items not studied. This is a procedure commonly used in research I have conducted on indirect memory (e.g., McBride, Coane, & Raulerson, 2006). Describing the indirect memory test in general or alternative terms that reduce demand characteristics is not the same as deceiving the participants, and the IRB will view these situations differently when reviewing a study for approval.

Most studies involve a debriefing process to fully explain the purpose of the study to the participants and the knowledge that the study will contribute, including expected results of the study. However, if the study uses deception, the debriefing process must thoroughly explain the nature of the study and the deception used, including the purpose of the deception in the study. The goal of the debriefing process is to allow the participant to leave the study with a positive attitude toward the research. Thus, if the participant has been stressed during the study, part of the debriefing process should attempt to reduce this stress. If the participant's mood has been negatively altered by the study, an attempt should be made during the debriefing process to restore the participant's mood to the state before the study began. The participants are also provided with an opportunity to gain new

Demand Characteristics: a source of bias that can occur in a study due to participants changing their behavior based on their perception of the study and its purpose

knowledge about their behavior in the debriefing through the explanation of the study provided by the researcher and through questions they may wish to ask about the study.

An Example

Consider the ethics of the following social psychology study: To investigate the effects on physiological behaviors of personal-space invasions, Middlemist, Knowles, and Matter (1976) arranged an interesting field experiment of urination behaviors in college males. They conducted their experiment in a men's restroom at a university, such that men using the restroom were selected as participants, and a field experiment was conducted (see Chapter 5 for a discussion of field experiments). Three urinals in the restroom were arranged so that men entering the restroom were forced to use (1) the end urinal with a confederate next to them (the urinal at the other end had a "being cleaned" sign and a bucket and sponge placed on it), (2) the end urinal with a confederate two urinals away (the middle urinal had the sign), or (c) the end urinal with no confederate nearby (both of the other urinals had signs). An experimenter in a stall measured the time it took for the participant to begin urination and the length of time he urinated. Participants were never informed that they were participating in a research study. The researchers found that the participants in the condition with the confederate at the urinal next to them took longer to begin urination and urinated for a shorter duration than the other two conditions, indicating that invasion of personal space affects physiological behaviors.

Imagine that you are a member of the IRB reviewing this study before it is conducted. What issues might you have with the research? What are the risks to the participants in this study? Do you feel that the risk to the participants outweighed the benefit of the knowledge gained? Why or why not? Can you think of any other way that this study could be designed to reduce the risks to the participants? One issue that you may have noticed is that no informed consent process or debriefing took place because the participants were never informed that they were involved in a research study. The informed consent process would likely have affected the participants' behavior, but a debriefing process may have alleviated any psychological discomfort caused by the presence of the confederate, especially in the condition with a confederate at the next urinal. However, the researchers may have argued that the process of debriefing the participants may have embarrassed them, thus causing harm. These are the sorts of issues that are considered by the members of an IRB as they review research.

Field Experiment: an experiment conducted in the participants' natural environment

---

Stop and Think

(3.4) Explain the purpose of the IRB.

(3.5) New drugs are sometimes tested just in male research participants for side effects. Explain how this practice violates the ethical guideline of justice as described in the Belmont Report.

(3.6) Explain why a debriefing typically takes place at the end of a research study. Include both ethical and reduction of bias purposes.

CURRENT ETHICAL GUIDELINES
FOR NONHUMAN ANIMAL SUBJECTS

Psychological research sometimes involves animal subjects (see Figure 3.4). Animals are often used as subjects when study procedures are considered too invasive or difficult to conduct with human participants. Important knowledge regarding basic human behaviors such as hunger, thirst, sensory processes, and learning has been gained through animal research in psychology (APA, n.d.). However, research with animal subjects represents a minority of the studies conducted in the field of psychology. Only about 7% to 8% of all psychological research involves animal subjects, mostly with bird and rodent subjects (APA, n.d.). Monkeys and other primates are rarely used in psychological research—only about 5% of animal studies in psychology involve primates (APA, n.d.). Yet just as

Figure 3.4   Rats Are a Common Species Used in Psychological Research With Animals

SOURCE: © iStockphoto.com/annedde.

there are guidelines for research with human participants, there are ethical guidelines that researchers must adhere to in research with animal subjects as well. The APA Ethics Code (APA, 2002) defines specific criteria that must be met for animal studies regarding justification of the study, personnel involved in the study, care and housing of the animals in the study, acquisition of the animals for the study, and procedures used in the study.

Justification

According to the APA Ethics Code (APA, 2002), justification of research with animal subjects must include a clear scientific purpose for the study. This ensures that frivolous studies with animals are not conducted. Any study with animal subjects must be shown to contribute important knowledge of behavior (for humans or other animals). The researcher must also justify the use of the specific species chosen for the study and why that species is best suited to the study. In other words, how will a study with that species contribute knowledge about behavior that can be generalized beyond that species? Researchers must consider alternative species and justify why animals are needed for the study. Just as is required in research with human participants, a risk-benefit analysis must be conducted to justify the research. The greater the risk of harm to the subjects, the greater potential benefit there must be from the study.

Personnel

The APA Ethics Code (APA, 2002) indicates that only trained and experienced personnel may be involved in research with animal subjects. Any researcher involved with a study that includes animals must be trained in the procedures to be used in the study to ensure that quality research is conducted and that effects on the animals are properly anticipated. Researchers must also have knowledge about the specific species being studied to properly care for the animals during the course of the study.

Care and Housing of the Animals

Researchers and the institutions where the research is conducted are responsible for the proper care of the animal subjects before, during, and after a research study has been conducted. The Animal Welfare Act (U.S. Department of Agriculture [USDA], 2007) provides specific standards for the acquisition, housing, and care of animals in the United States. Other countries also have specific standards for the care of animals that are used in research. The APA Ethics Code (2002) specifically states that researchers in psychology must meet or exceed the USDA guidelines for care of animals. Animals are to be provided with humane care and housing conditions that keep the animals in good health. Enrichment of the animals' environment is also encouraged.

Acquisition of the Animals

The APA Ethics Code (2002) describes criteria in a separate section of the guidelines to outline how animals used in psychological research may be ethically obtained. Animals not bred by the researcher's institution must be obtained in a manner that follows USDA regulations and local ordinances. Researchers must ensure that proper care of the animals is maintained during transport to the facility. Animals taken from the wild must be obtained humanely and lawfully. Finally, rules regarding the use of endangered or threatened species must be followed.

Procedures Used in the Study

Researchers must treat animals humanely during the study procedures. If the animals are to experience pain in the study, their discomfort should be minimized as much as possible. For example, animals must be given anesthesia during surgical procedures, and these procedures may be conducted only by trained researchers. As described above, a study with greater risk of harm to the animals requires greater justification of the study. Studies that harm animal subjects must have a greater potential to contribute important knowledge. Animals must be monitored during the study to look for unanticipated negative effects. For example, if food is withheld from the animal for a period of time during the study, the researchers must stop the study if the animal's body weight falls below a set criterion to ensure the health of the animal. Finally, animals cannot be released into the wild at the completion of the study, as it may be unsafe for the animals and the ecosystem into which they are released. Researchers conducting field studies in the wild must take care that their observations do not disturb that ecosystem.

Institutional Animal Care and Use Committee

The IRB equivalent for research with nonhuman animal subjects is the Institutional Animal Care and Use Committee (IACUC). Just as IRBs oversee research conducted with human participants, IACUCs oversee research conducted with nonhuman animal subjects at an institution. Thus, IACUC members must have knowledge of the APA Ethics Code regarding animal subjects, federal guidelines regarding the care and treatment of animals, and research procedures used in past studies with animals. Research proposals must be reviewed and approved by the IACUC before research with animals can commence.

For proposals of animal research, justification of the research is a particularly important issue. As discussed above, the risk-benefit analysis of research with human participants is important in justifying the need for the study and any risks the participants may experience as a result of the study. The benefit of the knowledge gained by the study must outweigh the risks to the participants. However, in the case of animal research this can be more difficult to determine. Human participants can refuse consent or choose to withdraw from a study if they wish. They can verbally indicate to the researcher if they are experiencing high levels of stress or pain during the study to alert the researcher to stop the study (as occurred in the 1973 Zimbardo prison study). Animal subjects do not have the choice to participate in a study and cannot terminate their participation during the course of a study. Animals cannot verbalize

Institutional Animal Care and Use Committee (IACUC): committee of knowledgeable individuals that oversees the ethics of research with nonhuman animal subjects at an institution

Figure 3.5   Animals Cannot Provide Informed Consent So Researchers Must Design Studies to Reduce Harm

"IF WE DIDN'T DO SO WELL IN THE EASY BOX, THEY WOULDN'T HAVE GIVEN US THIS COMPLICATED BOX."

SOURCE: Copyright by S. Harris, www.sciencecartoonsplus.com/scimags.html.

their discomfort level to the researcher, and it may be unclear how much discomfort an animal is experiencing during a study. Finally, some studies require that the animal be sacrificed to more closely examine brain tissue or other physiological aspects of the animal. Thus, justification of a study with animal subjects is an extremely important part of the approval process. The issue of when the discomfort of a few can be justified by the great benefit to the many, especially when the few have no choice but to endure the discomfort, is one that is debated by both psychologists and society at large.

An Example

As an example of ethical considerations for animals in psychological studies, consider a study reported by Nuseir, Heidenreich, and Proudfit (1999). Nuseir et al. were interested in the effects of an injection of a drug that reduces pain into a specific area of the brain to determine if that area of the brain is involved in pain perception. Rats were used as subjects in the experiment. Each rat was immobilized, injected with the drug, and then subjected to a heat source applied to its tail. A control group received a saline solution instead of the drug as a comparison group. The time it took for the rat to flick its tail (indicating it felt the heat on its tail) was measured for the rats. If the rat did not flick its tail within 10 seconds, the heat source was terminated to prevent burning of the rat's tail. At the end of the experiment, the rats were anaesthetized and injected with a lethal drug before brain removal. Tissue samples of the rats' brains were then analyzed to map the exact site of drug injection. Results indicated that initially, although the tail-flick response time was slower for the drug group than the saline group, over time their responses were quicker, indicating that the drug had worn off. Thus, the area of the brain the researchers were interested in was involved in pain perception in the rats.

What should the researchers consider in this study to ensure that their study meets ethical guidelines for research with animals? In the description above, did you notice any aspect of the study that shows the researchers included methodological details to make their study more ethical? You may have noticed, for example, that the researchers terminated the heat source after 10 seconds if the rats did not flick their tails to prevent harming them. They also anaesthetized the rats before removing their brains so that they would not feel any pain. In fact, the published report of the study contains a section titled "Animal Care and Use" that indicates that the study adhered to ethical guidelines for animal research and that efforts were made to reduce the rats' suffering (such as the procedures described above). What would need to change in the above study in order to include human participants? Would the same knowledge be gained if human participants were used instead? Why not? Should there be similar ethical guidelines for human and animal subjects? Why or why not? These are ethical issues that psychologists continue to ask themselves as research is designed to answer important societal questions.

ETHICS IN REPORTING RESEARCH

In addition to the treatment of participants/subjects in a study, the APA Ethics Code (2002) contains sections outlining ethical guidelines for reporting research in an ethical manner. Two primary issues are addressed in these sections: (1) errors in the data that are reported (either intended or unintended) and (2) plagiarism. These issues are just as important to the scientific process as the treatment of participants/subjects.

As you have seen, the scientific method relies on reports of previous studies for hypothesis development, designing valid methods, and anticipating negative consequences of study procedures on participants. Thus, the reports of psychological research must be accurate, or future research decreases in validity, an effect that can ripple through the literature for many years. Researchers are ethically bound to report data accurately. If an error is discovered in their report, the researcher must correct the error or make it known if correction is not possible.

Plagiarism: claiming another's work or ideas as one's own

Credit must also be given for information contained in the reports of research. Thus, researchers must properly cite the source of information they give in research reports. This includes both word-for-word reports from others (your university or college likely has a student code of conduct that forbids and punishes this type of plagiarism) and summarized representation of another's ideas. You have seen such citations throughout this text that provide sources for the information it contains. Research reports (even those that may not be published) must always cite sources for theories, methods, data, and other topics an author describes that came from another source. Even oral and poster presentations (see Chapter 8 for more discussion of these types of research reports) must include source information for material that is not original to the reporting author. Figures and pictures taken from previous studies or items posted on the web are included. Regardless of the form, the original source must be credited (e.g., see the source credits with the photos in this text).

When I teach scientific writing to students, my suggestion is to be especially careful when summarizing previous studies. If you are writing directly from the source, inadvertent plagiarism can easily occur. Thus, a better strategy is to first read the original source and take notes in your own words about the important information you want to use in your own writing. Then write using your notes, instead of the original source, to ensure that your writing is in your own summarized words. This strategy can help you avoid accidentally plagiarizing the words of the article's authors.

Violation of either of the above ethical guidelines (data errors or plagiarism) can seriously damage one's career. There have been several famous examples of such violations that damaged the standing of researchers in the scientific community. One such recent example was reported in 2011, when it was discovered that Diederik Stapel, a Dutch social psychologist, had falsified data in many of his published papers (Shea, 2011). All of his research has fallen under suspicion, including two particularly publicized findings: a paper published in *Psychological Science* titled "Power Increases Infidelity Among Men and Women" and a paper published in *Science* titled "Coping With Chaos: How Disordered Contexts Promote Stereotyping and Discrimination." The *Science* paper has been retracted (along with many of his other papers) and Stapel was criminally prosecuted. One reason such cases occur is the pressure on researchers to publish surprising and statistically significant (see Chapter 7) results. Often, there is a bias in publishing research studies for such findings (i.e., findings that are not surprising and/or and not statistically significant are less likely to be published), resulting in pressure on researchers to produce data that fit this description. However, this also creates another problem that you should be aware of: There may be many studies that have failed to find an effect that have never been published, meaning most researchers are unaware of them. This is also why it is important to replicate research findings that are new and surprising. If they can't be replicated, then it's possible they were due to chance factors in the studies that first reported them. This is how the falsified data are typically discovered—they cannot be replicated by other researchers.

From this example, you can see that false data reports can have very serious consequences, not just to the individual who falsified the data, but to the field of psychology as well in leading researchers in pursuit of findings that are not real as they attempt to replicate and expand on the falsified data. Researchers have an ethical duty to accurately report their methods and data in their research reports and to alert others to errors in their work if they are found (e.g., by having an erratum correcting a research article if the researcher finds an error after it is published). You are probably more likely, however, to be concerned about the second issue discussed here: plagiarism. Plagiarism can be intentional or unintentional; however, both are serious ethical violations as they both involve taking credit for someone's work or ideas. Students should exercise caution when writing about psychological research in their own reports to ensure that their own words are used and that information is properly cited. If you have any doubts about your own writing, it is always a good idea to check with your instructor to make sure your writing does not contain plagiarism.

Stop and Think

(3.7)   In what way(s) do ethical guidelines for research with humans and non-human animals differ?

(3.8)   Describe some ethical issues in reporting research.

CHAPTER SUMMARY

Reconsider the questions from the beginning of the chapter:

- Why do we need ethical guidelines for research? As described in this chapter, ethical guidelines are needed to define the appropriate treatment of subjects in psychological research.
- How were ethical guidelines for psychological research developed? Current ethical guidelines were derived over the years as the original Nuremberg Code was revised and adopted by the American Psychological Association (APA) and the U.S. Government in the Belmont Report.
- Were the Milgram (1963) and Zimbardo (1974) studies ethical? Why or why not? Due to the level of deception and stress caused by both the situation and the participants' experience in the Milgram study, and the level of stress experienced by the "prisoners" in the Zimbardo study, many researchers believe that these studies were not ethical.
- What are the current ethical guidelines for human participants? Current ethical guidelines for psychological research are summarized in Table 3.1.
- What is an institutional review board (IRB), and what purpose does it serve? The IRB oversees research conducted at each institution. In cases where the researchers may not be the most objective judge of the ethics of their study, the IRB provides a more objective review of the ethics of psychological research.
- What are the current ethical guidelines for animal subjects? Current ethical guidelines for animal subjects are also summarized in Table 3.1.
- How do ethics influence the way we report research? Ethical guidelines for reporting research necessitate accurate reports of results and proper citation of sources.

A summary of a research study in psychology is given below. As you read the summary, think about the following questions:

1. What are some ethical issues for this study regarding informed consent?

2. How would the consent process differ for the children and the chimpanzees/orangutans?

3. What steps should the researchers take to protect the confidentiality of the child participants in this study?

4. Ethically, what role is appropriate for parents/guardians to play in the participation of children in research studies? What role do you think they played in this particular study?

5. What are the possible risks to the animal subjects in this study? How about the risks for the children participants?

6. If you were an IRB member reviewing this study, what information would you ask the researchers to provide to allow you to determine the risk-benefit analysis for this study?

Research Study. Haun, D. B. M., Rekers, Y., & Tomasello, M. (2014). Children conform to the behavior of peers; Other great apes stick with what they know. *Psychological Science, 25,* 2160–2167. doi:10.1177/0956797614553235

Purpose of the Study. The study examined social learning behaviors in order to compare human social learning to social learning in nonhuman primates. Past studies (e.g., Laland & Galef, 2009) have shown that, similar to humans, many different animal species show evidence of social groups with behavioral differences. In addition, both humans and animals have shown evidence of social learning. In the current study, the researchers were interested in examining whether nonhuman primates show the same level of conformity to peer behavior that humans show. Study 1 was conducted to examine how often human children, chimpanzees, and orangutans change their current problem-solving strategy after watching peers perform a different strategy for the problem. Study 2 was conducted to examine whether the presence and number of peers during the strategy test phase would influence the children's strategy switching behavior.

Method of the Study. In Study 1, 18 children, 12 chimpanzees, and 12 orangutans participated. In Study 2, 72 children participated. Participants completed a task of dropping balls into one of three slots in boxes presented to them on a display (see Figure 3.6 for a diagram of the task). One of the boxes dispensed a reward (chocolate for children, peanuts for animals) when a ball was dropped into its top slot. Participants completed the task until they received the reward on 8 of 10 consecutive trials. In Study 1, they then watched three familiar peers (one at a time) perform the task for two trials each using a different box than the one the participant had used in the initial phase. Peers were rewarded on both of their trials. Participants were then tested on the task again while the peers watched. They performed three trials in the test phase. Each of the three trials was recorded as a "stay" response (they used their same box from the initial phase), a "switch" response (they used the box they had seen their peers use), or an "other" response (they used a different box from both the initial phase and their peers). In Study 2, this procedure was followed for the new children participants, but half of the participants had only

Figure 3.6   Task Performed by Participants in the Haun et al. (2014) Study

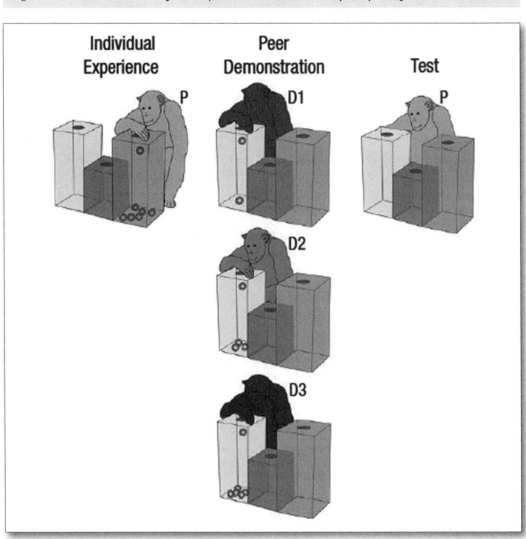

SOURCE: Figure 1 from Haun, Rekers, & Tomasello (2014).

one peer demonstration instead of three peer demonstrations. In addition, half of the children completed the testing phase alone with the experimenter (private condition) and half completed the test phase while the peer(s) watched as in Study 1 (public condition).

Results of the Study. A switch-stay score was calculated for each participant for the three trials they performed in the test phase. Positive scores indicate more "switch" responses, and negative scores indicate more "stay" responses. Figure 3.7 illustrates the results of Study 1. The graph shows that on average, children switched their responses to those shown by their peers, whereas animals stayed with their original responses, showing less influence of the peer demonstrations. Figure 3.8 shows the switch-stay scores for Study 2, where the children were exposed to different numbers of peers (one or three) and performed the test phase publicly or privately. The graph shows that switch responses were evident in the public conditions, but not in the private conditions.

Conclusions of the Study. From the results of the study, the researchers concluded that humans are more willing to adjust their behavior to match peers' behavior than are nonhuman primates. They also suggest that children change their behavior for social reasons, because in Study 2 they were more likely to switch their responses to match those of their peers when their peers were present (public condition) than when they were absent (private condition). They also showed that children adjust their responses to match peers' responses with as few as one peer illustrating the behavior and watching them perform the task. From these studies, the researchers concluded that nonhuman primates are not influenced socially by peers' behavior as much as humans are.

Figure 3.7   Mean Switch-Stay Scores for Study 1

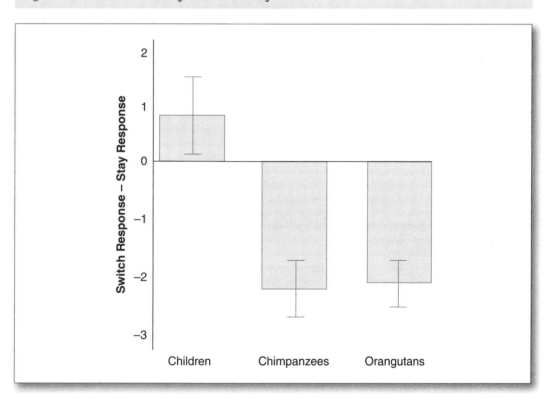

SOURCE: Figure 2 from Haun, Rekers, & Tomasello (2014).

Figure 3.8   Mean Switch-Stay Scores for Study 2

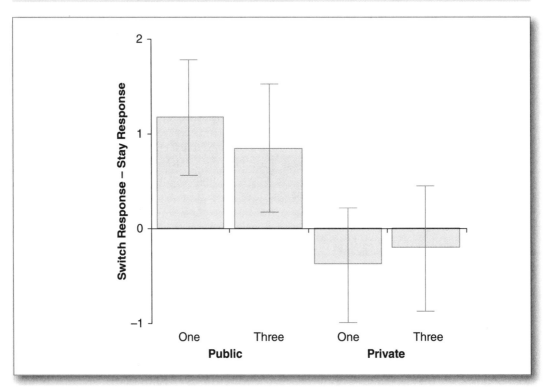

SOURCE: Figure 4 from Haun, Rekers, & Tomasello (2014).

COMMON PITFALLS AND HOW TO AVOID THEM

Problem: Confusing deception with full information—there can be confusion about what qualifies as deception in psychological research.

Solution: Holding back some information about the study does not usually qualify as deception. In many cases, researchers do not fully inform participants about the purpose of the study to prevent demand characteristics. Deception typically involves a more direct manipulation of the participants' understanding of the study.

Problem: Failure to identify risks—researchers often fail to see the possible risks to the participants in their own study.

Solution: Assume that there are always risks to the participants in a study. Sometimes these risks are minimal, such as boredom or fatigue. You should also think carefully about the different elements of the ethical guidelines (confidentiality, deception, informed consent, etc.) to attempt to identify situations where these elements could cause possible harm to the participants.

Problem: Inadequate debriefing—sometimes students designing a research study do not properly debrief participants at the end of a study.

Solution: Be sure to include a thorough debriefing for your study. It is your responsibility to ensure that participants do not have a negative experience in your study, and the debriefing is your opportunity to ensure that participants leave with as positive a view of the study as possible. Be sure to explain why the study was conducted to enrich the participants' understanding of psychological research. Also include information about where they can have further questions answered or learn about the final results if they wish.

TEST YOURSELF

1. Suppose you wanted to replicate the Milgram (1963) study to adhere to ethical guidelines currently in place for psychological research. What changes would you need to make to the procedures (described in this chapter) in order to conduct the study ethically?

2. Given what is described in this chapter regarding the informed consent process, make a list of information that should be provided on a consent form for participants in your modified Milgram (1963) study (see Question 1).

3. Why is the debriefing process especially important in studies that involve deception?

4. Write a debriefing statement that you think might be appropriate for the Middlemist et al. (1976) study on male urination described in the chapter.

5. Which of the following is part of the ethical guidelines for research with human participants?

    (a) No identifying information may be collected from the participants during the study.

    (b) Participants can withdraw from the study at any point before the study begins, but not after that point.

    (c) Participants must be informed about the study's procedures before they are asked to give consent for their participation.

    (d) All of the above.

6. Which of the following is part of the ethical guidelines for research with animal subjects?

    (a) Only trained personnel may be involved with the research.

    (b) Discomfort of the animals must be minimized as much as possible.

    (c) Use of animals and the particular species of animal used must be strongly justified for the study.

    (d) All of the above.

7. The _____ provides a set of ethical guidelines provided by the U.S. Government that must be adhered to by all researchers conducting studies with human participants.

    (a) Nuremberg Code

    (b) APA Ethical Code

    (c) Belmont Report

    (d) IACUC

8. At the conclusion of a study with animal subjects, the researcher

   (a) must provide for the care of the animals for the rest of their lives.

   (b) may release the animals into the wild to live the rest of their lives.

   (c) must use those animals for additional research studies before any new animals can be obtained.

   (d) (a) and (c) only.

9. The Belmont Report principle of _____ involves making certain that harm to the subjects in a research study is reduced such that the benefit of the study is greater than the risk.

10. If I were to discuss a research study without citing the source or authors of the study, I would be guilty of _____.

Answers can be found at edge.sagepub/mcbride3e.

STOP AND THINK ANSWERS

(3.1) Participation is voluntary, participants cannot be coerced and must be informed about the research, unnecessary harm/risk must be reduced and the benefits must outweigh the risks, and participants can end their participation at any time.

(3.2) Obtaining informed consent involves informing the participant about what will occur in the study, including any risks involved and their right to withdraw at any time and then obtaining their consent to participate after they have been informed about the research.

(3.3) Answers will vary, but may include coercion, risks outweighing the benefits, and/or not reducing unnecessary risks.

(3.4) The IRB reviews proposed research studies to ensure that ethical guidelines are followed.

(3.5) It does not provide opportunities for information about how the drug affects women. It violates the justice principle because if only men are tested, women do not obtain the benefits of the testing.

(3.6) Debriefing typically takes place to ensure that subjects understand the purpose of the research and any deception used without introducing bias from this information that might be present if debriefing occurred before the study.

(3.7) More care of the animals is needed than with humans and there is no informed consent process as with humans.

(3.8) Violations of ethics in reporting research occur if authors report false data or plagiarize from other sources without providing citations to those sources.

Visit edge.sagepub.com/mcbride3e for the tools you need to sharpen your study skills:

- Web Quizzes
- eFlashcards
- Thinking About Research

- SAGE Journal Articles
- Web and Multimedia Resources

Chapter 4

How Psychologists Use the Scientific Method

Data Collection Techniques and Research Designs

Consider the following questions as you read Chapter 4

- How do psychologists observe behavior?
- What are some common techniques for observing and recording behavior (i.e., collecting data) in different situations?
- How do psychologists use observations to learn about behavior?
- What questions about behavior do the different research methods allow psychologists to answer?
- Which research method is best when asking about the cause of behavior?

Imagine that you work in a busy corporate office. One day your boss comes to you for advice. A report found that productivity in the office tends to decline later in the afternoon and he or she wants to find a way to increase productivity during this time period. Your boss's suggestion is that having a cappuccino machine in the office lunchroom may cause workers to drink more coffee after lunch, in turn giving them more energy and productivity in the afternoon. You are asked to use your knowledge of research methods to find out if the suggestion is a good one. How would you conduct a study to provide the advice your boss is looking for?

In this chapter, we discuss the methods psychologists use to learn about behavior. This chapter provides an overview of some of the main data collection techniques and research designs used in psychological research to illustrate how psychologists apply the scientific methods described in Chapter 1 to the study of behavior. Figure 4.1 illustrates the steps involved in the research process while designing the study. The choices of data collection technique and research design are made by the researcher. These choices depend on the type of behavior that is of interest and what kinds of questions one wants to answer about the behavior. External and internal validities also play a role in these choices. External validity is the degree to which the behavior observed in the study is realistic, would occur naturally, and can be generalized beyond the boundaries of the study to other individuals and situations. How much external validity a study has is important because the goal of research is to gain knowledge about behavior that applies to a large group of individuals in their everyday lives, not just to the individual study participants with any situational restrictions the study included. In other words, the conclusions need to generalize beyond the study itself. Some of the observation techniques and research designs that psychologists use tend to allow for higher external validity than others. However, in many cases the higher the external validity in a study, the lower the internal validity.

Internal validity is the degree to which a study provides a good test of a causal hypothesis, where alternative explanations of the data can be ruled out. A study with high internal validity

Figure 4.1   Steps in the Research Process: Designing the Study

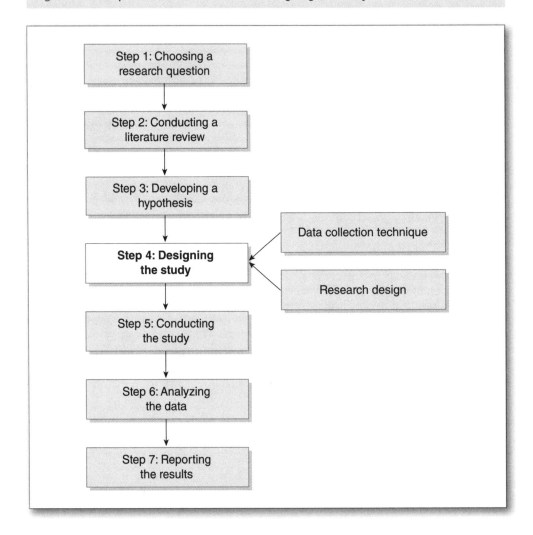

provides causal information about behavior. To increase the internal validity of a study, a researcher controls for extraneous factors that can affect the observations. With more control over the factors in a study, internal validity increases, but behavior may become more artificial and lower the external validity of that study. As we discuss the different types of studies that can be conducted by psychologists, you will see that internal and external validities are important concepts in research.

Another important issue in observing behavior is making certain that the observations are *reliable*. For some observation techniques, this means making sure that observers are categorizing behaviors the same way. For other techniques, this means making certain that different items on a survey or questionnaire designed to measure a specific behavior all provoke similar responses from the research participants. In other words, reliability in a survey means that the participants' responses are similar from item to item or from one time they complete the survey to the next. Thus, reliability is important to consider when you design a study and choose an observation technique, but how you increase reliability depends on the observation technique you are using.

External Validity: the degree to which the results of a study apply to individuals and realistic behaviors outside the study

Internal Validity: the degree to which a study provides causal information about behavior

Reliability: the degree to which the results of a study can be replicated under similar conditions

---

Stop and Think

(4.1)   For each description below, indicate if it is an issue with internal validity, external validity, or reliability:

- Subjects in a study complete a task in the lab in a different way than they would ordinarily do it.
- Subjects' scores on a mood questionnaire differ each time they complete the questionnaire.
- Different groups of subjects receive different teaching techniques to compare the effectiveness of the techniques on learning. However, the subjects in the different groups also differ in their pre-existing knowledge of the topic being taught.

DATA COLLECTION TECHNIQUES

How do psychologists observe behavior? When researchers are planning to observe a behavior, they must first decide how they are going to define that behavior. This is the operational definition of the behavior. An operational definition of an abstract concept (depression, memory ability, etc.) allows the researcher to define the concept for the purpose of measurement and data collection. Thus, an operational definition is a definition of an abstract concept that makes it concrete for the purpose of the research study. If *social behavior* is of interest, the researcher may define this as

---
❦

Operational Definition: the definition of an abstract concept used by a researcher to measure or manipulate the concept in a research study

---

"the number of people who spend time in groups," "the number of times an individual approaches another individual to interact with him or her," or "the score on a questionnaire that asks about social behaviors." There are clearly many ways to define a particular behavior for data collection. Researchers choose an operational definition for behavior that they expect will provide the best (i.e., accurate and reliable) method of learning about the behavior they are interested in. In other words, they define the concept so that it can be measured by a specific behavior (or set of behaviors). See Table 4.1 for some examples of operational definitions of different concepts. The techniques described in the following sections are different ways in which psychologists collect data about behavior. As you will see, the choice of technique is linked to the operational definition the researcher uses. Table 4.2 provides an overview and comparison of these techniques in terms of their realism (i.e., external validity).

Table 4.1   Examples of Operational Definitions

Concept	Possible Operational Definitions
Depression	Score on a mood questionnaire
	Number of times someone has thought about suicide in the last month
	Measure of certain neurotransmitters in areas of the brain
Problem-Solving Ability	Amount of time it takes to complete a puzzle
	Number of problems solved correctly
	Score on a standardized test
Learning	Difference in score from pretest to posttest
	Change in time to complete a problem or test
	Change in confidence ratings to perform a skill

Table 4.2   Comparing Data Collection Techniques

Technique	Definition	Realism
Naturalistic observation	Observing individuals' behavior in their normal environments	High, but decreases if observers fail to be unobtrusive
Surveys/questionnaires	Individuals respond to items in written form or on the Internet	Moderate, but decreases with inaccurate self-reports, phrasing of the questions, and the scale used to collect responses
Systematic observation	Collection of systematic behaviors in controlled tasks	Low, due to researcher control of task situation
Archival data	Using available records to collect observations	Varies with type of record

Naturalistic Observation

A once popular show on the Animal Planet cable network called *Meerkat Manor* follows packs of meerkats as they interact with each other within the pack, with other packs of meerkats, and with the environment they live

Naturalistic Observation: a data collection technique involving noninvasive observation of individuals in their natural environments

in. The show is narrated to make it more entertaining, but the animals' natural behaviors displayed on the show are observed and exhibited as they occur in their normal environment. In other words, the researchers for the show use naturalistic observation to learn about meerkat behaviors. Naturalistic observation is used when a researcher wants to learn about behavior that naturally occurs for an individual without influencing the behavior. The goal of naturalistic observation is to be unobtrusive so that the researcher does not affect the observed individuals' behavior. Naturalistic observation is often used by researchers interested in observing the behavior of animals in their natural environment or children who are in specific environments (both natural and contrived).

To understand observed behaviors using naturalistic observation, a researcher must develop a coding scheme to categorize the exhibited behaviors of the participants. This allows the researcher to quantify (i.e., count) and summarize the behaviors for the group of individuals observed. The coding scheme depends on the operational definition of the behavior the researcher is using. In other words, the behaviors the researcher indicates are part of the operational definition become categories of behaviors in the coding scheme. For example, if researchers are studying *helping* behaviors with naturalistic observations, they may define helping behavior as approaching someone who appears to need help (e.g., has dropped something, has a broken-down car, is unable to open a door, etc.) and offering help or acting to help the person. Thus, observers may sit on a university quad and count behaviors they observe that fit into categories such as "asking someone if he or she needs help," "helping someone pick something up," "giving someone directions when asked." This allows researchers to quantify the different behaviors they see. The researchers can then describe helping behaviors according to their coding scheme to indicate the frequency of helping behaviors overall for this situation and group of individuals, and which types of behaviors occur more often than others.

Developing a coding scheme generally involves defining categories of behavior that fit the type of behavior being observed. The operational definition of the behavior should guide the selection of categories of behaviors that qualify. It is important to clearly define these categories so that observers are clear about what behaviors they are looking for when they observe the individuals of interest in a study. Clear categories also help multiple observers be more consistent in how they classify the behaviors they are looking for (more on this issue below). Finally, the coding scheme can involve counting the number of certain types of behaviors and/or the amount of time individuals engage in the defined behaviors either in set time intervals or across the entire span of the observation period.

The primary advantage in using naturalistic observation to study behavior is that the behavior is likely to be more realistic compared to some of the other techniques. This can increase the external validity of a study. However, this technique has its disadvantages. It can sometimes be difficult to be unobtrusive. The presence of an observer can easily change the behavior of the individuals being observed. This is an issue that has come up for the *Meerkat Manor* show. Camera crews follow the meerkats closely all the time to record their behaviors for the show, and their presence may have affected the behaviors they observe. Thus, researchers using this

———————— ✥ ————————

Inter-observer/Inter-rater Reliability: a measure of the degree to which different observers observe or code behaviors in similar ways

technique must take great care to ensure that they are not influencing the behavior they are observing simply by being present in an individual's environment. Another drawback to naturalistic observation is that it can be very time-consuming. The observers must wait for the behavior they are interested in to be exhibited by the participants. Thus, this technique can be more time intensive and consume more resources than other observation techniques. A third disadvantage is that multiple observers (observing the same or different individuals) may not be recording the behaviors they observe in the same way. To deal with this problem, most studies that involve naturalistic observations include training of the observers to ensure that they are collecting the data in the same way. In fact, the similarity in coding of the data is typically measured and reported in such studies. This is known as inter-observer or inter-rater reliability (how similarly the observers are observing or coding the data). A measure of inter-observer/inter-rater reliability is usually reported based on the percentage overlap in the way the observations are classified across multiple observers. To illustrate this concept, consider the study described above that looked at helping behaviors. In this study, it is likely that more than one person would observe on the quad (either at the same time or at different times) to allow enough helping behaviors to occur and be observed. If the observers code the behaviors differently (e.g., one observer counts bending over to help as "helping someone pick something up," whereas another observer only counts this behavior if someone actually picks up something someone dropped), the internal validity of the study decreases because the observers will have different operational definitions of the behaviors.

Chiang (2008) provides an example of a study that used naturalistic observations. In this study, 32 children with autism were observed to investigate aspects of their spontaneous communication. The children were videotaped in their natural environments (classrooms at their school), while they completed normal, everyday activities (lunch, free time, academic activities, etc.). In the article reporting the study (published in the journal *Autism*), Chiang described the coding schemes developed to summarize and understand the communication behaviors that were seen in the tapes viewed by the observers coding those behaviors (speech or writing, vocalizations that were not identified as words, eye contact, common gestures such as hugging, waving, or nodding, etc.). The inter-observer/inter-rater reliability (above 80%) is also reported to provide evidence that the observers were coding the data in a similar manner. Chiang concluded that children with autism exhibit a range of communicative behaviors across the different settings and suggested a model for future studies of spontaneous communication in autistic individuals. The issue of intrusiveness can be considered for this study. How much did the presence of the video camera affect the participants' behavior? Were participants aware of the video camera? If so, were they more self-conscious or uncomfortable about their behavior because of its presence? The issue of obtrusiveness should be considered whenever naturalistic observations are used in a study.

Surveys/Questionnaires

The other data collection techniques we will discuss are more obtrusive than the naturalistic observation technique because they involve some type of interaction with the research participants. One of these techniques commonly used in psychological research is a survey in which individuals are asked about specific behaviors. (Although the terms *survey* and *questionnaire* are sometimes used in different contexts in research, in this text I will use these terms interchangeably.) Survey research is often conducted to measure mood, attitudes about a topic, or frequency of certain behaviors through self-reports from the participants. Typically, surveys contain a number of questions that ask the research participant to rate the presence or frequency of his or her own thoughts or behaviors. When surveys are used, participants are often asked to use a response scale (e.g., 1 to 5 or 1 to 7) or response category (e.g., often, sometimes, not very often, never) that matches how they feel about a behavior or how likely they are to exhibit the behavior. This means that the participants are limited in the types of responses they can make to the survey items. In other words, the survey uses a closed-ended response scale because only certain responses are valid responses to the items. The

Survey Research: a research study that uses the survey observational technique to measure behavior

Closed-Ended Response Scale: participants respond to survey questions according to the response options provided by the researcher

Open-Ended Response Scale: participants respond to survey questions in any manner they feel is appropriate for the question

Qualitative Data: nonnumerical participant responses

Quantitative Data: numerical data

scale in Table 4.3 was designed to assess how likely one is to discuss one's emotions and disclose personal problems to others. Scores on this scale have been shown to be related to higher self-esteem and general satisfaction with one's life (Kahn & Hessling, 2001). The Distress Disclosure Index provides an example of a closed-ended response scale, as a 5-point scale is given for responses.

Another way to design a survey is to ask participants to respond to questions on an open-ended response scale. In other words, they can respond in whatever way they wish to the questions you asked them. Analyzing the data from an open-ended response scale also requires the development of a coding scheme, because the responses are qualitative rather than quantitative. Such coding schemes are developed by researchers for some validated surveys used frequently in certain types of research. Using a closed-ended response scale allows the researcher to collect quantitative responses (i.e., numerical responses), so no coding scheme is needed for closed-ended scales. Surveys are often administered using pencil and paper or (as is becoming more frequent) over the Internet via website.

Researchers are often interested in testing the validity and reliability of the surveys and questionnaires they use. Checking the validity of a survey means making sure that the questions asked are really about the behavior the researcher is interested in. If a survey is designed to measure someone's level of anxiety, the questions have to be written to ask about behaviors that are related to anxiety, or the survey is not measuring what it is designed to measure. In other words, does the survey actually measure the construct it was designed to measure? Checking the reliability of a survey means making certain that the responses you get from an individual are similar either at different points in time or to similar items on the questionnaire. If an individual's responses change drastically from time to time or across similar items, even though the attitude or behavior being measured by the survey does not change, you will not get an accurate measure of that attitude or behavior. A more detailed discussion of the validity and reliability of surveys is presented in Chapter 9.

Typically, using a validated survey gives a researcher observations of behavior that are a step ahead of the other techniques discussed because the validity and reliability of a survey will

Table 4.3 Distress Disclosure Index

	1	2	3	4	5
1. When I feel upset, I usually confide in my friends.	1 Strongly disagree	2	3	4	5 Strongly agree
2. I prefer not to talk about my problems.	1 Strongly disagree	2	3	4	5 Strongly agree
3. When something unpleasant happens to me, I often look for someone to talk to.	1 Strongly disagree	2	3	4	5 Strongly agree
4. I typically don't discuss things that upset me.	1 Strongly disagree	2	3	4	5 Strongly agree
5. When I feel depressed or sad, I tend to keep those feelings to myself.	1 Strongly disagree	2	3	4	5 Strongly agree
6. I try to find people to talk with about my problems.	1 Strongly disagree	2	3	4	5 Strongly agree
7. When I am in a bad mood, I talk about it with my friends.	1 Strongly disagree	2	3	4	5 Strongly agree
8. If I have a bad day, the last thing I want to do is talk about it.	1 Strongly disagree	2	3	4	5 Strongly agree
9. I rarely look for people to talk with when I am having a problem.	1 Strongly disagree	2	3	4	5 Strongly agree
10. When I am distressed, I don't tell anyone.	1 Strongly disagree	2	3	4	5 Strongly agree
11. I usually seek out someone to talk to when I am in a bad mood.	1 Strongly disagree	2	3	4	5 Strongly agree
12. I am willing to tell others my distressing thoughts.	1 Strongly disagree	2	3	4	5 Strongly agree

SOURCE: Kahn and Hessling (2001).

already have been tested and the survey revised (if necessary) to maximize its accuracy. The primary disadvantage of using surveys to collect data is that the observations are considered self-reports, which means that they may not be correct representations of a person's behavior. Individuals do not always view their behavior accurately and may report who they think they are on a survey, not who they actually are. Participants may also want to portray themselves more positively to the researcher and intentionally respond in a way that achieves that goal (i.e., they self-monitor). This is called *social desirability* and it can bias the results of a survey or questionnaire. Thus, researchers must be careful in interpreting behaviors observed with this technique, as they may not be accurate representations of individuals' behaviors.

The Beck Depression Inventory–II (BDI–II; Beck, Steer, & Brown, 1996) and Beck Anxiety Inventory (BAI; Beck & Steer, 1993) are two commonly used surveys in psychological research on mood. These respective surveys contain items that ask individuals about the intensity of certain feelings and the intensity of specific behaviors related to depression and anxiety. For example, the BDI–II contains 21 items and asks respondents about feelings of sadness, being punished, and lack of interest in sex and behaviors such as difficulty in sleeping and changes in eating habits. Many studies use the BDI–II to measure depression or the BAI to measure anxiety, and the reliability and validity of these surveys have been frequently tested.

Interviews. Surveys can also be administered as interviews such that individuals respond to questions orally. Interviews can be done face-to-face, over the phone, or in focus groups. Like naturalistic observations, observing behaviors with interview data requires the researcher to

Interviews: a data collection technique that involves direct questioning of individuals about their behaviors and attitudes

develop a coding scheme to understand the behaviors described or exhibited in the interview. One advantage of using interviews is that you can ask about a specific behavior instead of waiting for the individual to exhibit the behavior spontaneously (as in naturalistic observations). Another advantage is that if the interview is structured to allow flexibility, different questions can be asked depending on the response that is given. For example, if a participant responds that a question particularly applies to him or her, the interviewer can follow up that response with additional questions on the topic tailored to the type of response made.

Focus groups are becoming a popular way to conduct interviews to learn about individuals' attitudes toward a societal issue, political candidate, or consumer product. Interviewing people in groups uses fewer resources and can sometimes elicit responses from individuals who may be more reluctant to voice an opinion when they are asked on their own. When reluctant individuals hear that others have an opinion similar to their own, they may be more likely to voice their opinion. However, this can also be a limitation to the use of interviews: If they are conducted in groups, individuals may go along with the group rather than voice an opinion that differs from others' (Ashe, 1955). In other words, conformity of responses occurs. Interviewees may also self-monitor during interviews, meaning that they can respond according to how they wish to appear to others instead of how they actually are (i.e., the social desirability bias can occur). Another drawback to the use of interviews is that the way a question is asked can affect the response that is given. Thus, great care must be taken in writing questions for interviews.

A study by Creasey and Ladd (2005) used interviews of individuals to investigate the relationship between parental attachment and conflict resolution behaviors in current romantic relationships. To understand attachment style to their parents, research participants were interviewed about their relationships with their parents. Responses were then coded to categorize individuals according to different types of attachments that children have with their parents. Creasey and Ladd reported that the success of conflict resolution strategies with a romantic partner depended on the type of attachment individuals had with their parents.

Systematic Observation

Systematic observations are typically used when the researchers want to exert the highest amount of control over behavior. This is typically done using a controlled task to indicate the behavior of interest (e.g., speed or accuracy for completing a task). Thus, systematic observation is often used to study behaviors that are least likely to be affected by the process of measuring them. Examples of these behaviors are often cognitive or biological in nature (e.g., memory accuracy, problem-solving speed, firing of a neuron, activity in a particular brain area). However, systematic observation can be used to study behaviors in other areas of psychology as well. A method for studying automatic social attitudes called the Implicit Association Test, or IAT (Greenwald, McGhee, & Schwartz, 1998), uses systematic observation of reaction times of participant responses to sets of word or picture stimuli to measure one's unconscious prejudicial attitudes. In the IAT, the speed with which people respond to items after certain associations have been formed is recorded to determine if some judgments take longer than others. The IAT works by associating a specific response to different dimensions of a concept (e.g., press the right key when you see a female name and the left key when you see a male name; press the right key when you see items a teacher might use and the left key when you see items a firefighter might use). The concepts are then combined (e.g., press the right key when you see a female name or an item used by a firefighter and the left key when you see a male name or an item used by a teacher). The assumption is that longer responses with one combination of concepts (e.g., female names and firefighter items both requiring a right-key response) than the other combination (e.g., female names and teacher items both requiring a right-key press) may reveal unconscious social biases people may have that they either are unaware of or consciously suppress when asked explicit questions about their beliefs (e.g., Is it appropriate for a woman to become a firefighter?). Figure 4.2 illustrates the IAT procedure. You can also try out the IAT procedure for yourself at Project Implicit (http://implicit.harvard.edu).

Systematic Observation: data collection technique where control is exerted over the conditions under which the behavior is observed

Because a high degree of control can be exerted on the measurements of behaviors observed using systematic observations, they typically add to the internal validity of a study. The situation in which the behaviors are measured is typically controlled to eliminate influences on the behaviors that are not the focus of the study. Thus, systematic observations are often collected in a laboratory setting, where distractions of normal life are minimized and tasks are presented and completed on a computer to maximize accuracy. The drawback of this level of control is that the behaviors being studied may be artificial. In other words, external validity can be lower for systematic observations than other data collection methods, though these observations may have better internal validity.

Figure 4.2   Simplified IAT Procedures

	Gender-Key Association	Occupation-Key Association	Common Associations Provide Baseline Condition	Test of Biased Association—Slower Responses Than Baseline Indicate Bias
Response-Dimension Pairing	Male (left key) Female (right key)	Teacher (left key) Firefighter (right key)	Male/firefighter (left key) Female/teacher (right key)	Male/teacher (left key) Female/firefighter (right key)
Stimuli (With Correct Response)	John (left) Mary (right) Angela (right) Steve (left)	Ladder (right) Books (left) Hose (right) Pencil (left)	Henry (left) Desk (right) Truck (left) Heather (right)	Rick (left) Book (left) Axe (right) Judy (right)

SOURCE: Greenwald, McGhee, and Schwartz (1998).

NOTES:

1. Conditions with keys (right, left) reversed (e.g., male with right key, female with left key) are also used.
2. Longer response times for biased test trials indicate unconscious social biases.

Using Archival Data

Sometimes when researchers have questions about behavior, they find that those behaviors they are interested in have already been observed. In other words, the data they wish to analyze to answer their research question

Archival Data: a data collection technique that involves analysis of preexisting data

already exist. Someone else has collected them. For example, if researchers are interested in health-related behaviors, they may wish to use existing hospital records as their observations. An example of this type of study was done in Pueblo, Colorado, a few years ago (Bartecchi et al., 2006). Pueblo is a small town with two hospitals where residents of the town and surrounding area receive medical care. After the town passed a smoking ban, researchers decided to look at hospital records to compare the number of hospitalizations for heart attacks during the year and a half before the smoking ban began (as a way to determine the number of heart-related illnesses that occurred when people were allowed to smoke in public places) with the number of hospitalizations for heart attacks that occurred during the year and a half after the smoking ban started. They found that the number of hospitalizations for heart attacks decreased significantly during the year and a half after the smoking ban and concluded that the decrease in public smoking was related to this decrease (by comparing heart attack hospitalization rate change for comparable areas without a smoking ban over the same period of time). The use of hospital records in this study is an example of how researchers use archival data as an observation technique.

Many archival data sets are collected by agencies on a periodic basis. A quick web search will show summary results for many of these observations. For example, one can find data related to presidential approval ratings, consumer confidence, consumer spending, and opinion polls. Figure 4.3 shows approval ratings (percentage of people who approve of the job the president is doing) for President Obama over a 2-year period near the end of his presidency. A web search will yield periodic ratings for the current president because presidential approval ratings are collected and published frequently each year by many news agencies. Many of these data sets are collected by governmental agencies and are available to researchers who wish to analyze the data on their own. Corporations may also make archival data sets available to researchers who wish to study workplace behaviors such as work productivity and absenteeism.

Archival data offer researchers a means of collecting data quickly. Few resources are needed, as the data are collected by another agency or institution. However, archival data offer the researcher no control over the circumstances under which the data are collected, the sampling technique used, or the measures used to observe behavior. Researchers using archival data also have no control over how the data are coded, which can make comparisons difficult across groups or areas if data are coded differently by different organizations.

Content Analysis. Content analysis is a specific type of archival data observation technique that involves analysis of what someone has said (as in a speech or interview) or written (as in a book

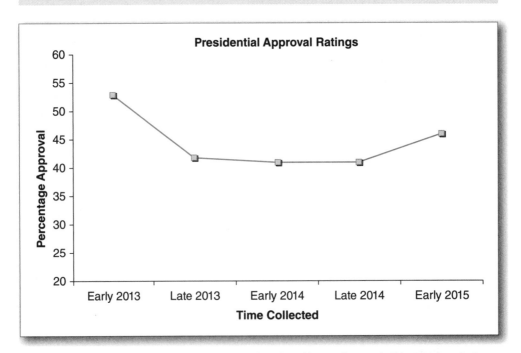

Figure 4.3   Approval Ratings for President Barack Obama

SOURCE: Gallup Poll Data retrieved February 10, 2015, from http://www.gallup.com/poll/116479/barack-obama-presidential-job-approval.aspx.

or article). This may involve analyzing the transcript of a speech someone gave, a written document, or a recorded statement. In content analysis, a researcher is analyzing a record of what someone has said or written in the past; thus, no interaction takes place between the research participant and the researcher. A coding scheme must be developed by the researcher to determine which behaviors will be considered in the analysis. This type of analysis can be resource intensive and time-consuming.

Content Analysis: an archival data collection technique that involves analysis of the content of an individual's spoken or written record

Table 4.4 contains some examples of behaviors that psychologists might want to observe. For each behavior, consider how psychologists might use each of the observation techniques described in this chapter to measure the behavior.

The discussion of data collection techniques presented here provides examples of the primary types of observations researchers use in psychological studies. In other words, they provide a means for the researcher to focus on the measured variables (i.e., a behavior, situation, or characteristic that can differ from individual to individual) of interest. Variables can be numeric and vary continuously from person to person or can be categorical so as to group individuals into different categories that can be compared. The behavior of interest in a study is typically one variable (or more) that is of primary interest in a research study. Observations of behavior (i.e., data) in a study constitute what is called a dependent or response variable. Dependent variables are measured in every research study. For some designs, only a single dependent variable is measured and the behavior is examined descriptively or causally (if the researcher is interested in a causal relationship and uses an experiment to study this relationship). Other designs examine relationships between

Variable: an attribute that can vary across individuals

Dependent/Response Variable: a variable that is measured or observed from an individual

---

Table 4.4   Thinking About Observations

For each behavior listed below, consider how you might observe the behavior using (a) naturalistic observation, (b) surveys and questionnaires, or (c) systematic observation. Be sure to operationally define the behavior before you describe how the observations would be collected. Also consider the limitations of each observation method as you choose one for each behavior.

1. How do humans (or animals) solve a problem?

2. How do people react to bad news?

3. What types of people are most likely to disclose personal problems to others?

4. How do groups of children organize themselves to complete a task?

5. What behaviors characterize people with attention-deficit/hyperactivity disorder (ADHD)?

6. What types of brain activity result when one consumes caffeine?

multiple dependent variables. As a result, how a dependent variable is measured depends on the data collection technique used, and what is learned about a dependent variable depends on the type of research design used. The next section describes some of the common research designs that psychologists use in their studies of behavior.

Stop and Think

(4.2) Describe a disadvantage of using closed-ended responses on a survey/questionnaire.

(4.3) For each description below, indicate which data collection technique would be best to use:

- You want to measure someone's ability to complete a task while controlling for sources of bias and increasing internal validity as much as possible.
- You want to know about how subjects judge their own behavior.
- You want to measure the most realistic behaviors possible to increase external validity.
- You want to know how Americans' confidence in the economy has changed across 4 decades of time.

TYPES OF RESEARCH DESIGNS

Research design types differ based on the type of question the researcher wants to answer. Each of the data collection techniques described earlier can be used in any of the major research designs; however, practically speaking, some techniques are more common in certain designs than in others. As each design is discussed, examples of the most common techniques used in that design will be described. In addition, some of the more common designs are discussed in further detail in Part II of this book. Note also that you may see the term *research design* applied to many aspects of a design. Here the term applies to the major categories of research designs that are used by psychologists to answer different types of research questions. What follows is a description of the major research designs used in psychological research with some examples of these designs.

Case Studies

In 1970, a woman walked into a welfare office in Southern California with her daughter Genie. After the woman was interviewed, it became clear that although Genie appeared to be about 6 or 7 years old, she was in fact 13 years old and had no language abilities. Her parents had kept her locked in her bedroom every day since she was very young. Genie did not attend school and had not been exposed to enough language from her family to learn how to speak. After Genie's situation was discovered, psychologists became interested in her case and hoped to learn from her about the development of language and whether it can occur at such a late age in a child (Fromkin, Krashen, Curtiss, Rigler, & Rigler, 1974). Genie became the subject of intensive study by a number of individuals. From the case study of Genie, evidence was gained for a critical period of language development because Genie was raised with little language interaction with others and had difficulty learning language after she was rescued.

The goal of a case study is to gain insight into and understanding of a single individual's (or just a couple of individuals') behavior. Case studies can also be conducted for a group of individuals, such as an agency or institution. Typically, a case study involves intensive observation of an individual's naturalistic behavior or set of behaviors. Thus, researchers often use naturalistic observations, interviews, or archival data (especially in the case of a famous individual) to learn about the individual's behavior, although some case studies have also included systematic observations and surveys to learn about an individual. Case studies are often exploratory studies, wherein a researcher can learn about a behavior when little is known about it (e.g., unusual symptoms of a new disorder). When a researcher is interested in testing theories about how behavior works or attempting to find a treatment that will help an individual or small set of individuals with a problem behavior, a small-n design is typically used instead of a case study. The primary difference between case studies and small-n designs is the goal of the researcher. In addition, small-n designs are often conducted as experiments (see section on Experiments later in this chapter). Small-n designs are further discussed in Chapter 14.

Some of the more well-known case studies conducted by psychologists have been with individuals who suffered a brain injury. Researchers study such individuals after their brain injury both while they are still alive (if possible) and after their death. Behaviors these individuals exhibit are then connected to the brain injury they suffered, which can be explored more extensively after their death. Physiological psychologists have gained a lot of important knowledge about brain functions through case studies of these individuals. A famous case is that of H.M. (typically these patients are identified by initials only or a pseudonym to keep the findings confidential for these individuals). H.M. suffered damage to a brain area known as the hippocampus during a surgery in 1953 that was done to help reduce his epileptic seizures (Hilts, 1996). As a result of the surgery, H.M. could no longer remember new experiences for longer than a few minutes. Through extensive study of this subject, psychologists learned that the hippocampus is an important structure for encoding or retrieving memories of events because H.M. lost the ability to retrieve memories of things that happened after his surgery (even though he still had access to memories of events he experienced before his surgery). From case studies of H.M. came a new set of questions about the hippocampus and exactly what function it serves in memory. In addition, researchers found that H.M. could improve on tasks over time, indicating that certain types of new memories were still available to him. For example, a study of H.M. (Bohbot & Corkin, 2007) found that his ability to learn a spatial memory task was quite good, despite having severe amnesia (his memory for things he experienced lasts only a few minutes). Case studies of H.M. are still conducted today. Although he died in 2008, H.M.'s brain will continue to be studied to further our understanding of the importance of specific brain areas in cognitive functioning.

Other case studies have used archival data or content analysis of a document to better understand an individual's behavior. For example, Lester (2006) recently examined the diaries

---

Case Study: a research design that involves intensive study of particular individuals and their behaviors

Small-n Design: an experiment conducted with one or a few participants to better understand the behavior of those individuals

of a man who committed suicide, in an attempt to identify specific events in his life that may have been connected to his choice to kill himself. Abramson (1984) conducted a case study of the sexual behaviors of a woman who called herself "Sarah," after receiving a letter from her. Sarah had been abused (physically and sexually) as a child and was recovering from those traumas at the time she wrote to Abramson, a psychologist at the University of California, Los Angeles. Abramson then conducted interviews with Sarah to better understand how individuals recover from such traumatic experiences. Abramson learned a good deal about psychological resilience and recovery in an individual despite traumatic childhood events.

Case studies can even be done after a person has died. When Albert Einstein died in 1955, portions of his brain were preserved to allow it to be studied. Since then scientists have examined these brain sections to look for ways in which Einstein's brain may differ from brains of other people. One difference that has been found is that Einstein's brain contains many more neuron cells in a section of his brain's cortex than in the brains of control participants that were used as a comparison (Anderson & Harvey, 1996). In addition, a section of Einstein's brain appears to have been improperly formed, allowing connections between areas of the brain that are not connected in other people's brains (Witelson, Kigar, & Harvey, 1999). These differences may account for the intellectual abilities Einstein possessed, but simply examining Einstein's brain does not allow researchers to make such strong conclusions. Instead, these studies allow researchers to start hypothesizing about which brain areas or characteristics may be important for advanced intellectual abilities, and these hypotheses can then be tested in further studies (see Figure 4.4).

Due to their exploratory nature, case studies often focus on rare or unusual cases to gain some information about a behavior that is not exhibited by all individuals. This means that the behaviors examined in case studies often cannot be generalized to all individuals. Because of the reduced generality of the behaviors, case studies do not allow for strong tests of the cause of the behavior (experiments are best for that—as explained in a later section), and researchers must be careful about drawing conclusions about the causes of the behaviors they are studying. However, case studies can give researchers a *starting place* for investigations of a behavior or a set of behaviors. Thus, they serve an important purpose in psychological research, drawing attention to new research questions that can be further explored with additional studies.

Correlational Studies

Correlational Study: a type of research design that examines the relationships between multiple dependent variables, without manipulating any of the variables

Predictor Variable: the dependent variable in a correlational study that is used to predict the score on another variable

Outcome Variable: the dependent variable in a correlational study that is being predicted by the predictor variable

Is insomnia related to depression? Do students who watch more TV have lower grade point averages (GPAs)? Do children who play violent video games behave more violently? Each of these questions can be explored in a correlational study (correlation means relationship). Correlational studies allow a researcher to examine relationships between variables and, if a relationship is found, predict values for one variable from values on the other variable(s). If a predictive relationship is examined, the variable that is used to make the prediction is called the predictor variable, and the variable that is being predicted is called the outcome variable. Therefore, the goal of a

Figure 4.4   Case Studies Can Provide a Unique View of an Individual

SOURCE: Copyright by S. Harris, www.sciencecartoonsplus.com/galpsych2.htm

correlational study is to determine if different behaviors are connected and occur together. This type of study, however, still does not allow us to determine if one variable *causes* another to occur (again, only well-designed experiments allow researchers to test causal relationships). All we can learn from a correlational study is if two variables covary (i.e., change together—up, down, or in opposite directions from each other). Then researchers may be able to predict one variable from another.

If a relationship is found in a correlational study between two variables, it can take one of two forms: a positive relationship or a negative relationship. A positive relationship means that the values on the variables change in the same direction (up or down) at the same time. A negative relationship indicates that as values on one variable increase, the values on the other

Figure 4.5   Positive (A), Negative (B), and (C) No Relationship Between Number of Hours of TV Watched and GPA

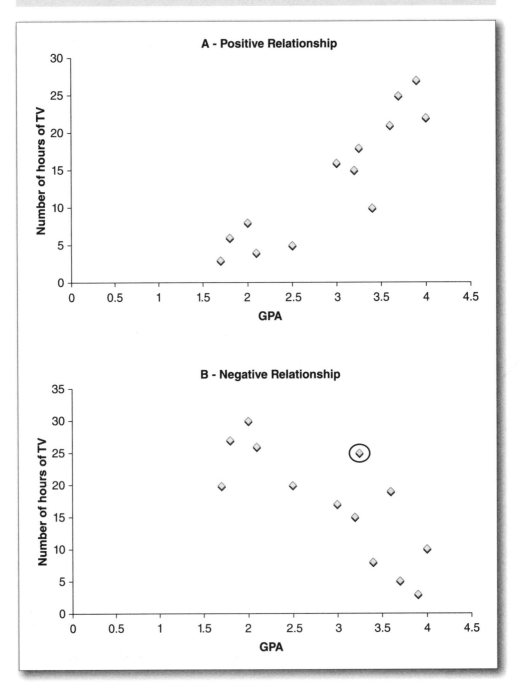

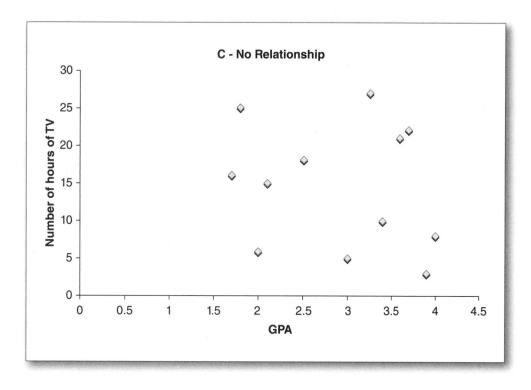

variable decrease. Figure 4.5 illustrates each type of relationship that might exist between GPA and the number of hours an individual watches TV per week. The graphs in Figure 4.5 are called scatterplots. In a scatterplot, one variable is placed on the *x*-axis, and the other variable is placed on the *y*-axis. The data points in the graph represent the scores on the two variables for each individual (horizontally for the first variable and vertically for the second variable). Thus, the data point that is circled in Panel B shows that one individual in this study reported watching 25 hours of TV per week and had a GPA of 3.25. You may also notice that there are very few data points below 1.0 on the GPA scale in the graph. This may be because very few students in college have GPAs lower than 1.0 (if they do, they do not remain in college very long).

Positive Relationship: the variables change together in the same direction (both increasing together or decreasing together)

Negative Relationship: a relationship between variables characterized by an increase in one variable that occurs with a decrease in the other variable

Scatterplot: a graph showing the relationship between two dependent variables for a group of individuals

Remember that a relationship between these variables does not mean that watching TV will *cause* one to have a higher or lower GPA or that having a higher or lower GPA will *cause* one to watch more TV. It is quite possible that a third variable (e.g., lack of interest in academic topics, a poor academic environment while growing up, good background in academic

---

Third-Variable Problem: the presence of extraneous factors in a study that affect the dependent variable and can decrease the internal validity of the study

---

topics that are covered in TV shows) is causing the number of hours of TV watched and GPA to change. This is called the third-variable problem and it is the reason that researchers cannot determine causation from correlational studies.

Experiments

Have you ever wondered why it took so long for scientists to learn that smoking causes cancer? People have been smoking for hundreds of years, and medical science has been studying the effects of smoking on health for many decades. Yet warnings on cigarette packages did not appear until 1966, and claims about smoking causing lung cancer were tentative for many years. Scientists could show that smoking and cancer were linked but could not show that smoking caused cancer in humans in a definitive way. The reason these findings were tentative for so long is that ethically it is very difficult (if not impossible) to conduct an experiment to examine whether smoking *causes* cancer in humans. An experiment involves manipulating the presumed causal variable known as the independent variable. This means that in the smoking experiment, one group of people would be assigned to smoke and a similar group of people (similar in age, weight, health, diet, etc.) would not be allowed to smoke. Obviously, researchers cannot force people to smoke (especially, if they have a hypothesis that it is harmful to them) or force

---

Experiment: a type of research design that involves manipulation of an independent variable, allowing control of extraneous variables that could affect the results

Independent Variable: a variable in an experiment that is manipulated by the researcher such that the levels of the variable change across or within subjects in the experiment

Levels of the Independent Variable: different situations or conditions that participants experience in an experiment because of the manipulation of the independent variable

Experimental Group: the group of participants in an experiment that experience the treatment level of the independent variable

Control Group: the group of participants in an experiment that do not experience the treatment level of the independent variable

---

people to never smoke. Thus, it has been very difficult (and has taken many correlational studies and animal experiments) to show that smoking is a cause of lung cancer, but this example illustrates what is required to test causal hypotheses: experiments.

As mentioned above, a key aspect of experiments that allows tests of causal relationships is the manipulation of the independent variable (or independent variables—an experiment can contain more than one independent variable). The independent variable is the factor that the researcher thinks may affect the observed behavior. Thus, data are collected from the participants in an experiment under at least two different conditions. The data from these conditions are then compared with one another to see if there are differences caused by the independent variable manipulation. These different conditions created from the independent variable make up the levels of the independent variable. For example, an experiment may involve subjecting one group of participants (randomly assigned) to treatment for depression, while another group receives no treatment. In this case, the treated group is the experimental group, because they receive the treatment condition, whereas the nontreated group is the control group, because they receive no treatment. Comparison of depression scores (the dependent variable in this experiment) for the two groups would allow the researcher to determine if the treatment was helpful (scores for the treatment group are higher than the control group's), harmful (scores for the treatment group are lower than the control group's), or makes no difference (scores for the treatment and control groups are similar). Another way to conduct this experiment would be to use two different treatments (e.g., talk therapy vs. drug therapy) for the two groups. In this case, there is no control group; both groups of participants receive some type of treatment. Comparison of the scores for the two groups in this experiment would indicate which of the two therapies was more helpful or if they are

Confounding Variable: an extraneous factor present in a study that may affect the results

Random Assignment: participants are randomly assigned to levels of the independent variable in an experiment to control for individual differences as an extraneous variable

Placebo: a sugar pill given to the control group in a drug study to allow all groups to believe that they are receiving a treatment

similar. In fact, this comparison is a key feature of an experiment. The goal in an experiment is to examine the effect of the independent variable on the dependent variable. We do that by comparing the data observed in the different levels of the independent variable; this comparison tells us if the independent variable has an effect. In other words, the comparison across the levels of the independent variable provides the test of the hypothesis.

Another key feature of experiments is the control of factors that could affect the results but are not part of the manipulation of the independent variable(s). These extraneous factors are called confounding variables. If confounding variables are not controlled, the causal relationship between the independent and dependent variables will be unclear. For example, in the depression examples discussed earlier, the severity of the depression the participants have before the experiment could be a confounding variable because participants with more severe depression may show less improvement with therapy than participants with less severe depression. If the participants with more severe depression are inadvertently assigned to the therapy group in the first example or to one of the therapy groups in the second example, they may show no effect of therapy, even if an effect does exist. In other words, the severity of the depression may mask the causal relationship between therapy group and depression at the end of the study. Thus, the researcher should control for this factor in the experiment, perhaps by randomly assigning participants to groups. The control aspect of experiments is discussed further in Chapter 11.

Another example of control used in experiments with a treatment as the independent variable is the use of a placebo for the control group. A placebo is typically given as a sugar pill in a study testing a drug treatment to the control group so that the subjects do not know whether they receive a treatment or not. This controls for the effects of the belief that one is being treated that can have an influence on the results of the study. People who believe they are receiving a treatment can improve from the belief alone so a placebo is often used to give both the experimental and control groups the belief that they may be receiving the treatment.

Systematic observations and surveys are the most common observation techniques used in experiments. These observation techniques allow for more control over the measurement of behavior than the other techniques (see Table 4.2). The IAT procedure described earlier (and in Figure 4.2) provides an example of the use of systematic observation in an experiment. An independent variable in an experiment using the IAT procedure is the type of word (or image) pairing the participant is responding to. The dependent variable is often the amount of time a participant takes to respond to the word pairings.

Quasi-Experiments

In some cases, researchers want to compare the behavior of groups of individuals but are unable to manipulate the characteristic on which the groups differ. For example, suppose you wanted to compare the behavior for older and younger adults. You cannot randomly assign individuals to be of a specific age, so age cannot be a manipulated variable. This means that you lose some control over alternative explanations of the data, because participants are not randomly assigned to the groups. In this example, if younger and older adults differ on the measured behavior, age may have caused the difference or something that varies with age (e.g., experiences of different generations with technology) may have caused the difference. Thus, conclusions from quasi-experiments must be more tentative than conclusions from experiments, where a true independent variable is manipulated. However, quasi-experiments involve group comparisons just as experiments do, and data from quasi-experiments are often analyzed the same way they are analyzed in experiments (see Chapter 15 for more on data analysis). The key difference between experiments and quasi-experiments is that the random assignment of participants to groups is missing in a quasi-experiment (Shadish, Cook, & Campbell, 2002).

One type of quasi-experiment design is called an ex post facto design, because the comparison of interest is based on a grouping that already exists instead of one the researcher assigns in the study. In other words, the grouping is based on something that already happened in the past (e.g., a subject decided to be a smoker or not, a subject was in an automobile accident in the last year or not). Based on these pre-existing characteristics of the subjects, a researcher can create groups of subjects to compare on a particular behavior (e.g., anxiety level, impulsivity). However, a design can be a quasi-experiment even if the researcher assigns subjects to groups if that assignment is not done randomly. Researchers might decide to assign subjects to groups based on their availability for participation in the study (e.g., morning or afternoon session). If the assignment is not random, then there could be additional factors (other than the grouping factor) that are responsible for the results found (e.g., people who sign up for the morning session are more alert and perform better on the task because of their energy level).

Some studies also have less control over conditions under which data are collected in a repeated-measures design. For example, suppose a researcher is interested in the change in attitude regarding trust of politicians after taking a political science class. In this study, attitude is measured before and after the class in what is called a pretest-posttest design. If attitude changes from pretest to posttest (getting either better or worse), this change may be either because of the class or because of other events that occurred in the time between the tests (e.g., a political scandal may have occurred in this time). Thus,

---

Quasi-Experiment: a type of research design where a comparison is made, as in an experiment, but no random assignment of participants to groups occurs

Ex Post Facto Design: a quasi-experiment where subjects are grouped based on a characteristic they already possess (e.g., age or gender)

Pretest-Posttest Design: a type of research design (often a quasi-experiment) where behavior is measured both before and after a treatment or condition is implemented

the causal relationship between the political science class and attitude change is less clear. For this reason, pretest-posttest designs (that do not include a control group) are considered quasi-experiments. Other types of quasi-experimental designs are considered in Chapter 13.

Stop and Think

(4.4) For each description below, indicate what research design is being used:

- To determine if there is a relationship between mood and weather, researchers measure subjects' moods and the temperature on the day that they complete the mood questionnaire.
- To examine the effect of temperature on mood, subjects are randomly assigned to a room at 86 degrees or a room at 72 degrees to complete their mood questionnaire.
- To determine if mood differs by room temperature, a researcher asks two of her classes to fill out a mood questionnaire at the end of class after adjusting the thermostat between classes. She then groups subjects by class and compares their mood scores.

(4.5) Explain why the results from a case study might be difficult to generalize to a large population of people.

(4.6) Imagine you wanted to learn about the factors that contribute to people quitting their jobs. Describe a study to examine this topic and identify the data collection technique and research design you would use.

CHAPTER SUMMARY

Reconsider the questions from the beginning of the chapter:

- How do psychologists observe behavior? There are some common techniques used by psychologists to observe behavior described in this chapter.
- What are some common techniques for observing and recording behavior in different situations? The common techniques used by psychologists to observe and record behavior are naturalistic observations, surveys/questionnaires, systematic observations, and archival data.
- How do psychologists use observations to learn about behavior? Each technique can be used in different research designs to allow psychologists to answer different types of questions about behavior.
- What questions about behavior do the different research methods allow psychologists to answer? Different research designs (e.g., case studies, correlational studies, experiments, and quasi-experiments) allow researchers to ask different questions about behavior. Case studies allow descriptive questions to be answered for a single individual or institution. Correlational studies allow descriptive and predictive questions to be answered about behavior. Quasi-experiments and experiments allow comparisons among groups, with experiments answering causal questions about behavior.
- Which research method is best when asking about the cause of behavior? Experiments are the best method to use when asking causal questions about behavior.

THINKING ABOUT RESEARCH

A summary of a research study in psychology is given below. As you read the summary, think about the following questions:

1. Two studies from a research article are described below. For each study, identify the data collection technique and the research design type.

2. Does Study 2 contain an independent variable? If so, what is it and what are its levels?

3. What controls did the researchers use in Study 2 to increase the internal validity of the study?

4. Would you consider Study 1 or Study 2 to have higher internal validity? Explain your answer.

5. How would you judge the external validity of this study?

Research Study. Nairne, J. S., VanArsdall, J. E., Pandeirada, J. N. S., Cogdill, M., & LeBreton, J. M. (2013). Adaptive memory: The mnemonic value of animacy. *Psychological Science, 24,* 2099–2105.

Purpose of the Study. The researchers conducted two studies to investigate whether living things have a memory advantage over nonliving things. Their research was motivated by an evolutionary perspective on the development of memory in that being able to distinguish between living and nonliving things is essential for survival. In their first study, they analyzed the relationship between the living/nonliving characteristic of words used in a past study (Rubin & Friendly, 1986) and recall of the words. They predicted a positive relationship between this living/nonliving status and recall. In their second study, they tested the hypothesis that subjects would recall more words of living objects than nonliving objects.

Method of the Study. Study 1: The researchers examined words from the Rubin and Friendly (1986) study. Three individuals separately coded the words according to whether they represented living or nonliving objects.

Study 2: Undergraduate students were asked to remember 24 words presented to them in random order. Twelve of the words represented living things; and 12 of the words represented nonliving things. The word sets were matched on several other characteristics (e.g., familiarity, how well an image could be brought to mind by the word, number of letters in the word, etc.). After studying the words, subjects completed a short task to categorize presented numbers as "odd" or "even." Subjects were then asked to recall the words in any order for 4 min. This entire procedure was repeated a total of three times (i.e., they studied and recalled the words three times).

Results of the Study. In Study 1, a strong positive relationship was found between the living/nonliving aspect of the words and recall of the words. In Study 2, subjects recalled more of the words for living objects than nonliving objects. Figure 4.6 presents the recall results from Study 2.

Conclusions of the Study. The researchers concluded that the living objects hold a memorial advantage, such that memory is attuned to this characteristic of objects. They suggest that this conclusion is consistent with an evolutionary perspective on the development of memory.

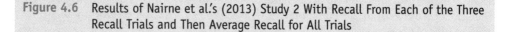

Figure 4.6   Results of Nairne et al.'s (2013) Study 2 With Recall From Each of the Three Recall Trials and Then Average Recall for All Trials

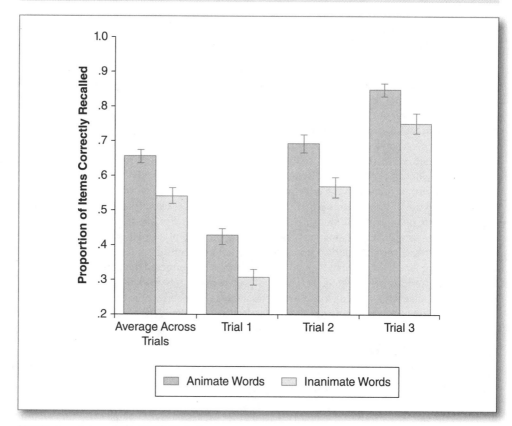

SOURCE: From Nairne et al.'s (2013) Study 2.

COMMON PITFALLS AND HOW TO AVOID THEM

Problem: Concluding cause without manipulation—nonexperimental studies are sometimes interpreted as providing causal information.

Solution: To test causal relationships, an experiment with a manipulated independent variable is needed.

Problem: External validity versus internal validity—some view external validity as more important than internal validity in all psychological research studies.

Solution: Be aware that high internal validity is required to test causal relationships but that internal and external validity typically trade off in psychological studies.

Problem: Use of control groups in experiments—students sometimes incorrectly believe that all experiments require a control group.

Solution: Remember that control groups are important in experiments if a single treatment is being evaluated or the effectiveness of multiple treatments is being tested, but control groups are not required in every type of experiment.

USING RESEARCH

In 1998, a group of British doctors published a paper suggesting that there may be a link between vaccines for measles, mumps, and rubella diseases and incidence of autism (Wakefield et al., 1998). This means the researchers were suggesting there is a positive relationship between these vaccinations and occurrence of autism in children that were tested. Their findings started a controversy over the causes of autism. Media sources in the United Kingdom (UK) reported the findings of this paper suggesting that having children vaccinated can cause them to develop autism. As a result, many parents in the UK and the United States refused to have their children vaccinated out of fear of their children becoming autistic, and the incidence of childhood diseases, such as measles, increased in the UK in the years after the paper was published. Based on the information you read in this chapter, why should parents hesitate to conclude from the findings of this paper that vaccinations can cause autism? What error did the media sources make in publicizing the study's findings? Why should the public refrain from making important decisions (such as refusing vaccinations) based on the findings of a single study? If this last question is a bit difficult to answer, consider what has happened more recently in this story: In February 2010, the journal that published the original paper describing this study retracted the paper because the study was found to have serious methodological flaws that were not entirely evident in the original report of the research. Consider what type of study would be necessary to show that vaccinations cause autism in children. How would such a study need to be done? Is this a realistic study to conduct? Why or why not?

TEST YOURSELF

Match each research design below with its appropriate description.

1. Experiment
2. Case study
3. Correlational study
4. Quasi-experiment

(a) Design that focuses on observing just one or a few individuals

(b) Design that will allow one to look for relationships between measured variables

(c) Best design for testing a causal relationship

(d) Design that allows comparison of groups but does not contain a true independent variable

5. Reread the scenario described at the beginning of the chapter about increasing work productivity. Use the concepts you read about in this chapter to design a study to test the boss's suggestion. Be sure to operationally define *work productivity* and decide what technique you will use to observe this behavior. Choose the research design that best fits the question you are trying to answer.

6. Suppose you are interested in testing the hypothesis "The herb ginkgo biloba causes one to have better memory."

   (a) What is the best research design to test this hypothesis? Why?

   (b) Describe the study you would conduct to test this hypothesis.

7. _____ validity indicates that a study's results can be generalized to other individuals and real-life situations. _____ validity indicates that a study's results provide causal information about the variables tested.

8. For each description below, indicate which data collection technique was used:

   (a) Medical records of patients with depression are examined to determine how often these patients attempt suicide based on what type of treatment they received

   (b) Participants are asked to perform a task on a computer where they must unscramble sentences as quickly as possible—the amount of time it takes to complete the task on each trial is recorded

   (c) A series of statements regarding their alcohol consumption behaviors is presented to participants—they are asked to rate their agreement with each statement on a scale from 1 to 5

   (d) Students in a college class are observed to record the number of times they exhibit behaviors indicating lack of attention to the lecture

9. If a study finds that as self-esteem goes up, symptoms of depression decrease, this study has found a _____ relationship.

10. _____ research designs are typically used when a researcher wants to explore the behavior of an individual or group of individuals to better understand unusual or atypical behaviors.

Answers can be found at edge.sagepub/mcbride3e.

STOP AND THINK ANSWERS

(4.1) External validity, internal validity, internal validity

(4.2) Closed-ended responses might be poorly written such that they bias subjects toward a particular response. They also don't allow for responses that do not fit the scale chosen by the researcher.

(4.3) Systematic observation, survey/questionnaire, naturalistic observation, archival data

(4.4) Correlational study, experiment, quasi-experiment

(4.5) Case studies examine just one or a small group of individuals. Thus, it may be difficult to generalize the results from a case study to others because the individual(s) tested may be unique.

(4.6) Answers will vary

$\$$SAGE edge™

Visit edge.sagepub.com/mcbride3e for the tools you need to sharpen your study skills:

- Web Quizzes
- eFlashcards
- Thinking About Research

- SAGE Journal Articles
- Web and Multimedia Resources

Chapter 5

Variables and Measurement in Research

> **Consider the following questions as you read Chapter 5**
>
> - What is a variable?
> - What are the different types of variables that researchers consider in their studies?
> - Which type of research method contains an independent variable? Why?
> - How do reliability and validity affect the results of a study?
> - What are some factors that affect the validity of a study, and how can a researcher control these factors?

When you hear that someone is *intelligent*, what does that mean to you? Do you think that the person gets good grades? Does the person excel in math and science courses? Does the person read a lot of books? Does it mean the person has a large brain? Or do you think that the person has an ability to solve complex problems quickly and easily? These are some of the same questions that psychologists attempt to answer when they try to study intelligence, and each of the suggestions above has at one time or another been used by researchers as a definition of *intelligence*.

The study of intelligence has a long history. Some attempts to measure intelligence in psychology have used intelligence tests that were designed to measure innate abilities that are not affected by culture or experiences (i.e., intelligence test scores were used as operational definitions of the concept of intelligence—see Chapter 4 for more discussion of operational definitions). Scores on these tests reflected a person's current ability level in reference to other people's abilities of the same chronological age. A score on these tests is called an intelligence quotient or IQ score. However, these tests are not always reliable or valid measures of innate abilities, and some psychologists have pointed out that these measures rely on a specific definition of intelligence that is expressed in the types of questions asked on the test.

More recently, other psychologists have suggested that there may be several forms of intelligence that can be measured in different ways. For example, Gardner (1999) suggested that intelligence comprises several different abilities. Some of the forms he proposed include the following: A person can be intelligent such that he or she has excellent verbal abilities (i.e., is a good writer), mathematical and logical abilities (i.e., excels at math and logical problems), or spatial abilities (i.e., navigates well or produces excellent drawings). Still other psychologists (e.g., Goleman, 1995) have suggested that people can have social intelligence (i.e., are skilled at interpersonal interactions) or emotional intelligence (i.e., understand others' emotions and manage their own emotions well).

From this example of the various measurements of intelligence in psychological research, you can see that how something is defined for the purpose of measurement can be controversial. Someone who has exceptional spatial abilities may still be considered unintelligent from the score he or she receives on a standard intelligence test, if the test is designed to measure other abilities. In other words, how one chooses to define the concept of intelligence affects the outcome of that measure. Thus, the goal of a measure of behavior is important to consider when a researcher is choosing to measure an abstract concept such as intelligence. Some of the intelligence tests described above have been used to predict future performance, even though they were not designed for this purpose. Other types of tests, called aptitude tests, were developed specifically to predict future performance (the SAT, or Scholastic Aptitude Test, and ACT, or American College Test, are that type of test, designed for high school students and used to predict their academic performance in college), and a person's score on these tests is often a fairly accurate prediction of his or her future academic performance. However, if one wishes to predict future success in life (e.g., type of job or salary), these tests may not be valid indicators because they were not developed for this purpose. These are some of the issues we will discuss in this chapter: the importance of how we measure and manipulate variables in a study, how these choices can affect how well the study tests a causal hypothesis (i.e., the internal validity of the study), how well the study applies to everyday behavior (i.e., the external validity of the study), and how well the study provides results that are reliable (Figure 5.1).

DEPENDENT VARIABLES

In Chapter 4, dependent/response variables were introduced as variables that are measured in a research study. In this chapter, we discuss how dependent variables are measured and how this affects reliability (how consistent the measurements are). Chapter 4 also introduced operational definitions, definitions of concepts that describe how they are measured or manipulated in a study. There are many ways to operationally define the abstract concepts that psychologists wish to study. Some examples of these concepts include depression, anxiety, intelligence, and memory. Some of the specific types of measurements that are used when dependent variables are operationally defined in psychological research are described below.

Dependent/Response Variable: a variable that is measured or observed from an individual

Reliability: the degree to which the results of a study can be replicated under similar conditions

Operational Definition: the definition of an abstract concept used by a researcher to measure or manipulate the concept in a research study

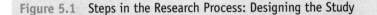

Figure 5.1   Steps in the Research Process: Designing the Study

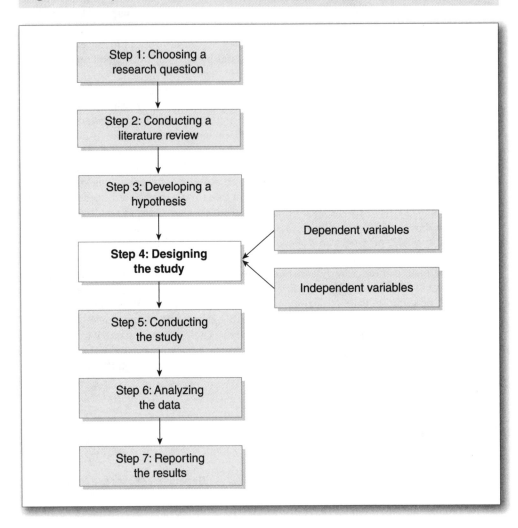

Scales of Measurement

As described above in the discussion of the concept of intelligence, how a researcher measures the dependent variable in a study can be important. Different types of measures allow different questions to be asked about the behaviors. In addition, some types of measures are more reliable than others. The choice of scale also constrains the types of statistical tests that are used to analyze the data. There are four primary scales of measurement for dependent variables: (1) nominal, (2) ordinal, (3) interval, and (4) ratio. Each of these scales is described below.

Nominal Scales. **The** simplest scale of measurement is a nominal scale, where nonordered categorical responses are collected. For example, if researchers are measuring a person's current mood, they may ask the respondent to choose from categories such as anxious, happy, depressed, and angry. These categories are not ordered on any continuum; they are merely different categories that reflect a person's mood. Another example of a nominal scale is a student's selection of a college major. Values on this scale are categories (e.g., English, education, psychology, philosophy) that are not

---

Nominal Scale: a scale of data measurement that involves nonordered categorical responses

Qualitative Data: nonnumerical participant responses

Quantitative Data: numerical data

Ordinal Scale: a scale of data measurement that involves ordered categorical responses

---

ordered in any particular way. Gender is another common nominal variable (e.g., male, female). The responses on a nominal scale do not involve numerical values; thus, nominal scales are considered qualitative data rather than quantitative data.

Ordinal Scales. When the response categories of a measure contain an ordering (i.e., can be ordered from lowest to highest) on a continuum of measurement, the measure is considered an ordinal scale. However, response categories on an ordinal scale are not assumed to be equally spaced on the continuum. They are merely ordered categories on the scale. For example, in measuring a person's mood, a researcher may ask respondents to rate their current anxiety level with possible response categories of "not at all anxious," "a little anxious," "fairly anxious," and "very anxious." These categories are ordered from lowest amount of anxiety to highest, but there is no implied equivalence in the difference between the "not at all anxious" and "a little anxious" response categories and the "a little anxious" and "fairly anxious" response categories. Thus, the response categories on this scale are not necessarily equally spaced. Another example of an ordinal scale might be asking students to indicate how often they consume alcohol during a typical week with response categories of "none," "once," "two to five times," and "more than five times." Again, these response categories are ordered from smallest to largest amount, but the difference between "none" and "once" is not the same as the difference between "once" and "two to five times."

Rank orderings of stimuli are also considered ordinal scales. For example, if preference for different products is being measured, the respondents may be asked to rank order (e.g., first, second, third, etc.) the products according to their preference. In rank orders, the difference between the first and second choices may be much larger or smaller than the difference between the second and third choices. Like nominal scales, ordinal scales involve qualitative data because the response values are not numerical.

Interval and Ratio Scales. Interval and ratio scales involve numerical response values; thus, they involve quantitative data. There are many measurement scales in psychology that are considered interval and ratio scales. Interval scales involve numerical categories that are equally spaced. Thus, a common interval scale is the Likert scale, where respondents are asked how much they agree or disagree with a statement on a 1 to 5 or a 1 to 7 scale (where possible responses are any whole value between these endpoints). Responses from surveys are often measured on a Likert scale with qualitative anchors provided to give the numerical values meaning (e.g., 1 = *item is*

❧

Interval Scale: a scale of data measurement that involves numerical responses that are equally spaced, but scores are not ratios of each other

Ratio Scale: a scale of data measurement that involves numerical responses, where scores are ratios of each other

Likert Scale: a scale of responses that measures a participant's agreement or disagreement with different types of statements, often with a rating from 1 to 5 or 1 to 7

Reaction Time: measurement of the length of time to complete a task

---

least like me, 3 = item is somewhat like me, 5 = item is most like me). However, the responses given by participants are the numerical ratings, with equal spacing between the different numbers on the scale.

Ratio scales also involve numerical measurements, but ratio scales allow a ratio comparison of values between individual scores. For example, a score of 50 on a ratio scale is twice as high as the score of 25. The amount of time to complete a task (sometimes called reaction time) is a common ratio scale used in psychological research. If one participant takes 250 milliseconds to complete a task and another participant takes 500 milliseconds to complete the same task, it can be said that the second participant took twice as long as the first participant. Accuracy for a task is also a ratio scale. In fact, measurement scales for distance, time, accuracy, height, or weight are ratio scales. For many ratio measurement scales (such as many of those listed above), 0 is the lowest value possible; however, some ratio scales do involve values lower than 0 (e.g., reaction times measured in a study can be negative, if the participant responds before the stimulus appears).

Temperature scales provide a good example of the difference between interval and ratio scales. Common temperature scales (Fahrenheit, Celsius) involve values of 0 that are not the coldest temperatures possible (anyone who has lived through a cold winter can tell you that negative temperatures are possible and can be unpleasant). In addition, Fahrenheit and Celsius temperature scales are interval scales because 20° is not twice as cold as 10° or four times as cold as 5°. The Kelvin scale for temperature, however, does include a 0 value that is the lowest possible value. The value of 0 on this scale indicates that it is the lowest temperature possible, and scores on the Kelvin scale are ratios of each other (e.g., 100 K is twice as hot as 50 K). Thus, the Kelvin scale of temperature is a ratio scale. See Table 5.1 for a comparison of the different measurement scales and some additional examples of each type of scale.

Correctly identifying the scale of measurement used for the dependent variable is an important step in conducting appropriate statistical analyses. Different scales may require different types of analyses in some designs. This issue will be discussed further in Chapters 7 and 15.

Table 5.1   Scales of Measurement

Scale	Definition	Example
Nominal	Unordered categories	University where degree was earned
Ordinal	Nonnumerical, ordered categories	Letter grades earned in a course (A, B, C, D, F)
Interval	Numerical categories without a true zero point	Ratings on personality surveys with values from 1 to 5
Ratio	Numerical categories with a true zero point	Age measured in days since birth

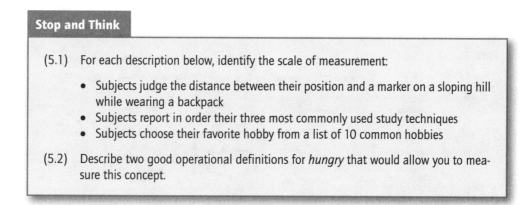

Stop and Think

(5.1) For each description below, identify the scale of measurement:

- Subjects judge the distance between their position and a marker on a sloping hill while wearing a backpack
- Subjects report in order their three most commonly used study techniques
- Subjects choose their favorite hobby from a list of 10 common hobbies

(5.2) Describe two good operational definitions for *hungry* that would allow you to measure this concept.

Validity and Response Scales

The choice of measurement can also affect the validity of a study (i.e., the study's accuracy in testing the researcher's hypothesis). For example, in many cases, the more response choices there are on the scale, the more accurate the measurement is of the behavior that is being measured. If you think about measuring height with a ruler, you can see how this works. Imagine you have a ruler that has

Construct Validity: indicates that a survey measures the behavior it is designed to measure

Nonverbal Scale: survey response scale that involves pictorial response categories for participants with low verbal skills (e.g., children)

increments marked only for every foot (1 ft, 2 ft, 3 ft, etc.). How accurate would your height measurement be if you used this ruler? The answer is "not very accurate," because you can choose only between values of 5 ft and 6 ft (or 7 ft for very tall people). If instead you use a ruler marked in inches, you can measure your height more accurately (5 ft 2 in., 5 ft 7 in., 6 ft 1 in., etc.). The ruler with more values on it will give you more accurate measurements. Response scales for behavior work the same way. The more values on the scale, the more accurate (and, thus, more valid) the scale will be.

In addition, if a poor operational definition of a concept is used, inaccurate conclusions from the data can also result. In this case, the measure has low construct validity. A measure with high construct validity provides an accurate measure of the behavior of interest. In other words, has the researcher used an appropriate operational definition of the variable of interest? For example, suppose a researcher is interested in measuring anxiety in children who are 5 years old. It is unlikely that children this young will understand the items on a standardized anxiety questionnaire such as the BAI (Beck Anxiety Inventory; Beck & Steer, 1993) or the response scale for the BAI. Thus, if this questionnaire (and response scale) is used in a study with young children, the responses are likely to be inaccurate and lower the validity of the study. While scores on the BAI may be a good operational definition of mood for adults, they are likely to provide a poor operational definition of mood for children. Thus, the BAI scores will have low construct validity in a study with children. For a study such as this, where mood responses from young children are required, it may be best to use a nonverbal scale to ensure that the children can provide valid responses. A series of faces with different expressions of mood may be a better (and more valid) measurement scale for

Figure 5.2   Example of a Nonverbal Response Scale

Choose the face below that matches how you feel today

Face Validity: on the surface, a study or scale appears to be intuitively valid

Inter-observer/Inter-rater Reliability: a measure of the degree to which different observers observe or code behaviors in similar ways

mood responses in 5-year-olds. See Figure 5.2 for an example of a nonverbal response scale (also see Egan, Santos, & Bloom, 2007, for an example of a study that used a similar nonverbal response scale with children).

When deciding on an appropriate operational definition to ensure that a study has good construct validity, a researcher can start by considering the face validity of a measure when it is chosen for a study. This means that, on the surface, the scale seems to measure what you think it does. For example, if you want to know how well someone performs a task under different conditions, an accuracy scale seems to be an intuitively good measure for this behavior. If you want to know about someone's mood, asking respondents about their mood seems as if it will measure what you want to measure. If items on a questionnaire seem to relate to the concept being measured, then the questionnaire has good face validity. We will consider more validity issues below as they relate to other variables in a research study.

Reliability of Measurements and Response Scales

The choice of measurement can also affect the reliability of the data collected in a study. Some scales are more reliable than others. For example, the reliability of a new survey is typically tested (in several ways) to ensure that responses do not change for a participant over time or across items on the survey, because the way survey items are written and the response scale chosen for a survey can affect the reliability of the scores on the survey. Typically, the reliability of a survey is tested by comparing scores for the same participants at different times or by comparing scores for the same participant on different parts of the survey. Reliability of surveys will be described further in Chapter 9.

Reliability is also an issue when a study involves multiple raters or coders of the behaviors of interest. The consistency of the recording of behaviors from different raters or coders is called inter-rater or inter-observer reliability. Inter-rater/inter-observer reliability was introduced in Chapter 4 with the naturalistic observation technique, as this form of reliability is most important with naturalistic observations. For example, in a study using naturalistic observations, there are typically multiple observers of the behaviors of interest, either observing at the same time to ensure that all behaviors are recorded or observing at different times to allow the participants to be observed for longer periods of time. In studies with multiple observers, you want to be sure that the different observers are making observations in the same way. In other words, it is important to have good inter-rater/inter-observer reliability. Consider a study where children are being observed for aggressive behaviors using naturalistic observations of the children, while they are at recess at school. For the study, aggressive behaviors have been operationally defined as aggressive contact with another person or yelling at another person. During the observation period, a child is seen yelling at other children. One observer codes the yelling as aggressive behavior because the behavior fits the operational definition. However, another observer codes the yelling as nonaggressive behavior, because he or she saw that the child was yelling from a distance to be heard, not to be aggressive. In this case, the two observers coded the same behavior in a different way, resulting in an inconsistency in the data. If the observers continue to code behaviors of other children this way, this inconsistency decreases the reliability of the data. To make certain that the inter-rater reliability in a study is good (and the inconsistencies just described do not occur), observers must be well trained to code behaviors in the same way, and their inter-rater reliability should be tested by having each observer code the same set of behaviors to look for a strong positive relationship between the data coded by the different observers. In other words, high inter-rater reliability means that there is a high rate of agreement in the way the different observers are recording behaviors.

Stop and Think

(5.3)   Explain what it means for a measure to have low reliability.

(5.4)   Suppose you created a new survey to measure mindfulness (i.e., one's ability to be "in the moment"). Describe how you could test the construct validity of your new survey.

(5.5)   Explain how lack of inter-observer/inter-rater reliability can lower the internal validity of a study.

INDEPENDENT VARIABLES

All research studies include at least one dependent variable, because the dependent variable is the measure of the behavior that is being observed. However, a subset of studies, classified as experiments, also includes an independent variable. In Chapter 4, we discussed experiments and how they differed from other research methods (i.e., they include an

Independent Variable: a variable in an experiment that is manipulated by the researcher such that the levels of the variable change across or within subjects in the experiment

independent variable that is manipulated and a comparison of the levels of the independent variable to test the hypothesis). Here we discuss some different ways that independent variables can be manipulated in a study and how the manipulation of independent variables can affect the validity of a study.

Types of Manipulations

There are three ways in which an independent variable can be manipulated to create levels of the independent variable: (1) as the presence and absence of a treatment or situation, (2) as a type of treatment or situation, and (3) as the amount of a factor in a treatment or situation.

Presence/absence variables typically include two levels, with one level being the presence of something and the other level being the absence of that thing. For presence/absence variables, the presence group is also called the experimental group and the absence group is called the control group (see Chapter 4 for more discussion of these concepts). The "something" that is manipulated could be a therapy (presence of therapy and absence of therapy), a drug treatment (presence of the drug and absence of the drug), or a time constraint for a task (presence of the time constraint and absence of the time constraint), depending on the type of study being conducted. Presence/absence variables are also called bivalent independent variables because they are independent variables that contain only two levels. Remember that an independent variable must have at least two levels, so a bivalent independent variable is the simplest type of independent variable.

Type variables include a different type of the "something" being manipulated in each level. For example, different types of drugs or therapies can be compared, different versions of an ad or product can be compared, or different types of instructions for a task can be compared. In each of these independent variables, all the levels include the factor being manipulated (drug, therapy, ad, product, instructions), but each level involves a different type or version of that factor.

Amount variables involve a manipulation of the amount of a factor in each level. For example, an experiment can investigate the amount of a drug (i.e., dosage) that is optimal for relieving symptoms such that each level of a variable includes a different amount of the same drug given to the participants. A common independent variable in memory research is the manipulation of the amount of time that passes between the study of material and the test on that material (i.e., a study–test delay) such that each level involves a different time delay (e.g., 5 minutes, 30 minutes, 2 hours, 1 day, 1 month, etc.). Whenever an independent variable contains three or more levels, it is considered a multivalent variable (i.e., multiple levels, more than two). See Figure 5.3 for a comparison of different independent variable manipulations.

——————— ❧ ———————

Presence/Absence Variable: a variable that involves a manipulation with a level that involves the treatment and a level that does not involve the treatment

Bivalent Independent Variable: an independent variable with two levels—a design is considered bivalent if it contains only one bivalent independent variable

Type Variable: a variable that involves a manipulation of types of a treatment

Amount Variable: a variable that includes levels with a different amount of the treatment changing from level to level

Multivalent Variable: an independent variable that includes three or more levels—a design is considered multivalent if there is only one independent variable that contains three or more levels

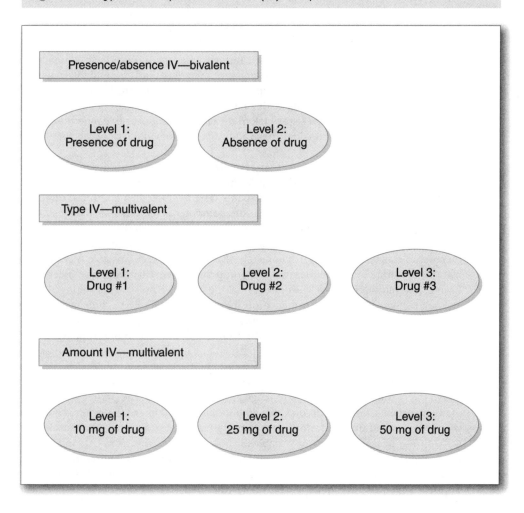

Figure 5.3 Types of Independent Variable (IV) Manipulations

Quasi-Independent Variables

So far in this chapter, we have been discussing true independent variables, or variables that are manipulated by the researcher. As described in Chapter 4, participants can also be separated into groups based on characteristics they already have. These groups create levels of a quasi-independent variable (also called a subject variable) based on characteristics that a researcher is unable to manipulate. The groups can then be compared in the same way as groups that are randomly assigned are

—✦—

Quasi-Independent/Subject Variable: variable that allows comparison of groups of participants without manipulation (i.e., no random assignment)

compared. Some examples of common quasi-independent variables used in psychological research include gender, age, personality types (e.g., introverts and extroverts), and ethnicity. Any characteristic that you can measure or observe from the participants can be used to group those participants and create a quasi-independent variable in a study.

The use of quasi-independent variables is very common in psychological research studies. However, researchers must be cautious when including these variables, because the causal relationship between the quasi-independent and dependent variables is not always as clear as it is with true independent variables. Without the manipulation by the researcher, it is always possible that additional factors (that are not part of the quasi-independent variable) are causing differences (or lack of differences) to occur between the groups. Thus, a researcher must always consider these additional factors when drawing conclusions from these factors.

For example, consider a study that compares different age groups on completion of a memory task to determine if memory declines as people age. Suppose the researcher for this study presented the items the participants were to study on a computer screen and then asked them to judge items presented on the computer screen as items they studied or not (i.e., they received a recognition test). The older participants in this study perform worse on the memory task than the younger participants. The researcher concludes that recognition memory of this type declines as people age. However, it is also possible that instead of having a deficit in memory abilities, the age group difference was due to the older participants having less familiarity with computers, making more errors in completing the computer task, and showing lower performance on the memory task due to their lack of experience with computers. The difference in computer experience between the two groups is one of those additional factors that must be considered here (and ruled out, if possible) before the researcher can conclude that the older participants had worse memory. In other words, the causal relationship between age and memory abilities has been clouded by the difference in computer experience between the two groups. Had the researcher been able to randomly assign the participants to the different age groups (or matched the participants based on previous experience with computers), this additional explanation of the results could have been more easily ruled out. Therefore, it is important to remember that the causal information gained from quasi-independent variables is not as clear as it is from true independent variables, and the researcher must be more cautious when interpreting differences across groups that were not manipulated (i.e., assigned) by the researcher. See Figure 5.4 for a comparison of true independent and quasi-independent variables.

Stop and Think

(5.6)   For each description below, identify the independent variable(s):

- Subjects are randomly assigned to one of three rooms of different size (small; medium, large) to complete a puzzle. Time to complete the puzzle is measured.
- Subjects play a computerized ball tossing game where a random half of the subjects are led to believe they are being included in the game by other subjects and the other half are led to believe they are being excluded by other subjects. Change in mood (before vs. after the game) is measured by a questionnaire.

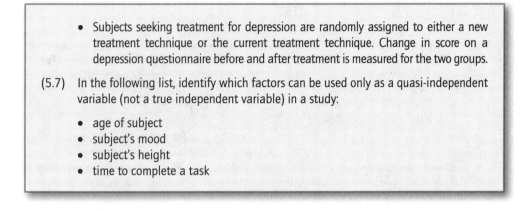

- Subjects seeking treatment for depression are randomly assigned to either a new treatment technique or the current treatment technique. Change in score on a depression questionnaire before and after treatment is measured for the two groups.

(5.7) In the following list, identify which factors can be used only as a quasi-independent variable (not a true independent variable) in a study:

- age of subject
- subject's mood
- subject's height
- time to complete a task

Figure 5.4 Independent and Quasi-Independent Variables

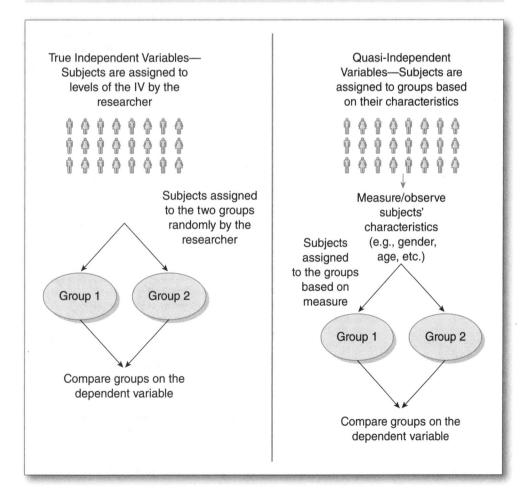

VALIDITY AND SOURCES OF BIAS

In this chapter, we have been discussing how the variables we examine in a study, as well as how we choose to measure or manipulate them, can affect the validity of the study. In fact, there are several different types of validity to consider when designing a study, and each has different implications. We will consider some basic types in this chapter and then further discuss validity as it relates to different research designs in the Nuts and Bolts chapters about each of those designs.

We have already considered choosing variables based on face validity (i.e., intuitively, does the variable seem to do what it should) and how a poor operational definition of a concept can lower the construct validity of a measure, but there are a few other types of validity that researchers should consider when designing a study. Some of the more common forms of validity and sources of bias that threaten these forms of validity are discussed below. Examples of these sources are provided in Table 5.2.

Internal Validity

Much of our discussion of validity has focused on internal validity. A study with good internal validity provides a good test of a causal hypothesis and controls for those extraneous factors that could affect the data but are not of interest in the study. In other words, a study with good

Table 5.2   A Summary of Sources of Bias

Bias	Definition	Examples	Type of Validity Threatened
Group differences	Participant groups are not equated on characteristics that can affect the data	Gender, previous knowledge or experience with the task, current mood state	Internal
Order effects	Order of conditions in a within-subjects design can affect data collected in different conditions	Easy versus difficult tasks, positive versus negative experiences	Internal
Testing effects	Multiple testing sessions—first testing affects subsequent testing	Practice effects, fatigue effects, accumulated knowledge of the task	Internal
Regression toward the mean	Extreme scores unlikely to recur	High score on test in class with low average grade, low score on test in class with high average grade, professional athlete has high-performing year compared with average performance	Internal
Hawthorne effect	Studying participants can change their behavior	Workers' productivity improves when they know they are being studied, participants perform better in a memory study than they would outside the study	External

internal validity provides a good test of a causal relationship by removing alternative explanations of the data (besides the independent variable). The discussion of different research designs in Chapter 4 indicated that the best way to test a causal relationship is to use the experimental method. Thus, well-designed experiments typically have higher internal validity than other research designs. The best way to design a good experiment (or even a good quasi-experiment) is to control for sources of bias that can make the causal relationship less clear (i.e., other factors besides the independent variable that might affect the dependent variable). These sources of bias are often called confounding variables (see Chapters 4 and 11 for more discussion of confounding variables).

Internal Validity: the degree to which a study provides causal information about behavior

Confounding Variable: an extraneous factor present in a study that may affect the results

Experimenter Bias: a source of bias in a study created when a researcher treats groups differently (often unknowingly) based on knowledge of the hypothesis

For example, suppose you were conducting a study on forgetting. You ask people to study some words and then they are tested on their memory for those words at some point in the future. Some people are tested after 5 min, others after 20 min, and still others after 2 hours. The people who are tested after 5 and 20 min are asked to complete some number puzzles between the study list and the test, but the people who are tested after 2 hours go to class and then come back after class for their test. The results of the study show that the people who were tested after 2 hours remembered fewer of the words that they had studied than the people who were tested after 5 and 20 min. What can explain these results? One possibility is that *forgetting* in memory has taken place and the people who were tested after 2 hours naturally forgot more than the people tested after 5 or 20 min. But another possible explanation for the results is that the people tested after 2 hours had to learn more information at their class, in the time between the study and the test, and that is the reason they could not remember as many of the words they studied as the people tested after 5 and 20 min, who completed number puzzles. In this example, the activity completed in the time between study and test is a confounding variable because it provides an alternative explanation for the results. The time between study and test changed across the groups but so did the activity they completed. Thus, it is unclear which thing caused the difference in memory scores.

There are several common sources of bias that can lower the internal validity of a study. As they apply to many different types of studies, it is a wise researcher who keeps these bias sources in mind when designing a study in order to control for or minimize these threats to internal validity.

Experimenter Bias. The first source of bias we discuss is one that can be caused by the researcher. Experimenter bias occurs when a researcher inadvertently treats groups differently in the study due to knowledge of the hypothesis for the study. For example, suppose an instructor is trying out a new type of assignment in a class that she thinks will help students learn a topic better than her old method. To test the effectiveness of the new assignment, she gives the assignment to one section of her class and the old assignment to another section of her class. She then compares the test scores of the two groups, with each section receiving the same exam. If the section with the new assignment scores higher than the section with the old assignment, there

---

Single-Blind Design: procedure used to hide the group assignment from the participants in a study to prevent their beliefs about the effectiveness of a treatment from affecting the results

Placebo: a sugar pill given to the control group in a drug study to allow all groups to believe that they are receiving a treatment

Double-Blind Design: procedure used to control for experimenter bias by keeping the knowledge of the group assignments from both the participants and the researchers who interact with the participants

---

are several possible reasons that this may have occurred. One explanation is that the new assignment is more effective than the old assignment in helping students learn the material. Another explanation is that there may be group differences (e.g., better students in the new assignment section) that caused the results, because the students were not randomly assigned to the two sections. A third explanation is that there may be experimenter bias in the study. In other words, because the instructor expected the new assignment section to perform better, she may have unknowingly been more enthusiastic with these students or encouraged them more than the other section. Alternatively, the instructor may have exhibited experimenter bias in the opposite manner by spending more time teaching the material to the old assignment section because she expected them to have more trouble learning the material. Either situation represents experimenter bias in the study.

To counter experimenter bias, a blind procedure is used in a study to hide the group assignment from the researcher and prevent inadvertent bias from occurring. A single-blind design is used to combat effects of subjects' knowledge of their group assignment. For example, when the effectiveness of a drug is tested, the control group typically receives a placebo to equate beliefs of effectiveness of treatment across groups. In a double-blind design, both the participants and the researchers who interact with the participants do not know which participants are assigned to the different groups. Thus, the instructor from the assignment study above could have used a double-blind design by trying out her assignment in a colleague's class or having a guest lecturer who is unaware of her hypothesis teach the material of interest. With this alternate procedure, the researcher who made the hypothesis does not interact with the participants during the course of the study.

Testing Effects. **Testing effects** can be an issue when multiple testing sessions occur in a study. They are more likely to occur in studies where participants are tested more than once or complete a task over a series of trials. Thus, testing effects are more likely in within-subjects experiments than between-subjects studies, as participants' behavior is measured under all levels of the independent variable(s) in within-subjects experiments (see Chapter 11 for more discussion of between-subjects and within-subjects experiments). Testing effects occur when an initial test affects data collected on subsequent tests. For example, in many tasks, participants improve over time due to practice effects. The more time participants spend completing a task (either across multiple levels of an independent variable or across many trials in a study), the more

---

Testing Effects: occur when participants are tested more than once in a study, with early testing affecting later testing

Within-Subjects Variable: each participant experiences all levels of the independent variable

Between-Subjects Variable: each participant experiences only one level of the independent variable

---

easily they complete the task due to experience with the task. Of course, the opposite can occur with extreme numbers of trials or many repeated testing sessions in a study. Participants can become fatigued over time, and their performance on a task declines over many repeated exposures to a task. Testing effects can be avoided in a study by minimizing the number of trials of a task as much as possible and counterbalancing levels of a within-subjects independent variable (see Chapter 11 for more discussion of counterbalancing). When questionnaires are

Counterbalancing: a control used in within-subjects experiments where equal numbers of participants are randomly assigned to different orders of the conditions

Regression Toward the Mean: can occur when participants score higher or lower than their personal average—the next time they are tested, they are more likely to score near their personal average, making scores unreliable

used in a study, different items may be used on different versions of the measure to minimize testing effects over repeated completions of a questionnaire. Testing effects are also discussed in the "nuts and bolts" chapters as they apply to specific types of studies: surveys in Chapter 9, experiments in Chapter 11, and quasi-experiments in Chapter 13.

Regression Toward the Mean. Regression toward the mean occurs when participants obtain an extreme score (high or low) on a questionnaire or task at one testing session but regress toward their mean score at another testing session. In other words, *regression toward the mean* signifies that extreme scores are not likely to recur. Regression toward the mean can be problematic in studies where a test or questionnaire is given more than once. If participants score very high or very low on the test the first time it is taken but obtain a more average score the next time the test is taken, it can make comparison of scores across conditions of a study difficult. Is the change in score due to the independent variable, or is it due to regression toward the mean? This can be a difficult question for a researcher to answer, but the more times the participants are tested, the more information a researcher will have to answer this question.

Consider your academic performance. Have you ever been performing very well in a class, but for one reason or another, you do poorly on one of the exams? Given that this is not your typical performance, this low score is not likely to reoccur. Now imagine that an instructor is trying out a new way of teaching material in a course. She gives the first exam with the old teaching technique and the second exam with the new teaching technique. If several people score unusually poorly on the first exam, but then regress to their more typical (and better) performance on the second exam, it may look like the new teaching technique was effective. But in reality, the difference in scores was simply due to several people regressing toward their mean performance.

Regression toward the mean can also hide an effect of a variable. If some people score unusually low on the first exam and more typically on the second exam while other people score typically on the first exam and unusually low on the second exam, it may look like the exam scores are similar for the two teaching techniques due to this regression toward the mean on both exams.

Regression toward the mean is a difficult source of bias to remove from a research study. The best way to minimize its effects is to use random assignment to conditions for between-subjects variables and to use several repetitions of the test for within-subjects variables (i.e., use more than two exams to compare teaching techniques). Random assignment should help spread any regression toward the mean that occurs in the study across the different groups so that it does not cause group differences. Using several repetitions of the test (e.g., having participants complete the test more than once for each level of the independent variable) will allow scores closer to each participant's true mean to occur in each condition. With a single testing for each level, you may end up with an extreme score for one of those levels. Trimming extreme scores from the data (when possible) also helps minimize regression toward the mean as a source of bias (see Chapter 7 for more information about trimming outliers). Splitting a group in half, based on high and low scores, can also control for regression toward the mean. Finally, using a large number of participants in a study (exactly how many depends on the type of study and the types of variables being tested) can help minimize the effect of a single extreme score on the data.

External Validity

External validity is the degree to which a study measures realistic behaviors and a study's results can be generalized beyond the study (i.e., to other individuals and situations). In other words, if participants behave in a research study the way they would in their everyday lives, then the study has good external validity. The results of the study can be generalized to behaviors, conditions, and individuals who were not specifically tested in the study. External validity can be reduced by attrition/mortality, where subjects decide not to complete a study, reducing the representativeness of the sample. There are also other factors that can reduce the external validity of a study. For example, as more control is imposed over sources of bias that reduce internal validity, the more external validity tends to suffer. When researchers include controls for internal sources of bias, they are typically restricting the situation under which the behavior of interest is expressed. Thus, the behavior may become more artificial and specific to the study being conducted. In other words, the behavior observed in the study becomes less like behavior that occurs in the participants' everyday lives.

❦

External Validity: the degree to which the results of a study apply to individuals and realistic behaviors outside the study

Attrition/Mortality: occurs when participants choose not to complete a study

---

For example, suppose a researcher was interested in the effects of work environment on work productivity. In the study, room size and the presence or absence of a window in the room are manipulated (i.e., these are the independent variables). The participants are asked to perform a task where they have to insert blocks of varying shapes into slots in a box for a 30-minute time period. At the end of the 30-minute period, the number of blocks correctly inserted is counted for each participant as a measure of work productivity (i.e., number correct on the block task is the operational definition of work productivity). The mean number of blocks correctly inserted is compared for the different room types. The study is conducted as a typical laboratory experiment such that the independent variables of interest are manipulated across room type, but the rooms are the same in all other ways.

Think about the internal and external validity of this study for a moment. The study appears to be fairly high in internal validity because the work environment is kept constant except for the manipulation of the two independent variables. The task is simple enough not to be affected by individual differences in ability. In other words, the study provides a good test of the hypothesis that room size and presence/absence of a window affect work productivity. However, one might question the external validity of the study. The block task might be a realistic type of task for a factory worker but may not be a good example of a daily task for an office worker. Thus, the results of the study may only generalize to a portion of all workers. In addition, the participants in the study know that they are participating in a study and may adjust their behavior accordingly. They may, for example, work harder than they would in their job because they know that they are being observed. Or, alternatively, they may not work as hard as they do in their job because they know that the task is just for a research study, and their performance does not affect them personally as it might in a job environment. This is known as the Hawthorne effect (see discussion below).

Now consider a similar study conducted in a factory by the factory's manager. Employees are placed in the different working environments as in the study described above (the rooms vary by size and whether or not a window is present). They complete their normal factory line task as usual. After a 30-minute period in the new environment, the factory manager counts up the number of assemblies completed by each employee to compare the different environments. The study described here is considered a field experiment, because the experiment (independent variables are still manipulated as in the laboratory experiment described above) is conducted in a naturalistic environment (i.e., in the "field").

Hawthorne Effect: a source of bias that can occur in a study due to participants changing their behavior because they are aware that they are being observed

Field Experiment: an experiment conducted in the participants' natural environment

Consider the internal and external validity of this experiment compared with the one described above. The external validity seems to be higher in the field experiment, because the factory workers' normal job task is used as the operational definition of work productivity. The behavior observed is more naturalistic for these workers. In addition, they are in their normal environment with other workers and normal factory sounds, making it more likely that they will exhibit more naturalistic work behaviors. However, several sources of bias have now been introduced into the experiment that might threaten the internal validity. Interactions with other coworkers are no longer controlled and could be different for different individuals across the experimental conditions. Noise is also a factor that might contribute to work productivity. It is not controlled across the room conditions in the field experiment as it is in the laboratory experiment. Thus, in this example with comparable laboratory and field experiments, the more controls there are that increase the internal validity in these experiments, the lower the external validity of the behaviors observed in the experiments.

Note that both studies described above are experiments. While experiments are typically higher in internal validity (and lower in external validity) than other research designs, this is not always the case and different types of experiments can vary greatly in internal validity based on the number of sources of bias controlled by the researcher. For example, in each of the above experiments, changes could be made in the method or design to increase internal or external validity as needed. How carefully a study is designed can make a big difference in how high the internal and external validity are, regardless of the research design employed. The design of the study can alter a participant's perception of the study, leading to a change in behavior that is less realistic simply because the participant knows that he or she is being observed. This issue will be discussed further below.

The Hawthorne Effect. The *Hawthorne effect* is a term coined by Landsberger (1955) as he was analyzing a set of studies conducted at the Hawthorne Plant, a factory that produced products for the Western Electric Company in the 1920s and 1930s in Chicago. Researchers conducted studies in the factory to determine the effects of different lighting conditions on worker productivity. The researchers found that all the lighting conditions they tried increased the workers' productivity. In other words, by the simple virtue of being studied, the workers' behavior changed. Other possible explanations have been offered for the results of this study (see Adair, 1984; Bramel & Friend, 1981), but the idea that studying individuals can change their behavior is now known as the Hawthorne effect. The act of studying individuals can alter their behavior and affect the results of a study, reducing its validity.

Demand Characteristics: a source of bias that can occur in a study due to participants changing their behavior based on their perception of the study and its purpose

---

A related concept known as demand characteristics can also affect the validity of a study. Demand characteristics occur when participants in a study attempt to "figure out" the purpose of the study and change their behavior based on their view of the purpose of the study. The participants' understanding of the study's purpose can be correct or incorrect, but they change their behavior based on whatever notion they have of the purpose (either to exhibit behavior that is consistent with what they think the researcher expects or to exhibit behavior different from what they think the researcher expects). This is a concept related to the Hawthorne effect, as demand characteristics occur as a result of a participant's involvement in a study.

One way to deal with the Hawthorne effect (and demand characteristics) is to observe the participants unobtrusively. This can be done using the naturalistic observation technique. However, this is not always possible for all behaviors. Another way to deal with the Hawthorne effect is to make the participants' responses in a study anonymous (or confidential). This may alleviate some of the effects of this source of bias. Deception may also be used to hide the purpose of the study. These issues are also addressed in the context of ethical standards for research with human participants in Chapter 3.

Sources of Bias Specific to a Field of Study

Some sources of bias are specific to a field of study. As a researcher becomes more familiar with an area of psychological study, these sources of bias become clearer, and ways to control for these biases can be built into the design of the studies—for example, in some memory research where study–test time delay is not an independent variable of interest, as in the example given earlier in this chapter. Instead, it can become a source of bias if different individuals are tested after different delays and delay is not a variable of interest in the study. Suppose that a researcher is interested in comparing two study conditions for their effect on memory ability. If one condition takes longer to complete, it is possible that the study–test delay will be longer in this condition than the study condition that can be completed in a shorter amount of time. Thus, memory researchers must consider the delay time in designing studies to ensure that different conditions are matched on this factor. Visual acuity is often controlled for in visual-perception experiments by requiring participants to have normal or corrected-to-normal vision. Each area of research has its own sources of bias.

As you become more familiar with a particular area of research, you can often learn about these sources of bias by examining the methods of other researchers to identify controls they have used to remove this bias. Discussion of internal and external validity will take place in the rest of the chapters of the text to help you identify situations in research where they are important.

Stop and Think

(5.8)   Describe the difference between a single-blind and double-blind design. Explain when each of these designs should be used.

(5.9)   An instructor wants to measure the amount of learning for students in his class. To measure learning, he gives subjects the final exam on the first day of class and then gives the same final exam at the end of the semester. Explain how testing effects could be a source of bias in this study.

CHAPTER SUMMARY

Reconsider the questions from the beginning of the chapter:

- What is a variable? A variable is an attribute, situation, or behavior that can change from individual to individual.
- What are the different types of variables that researchers consider in their studies? Dependent variables are measured from individuals and are present in all research studies. Confounding variables are variables that may affect the dependent variables in a study but are not of interest to the researchers (i.e., can bias the results). Independent variables are variables manipulated by the researcher in an experiment. Quasi-independent variables are present in quasi-experiments and experiments. They are similar to independent variables in that they involve a comparison of groups, but they are not manipulated (i.e., levels are not randomly assigned).
- Which type of research method contains an independent variable? Why? Experiments contain independent variables because experiments involve the manipulation of a variable that allows for additional control of confounding variables.
- How do reliability and validity affect the results of a study? Having good internal validity in a study means reducing bias that can affect the results and providing a good test of the hypothesis. Having good external validity means studying behaviors and obtaining results that generalize to individuals beyond the study in their everyday lives. Having reliable data in a study means having results that would occur again in a similar situation.
- What are some factors that affect the validity of a study, and how can a researcher control these factors? Several common sources of bias have been discussed in the chapter. Some are common to particular types of designs or behaviors. To control these sources of bias, researchers should first identify possible confounding variables in a study and then design the study in the best way to avoid having these variables bias the results.

THINKING ABOUT RESEARCH

A summary of a research study in psychology is given below. As you read the summary, think about the following questions:

1. Identify the independent variable. Was this independent variable manipulated between subjects or within subjects?

2. Identify the primary dependent variable. What scale of measurement was used for this dependent variable?

3. Consider the internal validity of this study. What aspects of the experiments increased the internal validity?

4. Consider the external validity of this study. Are the behaviors exhibited in the study realistic? Why or why not?

5. Would you characterize this study as higher on internal validity, external validity, or equal on each?

6. Why do you think the researchers used a confederate as the subjects' partner in the studies? What sources of bias does the use of a confederate allow them to control?

Research Study. Boothby, E. J., Clark, M. S., & Bargh, J. A. (2014). Shared experiences are amplified. *Psychological Science, 25,* 2209–2216.

Purpose of the Study. The researchers conducted two studies to examine the social effect on one's subjective experiences, based on past studies showing that shared experiences are psychologically stronger than unshared experiences. In their studies, they had subjects participate in both pleasant (Study 1) and unpleasant (Study 2) experiences. They predicted that when another person present was sharing the experience, the ratings of the experience would be stronger than when the other person present was engaged in a different activity.

Method of the Study. In both studies, participants completed both the shared experience and unshared experience conditions in a random order. In both studies, subjects and a research confederate were asked to complete some tasks based on a card draw. Subjects tasted the same chocolate in both conditions, but were led to believe that the chocolate was different in the two tasks. In Study 1, the chocolate was pleasant-tasting (pleasant experience) and in Study 2, the chocolate was bitter-tasting (unpleasant experience). In the shared condition, the confederate tasted the same chocolate as the subject. In the unshared experience, the confederate appeared to be tasting a different chocolate. The subjects were not allowed to communicate during the tasks. After tasting the chocolate, the subjects completed a survey about their rating of the chocolate (e.g., "How much do you like the chocolate? How flavorful is the chocolate?" etc.) and a survey about their impressions of the confederate. For both surveys, responses were made by checking a box on a 0 to 10 scale, with higher numbers indicating higher ratings.

Results of the Study. In both studies, ratings for the chocolate were stronger (higher for pleasant and lower for unpleasant) in the shared experience conditions. Figure 5.5 shows the ratings for liking of chocolate for both studies based on the social condition.

Figure 5.5 Mean Liking of Chocolate in Studies 1 and 2

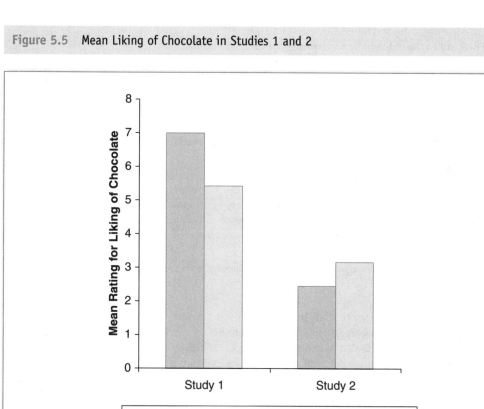

SOURCE: Results from Boothby et al.'s (2014) study.

Conclusions of the Study. The results of the study showed that shared experiences are more intense than unshared experiences, even when one does not communicate with someone else. This effect was present for both pleasant and unpleasant experiences, showing that the sharing of an experience does not simply make it more pleasurable, but makes it stronger overall.

COMMON PITFALLS AND HOW TO AVOID THEM

Problem: Confusing independent and dependent variables—students often get confused about which variable is which.

Solution: Remember that *dependent* means "relies on" and that must always be the variable that could change due to the "cause" or independent variable—thus, the dependent variable is the variable that is the behavior of interest measured from the participants and analyzed by the statistical tests.

Problem: Confusing independent and quasi-independent (subject) variables—students also have difficulty identifying a true independent variable that has been manipulated.

Solution: One method of identifying independent variables can be used for studies with different groups. For these studies, look for random assignment to levels for true independent variables that will indicate that a manipulation was made by the researcher.

Problem: Correctly identifying sources of bias—students sometimes have difficulty identifying sources of bias that can affect a study's results.

Solution: First identify the research design type (experiment, correlational study, etc.) and then consider sources of bias that are common for that design type; also consider the study from the participants' perspective and think through how their responses may be influenced by factors other than the variables of interest in the study.

Problem: Confusing scales of measurement—students sometimes have trouble distinguishing between different scales of measurement.

Solution: Consider first whether the scale involves categories or numbers. That will limit the scale to either a nominal/ordinal (category) or interval/ratio (number) scale. If the scale contains categories, consider whether the categories can be ordered from highest to lowest (ordinal) or not (nominal). If the scale involves numbers, determine whether the scale has a true zero point that indicates the absence of the variable being measured (ratio) or not (interval).

TEST YOURSELF

1. For each dependent variable below, indicate if it is measured on a nominal, an ordinal, an interval, or a ratio scale:

   (a) The amount of money you paid in tuition this year

   (b) Your hobbies, from most important to least important to you

   (c) Whether you plan to go to graduate school (yes or no)

   (d) Your last exam score as a measure of your performance on the exam (as percentage accuracy)

   (e) How much you are enjoying this class (on a 1 to 5 scale)

   (f) A list of your current career options

   (g) Your class standing (freshman, sophomore, junior, or senior)

2. For each of the following measures about aspects of beer, match each measure with the correct measurement scale: nominal, ordinal, interval, or ratio.

   (a) How dark the beer is with choices of lager (lightest), ale (medium light), porter (medium dark), and stout (darkest)

   (b) How long it takes one to identify the type of beer one is drinking

    (c)   Which brewery made the beer with choices of Yuengling, Leinenkugel, Blue Moon, Sam Adams, and Coors

    (d)   How much someone likes a beer being tasted, on a scale of 1 to 5

3. For the study described below, indicate all the information you can about how the independent variable was manipulated.

A psychologist conducted a study to compare the effect of different types of displays on participants' interest in a task. All participants in the study were asked to complete a set of math problems in the laboratory. Half of the participants just saw the text of the problem presented on the screen in black and white and typed in their answer on the computer keyboard. The other half of the participants saw the text of the problem in different colors, and small pictures that helped illustrate the problem were included. At the end of the task, all participants rated their interest in completing the task on a 1 to 10 scale.

4. For the study described in (3), list any possible sources of bias you can think of that might threaten the internal validity of the study and explain how the bias could affect the results of the study.

5. For the study described in (3), evaluate the external validity of the study. How could this study be redesigned as a field experiment?

6. If a score on a midterm is unusually high for a student and far above his or her mean grade in the class to date, this would represent _____ as a source of bias in using the midterm score to measure his or her learning in the course.

7. A _____ design is often used to prevent experimenter bias, such that neither the researcher nor the subject is aware of the condition the subject has been assigned to in the study.

8. Suppose a researcher wants to study work productivity in a factory. Video cameras are installed to see how much time workers spend on task during a workday. The workers are more productive on the day after the cameras are installed than on the day before. A possible cause of the increase in productivity that would represent a source of bias in the study is _____.

9. A researcher is interested in studying face recognition abilities. Subjects are tested in the lab on their recognition of photos of unknown faces presented on a computer screen. If the subjects process the photos of the faces in a way that is different from how they typically process faces in their daily lives, this study would suffer from low _____ validity.

10. Explain why attrition/mortality is a possible source of bias when it occurs in a research study.

Answers can be found at edge.sagepub/mcbride3e.

STOP AND THINK ANSWERS

(5.1)   Ratio, ordinal, nominal

(5.2)   Answers will vary, but two examples are (a) rating on a scale of 1 to 7 to indicate hunger and (b) how much food a person eats when food is offered.

(5.3)   Low reliability means that the scores on the scale are not consistent (either across time or across items).

(5.4)   You can compare the scores on your measure with other measures already known to measure mindfulness to see if they are similar.

(5.5)   If observers or raters measure behavior in different ways, this will add a source of bias to the results.

(5.6)   Room size (small, medium, large), game condition (inclusion, exclusion) and time of measure (before and after the game), treatment condition (current, new)

(5.7)   Age of subject, subject's height (unless you have them stand on something)

(5.8)   In single-blind designs the subject does not know which condition he or she receives. This design should be used when demand characteristics are of concern. In double-blind designs the researcher also does not know which condition a subject receives. This design is used when experimenter bias is of concern.

(5.9)   Because subjects take the same test both times, they could remember some of the questions and do better the second time simply because they have remembered them and paid attention to or looked up the answer.

⑤SAGE edge™

Visit edge.sagepub.com/mcbride3e for the tools you need to sharpen your study skills:

- Web Quizzes
- eFlashcards
- Thinking About Research

- SAGE Journal Articles
- Web and Multimedia Resources

Chapter 6
Sampling

Consider the following questions as you read Chapter 6

- What is the difference between a population and a sample?
- Why do we need to sample?
- What is the difference between probability and convenience samples?
- Which types of samples will reduce sampling error more than other types?
- In what situations would a researcher need to use a convenience sample?
- What is the advantage of using the Internet to sample?

Suppose you read in a magazine that 98% of women who responded to a survey reported being dissatisfied with their marriage and 75% reported having affairs. Would you conclude from this survey that 98% of all married women are unhappy being married? Would you believe that 75% of married women have affairs? Why or why not?

It is hoped that by now you have begun to recognize that not all research produces valid results and that whenever you are presented with statistics, such as those above about married women, you should be at least a little skeptical (even if the statistics seem believable) because there are many factors that can influence the observations collected in a study. How the study was conducted can tell you a lot about whether the results can be generalized to a larger group of individuals beyond the participants who participated in the study. We discussed some of these possible sources of bias in Chapter 5. In this chapter, we consider another possible source of bias in research studies: the sampling technique.

To give you an example of how sampling can affect a research study's results, consider the survey results described above. Hite (1987) reported these survey results in her book *Women and Love*. However, only 4.5% of the women who received Hite's survey responded to it (Reiniger, 2001; Wallis, 1987). This means that very few of the women who were contacted completed

---

Response Rate: the percentage of people out of the total number available who respond to a survey

---

the survey (4,500 out of 100,000 contacted for her survey). Her low response rate may help explain her results. Because individuals have a choice to complete a survey or not, the 4.5% who chose to complete the survey may have been different from the other women who chose not to complete the survey, resulting in a sample that did not represent how most women feel about the issues in the survey. For example, it is possible that the women who completed Hite's survey were particularly unhappy about their relationships and felt compelled to complete the survey to express their dissatisfaction.

To further investigate this issue, ABC News conducted a survey in 2004 that showed that only 14% of women who responded to their survey reported having an affair outside of a committed relationship. In their sample, 92% of the people who were asked to complete the survey did so (1,380 out of 1,501 contacted for the survey). In other words, the survey results obtained by ABC News were more likely to represent the responses of all American women (if all American women could have responded) than the results of Hite's survey, because the response rate was much higher in the ABC News survey. Thus, the higher response rate (i.e., a larger percentage of those contacted completed the survey) makes it more likely that the ABC News results better reflect the attitudes of American women, even though fewer individuals completed this survey than Hite's (1987) survey.

In this chapter, we consider the effect of sampling techniques on the results of research studies, discuss several common sampling techniques used in psychological research, compare different sampling techniques based on their potential to contribute bias to a study, and consider the practicality of the use of different sampling techniques in a study (Figure 6.1).

POPULATIONS AND SAMPLES

The goal of psychological research is to learn about behavior that applies to a group of individuals. The group can be all humans, all Americans, or all Europeans who have high levels of anxiety. The group a researcher wants to learn about depends on the study being conducted and the research question the study is designed to answer. This group is called the population. The population is typically a fairly large group of individuals. Thus, even though it is the population we want to learn about, it is usually impossible to test the entire population in a research study. There are often too many individuals in a population to include in a study, and researchers would have a difficult time locating each individual and persuading him or her to participate. Therefore, researchers select a sample of individuals from the population to serve as the participants in their study (Figure 6.2). This allows the researchers to learn about the population from the sample selected and to have a participant sample that is small enough that all individuals in the sample can participate in the study. The actual size of the sample depends on the type of study and the resources that researchers have for collecting data from their sample. In studies where

---

Population: a group of individuals a researcher seeks to learn about from a research study

Sample: the group of individuals chosen from the population to represent it in a research study

---

Figure 6.1   Steps in the Research Process: Creating a Sample

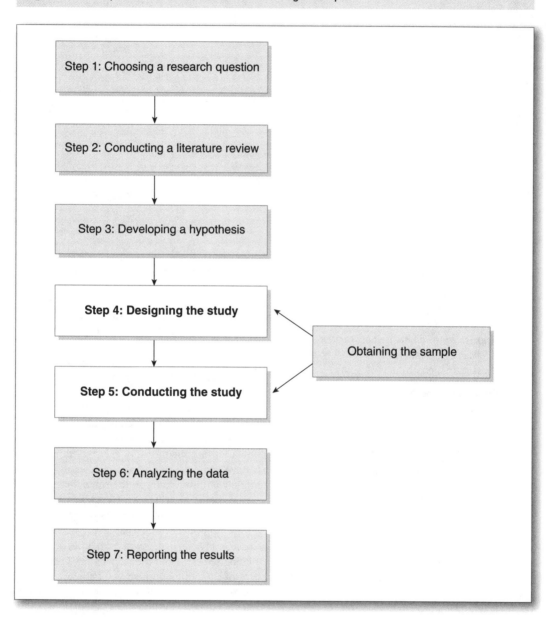

individuals must participate one at a time (as in some experiments using systematic observations—see Chapter 4), the sample may be smaller than in studies where individuals can participate simultaneously (as in correlational studies using surveys for data collection—see Chapter 4).

Figure 6.2   The Sample Is Chosen to Represent the Population in a Study

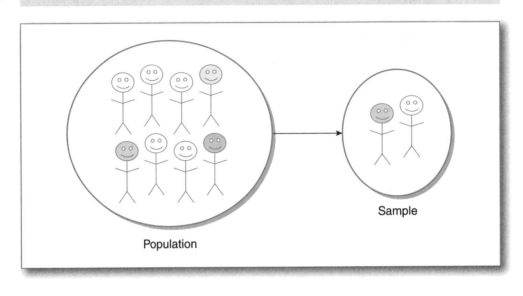

Population

Sample

Sampling Error: the difference between the observations in a population and in the sample that represents that population in a study

Probability Sample: sample chosen such that individuals are chosen with a specific probability

Convenience/Purposive Sample: sample chosen such that the probability of an individual being chosen cannot be determined

Regardless of the size of the sample obtained, the goal in participant sampling is to choose individuals for the sample who will represent the behaviors and attitudes of the entire population. In other words, you want to choose individuals for your sample whose overall observations are similar to the observations you would see in the complete population group—if you were able to study the entire population. Any difference in the observations between the sample and the population is called sampling error. All research studies have some amount of sampling error because the sample will never give you the same observations as the entire population. The best a researcher can do is to minimize the sampling error as much as possible.

One way to reduce sampling error is to choose a sampling technique that gives you the most representative sample for the population you want to study. We begin with probability samples, where individuals have a specific probability of being chosen from the population. Probability samples are those most likely to be representative of the population, so you should use these samples whenever it is feasible to do so. However, as you will see below, it is not always practical to use a probability sample. In many cases, a convenience sample (also called a purposive sample; Shadish et al., 2002) is needed. In convenience samples the probability of an individual being chosen from the population cannot be determined, because individuals are not chosen randomly. Thus, the sample may not represent the population as well as a probability sample but can be obtained more easily than a probability sample. Table 6.1 provides an overview of the sampling techniques discussed to help you choose the best sampling technique for a study.

Table 6.1   Overview of Sampling Techniques

Technique	Characteristics	Example	Advantages	Disadvantages
Simple random	Each member of the population has an equal probability of being selected using random sampling.	Students are chosen randomly from a list of all students at a university.	Reduces sampling error by choosing from all members of the population to best represent the population.	Difficult to ensure that each member of a large population can be chosen in a sample.
Cluster	Clusters of individuals are identified and then a subset of clusters is randomly chosen to sample from.	Doctors who work at hospitals are chosen for a sample by identifying all hospitals in different areas of the United States and then randomly choosing 10 hospitals in each area of the United States to sample from.	Makes it easier to choose members randomly from smaller clusters to better represent the population.	Can ignore segments of the population that are not in the clusters chosen for the sample.
Stratified random	Members of a population are selected such that the proportion of a group in the sample is equal to the proportion of that group in the population using random sampling.	Registered voters are randomly selected from lists of Democrats and Republicans to equal the proportion of registered Democrats and Republicans in the United States.	Reduces bias due to an identified characteristic of the population by equating proportions in the sample and the population for that characteristic to better represent the population.	Similar to simple random—can be difficult to ensure equal probability of being chosen from a large population.
Convenience	Members of population are chosen based on convenience and on who volunteers.	Sample is chosen from students who volunteer to complete an extra credit assignment in their psychology course.	Easier to obtain than probability samples.	May not represent the population properly due to selection bias because random sampling is not used.

PROBABILITY SAMPLES

Probability samples can reduce the amount of sampling error that exists in a study. Thus, it is important to use a probability sample when sampling error is likely to be large. Sampling error will increase whenever observations differ greatly from participant to participant in a sample or when a sample is chosen such that a segment of the population is not represented in the sample. For example, in small samples it is more likely that data will differ from participant to participant. We will consider three different types of probability samples (see Table 6.1) that researchers can consider when sampling error is likely to be high: simple random samples, cluster samples, and stratified random samples.

Simple Random Samples

A simple random sample is a sample in which each member of a population has an equal chance of being selected for the sample. Thus, if a population has 100 individuals, the chance of any one individual being selected for the sample is 1 in 100 or 1%. In most cases, using a simple random sample gives you the most representative sample possible for the population you are interested in, because the process of random sampling is less likely than any other selection mechanism to over- or underrepresent any particular subgroup of the population. The key to using a simple random sample is to find a way to choose individuals from the population such that they all have an equal chance of being selected. Suppose that the population for a study is all students at your university or college. If you want to choose a sample of 1,000 participants from this population, you could obtain a list of all the students at your school and choose 1,000 of them at random by having a computer generate a list of random numbers that correspond to numbers in your list of students. Many programs, such as Microsoft Excel, can do this for you. You can then contact each of the 1,000 students chosen randomly from the list to participate in your study (Figure 6.3).

However, simple random samples can be difficult to obtain for large populations. Suppose that you want to generalize the results of your study to *all* college students, not just the ones at

---

Simple Random Sample: sample chosen randomly from the population such that each individual has an equal chance of being selected

Cluster Sample: sample chosen randomly from clusters identified in the population

Stratified Random Sample: sample chosen from the population such that the proportion of individuals with a particular characteristic is equivalent in the population and the sample

---

Figure 6.3   Simple Random Sample

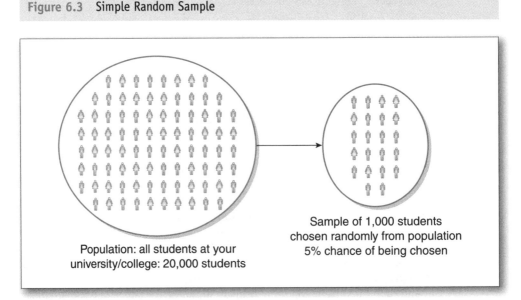

Population: all students at your university/college: 20,000 students

Sample of 1,000 students chosen randomly from population 5% chance of being chosen

NOTE: Each individual in the population has an equal chance of being chosen.

your school. In this case, your population is very large, and you do not have access to all the individuals in the population to choose them with equal probability. A simple random sample is not practical for this population and another sampling technique is a better choice.

Cluster Samples

A better way to sample all college students is to use a cluster sample. In a cluster sample, clusters of individuals (e.g., all students at each university/college) are first identified. Then a subset of the clusters is chosen to sample from (e.g., 25 of the universities/colleges on the list). Finally, individuals can be chosen at random from each of the target clusters in the subset (e.g., by randomly choosing 20 students from the list of all students at each of the 25 universities/colleges in the target cluster subset). Cluster samples allow researchers to obtain a probability sample from a large population more easily than they would with a simple random sample, because the list from which individuals are selected is more manageable and easier to obtain (i.e., it is easier to obtain lists of students at 25 universities/colleges than to obtain lists of students at *all* universities/colleges) (Figure 6.4).

From this example, you may be thinking that cluster sampling still seems rather difficult. However, cluster samples can be used more conveniently by using a hierarchy of clusters. For the example above, suppose that you were not able to obtain lists of all the students at each of the 25 universities/colleges that make up your target clusters. In this case, you could add a level

Figure 6.4   Cluster Sample: Clusters Randomly Chosen From a Population

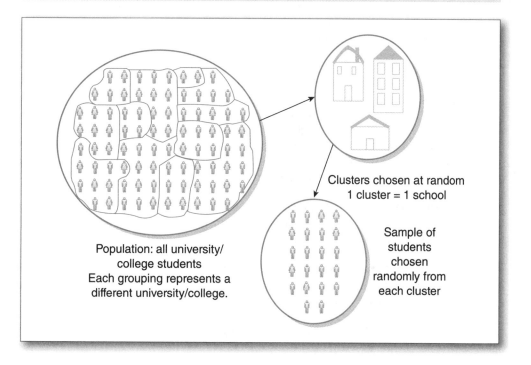

of clusters to your sampling technique. For example, instead of sampling randomly from the lists of all students at the 25 target universities/colleges, you could identify a course at each university/college chosen at random from the class list for the current semester and use the students in each class as your sample from that cluster. By using the classes as another level of clusters, you make the sampling job easier and still obtain a random sample from your population.

A disadvantage of cluster sampling is that a portion of the population may be missed in the sample, giving the researcher a sample that is not fully representative of the population. For example, suppose that all (or most) of the schools chosen at random as target clusters in the example above happened to be in the southern United States. In this case, significant portions of the population (college students in the other parts of the country or other countries) would be underrepresented in the sample. One way to fix this problem is to use another level of clusters in the sampling procedure that first groups schools by area before target cluster schools are chosen. Another solution to this problem is to use a stratified random sample.

Stratified Random Samples

A stratified random sample is used when researchers want to make sure that their sample contains equivalent percentages of individuals from subgroups as exist in the population. For example, approximately 60% of U.S. college students are female and 40% are male. Thus, if you are interested in the population of U.S. college students in your study and you want to ensure that the gender breakdown of students in the population is also represented in your sample, you would need to make certain that 60% of the students chosen at random from the population are female and 40% are male. This means that if your sample contained 100 students, 60 would be female, and 40 would be male. You could obtain lists of students organized by gender and randomly choose 60 females and 40 males from this list to obtain your sample. Using this method, your sample best represents U.S. college students by gender. If your sample does not follow this gender breakdown, then your sample might be biased depending on how much gender affects the results of your study.

A stratified random sample could also be used to solve the problem of location bias in the example above. Suppose you determined the breakdown of college students by area of the United States as 30% on the East Coast, 25% on the West Coast, 20% in the South, and 25% in the Midwest. To ensure that your sample contains a similar breakdown by area and best represents the population of college students, you can use the percentages of students by area to draw your sample. In other words, you would randomly choose 30% of your sample from students on the East Coast, 25% of your sample from students on the West Coast, and so on. In this way, your sample represents the current breakdown of students by area in the population (Figure 6.5).

An excellent example of stratified random sampling is provided in a study reported by Kahn and Schlosser (2010). These researchers were interested in evaluating several characteristics involving student and faculty satisfaction as well as student-faculty mentoring relationships in graduate programs in professional psychology. To obtain a sample of clinical, counseling, and school psychology doctoral programs from which to obtain their data, Kahn and Schlosser stratified programs by area and by size. In other words, they determined the percentage of psychology programs that were classified as clinical, counseling, or school and then considered the percentages of each of these area programs that were classified as "small" or "large." They then sampled a set of programs from all of these selections that fit the percentages by area and size of all the programs they identified. Thus, they did not sample all the doctoral programs

Figure 6.5 Stratified Random Sample

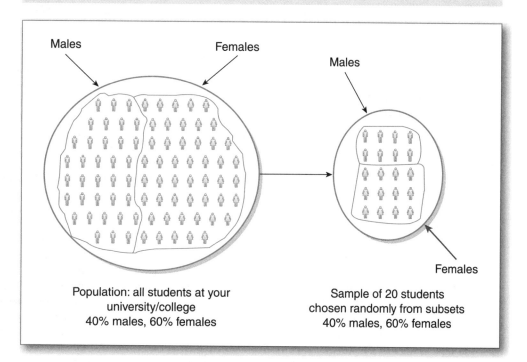

Population: all students at your
university/college
40% males, 60% females

Sample of 20 students
chosen randomly from subsets
40% males, 60% females

NOTE: Subsets of the population are identified based on demographics. A proportion of individuals is then randomly chosen from subsets to represent proportions in the population.

in clinical, counseling, and school psychology, but instead chose a subset of these programs such that the percentages in their sample matched the percentages of programs by area and size overall. This ensured that area and size of program were represented in their sample in the same proportions as exist in the population of all programs of this sort.

Stop and Think

(6.1) In what situation would a researcher want to use a stratified random sample?

(6.2) Explain why probability samples can be difficult to collect.

CONVENIENCE SAMPLES

In many cases, researchers would have a difficult time obtaining probability samples for their studies. As mentioned above, probability samples require access in some way to the entire population

---
— �֍ —

Internal Validity: the degree to which a study provides causal information about behavior

External Validity: the degree to which the results of a study apply to individuals and realistic behaviors outside the study

Volunteer Sample: sample chosen from the population such that available individuals are chosen based on who volunteers to participate

---

to select individuals according to a predetermined probability value. This is not always easy to achieve. For some studies, use of a probability sample can be important when sampling error is likely to be large. This is especially true for studies where results may be influenced by demographic factors such as gender, ethnicity, or location of residence, or in studies where participants are likely to differ from one another in their behaviors or attitudes. Sue (1999) argued, for example, that when ethnicity is not considered in a sample, ethnic differences that may exist will be ignored. However, in other studies, these factors are less important and less likely to influence the results. In many studies of basic cognitive functions, such as perception, memory, or psycholinguistics, demographic factors may be less influential and a convenience sample can be used without too much sampling error affecting the results (however, see Henrich, Heine, & Norenzayan, 2010, for some examples of the influence of demographic factors on cognitive effects). A convenience sample allows researchers to obtain a sample more easily when choosing at random from the population (or from subsets of the population) is not possible or necessary.

If a convenience sample is used in a study, a researcher should be aware of the limitations of these samples. Convenience samples likely increase the amount of sampling error in the study, lowering its internal validity by making a test of the hypotheses less accurate (Rosenthal & Rosnow, 2008). This can occur because some of the characteristics of individuals who volunteer to participate in studies may act as confounding variables and cloud a causal relationship tested in a study. See Chapters 4 and 5 for more discussion of internal validity and Chapter 7 for more discussion of sampling error. In addition, because individuals are chosen as a specific subset of the population that is not random, it is less likely that a convenience sample provides a good representation of the population in the study (a situation that leads to the increase in sampling error mentioned above). This makes it more difficult to generalize the results of the study to the population, lowering its external validity. See Chapters 4 and 5 for more discussion of external validity. External validity of a study should be considered when conclusions are drawn from results collected with a convenience sample.

Volunteer Samples

If you have ever participated in a research study at your school where you were recruited through a sign-up system (an online sign-up system, a sign-up bulletin board, etc.), then you have been part of a volunteer sample in a study. Volunteer samples are used when a researcher recruits individuals from a population (e.g., students at your school) by recruiting individuals to whom he or she has ready access (such as asking students in certain types of classes to sign up for the research studies). The incentive for students to sign up for these studies may be a research requirement or extra credit points in their course or a monetary compensation. You may have such a requirement or extra credit opportunity in the class for which you were assigned this text. If you have ever been asked to answer some survey questions by someone at the grocery store or in front of the student union building, then you have seen another example of volunteer sampling. The survey takers approach individuals they have easy access to and ask for volunteers to complete their survey (Figure 6.6).

Figure 6.6   Volunteer Sample

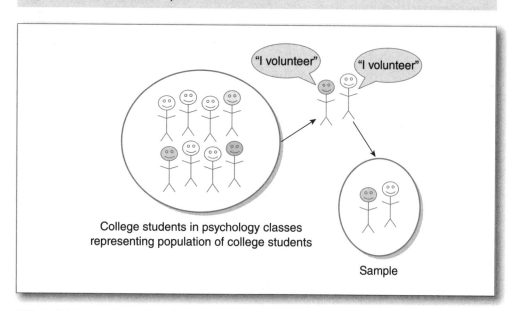

College students in psychology classes
representing population of college students

Sample

NOTE: Individuals are chosen from the population based on whom the researcher has easy access to and who volunteers from this group.

Volunteer samples are convenience samples because the probability of recruiting any individual from the population is not known due to a lack of random selection from the population or subset of the population. For example, when students at a university or college sign up to participate in psychological research studies, they are typically recruited from specific courses in which students are made aware of the research participation opportunities. Thus, the sample comes from students taking certain types of courses on campus (i.e., typically psychology courses). It is possible that these students are different from the students taking other courses on campus. In addition, the students are often given an incentive to sign up (e.g., credit in a course, monetary payment). The incentives may be influential to certain types of students. For example, a small monetary compensation or course credit may be more motivating to some students than to others. This means that the entire population of students at a university or college may not be represented in the sample, making it more difficult to generalize the results from the sample chosen to the broader population a researcher wishes to study.

Volunteer samples are quite common in psychological research. They are used because they are typically the most convenient means of obtaining a sample for a study and in most cases do not greatly reduce the generalizability of the results of a study. See below for further discussion of this issue.

Quota Samples

Quota samples are similar to stratified random samples without the random selection from subsets of the population. As with a stratified random sample, the goal of a quota sample is to

---

❧

Quota Sample: sample chosen from the population such that available individuals are chosen with equivalent proportions of individuals for a specific characteristic in the population and sample

---

represent subgroups of the population in the same proportions in the sample as exist in the population. Thus, if researchers wish to examine attitudes about college work habits, they may be concerned with their participants' class level, as participants at different class levels may have different attitudes based on the amount of experience they have with college-level work. If the population of students at their school is 30% freshmen, 20% sophomores, 25% juniors, and 25% seniors, then the sample contains the same breakdown of class level in a quota sample. However, unlike a stratified random sample, the quota sample makes use of convenience sampling techniques such as recruiting participants from a participant sign-up pool or asking students sitting in the library to fill out the survey. The researchers keep track of the percentage of different class levels in their sample to ensure they equate the class-level breakdown in their sample to the existing percentage in the population. Sampling continues until the quota is reached for each class level.

COMPARISON OF PROBABILITY AND CONVENIENCE SAMPLING TECHNIQUES

As described above, the advantage of convenience samples is that they are easier to obtain than probability samples. The disadvantage is that they may not be truly representative of the population a researcher wants to learn about, lowering the external validity of a study. The importance of external validity in psychological studies has been debated for decades. Many researchers have argued that results from psychological studies using volunteer college students for samples are not informative about the behavior in the general population (e.g., Rosnow, Rosenthal, McConochie, & Arms, 1969; Sears, 1986). However, convenience samples may be a lesser problem in studies examining certain types of behavior that are likely to generalize beyond the study. In addition, the purpose of the study may be to examine what is possible in human behavior, even if that behavior may not occur in the real world for a large group of individuals (Mook, 1983). Remember that studies will differ in how basic and how applied they are, based on the goals of the researcher. The more basic the research, the more external validity may be sacrificed due to the control required to meet the goal of gaining causal information about behavior. Important knowledge can still be gained about human behavior from studies where it is unclear how well the results generalize to everyday behaviors and populations that go beyond college students (Oakes, 1972). This issue also highlights the importance of replication in the scientific process. Results that generalize to one population may not generalize to another population. Thus, it is important to consider both the population and the goal of the research when choosing a sampling technique.

One should also consider the differences between a "target" population and the "accessible" population. The *target* population is the population that the researcher wishes to generalize the results of the sample study to. The "accessible" population is the population that the researcher has available to use as the sample pool. For example, a researcher may wish to generalize the results of a study to all human adults or to all U.S. citizens. However, it is unlikely that these populations are accessible to the researcher. It is more likely that a population of university students at the researcher's institution is accessible for sampling. In some cases, using an "accessible" population rather than the target population may affect the external validity of the study. However, in many situations, the results of a study that addresses a common behavior can be generalized to the "target" population as well.

Stop and Think

(6.3) The majority of psychological research studies utilize convenience samples. What consequence do you think this has for generalizing the results? Is this a serious problem? Why or why not?

(6.4) Suppose you wanted to collect survey responses from a quota sample that considered race/ethnicity of the participants. Explain how you might collect the sample in this case.

RECRUITING PARTICIPANTS

Regardless of the type of sampling technique chosen, researchers must consider how to actually recruit the participants for a study. In other words, how are the participants contacted to let them know about the study and what incentives are offered for their participation? The issue of how to contact the participants to recruit them is related to the selection mechanism in some types of studies. For example, if you are randomly choosing participants from the phone book, it may make sense to contact them by phone. If you are randomly choosing participants from a list of students at a university, you may only be provided with certain types of contact information (e.g., campus or permanent addresses, e-mail addresses) that will limit the means available for contacting the participants. Many university and college psychology departments have participant pools available to researchers that provide a standard means of contacting participants for volunteer samples (e.g., participant sign-up board or website). The means of contacting participants is an important issue, as it may affect the sample size obtained for a study. Researchers should carefully consider recruitment techniques that may be most effective for their population. For example, younger participants may be more likely to respond to e-mail contacts, whereas older participants may be more likely to respond to phone contacts. If you are considering recruiting acquaintances for a research study, the ethics of such recruitment should also be considered. For example, what is the best way to approach an acquaintance about participating in a study to maximize sample size but to also reduce coercion?

Incentives can also have an impact on the sample size obtained. For established, institution participant pools, there may be incentives built in to the recruitment process, such as completion of an assignment or extra credit in psychology courses. In these cases, an alternative assignment must also be available to students in the course to reduce coercion. Other incentives such as payment or entrance in a drawing may be possibilities available to researchers if the resources are available. Again, coercion issues should be considered for these incentives as well. Not all studies require incentives; individuals may be willing to participate in short studies without such incentives (e.g., completing a short survey on the street). Longer and more arduous studies may require an incentive to recruit a sufficient sample size. However, as described above, this may also create a situation where the incentive or lack of incentive adds bias to the study.

One question you may be thinking about (especially if you are working on your own research project for your methods course) is how many subjects is enough. The answer to this question depends on several factors, including the type of study you are conducting, the type of data you are collecting, the type of population you are sampling, and the practicality of your sampling technique. In some cases, you may be collecting several measurements for each dependent variable from each subject (e.g., as in cognitive studies). For this type of study, you may not need many subjects per condition. If you take a look at some studies on perception and memory, you will see that they include sample sizes of between 20 and 50 subjects per condition. However, if you are only collecting one measurement per subject or are asking subjects to complete surveys and questionnaires, you may need to include a larger sample. Many such studies include sample sizes in the hundreds. If you are sampling from a small population (e.g., autistic children), you may need to use a small sample of only 10 to 20 subjects due to lack of availability of individuals in this population and the difficulty you may have in recruiting such subjects. Thus, researchers must consider a number of factors when they decide how large a sample is sufficient for their study.

USING THE INTERNET TO SAMPLE

Samples obtained using the Internet are becoming more frequent in recent psychological research. Many types of observation techniques can be used with Internet samples, including surveys and systematic observations. Experiments that require systematic presentation of stimuli can be reproduced for presentation on the Internet to individual participants. See http://psych.hanover.edu/research/exponnet.html for a list of current psychological studies being conducted on the Internet ("Retrospection," 2008). According to Birnbaum (2001), advantages of Internet samples over laboratory studies include use of larger and more diverse samples, fewer opportunities for bias due to experimenter interactions with partici-

Internet Sample: sample chosen from the population by recruiting on the Internet

pants, fewer constraints on the time and location of data collection, less time needed to collect a sample, and fewer researchers needed to supervise the study procedures. Many researchers have also shown that data collected with Internet samples produced similar effects to samples collected in the laboratory (Birnbaum, 2001; Krantz & Dalal, 2000).

The studies comparing lab and Internet samples show that Internet samples tend to be more demographically diverse (Birnbaum, 2001). Thus, Internet sampling may yield samples that are a better representation of large, general populations. However, there are some issues that researchers should be aware of when they choose to use an Internet sample (Birnbaum, 2001). For example, some smaller subgroups in the population may require extra work to include in the sample because the number with access to the Internet may be too small to allow for adequate sampling. Researchers may need to contact special interest groups to recruit them for the study to achieve the best representation possible. In addition, it may be difficult to control who completes a study on the Internet, making stratified random and quota samples more difficult to obtain and making it difficult to monitor repeat participation from the same individuals. It may also be difficult to balance group size in between-subjects designs. Finally, it is more difficult to monitor participants during the study procedure to rule out sources of bias (such as distractions) for Internet samples. Nonetheless, Internet samples show great promise in making sampling easier for some types of psychological studies.

Also, providing incentives may be important for recruiting Internet samples. The type of incentive a researcher offers may affect the sample size obtained in an Internet sample more often than in studies where data collection is done in a laboratory or in other in-person environments because it may be harder to gain a participant's attention with an Internet study. On the other hand, the feeling of anonymity that comes with completing a study on the Internet may also be a benefit in recruiting Internet samples. Finally, Internet samples may be larger than samples obtained by other means; thus, researchers must also consider available resources when choosing an incentive for an Internet study.

CHAPTER SUMMARY

Reconsider the questions from the beginning of the chapter:

- What is the difference between a population and a sample? The population is the group of individuals a researcher wants to learn about. The sample is the subset of the population that participates in the study.
- Why do we need to sample? In most cases, it would be difficult or impossible to test the entire population in a study. Thus, a sample is used to represent the population in the study.
- What is the difference between probability and convenience samples? In probability samples, the probability of an individual being chosen from the population is known, and participants are chosen randomly from the population or a subset of the population. For convenience samples, the probability of an individual being chosen is not known, and the participants are chosen in a nonrandom manner.
- Which types of samples reduce sampling error more than other types? Probability samples are typically more representative of the population and have less sampling error.
- In what situations would a researcher need to use a convenience sample? In many cases, a population is too large to allow all individuals to be identified for sampling. Thus, a convenience sample is used. In other cases, the incentive for participation may apply only to a convenience sample.
- What is the advantage of using the Internet to sample? The Internet is a useful tool for recruiting a representative sample that may be larger than a sample that is recruited in person. Using the Internet can help a researcher access a subject sample that is more varied in age and ethnicity than convenience samples from college student populations.

THINKING ABOUT RESEARCH

A summary of a research study in psychology is given below. As you read the summary, think about the following questions:

1. Identify the most likely population of interest (i.e., "target" population) for this study based on the description below.

2. Each study described below used a different sampling technique. Can you identify the sampling technique used in each study?

3. Do you think the samples collected in these studies provided samples that were representative of the population of interest? Why or why not?

4. What are some of the disadvantages of the sampling techniques used in the study?

5. Suppose Study 2 had been conducted with a simple random sample of the population of all adults in the United States. Describe how a simple random sample might have been obtained for this study.

6. What would be the advantages and disadvantages of using the simple random sample you described in (5) above?

Research Study. Kumar, A., Killingsworth, M. A., & Gilovich, T. (2014). Waiting for Merlot: Anticipatory consumption of experiential and material purchases. *Psychological Science, 25*, 1924–1931. (Note: Only Studies 1 and 2 of this article are described below.)

Purpose of the Study. The researchers examined the finding that individuals show greater satisfaction with experiences they spend their money on than with material purchases (e.g., clothes, cars, etc.). They point out that most studies have focused on the outcome of the purchase (i.e., satisfaction after the experience or material purchase); thus, their study examined pre-purchase feelings. They examined pre-purchase feelings in a few studies. In Study 1, subjects thought about either an upcoming material or experiential purchase. They then rated their feelings about this purchase. In Study 2, subjects from an existing project were asked about their current thoughts and feelings about upcoming purchases of both types. The researchers predicted that subjects would feel more excitement than impatience about upcoming experiential purchases compared with upcoming material purchases.

Method of the Study. In Study 1, college students were asked to think about an upcoming purchase in the very near future that was for either an experience or a material thing. They then rated their feelings about the purchase on two scales, one with impatience and excitement end points and another for pleasantness of their feelings. Both scales included responses from − 4 to + 4. In Study 2, subjects were recruited from the trackyourhappiness.org project (Killingsworth & Gilbert, 2010) to be signaled by their iPhone to answer questions about their current thoughts or feelings. At random times during normal waking hours, subjects were asked if they were thinking about an upcoming purchase and, if so, what type of purchase (experiential or material). They then rated their feelings about the purchase on impatience/excitement and pleasantness scales with responses from 0 to 100.

Results of the Study. In both studies, subjects reported more excitement than impatience and a higher level of pleasantness for experiential purchases than for material purchases.

Conclusions of the Study. The results of this study showed that the finding that spending money on experiences is more positive than spending money on material things also applies to the anticipation of a purchase.

COMMON PITFALLS AND HOW TO AVOID THEM

Problem: Confusion of "volunteer" sample and the concept of informed consent—the use of the term *volunteer sample* can be inaccurately interpreted as a sample that consents to participate.

Solution: Remember that ethical guidelines require informed consent for research studies. The choice of sampling technique does not negate this obligation. All participants in the sample, regardless of the type of sample, have a right to informed consent.

Problem: Devaluation of volunteer samples—students often believe that if a study uses a volunteer sample, it is flawed.

Solution: While it is true that volunteer samples may not provide the most representative sample for some populations, they typically do not lower the external validity of a study very much and are quite common in psychological research. Consider the behavior that is examined in a research study before judging whether the sample may generalize. In many cases, the behavior can be generalized beyond the volunteer sample that was tested.

USING RESEARCH

In reading over my local paper one day, I came across a story that reported a study showing that Mississippi is the "fattest" state in the United States. Colorado was listed as the "thinnest" (Jalonick, 2011). My first thought was to question what the reporters meant by "fattest" and "thinnest." In other words, what was their operational definition of *fat*? I discovered that the study the paper was reporting operationally defined *fat* for each state as the percentage of obese individuals residing in that state. That led to another question: How is *obese* defined? Further reading indicated that *obesity* was defined as having a body mass index of 30 or more (a measurement that includes a person's height and weight). These definitions helped me better understand how the study reached its results, but there was still an important question remaining that the story in the newspaper did not answer: How did the researchers of this study determine the percentage of obese people in each state? It is likely they used a sample of individuals to collect their measurements, because it would be quite difficult (and likely impossible) to observe the body mass index of all the individuals residing in each state. Thus, the sampling technique they used was the information I was seeking. Did they conduct a survey and ask people if they were obese? If so, then they probably did not receive honest answers in many cases. Did they use medical records? If so, what were the restrictions on which records they could access and were there any important differences in the records they were able to access versus those records they did not access? If so, is it possible that the thinner individuals in the states would not have sought medical treatment recently and might have been missed in the medical records used? These are some of the important questions that should be asked when one encounters reports of studies in the media. Often there is important information missing that is needed to evaluate the conclusion of the study that is reported. In order to discover what sampling technique was used in this study, I had to read the original report published by the Robert Wood Johnson Foundation (2011), which produced the report (see http://www.rwjf.org/files/research/tfahfasinfat2011a.pdf). In the Appendix of their report, the authors state that the data were collected from a random sample of adults in each state in a telephone survey. Thus, the results of this study were in fact based on a self-report from the individuals in the sample regarding their weight. It is possible that not all subjects accurately reported their weight in the survey.

TEST YOURSELF

1. In what ways are probability samples preferable to convenience samples?

2. Despite the superiority of probability samples, why do many psychological studies use convenience samples?

3. Suppose you were conducting a survey study to learn about drinking behaviors for the population of students at your school with a quota sample. In your sample, you want to be sure that you represent the population according to year in school and gender. Describe how you might choose your sample for this study and how your survey would be administered.

4. What are some advantages of collecting samples using the Internet?

5. In a _____ sample, individuals are chosen at random from the population, but are chosen in proportions equivalent to proportions that exist in the population (e.g., 90% right handed, 10% left handed).

   (a) simple random

   (b) haphazard

   (c) quota

   (d) stratified random

6. In a _____ sample, individuals who volunteer from the population are chosen for the sample.

   (a) simple random

   (b) haphazard

   (c) quota

   (d) stratified random

7. Sampling error is

   (a) a type of sampling technique

   (b) the difference in observations between the population and the sample

   (c) an error introduced into a study by the researcher's bias

   (d) none of the above

8. The _____ is the group of individuals a researcher wants to learn about, whereas a _____ is the group of individuals who serve as subjects in a study.

9. In a _____ sample, all members of the population have an equal chance of being selected.

10. A biased sample will lower the _____ of the study.

    (a) reliability

    (b) validity

    (c) sampling error

    (d) independent variable

Answers can be found at edge.sagepub/mcbride3e.

STOP AND THINK ANSWERS

(6.1) When they are concerned about a characteristic in the population not being represented in equal proportions in the sample, stratified random samples are used to make sure the proportions are the same to make the sample more representative.

(6.2) Everyone in the population must have an equal chance of being selected and it can be difficult to identify everyone in a large population to make sure they have an equal selection chance.

(6.3) Answers will vary, but convenience samples may make some studies harder to generalize to larger populations. It may depend to some degree on the behavior being studied.

(6.4) You must first identify the proportions in the population for different race/ethnic groups. Then you must create your sample with the same proportion.

Visit edge.sagepub.com/mcbride3e for the tools you need to sharpen your study skills:

- Web Quizzes
- eFlashcards
- Thinking About Research

- SAGE Journal Articles
- Web and Multimedia Resources

Chapter 7

Summarizing and Interpreting Data

Using Statistics

Consider the following questions as you read Chapter 7

- How can we summarize a set of data to better understand it?
- How do the measures of central tendency of a distribution (mean, median, and mode) differ?
- How do inferential statistics allow us to learn about populations from the data collected from a sample?
- How do we make hypotheses about populations?
- What can we learn from significance testing?

Based on a survey conducted by Gallup (Morales, 2008), a large majority of Americans (82%) believe that smoking is "very harmful." The survey was based on responses from 1,016 American adults by telephone. In other words, the researchers for this survey collected a random sample of American adults for their survey. Does this mean that if all American adults were given this survey, 82% of them would say that smoking is very harmful? The answer is "probably not," because the 82% response is based on the reported sample, which represents the population but is unlikely to yield exactly the same values as the general population. In other words, due to sampling error, the difference between observations in the sample and the population, the sample value is unlikely to equal the population value exactly (see Chapter 6 for more discussion of sampling error). In fact, researchers reported a margin of error of + or −3% for this survey. This means that they are 95% sure that if all American adults were surveyed, between 79% and 85% of them would say that smoking is very harmful. But where did this margin of error of 3% come from, and why is it that the researchers cannot be 100% certain that the population value is in this range? The answers to these questions require a basic understanding of the principles of descriptive and inferential statistics, which are covered in this chapter. Descriptive statistics are techniques for summarizing raw data that allow researchers to get a sense of the data set without reviewing every score in the data set. Inferential statistics are techniques that use descriptive statistics from the sample to test hypotheses about the population the researcher is trying to study. The goal of this chapter is not to help you learn how to calculate the statistics. Calculations of statistics are described in the Appendix, and Chapter 15 covers use of the SPSS statistical software package. Instead, this chapter helps you understand the logic of how researchers use statistics to understand their data and test their hypotheses. Figure 7.1 illustrates where data analysis falls among the steps in the research process.

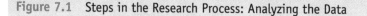

Sampling Error: the difference between the observations in a population and in the sample that represents that population in a study

Descriptive Statistics: measures that help us summarize data sets

Inferential Statistics: a set of statistical procedures used by researchers to test hypotheses about populations

Figure 7.1   Steps in the Research Process: Analyzing the Data

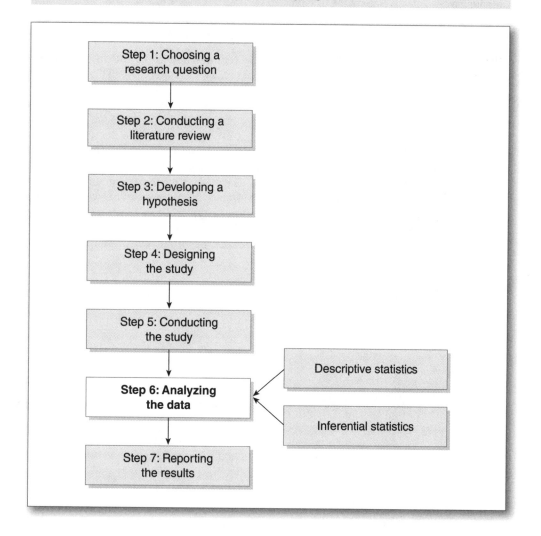

DESCRIPTIVE STATISTICS: SUMMARIZING THE DATA

Before we can understand how well our sample represents the population and whether our hypothesis was supported by the data, we need to first summarize what the data contain. It can be difficult to interpret what data reveal about behavior from just the raw data (i.e., the scores from each participant). Thus, researchers rarely report the raw data they have collected. Instead, researchers typically report descriptive statistics that summarize the set of data (also called a distribution). There are three main categories of descriptive statistics that help researchers summarize data. They are (1) the central tendency of the distribution, (2) the variability in the distribution, and (3) graphs or tables of the central tendency and variability.

---❧---

Distribution: a set of scores

Central Tendency: representation of a typical score in a distribution

Variability: the spread of scores in a distribution

Mean: the calculated average of the scores in a distribution

Median: the middle score in a distribution, such that half of the scores are above and half are below that value

Mode: the most common score in a distribution

Central Tendency

The central tendency of a distribution is a measure that indicates a *typical* score in the distribution. Three basic measures are commonly used to indicate the central tendency of a distribution: the mean, the median, and the mode. The mean is simply the calculated average score in the distribution (i.e., all the scores are added together and divided by the total number of scores in the distribution). The median is the middle score in the distribution, where half of the scores are above the median and half of the scores are below the median. The mode is the most common score (i.e., the one that appears most often in the distribution). Each of these measures can yield different values for any given distribution, but they all represent a typical score in the distribution. Table 7.1 provides a comparison of the three measures of central tendency for two different distributions, and the Appendix: Statistical Calculations, provides the formulas and examples of how to calculate these measures.

Table 7.1 Two Distributions and Their Measures of Central Tendency

Distribution	Mean	Median	Mode
1, 3, 4, 4, 4, 5, 7	4	4	4
1, 1, 1, 1, 2, 2, 13	3	1	1

The mean is the most commonly reported measure of central tendency. It is also an important value for inferential statistical tests, as you will see below. However, the mean can be greatly affected by extreme scores in a distribution. High or low extreme scores pull the mean value toward the top or bottom of the distribution's range because these extreme scores are included in the calculation of the average value. This is illustrated by the second distribution of scores in Table 7.1. The extreme score of "13" in this distribution pulls the mean toward it. The mean for this distribution is higher than the median or mode due to this extreme score. Thus, when a distribution includes several extreme scores, sometimes

---
❀

Outliers: extreme high or low scores in a distribution

Reaction Time: measurement of the length of time to complete a task

---

called outliers, researchers often report the median score in addition to or instead of the mean. One example of a distribution that is likely to include outliers is a distribution of salaries at a company. The majority of the workers at most companies earn a salary that may be within a particular range (e.g., $30,000 to $60,000 per year). However, there are also likely to be a few top executives at the company who earn a salary much higher than this range (e.g., $800,000 per year). If you were to calculate the mean salary at the company, the top executives' large salaries would skew the mean higher than the typical salary in the company and make it appear as though typical salaries are higher than they really are. Thus, the median value is typically reported for salary distributions. Another example of this type of distribution is reaction time (i.e., how long it takes someone to make a response in a task). Reaction-time distributions typically include scores that are clustered around an average score that represents the typical speed of response with a few scores that are slower than the rest. These slower scores often result from cases where people take longer than typical to respond or lose their attention focus in a task. Thus, these slower scores are extreme compared with the typical reaction-time score in a distribution and draw the mean score higher when they are included.

The mode is often reported when the distribution includes frequencies of responses (i.e., nominal scales). For example, if a survey is given where people must choose their current mood from categories such as happy, sad, anxious, or excited, the mode is typically reported (e.g., most participants reported feeling anxious).

Variability

The variability of a distribution indicates how much the scores in the distribution differ from each other across the response scale. For example, if a 1 to 5 rating scale is given for survey items and most participants use the values from 2 to 4, the distribution has low variability, as most of the scores are similar to one another and do not use the entire response scale. However, if the participants use all the values from 1 to 5 for their responses, the variability in the distribution is higher. High variability can also occur in a distribution when some participants' responses differ greatly from other participants' responses. Figure 7.2 illustrates distributions with high and low variability. In the left graph, you can see that the scores are clustered close together, representing low variability. In the right graph, the scores are more spread out and do not cluster as much in the middle of the distribution.

As with central tendency, there are a few different measures of variability that researchers typically report for a distribution: range, standard deviation, and variance. The range is the most basic measure and is simply the difference between the highest and lowest scores in a distribution. However, the range ignores all the scores between the most extreme scores and therefore is a crude measure of variability. The standard deviation and variance are much more precise measures of variability. The standard deviation is a measure representing the average

Figure 7.2   Low and High Variability Distributions

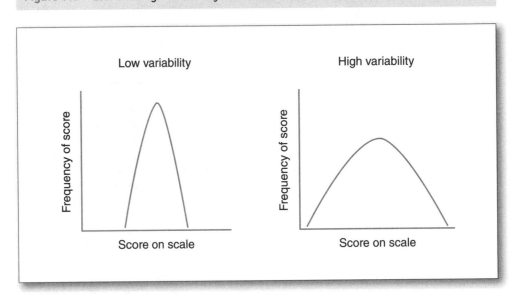

Range: the difference between the highest and lowest scores in a distribution

Standard Deviation: a measure representing the average difference between the scores and the mean of a distribution

Variance: the standard deviation of a distribution squared

Degrees of Freedom: number of scores that can vary in the calculation of a statistic

---

difference between the scores and the mean of the distribution. However, if you were to simply calculate the differences between the scores and the mean and add them up, you would find that the value is always 0. Thus, the standard deviation is determined by calculating the difference between each score and the mean, squaring those values, adding them up, and dividing by $n - 1$ (where n is the number of scores). See the Appendix for an example of this calculation. We divide by $n - 1$ because the scores are from a sample that represents the population (see Chapter 6), not from the population itself. This $n - 1$ value is called the degrees of freedom term, and it is used in the calculation of both descriptive and inferential statistics.

Unlike the range, all the scores are considered in the calculation of standard deviation. The variance is simply the standard deviation squared. Standard deviation and variance measures are important for inferential statistical tests, as you will see below. See the Appendix for the formulas and examples of how to calculate these measures of variability.

Graphs/Tables

Graphs (also called figures) and tables of data are useful tools for quickly summarizing data in a visual way. They can represent a frequency distribution for a data set, which indicates how often each score or category appears in a distribution. In a frequency distribution, the different responses or scores are graphed on the *x*-axis (the horizontal axis) and the frequency of each response in the distribution is graphed on the *y*-axis (the vertical axis). Figure

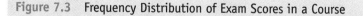

Frequency Distribution: a graph of a distribution showing the frequency of each response in the distribution

7.3 illustrates a frequency distribution of exam scores in a methods course. The *x*-axis shows the score out of 100 % and the *y*-axis shows the number of students in the class who earned each score. Frequency distributions can be useful in quickly identifying whether there are outliers in a distribution of scores that may affect the measures of central tendency. Another way to represent a distribution in a graph or table is to include a measure of central tendency (typically the mean) in the graph or table. A table is organized to include the mean score for different conditions or groups in a study. A graph can be organized in the same way as a table but can be

Figure 7.3   Frequency Distribution of Exam Scores in a Course

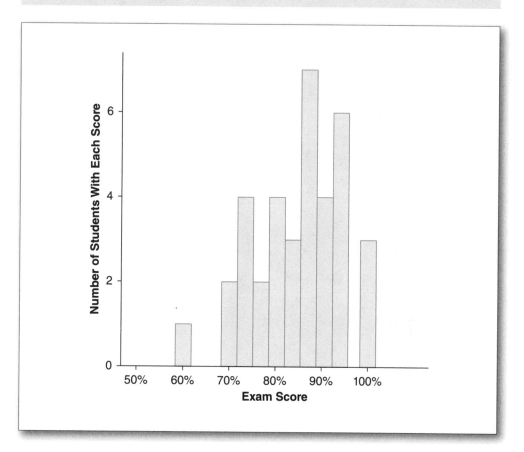

Figure 7.4　(a) Bar Graph Showing the Comparison of Mean Memory Scores for Children and Adults, (b) Line Graph Showing the Comparison of Mean Memory Scores Based on Years of Education

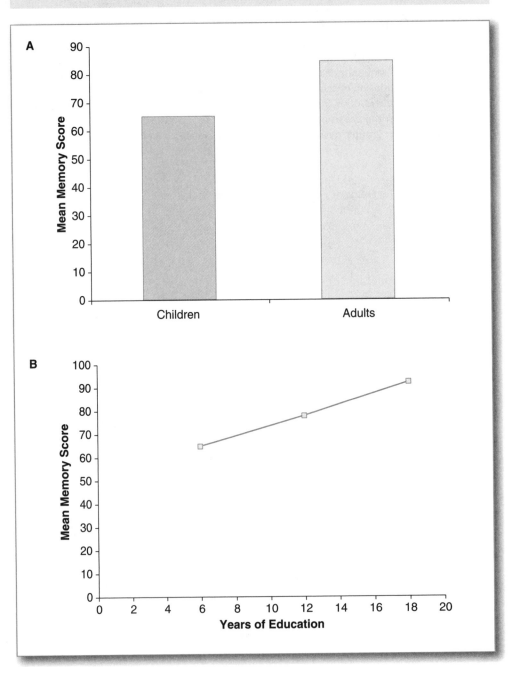

visually presented as a bar graph or a line graph. Figure 7.4 shows a bar graph and a line graph for the mean scores in a study according to two different variables, age group and years of education. In the bar graph, the condition or group is indicated on the x-axis, and the mean score is indicated on the y-axis. In the line graph, the continuous predictor variable (years of education) is indicated on the x-axis and the mean score is indicated on the y-axis.

One should use caution in viewing graphs of data, as they can be created in such a way as to confuse or mislead the reader. Consider the graphs presented in Figure 7.5. Both graphs show the same mean data from a study measuring percentage of individuals reporting symptoms of an illness for a new drug compared to a placebo. Graph A shows the means with a y-axis that ranges from 60% to 67%, whereas Graph B shows the full range of scores with a y-axis from 0% to 67%. Suppose that you saw Graph A in an ad for the new drug touting its benefits. You should be skeptical

Bar Graph: a graph of the means for different conditions in a study where the bar height represents the size of the mean

Line Graph: a graph of the means for different conditions in a study where each mean is graphed as a point and the points are connected in a line to show differences between mean scores

Scatterplot: a graph showing the relationship between two dependent variables for a group of individuals

Predictor Variable: the dependent variable in a correlational study that is used to predict the score on another variable

Outcome Variable: the dependent variable in a correlational study that is being predicted by the predictor variable

about whether the benefits of the new drug are real, given the presentation of the data provided by the company. In fact, the best way to determine if the new drug is beneficial is to consider the outcome of an inferential statistical test that indicates whether the difference between the drug and placebo groups is big enough. These types of tests will be discussed later in this chapter. From this example, you can see that one should use caution in creating and reading graphs so as not to be misled by the presentation of the data into drawing incorrect conclusions.

In Chapter 4, we discussed another type of graph that can be used to describe the relationship between two distributions called a scatterplot. As shown in Figure 4.5 in Chapter 4, a scatterplot is a graph that includes data points from each participant in a study for two different dependent variables. One variable is plotted on the x-axis and one is plotted on the y-axis. For correlational studies with a predictor and outcome variable (see Chapters 4 and 10 for more discussion of these variables), the predictor variable is typically plotted on the x-axis, and the outcome variable is plotted on the y-axis. How well the data points cluster together in the graphs indicates the strength of the relationship between the two variables.

Stop and Think

(7.1) Of the three measures of central tendency, which one is most affected by extreme scores?

(7.2) Describe the difference between a scatterplot and a line graph.

Figure 7.5   Two Bar Graphs Showing the Comparison of Individuals Reporting Symptoms for a New Drug and a Placebo

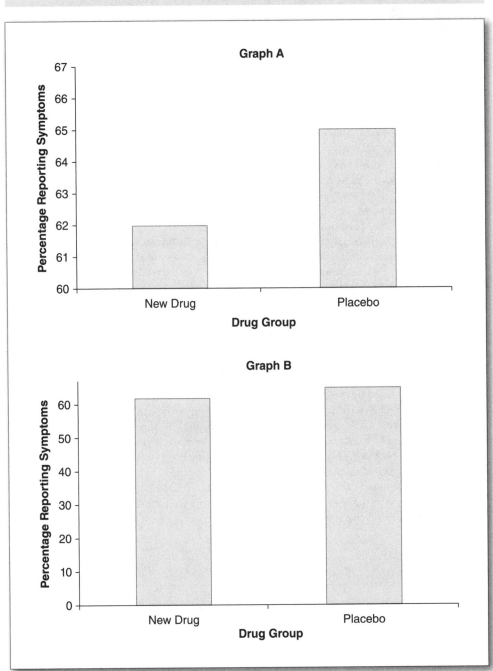

INFERENTIAL STATISTICS: TESTING HYPOTHESES

As indicated above, descriptive statistics help researchers summarize and understand their data. However, they are also useful in testing hypotheses about the populations researchers want to study. In some studies, researchers are interested in testing a hypothesis by comparing means across groups of participants or conditions. Remember that the descriptive statistics that come from the sample are similar to those that are produced by the entire population, because the sample is chosen to represent the population in the research study. However, the sample statistics are often not exactly the same as those that would be produced by the population because sampling error is always present. This is why we can never be 100% certain of what the population mean is just from looking at the sample mean (e.g., see the smoking survey study description at the beginning of the chapter). Without testing the entire population, we can estimate the population mean only with a particular level of certainty. The more variability there is in the data, the more sampling error there is, and the less certain we are about the value of the population mean (i.e., the margin of error). Thus, researchers use *inferential statistics* to determine what can be learned about the population from the sample. As you will see below, descriptive statistics are an important part of the inferential process.

Hypotheses

We begin our examination of inferential statistics with a discussion of different types of hypotheses that we are testing with the statistical procedures. Recall from Chapter 2 that making a hypothesis is an important step in the research process. The literature review helps us determine what we should predict for the data in our study. In inferential statistics, this hypothesis made by the researcher is usually the scientific or alternative hypothesis (why it is called the alternative hypothesis becomes clearer as you read). The scientific or

Scientific/Alternative Hypothesis: the hypothesis that an effect or relationship exists (or exists in a specific direction) in the population

Null Hypothesis: the hypothesis that an effect or relationship does not exist (or exists in the opposite direction of the alternative hypothesis) in the population

alternative hypothesis is the hypothesis either that an effect of the independent variable exists (for an experiment or quasi-experiment) or a relationship between the variables exists (for a correlational study). This hypothesis is stated in terms of an effect or relationship that exists in the population because it is the population that the researcher wants to learn about. The null hypothesis is the opposite hypothesis to the scientific or alternative hypothesis: that an effect or relationship does not exist in the population.

Let's consider an example to state these hypotheses more concretely. Imagine that you are conducting a study to examine the research question: *Do memory abilities change as people age?* (see Figure 7.4 for sample data from such a study). You conduct a literature review (see Chapter 2 for discussion of how to conduct a literature review), and the previous studies you read seem to indicate that memory abilities do change as people age. Thus, an appropriate hypothesis for your study is: *Memory abilities change with age.* This becomes the scientific or alternative hypothesis for your inferential statistics. The scientific or alternative hypothesis is often denoted by H_a or H_1. Thus,

H_1: *In the general population, memory abilities change with age.* OR *In the general population, different age groups have different mean memory scores.*

The null hypothesis (denoted by H_0) makes the opposite prediction: *that memory abilities do not change with age.* Thus,

H_0: *In the general population, memory abilities do not change with age.* OR *In the general population, different age groups have the same mean memory scores.*

Two-Tailed Hypothesis: both directions of an effect or relationship are considered in the alternative hypothesis of the test

One-Tailed Hypothesis: only one direction of an effect or relationship is predicted in the alternative hypothesis of the test

What we have considered above is called a two-tailed hypothesis because we are considering both possible directions of difference in the hypothesis. In other words, our alternative hypothesis above does not predict whether younger or older individuals will have higher memory scores. It simply states that the mean scores for younger and older individuals in the population will be *different*. It does not include a prediction about which population will have higher scores. However, for this study, you might find previous studies that indicate that as people age, their memory abilities decline. Thus, you could make a directional or one-tailed hypothesis. As a one-tailed hypothesis, our alternative hypothesis could be stated thus:

H_1: *In the general population, older individuals have lower memory scores than younger individuals.*

We could also make the opposite prediction (e.g., H_1: *In the general population, older individuals have higher memory scores than younger individuals*), but the first hypothesis stated is more likely to be consistent with the results of previous studies. For this alternative hypothesis, our null hypothesis must include any other possible outcome, so our null hypothesis is this:

H_0: *In the general population, older individuals have higher memory scores than younger individuals or the memory scores of the two age groups are the same.*

For a one-tailed hypothesis, the null hypothesis contains the predictions of no effect or relationship *and* the effect or relationship in the direction opposite to that predicted in the alternative hypothesis. See the top portion of the flowchart in Figure 7.6 for a comparison of one-tailed and two-tailed hypotheses for this study.

One-tailed hypotheses are typically made only when a researcher has a logical reason to believe that one particular direction of the effect will occur. Thus, one-tailed hypotheses are often made when the other direction of the effect logically should not occur or does not answer the research question. They may also be made when the literature review of an area indicates that one direction of the effect has been shown consistently over a number of research studies.

The study described above could also be done to look for a relationship between age and memory ability. In this case, the hypotheses can be stated with regard to relationships that might exist (or not) in the population. The two-tailed alternative hypothesis in this case would be this:

H_1: *In the population, age and memory scores are related.*

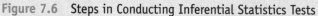

Figure 7.6   Steps in Conducting Inferential Statistics Tests

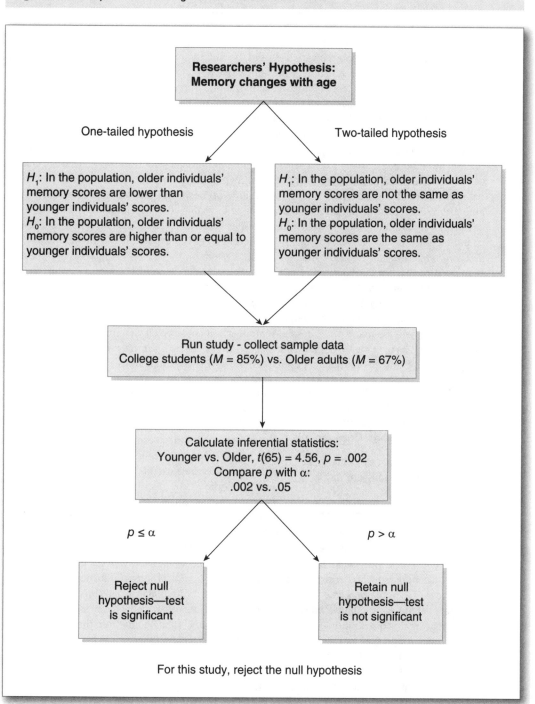

The null hypothesis would be:

H_0: *In the population, age and memory scores are not related.*

A one-tailed alternative hypothesis for a test about relationships predicts a specific relationship (positive or negative) between the variables, and the null hypothesis predicts no relationship or a relationship in the opposite direction of the alternative hypothesis.

An inferential statistical test provides a test of the null hypothesis for either one-tailed or two-tailed hypotheses. These tests allow researchers to determine whether there is enough evidence to reject the null hypothesis for their study and accept the scientific or alternative hypothesis. This is why it is called the alternative hypothesis: It is the alternative to the null hypothesis. The evidence provided by the inferential test is the likelihood of obtaining the data in the study when the null hypothesis is actually true. That is what the inferential test focuses on: What is the chance of obtaining the data in this study when the null hypothesis is in fact true? If the chance is fairly high, then there is no evidence to reject the null hypothesis. In other words, there may not be an effect or relationship (although the test does not speak to this possibility specifically). If the chance is very low, then the researcher takes that as evidence against the null hypothesis, rejects it, and accepts the alternative hypothesis that there is an effect or relationship. *In other words, the decision to reject or not reject the null hypothesis is based on the probability of obtaining the data from the sample when the null hypothesis is true.* The strength of the effect or relationship and the amount of sampling error in the data are also considered in determining this probability.

Now consider this inferential process more specifically in terms of populations and samples. When we choose a sample from a population, we are choosing one possible sample from this population. There are many other possible samples that could be chosen instead, and each sample would have its own mean. But if we considered all the possible sample means that could come from samples from this particular population, we would find that most of the sample means would be fairly close to the actual population mean and a few would be quite far away. Figure 7.7 represents a distribution of possible sample means that can occur for a particular population. Notice that a few of the sample means are at the far ends of the distribution and are far off of the population mean, but most of the sample means are close to the actual population mean in the middle of the distribution. This distribution is called the distribution of sample means and is used to determine how likely it is that a particular sample mean occurs for a population. This distribution represents the different sample means that can occur when the null hypothesis is true. In fact, the exact probability of a sample mean falling into portions of this distribution can be determined and is a value obtained when the inferential statistical test is conducted. Thus, researchers know the likelihood that their sample mean would occur when the null hypothesis is true after they conduct their inferential test. This information allows them to determine if they have an extreme enough sample mean to decide that it probably did not come from this distribution (i.e., the chance is very small that it came from the distribution of sample means), and they can reject the null hypothesis, because their sample mean probably did not come from this distribution. This is the general logic used in significance tests, regardless of the type of test that researchers conduct.

One way that researchers sometimes estimate the population mean from the sample mean is with a confidence interval. A confidence interval provides a range of values that the population

---

Distribution of Sample Means: the distribution of all possible sample means for all possible samples from a population

Confidence Interval: a range of values that the population mean likely falls into with a specific level of certainty

Figure 7.7 Distribution of Sample Means From a Population When the Null Hypothesis Is True

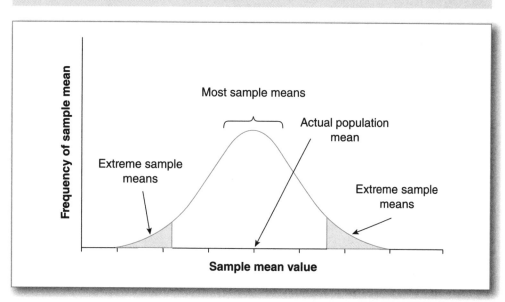

mean likely falls into with a particular level of certainty. For example, using the sample mean from their data set and the distribution of sample means, researchers can estimate a range of values for the population mean they are interested in with a 95% or a 99% probability level. If you look back at the example at the beginning of this chapter, you will see that a margin of error value of + or −3% was reported for the survey with a sample mean value of 82%. The + or −3% reported was the confidence interval (i.e., 79% to 85%) around the sample mean that the researchers were 95% sure the population mean would fall into. Confidence intervals provide a way of looking at how large a range is possible for the population mean given the data collected.

Stop and Think

(7.3)   For each of the following statements, indicate whether a one- or two-tailed test is most appropriate:

- Taking aspirin reduces the chance of a heart attack
- Quizzing yourself before a test will increase your test score compared with simply re-reading your notes
- Completing a puzzle under time constraint will affect your accuracy
- Sleep affects depression

(7.4)   For each statement above, provide the null and alternative hypotheses.

Significance Testing

How unlikely does a sample mean have to be before we decide it did not come from the distribution of sample means? That is a value determined by the researcher, and it is typically set at 5% or less. In other words, there has to be a 5% or less chance that the sample mean came from the distribution of sample means for a researcher to reject the null hypothesis. This probability value is called the alpha level (often denoted by the Greek letter α) in inferential statistics. It is the highest probability that a sample mean came from this distribution that still provides evidence against the null hypothesis. It is set by the researcher at a low value to allow rejection of the null hypothesis only when it is very unlikely that the sample mean came from the distribution of sample means for the null hypothesis. The probability of a sample mean occurring in the distribution of sample means is compared with the alpha level in an inferential test. Remember that most sample means occur near the actual population mean, so if the probability is high that the sample mean came from this distribution, then it is more likely that the null hypothesis is true. If the probability value (also called a *p* value) is equal to or lower than alpha, then the researcher rejects the null hypothesis as unlikely to be true. If the *p* value is higher than alpha, the researcher cannot reject the null hypothesis, as it might be true (again, the test does *not* provide evidence *for* the null hypothesis, only against it). If the *p* value is less than or equal to alpha, the test is said to be significant. In other words, a significant inferential test means that the null hypothesis can be rejected, the alternative hypothesis can be accepted, and the researcher can conclude that there is an effect or relationship for the data in the current study.

Consider the distribution of sample means again (see Figure 7.7). Suppose that an inferential test you conducted indicated that the probability of the sample mean when the null hypothesis is true is .70. This means that there is a 70% chance of obtaining your sample mean when the null hypothesis is true (i.e., there is a 70% chance that the null hypothesis is true given your data). In this case, it is very likely that the null hypothesis is true and you cannot reject it. However, suppose instead that the *p* value for your data was .03. This means that there is only a 3% chance of obtaining your sample mean when the null hypothesis is true. Your sample mean falls in the most extreme portion of this distribution. This portion of the distribution is called the critical region of the distribution. The shaded portions in Figure 7.7 indicate the critical regions for a two-tailed hypothesis, and the identified area (with hash marks) in Figure 7.8 indicates the critical region for a one-tailed hypothesis. When your calculated statistic falls in this region, you can take this as evidence against the null hypothesis and reject it. For the *p* value of .03, the value falls in the critical region of the distribution, indicating that your value is unlikely to occur when the null hypothesis is true. In other words, the chance of obtaining your data when the null hypothesis is true is very low, and you can be fairly confident that it is wrong in this case and reject it.

Now consider the study discussed above regarding the comparison of younger and older individuals' memory abilities. Suppose this study had been conducted comparing scores on a memory test for college students and older adults (refer back to Figure 7.6 for a flowchart of this study). In the study, the college

———— ✂ ————

Alpha Level: the probability level used by researchers to indicate the cutoff probability level (highest value) that allows them to reject the null hypothesis

***p* Value:** probability value associated with an inferential test that indicates the likelihood of obtaining the data in a study when the null hypothesis is true

Significant Test: the *p* value is less than or equal to alpha in an inferential test, and the null hypothesis can be rejected

Critical Region: the most extreme portion of a distribution of statistical values for the null hypothesis determined by the alpha level (typically 5%)

students' mean score was 85%, and the older adults' mean score was 67%. The inferential test indicates the likelihood that these two sample means both came from the same population with a single mean (consistent with the two-tailed null hypothesis that the scores are the same for younger and older individuals) or from different populations with different means (consistent with the two-tailed alternative hypothesis that the scores are different for younger and older individuals). The p value given for the statistical test indicates the chance of obtaining these means from the same distribution of scores (i.e., when the null hypothesis is true). As seen in Figure 7.6, the p value calculated in the statistical test for this study is .002, which means that the chance of obtaining these data when the null hypothesis is true is only 0.2%.

Statistic Distributions. The process just described is followed when an inferential statistical test is conducted. However, depending on the statistic being used, a researcher may be considering the difference between sample means or whether a relationship exists between distributions. Thus, instead of considering the probability of a single sample mean in the distribution of sample means, a distribution for the statistic being calculated is the distribution that is used to determine the p value. Different types of statistics are used for different measurement scales and research design types (see Chapters 4 and 5 for a discussion of research designs and measurement scales). The p value obtained represents the probability of obtaining that statistic in a distribution corresponding to the null hypothesis. Thus, the p value has the same meaning regardless of which statistic you are using. Figure 7.8 indicates how p values are useful in the process of conducting the statistical test. We will consider different types of statistics and when to use them more specifically in Chapter 15.

Significance Test Outcomes. Table 7.2 illustrates the different possible outcomes of a significance test. The columns represent the reality for the population being studied: Either the null hypothesis is true and there is no effect/relationship, or the null hypothesis is false and there is

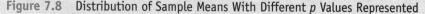

Figure 7.8 Distribution of Sample Means With Different p Values Represented

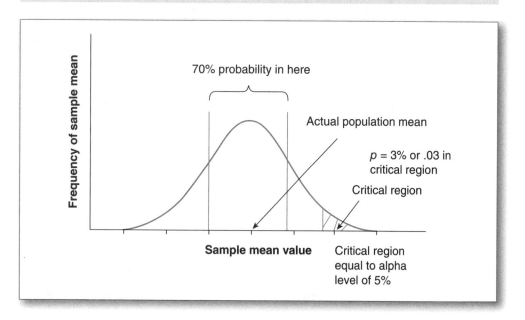

—————————— ❧ ——————————

Type I Error: error made in a significance test when the researcher rejects the null hypothesis when it is actually true

Type II Error: error made in a significance test when the researcher fails to reject the null hypothesis when it is actually false

Power: ability of a significance test to detect an effect or relationship when one exists (equal to 1—the probability of a Type II error)

an effect/relationship. When a significance test is conducted, the researcher does not know whether the null hypothesis is actually true or false. However, the test is conducted to look for evidence that the null hypothesis is not true. If that evidence is found, the researcher can decide that the null hypothesis is false and reject it. This is the outcome represented in the first row of Table 7.2. If in fact the null hypothesis is actually false, the researcher has made a correct decision in the test, because the decision matches the reality about the null hypothesis. However, remember that the researcher will never know whether the null hypothesis is really true, so it is possible to make the wrong decision. Thus, the outcome to reject the null hypothesis in the first row under the column where the null hypothesis is really true is an error. The researcher's decision does not match the reality for the null hypothesis. This is called a Type I error and indicates that the researcher has rejected the null hypothesis when it is really true. The chance of making a Type I error is determined ahead of time by the researcher when an alpha level is chosen. Alpha is very often set at 5% (or .05) by researchers. It is the standard alpha level used in psychological research. Thus, in tests with $\alpha = .05$, there is a 5% chance of making a Type I error.

The second row in Table 7.2 illustrates test outcomes for the other decision that can be made in the significance test: failing to reject the null hypothesis, which occurs when evidence against it is not found in the test. A correct decision is made in the test when the decision is to fail to reject the null hypothesis and this hypothesis is really false (bottom right box). However, another type of error, called a Type II error, can be made when the null hypothesis is not rejected but is actually false. This means that an effect or relationship exists in the population but was not detected in the data from the sample. The chance of a Type II error is more difficult to determine. There are several factors that can influence the probability of a Type II error, including the alpha level chosen, the size of the effect or relationship, and the sample size in the study. The researcher can lower the chance of a Type II error by using an optimal sample size and making sure that the study is designed to maximize the effect or relationship being studied. By keeping the Type II error rate low, you are increasing the power of your significance test to detect an effect or relationship that actually exists. Thus, it is important to keep Type II errors in mind as you design your study to conduct a powerful test of the hypothesis.

Up to this point, we have discussed inferential statistics generally as they can be applied to different types of hypotheses. Chapter 15 continues this discussion with the "nuts and bolts" of how to use the different statistical tests that are based on this hypothesis-test logic. For a discussion of how common statistics are calculated and how SPSS software is used to calculate and interpret the statistics, refer to Chapter 15.

Table 7.2   Possible Outcomes of a Statistical Test

Decisions	Null Hypothesis Is Actually False	Null Hypothesis Is Actually True
Reject the null hypothesis	Correct decision!	Type I error
Fail to reject the null hypothesis	Type II error	Correct decision!

Predicting the Null Hypothesis

As mentioned above, in many cases, the alternative hypothesis is also the researcher's hypothesis. The researcher predicts that an effect or relationship exists in the population. However, in some cases, the researcher may wish to predict that an effect or relationship does not exist in the population. Is this an appropriate thing for a researcher to do when using inferential statistics? Many would argue that it is not appropriate for a researcher to predict the null hypothesis because significance tests do not provide evidence for the null hypothesis. In fact, most papers that are published in psychological journals describe studies that showed significant results (Greenwald, 1975), because it can be difficult to draw strong conclusions from studies that do not show significant results. However, power analyses can be used to estimate the chance of a Type II error occurring and the null hypothesis being falsely retained. While any single study with nonsignificant results is not sufficient to provide support for the null hypothesis, a series of studies that have a reasonable level of power to detect effects (80 % or higher is the generally accepted level; Cohen, 1988) that all show the same nonsignificant results may provide some support for the null hypothesis. Thus, if researchers want to predict the null hypothesis, they must be prepared to conduct several studies in order to obtain some support for their hypothesis. Greenwald (1975) also argued that a bias against the null hypothesis can result in researchers' ignoring studies that do not find significant effects (which can be caused by the bias against publishing them). In addition, because it is important that theories of behavior can be falsified (see Chapter 1), it is sometimes necessary to predict the null hypothesis in order to truly test a theory. Finally, in order to get around this issue several researchers (e.g., Cohen, 1990, 1994; Loftus, 1993) have suggested alternatives to significance testing as a means of interpreting data.

Stop and Think

(7.5)   For each description below, indicate the situation (correct decision, Type I error, Type II error):

- An effect of amount of sleep on mood exists, but the results of the study were not significant.
- A relationship between early reading and later academic achievement exists and the results of the study were significant.
- An effect of caffeine on work productivity does not exist, but the results of the study were significant.

CHAPTER SUMMARY

Reconsider the questions from the beginning of the chapter:

- How can we summarize a set of data to better understand it? Data can be summarized with descriptive statistics. Measures of central tendency indicate a typical score in a distribution. Measures of variability indicate the spread of the scores in a distribution. Graphs and tables can also provide a visual summary of the data.

- How do the measures of central tendency of a distribution (mean, median, and mode) differ? The mean is the average of the scores in the distribution. The median is the middle score in the distribution. The mode is the most frequent score in a distribution.
- How do inferential statistics allow us to learn about populations from the data collected from a sample? Inferential statistics estimate sampling error to adjust for how well the sample represents the population in hypothesis tests. Then an inferential statistic is calculated from the sample values with an estimate of sampling error included in the calculation. For each statistic, a p value is determined that indicates the likelihood of obtaining the sample data when the null hypothesis is true. If the p value is less than or equal to alpha, this is taken as evidence against the null hypothesis about the population, and it can be rejected. Otherwise, the null hypothesis about the population must be retained. See Figure 7.6 for an illustration of this process.
- How do we make hypotheses about populations? Null and alternative hypotheses about populations are stated for studies as either comparisons of conditions or predictions about relationships.
- What can we learn from significance testing? We can determine if there is enough evidence against the null hypothesis to reject it and conclude that the alternative hypothesis is true.

THINKING ABOUT RESEARCH

A summary of a research study in psychology is given below. As you read the summary, think about the following questions:

1. What research design is used in this study (i.e., experiment, quasi-experiment, correlational study, case study)? Describe any independent and dependent variables in the design.

2. Should the authors make one-tailed or two-tailed hypotheses for their statistical analysis? Explain why.

3. State the null and alternative hypotheses for this study.

4. Suppose the test the researchers conducted to compare the "glucose" and "no glucose" conditions provide a p value of .001. Assuming they used an alpha level of .05, what decision should the researchers make regarding the null hypothesis for this comparison?

5. For the decision made in (4) above, suppose that the null hypothesis is actually true. What type of error have the researchers made in this case?

6. Suppose that the subjects given the glucose laced lemonade rated the lemonade as more pleasant than the no glucose group did. Describe the alternative conclusion this result would provide to the Stroop reaction time results presented in Figure 7.9.

Research Study. Sanders, M. A., Shirk, S. D., Burgin, C. J., & Martin, L. L. (2012). The gargle effect: Rinsing the mouth with glucose enhances self-control. *Psychological Science, 23,* 1470–1472.

Purpose of the Study. The researchers examined possible causes of the impairment of self-control. Previous studies have shown that there is a limited amount of self-control that one can engage in, such that if one task requires self-control, performance on a second task that requires self-control will be impaired. This study tested the idea that self-control energy is influenced by the presence of glucose. Two groups of subjects were compared on their task performance for a task that required self-control: one that was given glucose and one that was not. The researchers predicted that the group given glucose would show better performance on the self-control task than the group not given glucose.

Method of the Study. Students completed the study to fulfill a course requirement. They first completed a task that required self-control: crossing out *e*'s in a page of text based on a complex rule (i.e., cross out some *e*'s, but not others). Then all subjects completed a second task requiring self-control while swishing lemonade around in their mouths. They did not swallow the drink. For half of the subjects, the lemonade was sweetened with glucose and for the other half, the lemonade was sweetened with Splenda (no glucose). The task they completed was a Stroop task where words were presented in colored font. Subjects were asked to name the font color as quickly as possible. On some trials, the word was a color word that was different from the font color (e.g., the word *BLUE* printed in red font). These trials require self-control because it is hard not to read the word that interferes with the font color. Reaction time to name the font color was recorded on the Stroop trials. Subjects then rated the sweetness and pleasantness of the lemonade.

Results of the Study. Figure 7.9 presents the mean reaction time results on the Stroop task for each group of subjects. Lower reaction times indicate more self-control. The statistical test run on these data showed that the glucose group has a significantly lower mean reaction time than the no glucose group.

Conclusions of the Study. The results of the study support the idea that the presence of glucose can provide more energy for self-control in tasks that require it.

Figure 7.9   Mean Reaction Time Results for the Two Groups

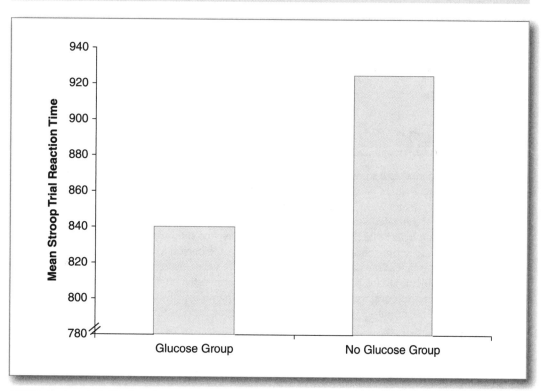

SOURCE: Sanders et al. (2012) study.

COMMON PITFALLS AND HOW TO AVOID THEM

Problem: Supporting the null hypothesis—students often make the error of stating that the null hypothesis is supported with a nonsignificant result.

Solution: Always remember that hypothesis testing procedures with inferential statistics are designed to provide evidence against the null hypothesis, never to support it. When a decision to retain the null hypothesis is made, this simply means that there is not enough evidence to reject it, not that it is supported by the data.

Problem: Stating that results "prove" the hypothesis is true—students sometimes make the mistake of stating that statistical results prove that an effect exists or that a hypothesis is supported.

Solution: Remember that any single study cannot prove something is true in psychological research. Hypotheses are supported by the data but are never proven true or false, because it is always possible that a Type I or Type II error has occurred. It is a good idea to avoid using the word *prove* when you report results of a psychological study.

Problem: Ignoring the power of the test—researchers sometimes do not consider the power of their tests carefully enough, concluding that a nonsignificant result can be relied on with the same certainty as a significant result.

Solution: Remember that although the Type I error rate is set as alpha by the researcher (usually .05 in psychological studies), the Type II error rate is typically unknown at the start of a study and is usually much higher than .05. Thus, researchers should not view nonsignificant results with the same level of certainty as significant results.

TEST YOURSELF

1. Suppose you conducted a study to test the hypothesis that social pressure affects memory accuracy. You set up a study where participants view a video of a person robbing a convenience store. Then half of the participants watch a video of other "participants" discussing the crime. In reality, the "participants" in the video are part of the experiment, and some of the details of the crime that are discussed are inaccurate. The actual participants are told they should consider other people's perspectives on the crime because it is difficult for any one person to accurately remember all the details. The other half of the participants do not view the video discussion of the crime but are also told that it is difficult for any one person to accurately remember all the details of the crime. Thirty min after viewing the original crime video, all participants are given a recognition memory test about details of the crime. For this study, answer the following questions:

   (a) What are the independent and dependent variables?

   (b) State the alternative and null hypotheses for this study.

   (c) Suppose you collected the data for this study, calculated the appropriate statistic to compare the means for the two groups (see Chapter 15 for discussion of statistical tests appropriate for this design), and obtained a *p* value of .013 for the statistic. What decision should be made (assuming α = .05) about the null hypothesis? What can you conclude about the independent variable from this decision?

(d) Now suppose that in reality, the null hypothesis is true. What type of decision have you made in (c): correct decision, Type I error, or Type II error?

2. Suppose you conducted a study to determine if some people have the ability to predict which of two cards a poker player has been dealt for a poker hand. The study involves a single sample of people who claim to be "better than average poker players." In the study, all participants are asked to view a poker player being given a card from the dealer. They are asked to judge from the player's reaction whether the card is a card dealt to the player that will "complete a four of a kind hand" or "not complete a four of a kind hand." They complete 100 judgment trials, and their overall percentage accuracy is calculated. In other words, across all trials, the participants have a 50% chance of being correct if they have no ability to interpret the player's "poker face" (i.e., they are guessing). If they are able to interpret the player's poker face, the participants should perform better than chance (50%) in correctly choosing which type of card the player has been dealt.

(a) Should a one-tailed or two-tailed test be used for this study? How do you know?

(b) State the null and alternative hypotheses for this study.

(c) Suppose that the test statistic calculated for this study yields a *p* value of .18. What decision should be made with regard to the null hypothesis (assume α = .05)? What can the researcher conclude about the poker players' abilities?

(d) Suppose that in reality poker players are able to predict another player's hand with better than chance accuracy. In this case, what type of decision was made in (c) above?

3. Explain the difference between Type I and Type II errors that can be made in significance testing. Which type of error has probability equal to alpha?

4. For the study reported in Figure 7.5, what type of research design is this study (see Chapter 4 for a review of research designs)?

5. A _____ hypothesis is a directional hypothesis, whereas a _____ is not.

6. Alpha is the highest probability that can be obtained and still _____ the null hypothesis.

7. The most common score in a distribution is called the

(a) mean.

(b) median.

(c) mode.

(d) all of the above.

8. An extremely high or low score in a distribution is called a(n) _____.

9. When scores cover a wide range of values in a data set and differ greatly from one another, the distribution of scores is said to have _____ variability.

10. Inferential statistics provide a probability value about the _____ hypothesis.

Answers can be found at edge.sagepub/mcbride3e.

STOP AND THINK ANSWERS

(7.1)   The mean is most affected by extreme scores (i.e., outliers).

(7.2)   A scatterplot shows a data point for each individual with one measure on the *x*-axis and one measure on the *y*-axis. A line graph shows data points for means for a continuous independent (or quasi-independent) variable on the *x*-axis and the dependent variable on the *y*-axis.

(7.3)   One-tailed test, one-tailed test, two-tailed test, two-tailed test

(7.4)   Alternative: A population who takes aspirin will have fewer heart attacks than a population who does not take aspirin.

Null: A population who takes aspirin will have more or the same number of heart attacks as a population who does not take aspirin.

Alternative: A population who quizzes themselves will have higher test scores than a population who re-reads their notes.

Null: A population who quizzes themselves will have lower test scores than or equal test scores to a population who re-reads their notes.

Alternative: A population who completes a puzzle with time constraint will have different accuracy than a population with no time constraint.

Null: A population who completes a puzzle with time constraint will the same accuracy as a population with no time constraint.

Alternative: A population who sleeps a lot will have different depression levels than a population who does not sleep a lot.

Null: A population who sleeps a lot will have the same depression levels as a population who does not sleep a lot.

(7.5)   Type II error, correct decision, Type I error

Visit edge.sagepub.com/mcbride3e for the tools you need to sharpen your study skills:

- Web Quizzes
- eFlashcards
- Thinking About Research

- SAGE Journal Articles
- Web and Multimedia Resources

Chapter 8

Reporting Research

Consider the following questions as you read Chapter 8

- What are the different ways that psychologists present research?
- How do we write an APA-style article? What information goes into each section of the article? How do we format the article?
- What is an appropriate format for an oral presentation of research?
- How do we prepare a conference-style poster presentation of research?

Once you have completed your first research project, you may be asked to present the study to a group. You may be asked to write an article in APA (American Psychological Association) style, give an oral presentation, or prepare a poster presentation of your research. This is how psychologists communicate with each other about research that they have conducted. It is an important part of the scientific method to tell others about your study and its results. This is how knowledge accumulates and science progresses.

You should already be somewhat familiar with an APA-style article by reading the published journal articles that other psychologists have written. However, the focus up to this point in the text has been on how to read and understand these articles. In this chapter, we focus more on how to write one of these articles as a researcher who has completed a study and is getting ready to present it to others. We will also discuss the other common forms of presentation: the oral presentation and the poster presentation. Oral and poster presentations are common at conferences as methods of presenting research one has completed. They are sometimes given before an APA-style article is written for publication and, thus, represent the most up-to-date findings in an area. There are many undergraduate conferences that are held regionally each year, and your college may hold its own as well. Thus, as a student you are more likely to be involved in an oral or poster presentation if you present research outside your class. However, all the presentation styles help you learn how to organize a presentation of research, and learning to write APA-style articles also helps you better understand journal articles that others have written. We begin with the APA-style article as a mode of research presentation (see Figure 8.1).

Figure 8.1   Steps in the Research Process: Reporting the Results

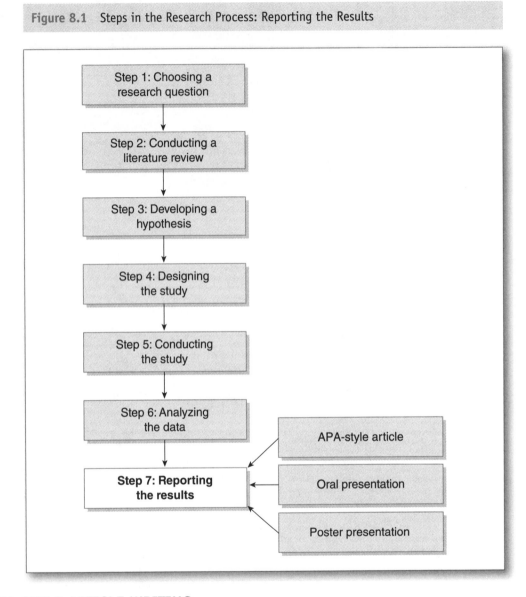

APA-STYLE ARTICLE WRITING

As you have seen in the journal articles you have read (and from the description of these articles in Chapter 2 of this text), APA-style articles follow a particular organizational style. APA style refers to the writing style proposed by the American Psychological Association (APA, 2009) for research articles in psychology and related fields. There are other formatting styles for research articles, but APA style is the most commonly used style in psychology, and most psychological journals require submissions of articles for publication to be written in APA style. Figure 8.2 illustrates the formatting of an APA-style article that has been typed in by a

Figure 8.2 Sample APA-Style Report

Running head: DELAY AND PROSPECTIVE MEMORY ACCURACY 1

Does Delay Affect

Prospective Memory Accuracy?

Jackie K. Cavallo

Illinois State University

(Continued)

Figure 8.2   (Continued)

DELAY AND PROSPECTIVE MEMORY ACCURACY   2

Abstract

The present experiment was designed to test the effect of delay on prospective memory. Prospective memory is remembering to complete a task in the future (Einstein & McDaniel, 2005). Previous studies that measured forgetting of prospective memory have reported mixed results. Thus, the current study tested the effect of delay in an attempt to clarify the effect. Delay between the presentation of the prospective memory instructions and the prospective memory cue was manipulated. Delays of 5 to 20 min were tested. Results indicated that prospective memory performance did not change as delay increased. Thus, there was no evidence that delay affects prospective memory for this range of delays.

Keywords: prospective memory, forgetting

Does Delay Affect Prospective Memory Accuracy?

Prospective memory (PM) is the act of remembering to perform a task at some point in the future (Einstein & McDaniel, 2005). More and more research is taking place on this topic. Researchers in this area have been examining the effect of delay on PM. In these studies, the delay between the PM instructions and the presentation of the PM cue was manipulated. Knowing how delay affects PM may indicate how similar PM is to retrospective memory (i.e., remembering something you have experienced in the past).

Previous studies have reported mixed results for the effect of delay on PM. For example, in a study by Nigro and Cicogna (2000), university students answered two standardized questionnaires. After completing the first questionnaire, participants were told to relay a message to the experimenter in charge of giving the second questionnaire. The message was the same for all participants. Random assignment was used to place the participants in one of three delay conditions: 10 min, 2 days, or 2 weeks. On seeing the second experimenter at their designated time, participants were to give the message. Results showed that PM accuracy was not affected by delay of the second session. However, Hicks, Marsh, and Russell (2000) did find an effect of delay on PM performance. They manipulated delay in a laboratory study of PM and found that PM performance increased from a delay of 2.5 min to a delay of 15 min. Thus, the effect of delay on PM is unclear.

Contrary to the results of Hicks et al. (2000), Meier, Zimmerman, and Perrig (2006) found that PM performance decreased with longer delays. In their second experiment, they administered delays of 5, 15, and 45 min using two distractor tasks. Results suggested that as the delays got longer the PM accuracy decreased.

The purpose of the current study was to find out if delays between the PM instructions and the presentation of the PM cue significantly affect PM accuracy. Delays of 5, 10, 15, and 20 min were used. Based on the results of Meier et al. (2006) for delays in this range, I hypothesized that as delay increased, PM accuracy would decrease.

(Continued)

Figure 8.2 (Continued)

DELAY AND PROSPECTIVE MEMORY ACCURACY   4

Method

Participants

The participants were 80 undergraduate students from a psychology department subject pool at Illinois State University. They completed the experiment voluntarily and received extra credit in their courses for their participation. Participants were randomly assigned to one of the four conditions—5-, 10-, 15-, or 20-min delay—with 20 participants per condition.

Design

A between-subjects design was used to examine the differences between the four delay conditions and PM accuracy. The independent variable was delay between instruction of the PM task and the PM cue. The levels of the independent variable were 5-, 10-, 15-, and 20-min delays. The dependent variable in the study was PM accuracy.

Materials

The stimuli consisted of categories and items that did or did not belong to a specific category. The stimuli were drawn from Battig and Montague's (1969) category norms. There were 11 categories presented to the participants with exemplars: fruit, vegetable, human body part, metal, fish, flower, city, color, sport, musical instrument, and places to sleep. There were 280 category and exemplar pairings in the experiment, divided into four blocks of trials. Trials were numbered for participant accuracy in recording judgments on the record sheet. Half the exemplars belonged to the category presented, whereas the other half did not belong. The participants were given response sheets numbered from 1 to 280. They circled "yes" or "no" on each trial according to whether or not the exemplar belonged in the category. Four PM cues appeared in the category-judgment trials: hotel, dormitory, library, and restaurant. Two of these cues were presented with a correct category, and two were presented with an incorrect category. The trials were presented with PowerPoint. In each trial, categories and exemplars were presented in the center of the computer screen.

Procedure

Participants were run individually. Participants first read and signed an informed consent form. The ongoing task for the four conditions was to identify whether the item exemplar on the right of the screen belonged in the category presented on the left of the screen. In addition, the PM task for all participants was to mark an "X" next to the trial number when a building was displayed in the trial. Both the ongoing and PM task instructions were read to the participant by the researcher. Ten practice trials followed. At that time, if participants had any questions, they were answered before the rest of the experiment continued.

Each of the 280 trials remained on the screen for 5 s. There were three breaks of 30 s between each block of trials. The four PM cues appeared within a minute period at the delay time for each delay group. At the end of the experiment, the participants were debriefed.

Results

The effect of delay on prospective memory accuracy was tested. A one-way analysis of variance (ANOVA) was run on the accuracy data with an alpha level of .05. Means and standard deviations for PM accuracy can be found in Figure 1. PM accuracy in all conditions was relatively low. We found that the effect of delay on PM accuracy was not significant: $F(3, 37) = 0.06$, $p = .98$.

In addition to PM accuracy, we analyzed the ongoing task accuracy for each delay. With an alpha level of .05, a one-way ANOVA was used to analyze these data. Means and standard deviations for the ongoing-task accuracy can be found in Table 1. The ongoing-task accuracy was high in all conditions. Results indicated that the effect of delay on the ongoing task accuracy was not significant: $F(3, 37) = 1.44$, $p = .25$.

Discussion

The current study was designed to examine how the amount of time between the PM instructions and the presentation of the PM cue affects PM accuracy. The hypothesis was that as

(Continued)

Figure 8.2 (Continued)

DELAY AND PROSPECTIVE MEMORY ACCURACY   6

delay increased, PM accuracy would decrease. The results of the current study indicated that PM accuracy was not significantly affected by delay. The overall PM accuracy was low for all conditions. It was also found that delay did not affect the accuracy of the ongoing task. The overall ongoing-task accuracy was high in all conditions.

The present results are consistent with some previous studies that found no effect of delay on PM accuracy. An example of such a study is that of Nigro and Cicogna (2000), where they found no effect of delay for delays from 10 min to 2 weeks. In the current study, results consistent with Nigro and Cicogna's were found for delays from 5 to 20 min. However, the present results are inconsistent with those reported by Meier et al. (2006). They found significant effects of delay for delays of 5 to 45 min. The inconsistency could be due to the way delay was manipulated (e.g., no distractor task was used in the present study) or the shorter delays used in the present study.

This study examined the effects of delay on PM accuracy in the hope of better understanding factors that affect PM and how similar PM is to retrospective memory, which typically shows an effect of delay. The results of this study indicated no effect of delay on PM. Future studies should continue to explore delay as a possible factor that affects PM to allow us to fully understand how PM works.

References

Battig, W. F., & Montague, W. E. (1969). Category norms for verbal items in 56 categories: A replication and extension of the Connecticut category norms. *Journal of Experimental Psychology Monographs, 80*(3, Pt. 2).

Einstein, G. O., & McDaniel, M. A. (2005). Prospective memory: Multiple retrieval processes. *Current Directions in Psychological Science, 14,* 286–290.

Hicks, J. L., Marsh, R. L., & Russell, E. J. (2000). The properties of retention intervals and their affect on retaining prospective memories. *Journal of Experimental Psychology: Learning, Memory, and Cognition, 26,* 1160–1169. doi: 10.1037//0278–7393.26.5.1160

Meier, B., Zimmerman, T. D., & Perrig, W. (2006). Retrieval experience in prospective memory: Strategic monitoring and spontaneous retrieval. *Memory, 14,* 872–889.

Nigro, G., & Cicogna, P. C. (2000). Does delay affect PM performance? *European Psychologist, 5,* 228–233.

(Continued)

Figure 8.2 (Continued)

DELAY AND PROSPECTIVE MEMORY ACCURACY 8

Table 1
Mean Ongoing Task Performance

Delay	Mean	Standard Deviation
5 min	.97	05
10 min	.95	.04
15 min	.98	.04
20 min	.96	.03

Figure 1.   *Mean proportion accuracy for prospective memory task as a function of delay*

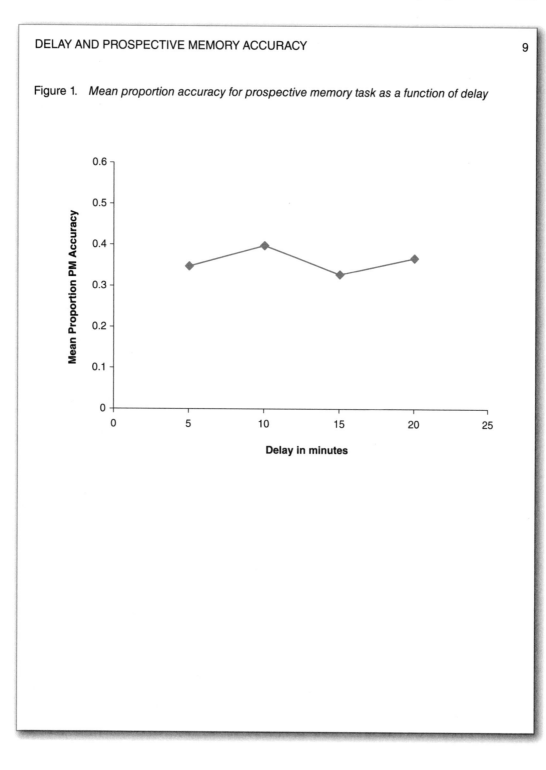

Delay in minutes

researcher. We are going to discuss each section of the APA-style article and the information that should be included in each section. Some important APA style rules are also covered to help you format your article as you type it. All information described in the section below is also covered in the *Publication Manual of the American Psychological Association* (APA, 2009). In addition, an article describing what belongs in the sections of an APA-style article that is also formatted in APA style is available at http://about.illinoisstate.edu/dmmcbri/Pages/Research-Methods-in-Psychology.aspx.

Sections of an APA-Style Article

Title Page. The first page of your article is the Title Page. It includes the title of the article, the authors' names, and the authors' affiliations centered on the page. Your title should be concise and informative. Someone should be able to determine the general topic of your study from the title you choose. The Title Page also contains a running head that is a shortened version of the title (50 or fewer characters including spaces). The purpose of the running head is to include a shortened version of your title that runs along the top of every other page of a published article to identify the article within the journal. Take a look at an article published in APA style and you will see the running head in the top margin of every other page. The running head is typed in all capital letters and appears in the header on each page, left margin justified. Finally, the page number appears in the header, right margin justified, of every page in the article (including the Title Page, which is Page 1).

Abstract. The second page of your article contains your Abstract. The Abstract is a short paragraph (not indented) that describes the important aspects of your article. In other words, your Abstract contains a sentence or two for each of the four major sections of your article: Introduction, Method, Results, and Discussion. For example, a sentence or two that explains the purpose of your article begins your Abstract. A sentence or two that describes the method follows. Be sure to describe the primary variables in your study. The primary result(s) are described in a sentence or two, and your Abstract ends with the primary conclusion of the study. However, the length of your Abstract is limited (in most cases to 120 to 150 or fewer words), so you must be selective in what you discuss in your Abstract. Do not include too many details of the method, and do not include all results. If you use numbers in your Abstract, they are typed in numerical form. Finally, the heading "Abstract" is centered in bold at the top of the page.

Introduction. Your Introduction begins on the third page of your article. Your full title (not the heading "Introduction") is centered at the top of the page. Your Introduction should cover several things. It should inform your reader about the general topic of your study (e.g., the bystander effect, visual short-term memory, therapeutic treatments for depression). Be careful not to begin your Introduction too generally. Your Introduction should not begin with statements about all of psychology or all human behavior. Begin by explaining what behavior your study addresses and which aspects of that behavior are most relevant to your study. Be sure to indicate what your research question is. You should also review relevant background studies that tell your reader what is already known about your research question and how it has been studied previously. Be careful not to simply summarize the background literature. Instead, you should discuss only the aspects of these studies that are particularly relevant for the development of your study.

Your Introduction should become more specific as it progresses, with some details about your study's design being discussed (e.g., simply indicating the variables that were studied) to inform the reader how your study addresses your stated research question. State your hypotheses toward the end of your Introduction. Be sure to explain (briefly) why you are making those hypotheses, tying them to the background literature you discussed earlier in your Introduction. One of the main purposes of your Introduction is to make the argument that your study contributes important knowledge to the topic area you have chosen and that you are justified in making the hypotheses you are making. In other words, if you have written a good Introduction, your readers should have a good idea what your hypotheses are before you state them and be convinced that they are the best hypotheses to make for your study. By the time readers reach the end of your Introduction, they should also be convinced that the study you are describing is important and worthy of reading. Be sure to keep your argument in mind as your write your Introduction.

Method. The Method section begins on the next line after your Introduction ends. To begin the Method, type the heading "Method" in bold centered on the page. Do not begin a new page for the Method section. A general rule of thumb to use in deciding what information to include in your Method section is enough information that researchers could replicate your study if they wanted to. For example, your Method section should contain a description of your stimuli or survey but should not include the type of writing instrument used by your participants (unless it is relevant to the design of your study). The Method section has four subsections: Participants, Design, Materials or Apparatus, and Procedure. Each subsection should begin with the subsection heading left justified and in bold. You may not need to include each subsection in every Method section you write. If you take a look at some different journal articles published in APA style, you will see that some authors choose to combine some of these subsections, and in very short articles (e.g., Short Reports of the journal *Psychological Science*), the subsections are all combined into one Method section that contains the relevant details of all the subsections. In addition, in many articles, you may see that the Design section has been omitted or combined with the Materials section.

Participants. In the Participants subsection, describe the relevant details of the participants or subjects in your study (humans are typically referred to as "participants" and nonhuman animals as "subjects"). For example, how many participants took part in the study? How were the participants recruited? How were they compensated? Who were the participants? Were they college students or individuals living in retirement communities? Or did the researcher use Sprague-Dawley rats as subjects? Also include demographic information about the participants that is relevant to your study, such as gender breakdown, socioeconomic status, education level, and age. How participants were assigned to study conditions (e.g., randomly) is also indicated in this section.

Design. Although not explicitly listed in the *Publication Manual of the American Psychological Association* (2010), the Design subsection is often included by authors for studies with more complex designs (e.g., experiments) to improve the clarity of the method. The Design subsection describes the variables in your study and how they were measured and manipulated. Be sure to indicate any independent and dependent variables included in your study. Describe levels of any independent variables. In other words, provide operational definitions of the variables in the

Method section. In many cases, the materials used in the study (e.g., stimuli, questionnaires) are too closely tied to the design to separate them, and the author combines these two sections.

Materials/Apparatus. The Materials or Apparatus subsection contains information about what was used to run the study. Any stimuli or questionnaires presented in the study are described in this subsection, including the origin of these materials and number of items. Assignment of stimuli to conditions is also described in this section. If complex equipment is used in a study, this section may be labeled "Apparatus," or the author may include a separate Apparatus section.

Procedure. The Procedure subsection describes what the participants/subjects experience in the study in chronological order. Information about the instructions they were given in the study and the tasks they performed is included. Timing of any stimulus presentations is described in the Procedure. In addition, how the participants/subjects were assigned to conditions is included for studies that are experiments, and debriefing is described for studies that involve deception. A statement indicating that participants/subjects were treated according to ethical standards is often included in this section or in the Participants section.

Results. The Results section begins on the next line after the end of the Method section. Do not begin a new page for the Results section. The section begins with the heading "Results" centered on the page in bold. The Results section states the dependent variables that were analyzed and the tests used to analyze them. The alpha level for the statistical tests is given, and the tests that were run are described. You should make statements about the results, indicating what differences or relationships were found, with support for the statements provided by the statistical values. For example, your Results section may contain a statement such as "The difference between the two age groups was significant, $t(65) = 4.56, p = .002$, with older participants scoring higher ($M = 85.00, SD = 7.89$) than younger participants ($M = 67.00, SD = 7.32$)." Notice that the statistics are not the focus of the sentence. The difference is the focus, with support provided by the t and p values and the mean values for each condition. Also note that statistical values are generally rounded to two decimal places. Be sure to format statistics according to APA style, with italics for statistics, degrees of freedom provided, and spaces surrounding equal signs. Consult the *Publication Manual* (APA, 2009) for APA style for specific statistics.

The Results section also includes any tables or figures that help illustrate the important results of the study. Choose one or the other for any set of results. Do not provide both a table and a figure for the same results. Figures may take the form of one of the graph types described in Chapter 7 (e.g., line graph of means, bar graph of means, scatterplot). Be sure to refer to the table or figure in the text of the Results section. However, tables and figures are positioned near the end of the typed article. They are not embedded in the text of the Results section. All figures have a figure caption that is typed above the figure. See Figure 8.2 for examples of formatted tables and figures in APA style.

Discussion. The last section of text in your article is the Discussion section. Begin the section with the heading "Discussion" on the next line after your Results section ends. The Discussion section continues where your Introduction left off, beginning with a review of the hypotheses and some statements about whether these hypotheses were supported and which results provide that support. The Discussion section also contains a comparison of your results with those from past studies, especially the studies you described in the Introduction section. For example, are your results consistent with those from previous studies? If not, why not? Limitations of the study are also discussed in this section of the article. However, be careful not to argue that the study was conducted poorly. You are still making an argument (as you did in the Introduction) that the study contributes to scientific knowledge. As part of that argument, you can point out, based on the results you found, issues your study does not address or limitations of the research method chosen for the study, and you may also wish to suggest directions for future studies in your area of research. Your Discussion section ends with a summary paragraph, describing what you learned overall from the study.

References. The Reference section provides a complete listing of all the sources cited in the article. The references are listed in alphabetical order by the last name of the first author. All subsequent authors are listed in the reference in the order in which they appear in the publication. You also provide the publication year, title of the source, where the source was published, and additional information about the publication source. For example, a reference for the journal article described in the Thinking About Research section at the end of the chapter should appear as follows:

Geraerts, E., Bernstein, D. M., Merekelbach, H., Linders, C., Raymaekers, L., & Loftus, E. F. (2008). Lasting false beliefs and their behavioral consequences. *Psychological Science, 19,* 749–753.

See the References section of Figure 8.2 for some additional examples of reference formatting. Begin a new page for the Reference section. Reference organization packages, such as RefWorks and EndNote, can help you format source references into APA style.

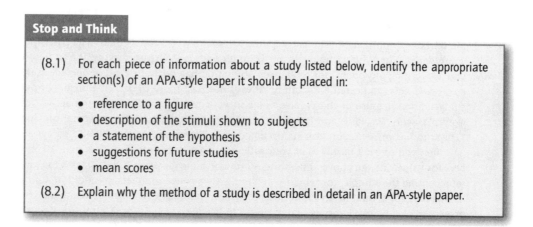

Stop and Think

(8.1) For each piece of information about a study listed below, identify the appropriate section(s) of an APA-style paper it should be placed in:

- reference to a figure
- description of the stimuli shown to subjects
- a statement of the hypothesis
- suggestions for future studies
- mean scores

(8.2) Explain why the method of a study is described in detail in an APA-style paper.

Multiple-Study Articles

For some APA-style articles, you may be describing multiple related studies in one article. For multiple-study articles, you include one Introduction section that provides background for all your studies, a Method for each study, a Results section for each study, and a general Discussion section that describes conclusions for all the studies combined. The Method and Results sections of each study are preceded by headings that indicate the study number, such as "Study 1" or "Experiment 1," centered on the page. A new hierarchy of headings follows for the Method, Results, and subsections of the Method. In multiple-study articles, Method and Results headings are left justified in bold and the subsections of the Method are indented with the paragraph and end with a period. See the *Publication Manual* (APA, 2009) for additional information about formatting multiple-study articles.

Research Proposals

In some situations, researchers must write a proposal for a research project before they conduct the study. Proposals are typically written to convince someone else that a research project should be conducted. The purpose may be to obtain grant funds to conduct the project or to propose a project for a class. To write a research proposal, the APA-style structure described above is generally followed, but a few modifications are made to account for the fact that the study has not yet been completed. For example, the Results section typically contains a plan for the analysis of the data and predicted results for the study. Likewise, the Discussion section contains a discussion of what may be learned in the cases where the hypotheses are supported and not supported. In addition, the details of the study (method details, etc.) are described in the future tense (e.g., "The participants will be recruited from a population of university students"), because the study will take place in the future.

General Formatting

When you type your APA-style article, you should format it according to the following APA style guidelines. The entire article should be double spaced. Use 1-in. margins all around the pages. Type the running head in the top left header and page number in the top right header of each page. Use past tense when you describe any study (including yours) that has already been completed. For example, state "The participants volunteered . . ." rather than "The participants will volunteer . . ." or "The participants are volunteering. . . ." The only exception to this rule is if you are writing a proposal for a research study that has not yet been conducted. In this case, use future tense to describe the study. Always use past tense to describe details of published studies. Minimize use of the passive voice in your writing. Instead, use the active voice. For example, state "Williams and Jones (2006) manipulated the stimulus presentation" instead of "The stimulus presentation was manipulated by Williams and Jones (2006)."

When you present numbers in your article, use words for numbers less than 10, and numbers for values 10 and above, unless the number is a measurement, statistical value, or a value representing the sample, for which you should always use numbers. In addition, all numbers in the abstract should be in numerical form. Any number that begins a sentence should be presented as a word. Numbers that are used in lists (Study 1, Study 2, Group 1, Group 2, etc.) should be given in numerical form. Check the *Publication Manual of the American Psychological Association* (2010) for more rules regarding use of numbers. If you use abbreviations in your article, you must define the abbreviation the first time you use it. For example, on the first page of this chapter, I defined American Psychological Association (APA) and then used this abbreviation throughout the chapter. APA style provides for a few exceptions for some abbreviations that do not need to be defined, such as M for mean, min for minute, and so on, when they are presented with a value.

Citation Format

It is important to cite the sources where you obtain information for your article. You should cite sources for definitions of concepts, review of previous studies, sources for stimuli or questionnaires, and so on. APA-style citation format is to include the last names of the authors in the order they appear in the publication and then the year of publication. For articles with five or fewer authors, list all authors the first time you cite the article. If you cite a source with three or more authors a second time or more than five authors at any time, include just the last name of the first author and et al. to indicate there are other authors. For single- or double-author articles, continue to cite all authors' last names.

Sources can be cited by naming the authors in the text and including the publication year in parentheses. An example of a citation of this type is "Hamilton and Mayes (2006) stated that. . . ." Alternatively, the entire citation can be provided in parentheses to indicate the source of a statement. An example of a citation of this type is "Prospective memory is defined as remembering to perform a task at a future time (Einstein & McDaniel, 2005)." Note that this statement is not a quote from the Einstein and McDaniel article. It is a summarization of the definition in the writer's own words. Quotes are rarely used in psychological articles, but if you do include a direct quote from a source, you should also include the page number on which you found the quote in the article. Also note that the word *and* is used for citations where the authors are directly referred to in the text, whereas an ampersand (&) is used for citations enclosed in parentheses. Remember to include a full reference for each citation in the Reference section.

Proper citation of sources is an important part of avoiding plagiarism (taking credit for someone else's work or ideas). Any description of another study or of someone's theory must include the citation of the source of the study or theory to give proper credit to the author(s) of the source. In addition, presenting another author's written work verbatim or in a manner similar to the written form produced by the author without quotations also constitutes plagiarism. Thus, students should be extremely careful when writing from sources to ensure that quotation marks or original writing is included.

Plagiarism: claiming another's work or ideas as one's own

ORAL PRESENTATIONS

The most common venue for oral presentations of psychological research is a psychological conference. While you may not experience psychology conferences as an undergraduate student, there are many conferences held each year to showcase research conducted by undergraduate students. Your college or university may hold one of these each year. There are also regional conferences such as the Mid-America Undergraduate Psychology Research Conference (MAUPR) and undergraduate psychology conferences in many U.S. states (e.g., ILLOWA Undergraduate Psychology Conference for Illinois and Iowa) that may be of interest to you. Compared with poster presentations, oral presentations of research studies are less likely to be given by undergraduate students at conferences, although the class in which you were assigned this text may have such an assignment.

Preparing an oral presentation of a research study is not very different from writing an APA-style article. The primary differences are that you present the information orally to an audience, and there is usually a time limit, so you must work out ahead of time how much information you can reasonably include in the presentation. The type of information you present, however, is very similar. You begin an oral presentation by introducing the main concepts (e.g., the bystander effect, visual short-term memory, therapeutic treatments for depression), and then present your research question and review what is already known about the research question. You present hypotheses for your study. You then explain the method of the study and review the results, typically using tables or figures to illustrate the main results. Finally, you state conclusions of the study, including whether the hypotheses were supported (or not) by the results and what you learned from the study. Throughout the presentation, you cite sources for your information, just as you would in an APA-style article.

Organization is very important for an oral presentation, just as it is for a paper presentation of research. You must present a coherent argument for your study and your hypotheses. In fact, it can be more difficult to organize an oral presentation, because you must choose carefully what information to present to fit into the time limit you are given. For example, many conference-style oral presentations are limited to 10 or 15 min. Thus, presenters must be very clear in what they present to make themselves understood by their audience in such a short time. A good oral presentation is accompanied by visual aids, typically presented as PowerPoint slides. Because audience members must absorb the information quickly, visual displays of information are more important in oral and poster presentations than in written papers.

POSTER PRESENTATIONS

As with oral presentations, you are most likely to encounter a poster presentation of psychology research at a psychology conference. You may also have been assigned a poster presentation in the course you are taking that assigned this text. Poster presentations are essentially mini-APA-style articles that are condensed to allow a visual presentation rather than a text presentation. They contain the same information as an oral presentation but may be even further condensed according to the space allowed for the poster. See Figure 8.3 for an example of a poster presentation of research. Notice that each of the main APA-style sections is included as well as visual presentations of stimuli and results. Bullet points are used in many places instead of full sentences to make the poster more easily read and to save space.

The organization of a poster presentation should be as visual as possible. Include examples of sample stimuli and organize sections so that they flow. Include a title and authors at the top of the poster. The body of the poster is often organized into segments to make information easier to find and comprehend. Place the introductory information at the left of the poster and then direct the flow of information down each segment, with new segments placed to the right. See the sample poster in Figure 8.3 for the organization style used in a poster.

During a poster presentation, the authors typically stand by their poster, prepared to offer a short summary to interested viewers and answer questions viewers may have as they read the poster. If you are preparing to give a poster presentation, it is a good idea to think through what you will say ahead of time so you give clear and concise descriptions of the research study described in the poster.

Figure 8.3   Poster Presentation of Research

The Relation Between Mood and False Memory Creation of Negative Stimuli

Diana M. Steakley-Freeman and Dawn M. McBride
Illinois State University

Introduction

- The constructive nature of memory has been a highly controversial topic attracting a growing body of research over the last twenty years (Loftus, 1993, 2003)

- False memories of traumatic and otherwise negative events have been of particular interest to cognitive and clinical psychologists (Gallo, 2010; McNallly, 2006).

- Despite continued intradisciplinary debate surrounding the most ecologically valid mode of inquiry, laboratory investigations allow for controlled examination of false memory creation.

- Though there is little consensus on the directionality of the relation between mood and false memory creation, there is clear evidence of an association between these constructs (Corson & Verrier, 2007; Storbeck & Clore, 2005).

- More recently, investigators have begun to study *negative* false memory creation as a distinct phenomenon (Howe & Malone, 2011; Otgaar, Candel, & Merckelbach, 2008)

- The present study investigated individual differences in negative affect and cognitive style as a predictor of negative false memory creation.

Hypotheses

H_1: Depression scores, regardless of clinical significance, will be correlated with negative, but not neutral false memory creation

H_2: After statistically controlling for mood, negative cognitive styles will be a stronger predictor of negative false memory than of neutral false memory

H_3: Production of negative false memories will be related to future negative event forecasting

Method

Participants
N=144 (12 exclusions) undergraduate students ranging in age from 18-25 years-old ($M = 20.40$, $SD = 1.64$)

Measures/Paradigms
Cognitive Style Questionnaire (α=.83; Meins et al., 2012)
Example items: Imagine you are getting along badly with your parents...
"It is my fault I get along badly with my parents."
"Getting along badly with my parents does not say anything bad about me as a person" (reversed scored)

Future Events Questionnaire (α=.84; Miranda & Menin, 2007)
Example items: Rate how like you are to...
"...be socially inadequate"
"...have a successful career" (reverse scored)

Beck Depression Inventory-II (α=.85; Beck, 1996)
Example items:
Sadness
0 I do not feel sad
1 I feel sad much of the time
2 I am sad all the time
3 I am so sad or unhappy that I can't stand it

Deese-Roediger-McDermott List Learning Procedure (DRM; Roediger & McDermott, 1995)

Participants listened to lists of negative and neutral words designed to prime *Critical Lures* (CL) – words that are semantically related to the lists, but not presented. After a distractor task, we asked participants to recall as many words as they could remember.

Example Negative list:
Cry (CL): Tears, Laugh, Baby, Sob, Weep, Upset, Sorrow, Emotional, Scare, Onion, Emotion, Sensitive, Handkerchief, Grief, Fuss

Results

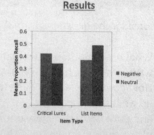

Overall, more items from negative lists were falsely recalled, $t(142) = 2.63$, $p = .009$, However, for studied list items, more neutral list items were recalled than negative list items, $t(142)= 14.73$, $p < .001$.

A linear regression analysis revealed that depression scores were a significant predictor of false recollection of negative stimuli ($\beta = .21$, $p = .02$), but only a marginally significant predictor of neutral stimuli ($\beta = .16$, $p = .06$). Neither of the other measures (CSQ, FEQ) were significant predictors of false memory creation (r's < .10, p's > .10).

To further examine the predictive value of the BDI on false memory creation, we conducted an exploratory factor analysis (oblique rotation assuming correlated latent factors). Negative FM was most strongly related to the factors of cognitive depression ($r = .20$, $p = .02$), and affective instability ($r = .21$, $p = 01$).

Correlations	Negative FM	Neutral FM
Cognitive Depression	.201*	.108
Somatic Depression	.140	.083
Survival Avoidance	-.036	.154
Self Punishment	.028	.061
Anhedonia	.145⁺	.180*
Affective Instability	.213**	.085

Discussion and Future Directions

These data suggest that cognitive patterns associated with negative affect may be stronger predictors of Negative FM than affect alone. Further, our data also suggest that anhedonia may play a role in memory creation as well, though the current study may lack sufficient power to detect this effect. Future studies will investigate the relation between cognition, emotional regulation, and memory creation in an effort to better understand this relation.

Presented at the 2014 Meeting of the Psychonomic Society, Long Beach CA. This project was supported by a Research and Sponsored Programs Grant at Illinois State

Stop and Think

(8.3)   In what ways do paper presentations of a study differ from poster and oral presentations of a study? In what ways are they similar?

CHAPTER SUMMARY

Reconsider the questions from the beginning of the chapter:

- What are the different ways that psychologists present research? Psychologists present research as written reports, oral presentations, and poster presentations.
- How do we write an APA-style article? What information goes in each section of the article? How do we format the article? An APA-style article is organized into sections that present the background and purpose of the study (Introduction), Method of the study, Results of the study, and conclusions of the study (Discussion). Additional format information is described in this chapter and in the APA publication manual (APA, 2010).
- What is an appropriate format for an oral presentation of research? An oral presentation is organized according to the major sections of an APA-style article, but presented orally, and often employs visual aids such as PowerPoint slides.
- How do we prepare a conference-style poster presentation of research? A poster presentation is also organized according the sections of an APA-style article, but provides a more visual representation of the most important information that is presented in those sections.

THINKING ABOUT RESEARCH

A summary of a research study in psychology is given below. As you read the summary, think about the following questions:

1. Notice that the sections of the following summary are identical to the four main sections of an APA-style article. Describe the four subsections of the Method and describe what the authors of this article likely included in each Method subsection of their article beyond what is already described below.

2. Read the Results section below and determine what is missing that should be included in an APA-style Results section.

3. Use the means provided in the Results section below to create an APA-style figure or table to present the means. Be sure to include a figure caption if you create a figure.

4. Use PsycINFO (or another journal article search tool) to find the reference for the Loftus (2005) review article published in *Learning and Memory*. Be sure to locate the reference that is the most appropriate for the citation. Type the reference in APA style.

5. The study described below involved deceiving the participants. Explain how deception was used in the study and describe how the authors should design the study to adhere to ethical guidelines. Also indicate in which section of the APA-style article they report the ethical aspects of the study.

Research Study. Geraerts, E., Bernstein, D. M., Merekelbach, H., Linders, C., Raymaekers, L., & Loftus, E. F. (2008). Lasting false beliefs and their behavioral consequences. *Psychological Science, 19,* 749–753.

Purpose of the Study. Numerous previous studies have shown that false memories can be created for life events that were never experienced (see Loftus, 2005, for a review). However, previous research has not addressed the question of how these false memories affect the future behavior of participants. The current study planted a false memory in participants that they had become ill after eating egg salad when they were children. Their behavior with regard to egg salad was then tested after 1 week and then again 4 months later.

Method of the Study. Undergraduate students were randomly assigned to either an egg salad group ($n = 120$) or a control group ($n = 60$). All participants completed three study sessions. At the first session, the participants completed a questionnaire regarding their food preferences and experiences, including whether they had ever been sick as a child from egg salad and how much they liked egg salad. Data for participants who had actually gotten sick from egg salad as children (as verified by their parents, $n = 5$) were omitted from the study. At the second session that occurred 1 week later, participants received feedback about their responses to the questionnaire. The feedback was false, but the participants were told that a computer generated the information they were given based on their responses to the questionnaire. The egg salad group was told that they had gotten sick from egg salad as a child. The control group was not given this information. Participants then completed another series of questionnaires, including a memory belief questionnaire to determine whether they believed they had gotten sick from egg salad as a child. Finally, participants were placed in a room for a false debriefing session with various foods present, including egg salad sandwiches. The type of sandwich participants chose was recorded. Four months after the first session, the participants were contacted to take part in a taste-test study. They were asked to rate various foods on an 8-point scale, including egg salad sandwiches. Finally, participants were given the opportunity to eat the leftover food. The number of egg salad sandwiches eaten was again recorded.

Results of the Study. Participants in the egg salad group were first divided into believers and nonbelievers, based on their responses to the memory belief questionnaire. This division created three groups of participants for comparison: egg salad believers ($n = 41$), egg salad nonbelievers ($n = 58$), and control participants ($n = 58$). Results showed that fewer participants in the two egg salad groups ($M = 7\%$ for believers, $M = 4\%$ for nonbelievers) ate egg salad sandwiches at the second session than the participants in the control group ($M = 33\%$). The believer and nonbeliever groups did not differ. For the third session, participants who were believers ($M = 11\%$) ate fewer egg salad sandwiches than participants in the control ($M = 44\%$) and nonbeliever groups ($M = 37\%$). None of the groups differed in the mean number of other sandwiches eaten at either session. (*Note:* The means in this section were estimated from Figure 2 in the article.)

Conclusions of the Study. The results showed that exposing participants to a false belief about a life event (e.g., getting sick from egg salad as a child) affected their future behavior with regard to the objects of the event (e.g., they ate fewer egg salad sandwiches). Over time, this effect was evident for the believers, but not for the nonbelievers. These results indicate that future behavior is affected by a false belief, but the effect will dissipate over time if the false belief is not well accepted by the participants.

COMMON PITFALLS AND HOW TO AVOID THEM

Problem: Misuse of citations and quotes—students tend to overuse quotes in research reports and incorrectly cite sources.

Solution: Remember that quotes are rarely used in psychological reports. Instead, you should summarize another author's ideas in your words, being careful not to plagiarize other authors' writings. Always cite sources for ideas, definitions, theories, methods, and so on that are from another author.

Problem: Incorrect uses of verb tense—students often use the wrong verb tense to describe their studies.

Solution: If you are reporting a study that has already been completed, use the past tense to describe the study (yours or someone else's). If you are writing a research proposal, use the future tense to describe a study that will be completed in the future.

Problem: Providing too many details of background studies—writing a full summary of a past study in the Introduction of a research report.

Solution: The goal of the Introduction is to motivate the study you did (or will do), not to provide a full review of all the studies done in an area. Thus, you should describe only the most relevant background studies in your Introduction (i.e., those that help motivate your study or your hypotheses) and only describe aspects of those studies that help you make the point you want to make.

Problem: Describing background literature from secondary sources—students often use secondary sources (see Chapter 2 for more information) for literature reviews leading to problems with misrepresentation of the primary source.

Solution: In your Introduction, be sure to describe primary sources you have read in reviewing background literature. This allows citations of the primary source and more accurate presentation of background studies. You should never cite sources that you have not read.

Problem: Focus on statistics in the Results section—making statements about the statistics instead of the effect or relationship tested.

Solution: Remember that statistical values should be used to support statements about effects or relationships, not as the focus of your statements. For example, indicate that the effect of the independent variable on the dependent variable was significant and support this statement with statistics. Do not make statements that the statistic itself was significant or not significant.

TEST YOURSELF

1. In which section of an APA-style article would you include the following information about your study?

   (a) Statements of hypotheses

   (b) Graphs of the means for each condition

   (c) A description of the questionnaire the participants completed

   (d) The number of participants or subjects in the study

   (e) A citation for a published source

   (f) Instructions that were given to the participants

2. Which of the following is true about formatting an APA-style article? (Choose all that apply.)

   (a) Two-in. margins should be used.

   (b) The entire article should be double spaced.

   (c) Tables and figures should be embedded into the Results section.

   (d) You need to provide citations only when you quote from a source.

   (e) You should begin a new page for the References section.

3. For the citation examples below, indicate which ones display correct APA style:

   (a) Regia-Corte and Wagman (2008) reported that participants perceived a slope to be more difficult to stand on when wearing a weighted backpack.

   (b) In a review of how scientific thinking skills develop, Corinne Zimmerman reported many studies that support this theory.

   (c) The list-strength effect is exhibited when stronger items (studied for a longer time, studied to a deeper level, etc.) in a list produce better memory than weaker items (Verde, 2009).

   (d) The method used in the current study is based on the method described by Garrison (Feb, 2009).

4. Place the following APA-style sections into the correct order in which they should appear in a manuscript: Results, Introduction, Procedure, Discussion, Abstract, References, Title Page, Participants.

5. Which of the following illustrates correct APA style for references of journal articles?

   (a) Reese-Weber, Marla (2008). A new experimental method assessing attitudes toward adolescent dating and sibling violence using observations of violent interactions. *Journal of Adolescence, 31,* 857–876.

   (b) Reese-Weber, M. (2008). A new experimental method assessing attitudes toward adolescent dating and sibling violence using observations of violent interactions. *Journal of Adolescence, 31,* 857–876.

   (c) Marla Reese-Weber (2008). A New Experimental Method Assessing Attitudes Toward Adolescent Dating and Sibling Violence Using Observations of Violent Interactions. *Journal of Adolescence, 31,* 857–876.

   (d) Reese-Weber, M. (March, 2008). A new experimental method assessing attitudes toward adolescent dating and sibling violence using observations of violent interactions. *Journal of Adolescence, Vol. 31,* pp. 857–876.

6. Explain how an oral presentation differs from a poster presentation.

7. In APA-style, the Participants section is a subsection of the _____ section.

8. Figures and tables will most likely be referred to in the _____ section of an APA-style paper.

9. A(n) _____ is a short summary of a study that appears on the second page of a research report.

10. The Reference section should include _____.

Answers can be found at edge.sagepub/mcbride3e.

STOP AND THINK ANSWERS

(8.1) Results; Method (Materials subsection); Abstract (maybe), Introduction, and Discussion; Discussion; Results (also possibly a table/figure)

(8.2) The goal of a Method section is to provide enough detail that someone could replicate the study if they wish. This will also ensure that the reader has enough information to understand how the study was conducted in order to evaluate the conclusions made.

(8.3) More detailed information is provided in a paper report than in oral/poster presentations. Oral/poster presentations typically cover main ideas about the study in bullet points for speedy understanding of the study. However, the main ideas of the study (why, how, what was found, and what was learned) are provided in all types of presentations.

$SAGE edge™

Visit edge.sagepub.com/mcbride3e for the tools you need to sharpen your study skills:

- Web Quizzes
- eFlashcards
- Thinking About Research

- SAGE Journal Articles
- Web and Multimedia Resources

Chapter 9

The Nuts and Bolts of Survey Research

Consider the following questions as you read Chapter 9

- What types of research questions can be answered with survey observations?
- How are surveys constructed?
- What makes responses for a survey valid?
- How is reliability tested for a survey?
- What are some different ways that surveys can be administered?

$\mathbf{A}$s legislative battles continue in places around the world regarding the issue of same-sex marriage, you may have your own opinion about whether same-sex marriage should be legal or not. And you may be wondering whether your opinion is similar to others' in your country or not. One way to find out how your opinion compares with others' is to consider the results of a survey conducted to determine the opinions of a population of people on a particular issue. From a Gallup poll conducted in July, 2013 (retrieved from http://www.gallup.com/poll/163730/back-law-legalize-gay-marriage-states.aspx on March 2, 2015), 52% of Americans favor the legalization of same-sex marriage in the United States. By May 2015, this number had risen to 60%. One question you may be asking is how do they know that these numbers are accurate? If they did not sample from the entire population (which they did not), then how many people is this survey based on and how many do we need to survey in order to determine that 60% is accurate? Surveys conducted with good methodology will report this information to allow you to answer these questions and judge for yourself how accurate (or valid) the survey results are. For this survey, these results were based on a phone survey, where landline and cell phone numbers in the continental United States were randomly selected to be called for the survey with 2,027 people sampled. They also considered demographic characteristics of the individuals such that a stratified sample (see Chapter 6) was used to ensure a representative sample for the population of U.S. adults. The sampling error reported was + or −3%, indicating that the population value is between 49% and 55% with 95% certainty (see Chapter 7).

Surveys are a common data collection technique used in psychological research, but it can be difficult to construct a valid survey. In fact, this is one of the most important issues to consider when designing a new survey: how to maximize the validity of the scores from the survey. Consider surveys you may have taken for fun in a magazine or online. They may have asked you questions such as "What is your favorite color?" and "If you could be any animal, what would you be?" to tell you about your personality. How valid do you think these surveys are? Does your favorite color or preferred animal really indicate aspects of your personality? This is what researchers try to determine when they test the validity of the scores from a survey. In addition, how much can be learned from a survey if people's responses change each time they take the survey (e.g., your favorite color this month is purple, but last month you were really into blue)? Wording of the questions, choice of response scale (see Chapter 5 for more discussion of response scales), and the sampling technique used can all affect the validity and reliability of the survey results. Accordingly, this chapter describes the "nuts and bolts" of survey research, including issues that affect the validity and reliability of surveys that researchers should consider as they construct a survey (Figure 9.1). Note that in this chapter, I will use the terms "survey" and "questionnaire" similarly, but many researchers distinguish these as different types of instruments.

Survey Research: a research study that uses the survey observational technique to measure behavior

---

ANSWERING RESEARCH QUESTIONS WITH SURVEYS

Using surveys to learn about behavior is fairly common in personality, clinical, counseling, industrial-organizational, and social psychology. In these areas of psychology, surveys allow a researcher to learn about behaviors that would be difficult or impossible to directly observe in the behaviors of the participants: their thoughts and attitudes. In other words, surveys allow a researcher to obtain self-reports from participants about the behaviors and attitudes they report. They can also be used to ask people to describe other people's behaviors (e.g., parents describing their children's behaviors, teachers describing their students' behaviors). Surveys can be short, such as a single question, or they can be very long, containing hundreds of items. Longer, standardized surveys are often called questionnaires, but many psychologists use these terms interchangeably.

The majority of survey research is conducted to answer descriptive or predictive research questions. For example, "How do Americans (or people in the United Kingdom or people in Canada, etc.) currently feel about the economy?" is a descriptive question about an attitude that can be answered by administering a survey to Americans (or individuals in another country) with questions about the economy. Or a researcher could instead ask the question "Can the consumer behaviors of Americans (or others) be predicted from how

---

Descriptive Research Question: a research question that asks about the presence of behavior, how frequently it is exhibited, or whether there is a relationship between different behaviors

Predictive Research Question: a research question that asks if one behavior can be predicted from another behavior to allow predictions of future behavior

---

Figure 9.1   Steps in the Research Process: Designing the Study

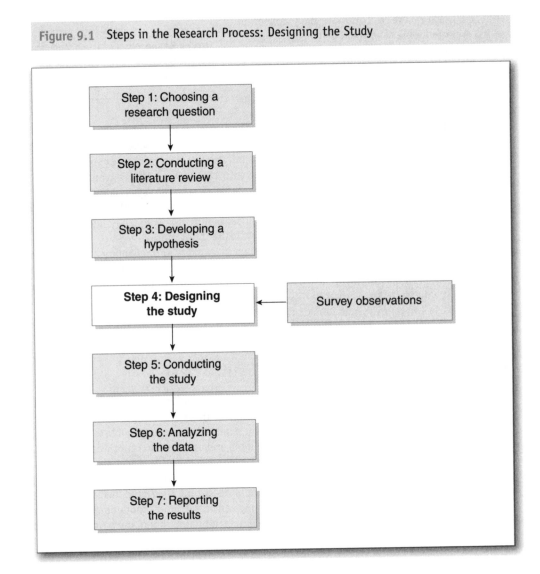

Causal Research Question: a research question that asks what causes specific behaviors to occur

they currently feel about the economy?" In this case, the goal is to determine whether a predictive relationship exists between the attitudes collected from the survey and the consumer behaviors of Americans (or others). In some cases, researchers use surveys to test causal relationships in experiments. For example, suppose a researcher wants to answer the causal research question, "Which of a series of treatments causes the largest reduction in depression symptoms?" This researcher might conduct an experiment to compare the therapies' effect on scores from a depression questionnaire, such as the Beck Depression Inventory II (BDI-II), where the survey is used to measure the dependent variable of depression symptoms. Another example of experiments that involve surveys is in testing the effect of new products on consumer behaviors and attitudes. This type of research is often done by presenting participants with different products or different variations of a product and asking them to complete a short survey about each product. Thus, although surveys are used most commonly to describe or predict behavior, they can be used to test a variety of research questions. The difference between these types of questions is based on the researcher's goals for the study.

CREATING A SURVEY

For many behaviors of common interest in psychology, a researcher is able to find a questionnaire that has already been developed, tested, and validated for use in asking participants about these behaviors. There are two good sources for standardized questionnaires that may contain the type of survey you are looking for. One is called the Health and Psychosocial Instruments (HAPI) database. If your institution's library connects to the EBSCO database, you may find HAPI through your library's web database. The other source is called the Mental Measurements Yearbook (also available through EBSCO if you have access to that database). Each of these sources contains references to standardized questionnaires on different topics, and in some cases, the questionnaires themselves are available on the sites. For example, there are many standardized questionnaires that measure various mood states of interest.

There are also situations where a researcher wants to ask participants about their thoughts and behaviors on a topic for which a questionnaire has not yet been developed and/or tested. In these cases, researchers may need to develop their own questionnaires to ask questions about a specific topic that has not yet been investigated with a survey. This is an area of psychological research called psychometrics, which involves the development, validation, and refinement of surveys and tests for measuring different psychological constructs, such as intelligence and aspects of personality (Vogt, 2005). When a new survey or test is developed, it is important that the validity and reliability of the measure be tested. Thus, we next discuss some important issues that are considered when a new survey is being developed, as these issues can affect the validity and reliability of surveys.

Psychometrics: area of psychological research that involves the development, validation, and refinement of surveys and tests for measuring psychological constructs

Construct Validity: indicates that a survey measures the behavior it is designed to measure

Survey Questions

The types of questions included in a questionnaire can affect the construct validity or accuracy of measurement (see Chapters 4 and 5 for more discussion of validity) of the scores from the questionnaire by influencing the responses of the research participants. Hence, it is important to write questions carefully so as to reduce bias in responses. To ensure that your survey includes the best set of questions, it is a good idea to pilot test sets of questions to determine the specific wording that is most easily understood by your participants.

Face Validity: on the surface, a study or scale appears to be intuitively valid

Factor Analysis: a set of statistical techniques used to analyze responses from a survey or questionnaire to group items together by concept

Open-Ended Response Scale: participants respond to survey questions in any manner they feel is appropriate for the question

Closed-Ended Response Scale: participants respond to survey questions according to the response options provided by the researcher

---

Dillman (2000) makes several important suggestions to researchers writing survey questions. For example, consider how your participants perceive the question. Are the questions confusing? Will it be unclear how the participants should respond in some cases? If you ask a question such as "When you go to the movies, do you tend to go with your friends, family, or on your own?" it is unclear how a participant who does not go to the movies can respond. Consider whether participants are able to recall the behaviors you are asking about. If you ask older adults a question such as "When you were a child, how many days a week did your parents talk about finances in your presence?" it may be difficult for participants to remember an accurate response. Avoid double-barreled questions that are actually two questions in one, where each question may require a different answer. For example, a question such as "Do you often get depressed and talk to others about it?" is actually two separate questions: "Do you get depressed?" and "If you get depressed, do you talk to others about it?" In addition, avoid loaded questions that assume too much (e.g., "When you talk about depression to your friends, whom do you speak to about it?"). In summary, strive to create simple and clear questions that can be unambiguously interpreted by the respondents. Researchers consider these issues when they write questions to ensure that the questions elicit valid responses from the participants.

When a researcher develops a new survey, there are several steps that must be followed to ensure the survey has good validity. The first step is to write the questions. This typically involves writing more questions than will be used in the final survey, because some questions may be biased or duplicate other questions on the survey. The next step is to consider the face validity of the questions. On the surface, do the questions seem to address the concept the researcher wishes to measure? If the questions seem to have face validity, then presenting them to a group for pilot testing is the next step. Are the responses as expected for these questions or are some of them confusing or biased toward a particular response? Further refining of the questions is typically done at this point. The researcher may also conduct a factor analysis of the questions to determine which questions naturally group together based on the responses in the pilot testing. A factor analysis is a statistical technique that will analyze responses from a survey or questionnaire to indicate which questions seem to measure the same concept based on the responses made by individuals to all the questions. This will allow the researcher to determine if there are too many questions about one concept or if there are distinct concepts being measured in the survey. Finally, the survey will be tested for item reliability (see Reliability section later in this chapter) to determine whether the scores on the different items are internally consistent.

Types of Survey Response Scales

When researchers write a survey, an important decision they need to make is the type(s) of response scales that are included in the survey. As described in Chapter 4, question responses can be either open-ended or closed-ended. Open-ended responses allow the participants to respond in any way they feel is appropriate for the question. An example of an open-ended question is "How do you feel today?" For this question, participants may respond with a single word describing their current mental state or they may write a longer response that describes several aspects of their current mental state. Closed-ended questions provide a set of responses that the participants must choose from. For example, if the question above were followed with choices of "happy," "sad," "excited," "anxious," and "frustrated," the question would become closed-ended, because the participants are asked to choose one of the given responses for the question. A Likert rating scale (i.e., rating agreement on a 1 to 5 scale) is another example of a closed-ended response scale (see Chapter 5 for more discussion of Likert scales). The choice between these two response options determines the type of data you collect with your survey. Collecting open-ended responses requires developing a coding scheme to categorize the different types of responses. Collecting closed-ended responses involves use of one of the different types of measurement scales described in Chapter 5. Specifically, nominal, ordinal, or interval scales can be used, depending on the type of response options given to the participants.

If you choose to include closed-ended response scales in your survey, Dillman (2000) suggests following a similar process in the wording of questions. Consider how your participants view the response choices you provide. Will the response categories be confusing to your participants or bias the way they respond? For example, if you ask "How much TV do you watch each day?" you may bias the response you get from participants with different types of closed-ended response categories. Giving choices of "(a) less than 1 hour per day, (b) 1 to 2 hours per day, or (c) more than 2 hours per day" may lead participants to respond differently than choices of "(a) less than 5 hours per day, (b) 5 to 7 hours per day, or (c) more than 7 hours per day." Carefully consider the number of response categories provided to the participants. Including too few choices can bias the participants' responses, but including too many choices may confuse the participants. However, more response options allow for more varied responses, which can increase the validity of the scores (see Chapter 7 for more discussion of the importance of variability in data distributions), so researchers should carefully consider the number of response options provided. Also, consider that the use of ordinal response scales, such as those described above, may not provide choices that match the participants' exact behavior. Thus, an open-ended ratio scale that allows participants to report the exact number of hours of TV they watch per day may be accurate.

Some other considerations: Avoid response categories that overlap, but make certain that categories are comparable and unbiased. Include equal numbers of positive and negative response categories. Try to include response categories that allow a response for all possible behaviors and attitudes. Decide whether you will include neutral and/or undecided response categories to allow participants to indicate when they have no opinion on a topic. Consider how the respondents interpret the response categories you have provided. If a rating scale is used, be certain to provide labels for the endpoints and perhaps the midpoint of the scale. Piloting your questions with the response categories helps determine the best categories to include in your survey (Figure 9.2). See Table 9.1 for some examples of different types of response scales.

Stop and Think

(9.1)   Explain how face validity can contribute to the construct validity of a survey.

(9.2)   If you were constructing a survey, would you include open-ended or closed-ended responses on the scale? Explain your answer.

Table 9.1   Examples of Different Types of Response Scales for Survey Questions

Response Scale	Examples
Open-Ended	How do you feel today? _____ What is your political affiliation? _____ Why did you decide to go to college? _____
Closed-Ended	How do you feel today? __ Happy __ Sad __Anxious __ Excited __ Frustrated Indicate where your political affiliation falls on the following scale: X X X X X Liberal Neutral Conservative Rate how strongly you wanted to go to college when you were a high school senior: 1 2 3 4 5 6 7 Weak Neutral Strong Desire Desire Desire

Figure 9.2   Consider the Response Choices You Include in Your Response Scale

SOURCE: Copyright by Getty Images, www.gettyimages.com.

Validity of Scores From a Survey

The concept of validity has been discussed in several contexts in the different chapters of this text. In Chapter 5, *construct validity* as it pertains to response scales was introduced. Construct validity is particularly relevant to survey research because a survey with construct validity is one that accurately measures the behavior it was designed to measure. Some researchers argue that all tests of validity of scores from a survey contribute to the construct validity of the survey (e.g., Messick, 1995). However, the method researchers use to test the validity of the scores from a survey depends on the goals they have for the research study in which the survey is used. For example, the validity of a survey may allow a researcher to test a theoretical assumption about behaviors. Alternatively, testing the validity of the scores from a survey may allow a researcher to determine if the survey can be used to predict related behaviors.

If researchers are designing their own survey, it is very important that they write survey items carefully to ensure that they address the behaviors that they intend to measure. This helps maximize the validity of the scores from the survey. Issues related to sampling, discussed in Chapter 6, also affect the validity of the scores from a survey. A biased sample that does not accurately represent the population of interest reduces the validity of the survey measure. For example, the survey described at the beginning of the chapter about opinions on same-sex marriage was conducted by calling people with only landline or cellular telephones. Thus, a bias may be present because the sample excluded people who were unavailable to answer their phone at the time they were called for the survey. In addition, nonresponse errors can decrease the validity of the scores from the survey measure in a similar way by biasing the sample. Nonresponse errors occur when individuals chosen for the sample choose not to respond to the survey. Therefore, even when an appropriate sampling technique is used, nonresponse errors can still occur, making the sample less representative. However, if a survey is being administered in a laboratory setting, as compared with a survey that is mailed, conducted by phone, or completed on the web, nonresponse errors are less problematic because a different sampling technique is involved. Nonresponse errors are a particular type of coverage error that occurs when the sample completing the survey does not represent the entire population that the researchers wish to use to generalize the scores. In other words, coverage errors occur when the sampling technique used is not successful in collecting a representative sample. This type of error can occur in several ways, including from nonresponse errors, from a sample that does not include a particular subgroup of the population (e.g., a sample of mostly males or mostly females), or from a volunteer sample where volunteers are different from individuals who do not volunteer (e.g., individuals with strong feelings on a topic respond to a survey, but individuals with more neutral feelings do not respond). Coverage errors reduce the external validity of your survey, such that responses from the sample do not generalize to the researcher's study population. See Chapter 6 for more discussion of sampling techniques and their effects on validity.

Previously validated surveys are useful to researchers. If used with the same population for which they were validated, previously tested surveys can be used with more confidence and the knowledge that they measure the intended behaviors with reasonable accuracy. However, if you must validate your own survey, there are some different ways this can

Nonresponse Error: a sampling error that occurs when individuals chosen for the sample do not respond to the survey, biasing the sample

Coverage Error: a sampling error that occurs when the sample chosen to complete a survey does not provide a good representation of the population

---

❧

Criterion-Related Validity: determining the validity of the scores of a survey by examining the relationship between the survey scores and other established measures of the behavior of interest

Social Desirability Bias: bias created in survey responses from respondents' desire to be viewed more favorably by others, typically resulting in overreporting of "positive" behaviors and underreporting of "negative" behaviors

---

be done. One method of validation is to examine relationships between your survey and other measures of the behaviors of interest, such as other surveys that have already been validated or direct observations that indicate the behaviors of interest (e.g., seeking counseling for mood problems, voting for a particular candidate or issue, exhibiting social behaviors). This is called criterion-related validity, and it is based on the relationship between your survey and the criterion measures or behaviors that have previously been used as operational definitions of the behavior of interest. Often, a researcher tests the criterion-related validity of a survey to determine if the survey can predict other behaviors. For example, the SAT (Scholastic Aptitude Test) and ACT (American College Test) are used as college entrance exams because the criterion-related validity of the scores on these tests has been correlated to academic achievement in college. In some cases, these tests do predict academic achievement (e.g., first-year college GPA [grade point average]; Coyle & Pillow, 2008); however, they have not been found to predict all types of academic achievement (see Sackett, Kuncel, Arneson, Cooper, & Waters, 2009, for a recent review of research on this issue). Thus, their validity may be limited to certain types of academic measures.

Another threat to the validity of survey responses is the willingness of respondents to accurately represent their true attitudes and behaviors in their responses. Because surveys involve self-reports from the research participants instead of direct behavior measurements by the researchers, it is often unclear if the data are being reported accurately by the subjects. In some cases, participants completing a survey alter their responses to present themselves in a more positive way. This effect is called the social desirability bias and can be present when surveys are used to measure behavior or attitudes from individuals. One way researchers try to deal with social desirability bias in survey responses is to include a measure of this bias such as the Marlowe-Crowne social desirability scale (Crowne & Marlowe, 1960). These measures include items designed to test a respondent's level of social desirability in order to allow a measurement of the bias within the sample. Social desirability measures are typically included along with the main survey.

Reliability of Responses

The reliability of responses to a survey is also important to determine because unreliable surveys reduce the validity of the scores of a study. If participants respond to the questions in a different way at different times or respond in different ways to different sets of similar questions in the survey, the researcher is unable to draw accurate conclusions from the survey responses. Thus, using a measure with high reliability increases the likelihood of high validity for a study that includes a survey. One way to increase the reliability of scores on a survey is to use a longer survey. Surveys with more items typically yield more reliable scores than shorter surveys. Shorter surveys tend to be less reliable, because an unusual response on a single item can skew the results quite a bit. However, with more items on a survey, a single unusual response does not affect the results as much. In addition, there are different types of reliability that are of interest depending on the purpose of the study. Two common types of reliability that are important to consider for a survey are discussed below.

Test-Retest Reliability. Test-retest reliability means that the scores on a measure are consistent over time. If a questionnaire has good test-retest reliability, then each time a person takes the questionnaire, his or her scores should be similar. Test-retest reliability is typically determined from the relationship between the same individual's scores on a questionnaire when he or she takes the questionnaire at different points in time. For example, if you were designing a new questionnaire, you might check its test-retest reliability by having a group of participants take the questionnaire once, recording their scores, and then have them take the questionnaire again 2 months later. If the scores from the first time they take the questionnaire are positively related to the scores from the second time they take the questionnaire 2 months later (with a strong relationship between the two), then the questionnaire has good test-retest reliability. However, getting the same participants to take a questionnaire twice can be problematic for two reasons: (1) participants may not come back the second time, and the sample size is then reduced—an issue known as attrition/mortality (attrition was introduced as a form of bias in Chapter 5) and (2) having participants take the same questionnaire more than once can change their results through testing effects—these occur when taking a test or questionnaire once affects future scores on the scale (testing effects were also introduced in Chapter 5). Thus, other methods of evaluating the reliability of a questionnaire have been developed to deal with these problems. In addition, there may be occasions when researchers expect to find changes in scores over time based on changes in personality or attitudes as individuals develop or events that individuals experience (e.g., starting a new job, getting married) between testings. Thus, test-retest reliability may only be desirable for some surveys tested with specific populations.

Test-Retest Reliability: indicates that the scores on a survey will be similar when participants complete the survey more than once

Attrition/Mortality: occurs when participants choose not to complete a study

Testing Effects: occur when participants are tested more than once in a study, with early testing affecting later testing

Internal Consistency of Scores. Internal consistency of scores indicates how similar scores on the different items of a survey are compared to one another. This is another means of evaluating the reliability of the scores on a survey. One way to determine internal consistency is to examine the correlation between scores for subsets of items. In other words, the items on the questionnaire are split into two halves or sections and the relationship between the scores on the two sets of items is tested. This is called split-half reliability. If a strong, positive relationship exists between the scores on the two sets of items, then the questionnaire has good split-half reliability. The advantage of split-half reliability as a method of testing the reliability of a questionnaire is that you can test the reliability with a single testing of a group of participants. You do not need to retest the participants and wait for the second set of results. However, split-half reliability provides a fairly crude measure of reliability and can depend on how the items are divided in the survey.

Internal Consistency: a form of reliability that tests relationships between scores on different items of a survey

Split-Half Reliability: method of testing scores' internal consistency that indicates if the scores are similar on different sets of questions on a survey that address similar topics

—————— ✤ ——————

Cronbach's Alpha (α): method of testing scores' internal consistency that indicates the average correlation between scores on all pairs of items on a survey

Another method of testing the internal consistency of scores is to examine the overall correlation between pairs of items. In other words, the relationship between the scores for each pair of items on a survey is calculated, and then a statistical averaging of these correlations is determined for the whole survey. This method is called Cronbach's alpha (α), which is also the name of the statistical test that is used to calculate the overall correlation (Green & Salkind, 2007). Note that Cronbach's alpha is different from the alpha level used to set the Type I error rate in an inferential statistical test (see discussion of alpha level in Chapter 7). Cronbach's alpha is a commonly used measure of reliability of scores for a survey and is provided in many studies for the responses collected from a survey.

SURVEY ADMINISTRATION

Researchers have a few options for administering surveys. Surveys can be given in person using a paper form of the survey, by computer, or by oral administration (in person or over the phone). Surveys can be administered by mail (using a mailing list to send a paper copy or web address for the survey) or by phone using a phone list to choose participants. Many of the survey results you hear reported in the media (e.g., the example presented at the start of this chapter) are obtained with phone surveys. Phone surveys are used to collect data from a large number of individuals quickly, especially if they only involve a few short questions. Mailings are expensive due to the large number of surveys that need to be sent out in order to obtain a large enough sample. They also typically require a postage-paid return envelope if a paper survey is to be mailed back to the researcher. In addition, mailed surveys and phone surveys have the disadvantage of low response rates that can create nonresponse errors as described above. Participants can easily ignore a mailing or choose not to answer the phone for numbers they do not recognize. There may also be issues obtaining representative phone lists, as many individuals now exclusively use a cellular phone or may not have their number listed. Surveys typically require a large number of responses in order for the researcher to be able to generalize the results to a large population, so low response rates are an important issue in using surveys.

If they can be obtained, e-mail lists are also used to contact individuals to ask them to complete an attached survey or to provide a web address that administers the survey on the Internet. Surveys administered on the Internet can yield larger and more diverse samples, but they may also restrict the sample to individuals who are comfortable using the Internet or who have Internet access. This can restrict the sample to certain types of individuals (e.g., younger) and may mean the survey results do not generalize to the larger population. Internet surveys also require access to technological support. See Chapter 6 for more discussion of the issues involved in collecting data using the Internet.

Recruiting participants and getting them to complete a survey requires extra steps. The more participants in your sample who are willing to complete the survey, the lower chance there will be of nonresponse error in your study. Dillman (2000) made several suggestions for improving response rates of surveys. How the survey is presented can influence whether a participant chooses to complete the survey. Using printed fonts and formatting that make the survey easy to read increases completion rates. Some of the controversy over the outcome of the 2000 U.S. presidential election occurred because the Florida ballot had a confusing format, which led to many voters reporting that they may have marked their ballot for a different candidate than they had intended to vote for. Providing clear instructions also helps encourage responses. If surveys are administered orally (e.g., by phone), it can also be useful to begin with a friendly greeting to put the person at ease and make it more likely he or she will complete your survey. In addition, contacting participants multiple times increases completion rates. For example, sending an introduction letter or e-mail before the survey is sent, sending personalized correspondence, sending information about the importance of the survey with the survey itself, and sending follow-up reminders encourages participants to complete the survey (Dillman, 2000). Finally, including an incentive (e.g., a small amount of money or a small gift) encourages completion.

Stop and Think

(9.3)   Explain the difference between test-retest reliability and split-half reliability.

(9.4)   How can attrition and testing effects biases decrease the reliability of a survey?

(9.5)   Describe some ways to decrease nonresponse errors in the administration of a survey.

CHAPTER SUMMARY

Reconsider the questions from the beginning of the chapter:

- What types of research questions can be answered with survey observations? Most surveys are used to answer descriptive or predictive research questions in correlational studies. However, if a survey is used to measure behavior in an experiment, then it can be used to answer causal research questions as well.
- How are surveys constructed? Surveys are constructed with questions or items that address behaviors and attitudes on specific topics. Open-ended or closed-ended items may be included. The goal is to construct the survey such that its validity and reliability are maximized. Thus, validity and reliability are typically evaluated for new surveys that researchers construct.
- What makes responses for a survey valid? If survey scores truly represent the behavior the survey was designed to measure, then the responses on the survey have good validity.
- How is reliability tested for a survey? There are several methods for testing the reliability of the scores from a survey. For example, correlations between scores on different items of the survey can be measured. Alternatively, correlations between scores on the same survey taken at different times can be measured. Strong, positive correlations in these cases would indicate reliable scores on the survey.
- What are some different ways that surveys can be administered? Surveys can be administered in paper booklets to groups or individuals, as oral questions posed to groups or individuals, or on the web to individuals.

THINKING ABOUT RESEARCH

A summary of a research study in psychology is given below. As you read the summary, think about the following questions:

1. Describe the purpose of the survey used in this study. What construct was it intended to measure?

2. Imagine that you have been tasked with creating a sexual interest survey to be used in a study like this one. Write three items for this survey that could be responded to on a 5-point Likert scale (see Chapter 5 for a discussion of Likert scales).

3. Cronbach's α was reported in the article for the survey used. Explain what this value indicates about the survey.

4. Why was it important for the researchers to replicate the past findings in a non-student sample? What source of bias does this rule out?

5. The standard deviation (*SD*) for women's ratings was higher than that for men's ratings. Explain what this tells us about the ratings. (Hint: See Chapter 7 for discussion of standard deviation.)

Research Study. Perilloux, C., & Kuzban, R. (2015). Do men overperceive women's sexual interest? *Psychological Science, 26,* 70–77. (NOTE: Study 1 from this article is described below.)

Purpose of the Study. The purpose of the study was to examine past findings that men overestimate women's sexual interest. Two possible interpretations of these findings were explored: (1) that men really do overestimate women's sexual interest or (2) that men's perceptions are accurate and that women are underreporting their sexual interest. In their first study, Perilloux and Kuzban (2015) examined responses from men and women on a dating-behaviors scale to compare sexual intentions based on reported behaviors from a sample of individuals from the general population.

Method of the Study. Participants were recruited from Amazon's survey site, Mechanical Turk. They completed the dating-behaviors scale (Haselton & Buss, 2000, Cronbach's α = .93) that includes 15 sexual behaviors. For each behavior listed, the participant was asked to rate their how likely they would be to have sex (with a man for female participants and with a woman exhibiting the behavior for male participants) on a scale from −3 (extremely unlikely) to +3 (extremely likely). An average score was calculated for each participant based on their responses to these items.

Results of the Study. The researchers compared scores on the survey for men and women using a *t* test (see Chapter 15). They found that men (*M* = 1.44, *SD* = 0.76) provided higher average ratings of sexual interest than did women (*M* = 0.77, *SD* = 1.21). These results show that the past findings of higher sexual interest ratings from men than women replicate in a nonstudent sample.

Conclusions of the Study. The results of the study showed consistent results across student samples from past studies and the nonstudent sample collected in the current study. The additional studies conducted by these researchers described in this article suggest that men's perceptions of women's sexual interest are fairly accurate and that differences in ratings are due to women underreporting their actual sexual interest. (See the Student Study Site for the entire article that describes all of their studies.)

COMMON PITFALLS AND HOW TO AVOID THEM

Problem: Biased question/item wording—the wording of questions/items on surveys can affect the participants' responses.

Solution: When wording questions/items on a survey, consider how they will be interpreted by the participants. If participants can have different responses to different parts of a question/item, consider breaking the question into two items. If a question/item can be misinterpreted by a participant, consider rewording the item.

Problem: Equating survey responses with direct measures of behavior—overestimating the validity of self-report measures can occur.

Solution: Remember that survey responses are based on what the participants are willing to report about their behaviors and attitudes. In some cases, participants may feel the need to present themselves in a more positive way than is real, reducing the validity of responses on the survey. In addition, it is also possible that participants see themselves differently than they really are. Thus, they do not intentionally mislead with their responses, but their responses still do not match their actual behaviors or attitudes.

TEST YOURSELF

1. What types of research questions can be answered with surveys?

2. Survey items that can be completed with any response chosen by the participant are called _____ questions, whereas survey items that must be completed with one of the response options provided by the researcher are called _____ questions.

3. Describe two ways that reliability can be tested for a survey.

4. Rewrite the survey question to improve its clarity:

   Do you prefer dogs or cats? ___ dogs ___ cats

5. Given the outcome of the U.S. presidential election in 2008, evaluate the survey described at the beginning of this chapter. What aspects of the survey allowed the researchers to accurately predict the winner of the election?

Match each concept below with its correct definition.

6. construct validity

7. test-retest reliability

   (a) participants are not restricted in the types of responses they can make to survey items

   (b) a measure of reliability based on the average correlations between pairs of items on a survey

8. open-ended scale

9. testing effects

10. Cronbach's alpha

(c) the scores are similar each time a participant takes the survey

(d) the scores are indicative of the psychological construct the survey was designed to measure

(e) scores at later testings are affected by a participant's having taken the survey or test previously

Answers can be found at edge.sagepub/mcbride3e.

STOP AND THINK ANSWERS

(9.1) Face validity gives you an intuitive sense of whether your survey measures what you think it measures.

(9.2) Answers will vary.

(9.3) Test-retest reliability measures whether scores are similar over different administrations of the survey. Split-half reliability measures whether scores are similar within the survey over items that measure the same concept in different parts of the survey.

(9.4) Attrition can affect the reliability of a survey in having people with specific characteristics drop out before the survey is complete (e.g., across different administrations). Testing effects can affect reliability by affecting scores with some subjects changing their responses as the survey continues (e.g., from fatigue or practice effects).

(9.5) Answers will vary, but the goal is to encourage all the individuals chosen in a population for the sample to complete the survey.

$SAGE edge™

Visit edge.sagepub.com/mcbride3e for the tools you need to sharpen your study skills:

- Web Quizzes
- eFlashcards
- Thinking About Research

- SAGE Journal Articles
- Web and Multimedia Resources

Chapter 10

The Nuts and Bolts of Correlational Studies

Consider the following questions as you read Chapter 10

- What types of research questions can be answered with correlational studies?
- What is the difference between correlational and causal hypotheses?
- What aspects of correlational studies prohibit testing causal hypotheses?
- How do correlational studies allow us to predict behavior?

For the past several years, the popular press has been recommending that to ward off dementia, older people should continue to engage in activities that exercise their minds, such as solving crossword puzzles and playing other word games (Brody, 1996). These recommendations are based on research showing that people who engaged in more cognitive activities were less likely to develop Alzheimer's disease (Wilson, Scherr, Schneider, Tang, & Bennett, 2007). Note that this claim is based on a correlation between variables (i.e., frequency of Alzheimer's disease and level of cognitive activity). In other words, the researchers are claiming that one variable tends to be higher with the absence of another variable (Alzheimer's disease and frequency of cognitive activity), not that one variable (frequency of cognitive activity) causes another (lower incidence of Alzheimer's disease). Yet the media report recommendations as if a causal relationship exists. Is this appropriate?

The answer to this question is "maybe not." The research findings reported above suggest several possibilities. One possibility is the causal relationship suggested by the media: engaging in cognitive activity as we age prevents Alzheimer's disease. Another possibility, however, is that development of Alzheimer's disease reduces the cognitive activities of people, perhaps because these activities become more difficult as the disease begins to develop. Finally, a third possibility is that a third variable causes both greater cognitive activity and lower incidence of Alzheimer's disease. For example, genetic factors could cause both interest in cognitive activities (making it more likely that someone engages in these activities) and the predisposition (or

—————————— ❧ ——————————

Correlational Study: a type of research design that examines the relationships between multiple dependent variables, without manipulating any of the variables

lack thereof) to Alzheimer's disease. In other words, the simple finding of a relationship among variables does not provide information about the causal relationship between those variables. This is the most important issue to consider when designing a correlational study (Figure 10.1). In correlational studies, researchers examine two or more measures to determine whether those measures are related. Notice that this is different from a quasi-experiment (see Chapter 4) in that no groups of subjects are compared in a correlational study as they are

Figure 10.1 Steps in the Research Process: Designing the Study

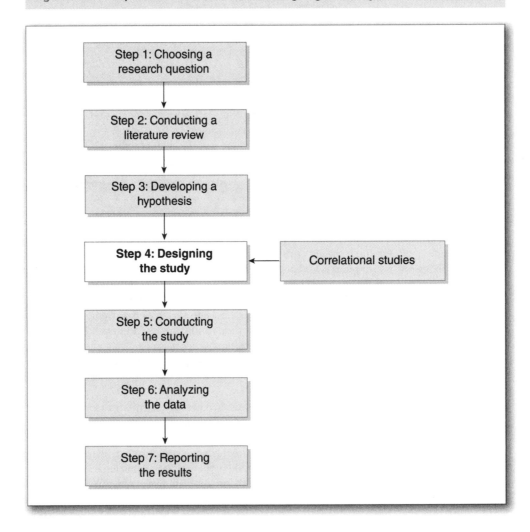

in quasi-experiments. Instead, multiple measures are simply collected from a single group of subjects to determine if those measures co-vary (i.e., change together) across that group of subjects.

Despite the lack of causal information, however, correlational studies do provide information that allows researchers to determine which variables should be considered when they design tests of causal relationships. This is especially important when manipulating a variable to test the causal relationship is difficult or impossible. The results described above regarding incidence of Alzheimer's disease suggested to researchers that a causal relationship might exist between this factor and cognitive activities to allow additional studies to be done to provide further research examining possible causal relationships. For example, programs that include various cognitive activities can be tested to determine if they are effective in reducing the incidence of Alzheimer's disease (Szekely, Breitner, & Zandi, 2007). However, these studies will take time to complete, as Alzheimer's disease takes time to develop and is typically confirmed by examining brain tissue after someone has died. Correlational studies can also suggest the incidence or likelihood of something occurring in the presence or absence of something else. In many studies related to health, for example, correlational studies are the only options because we cannot subject someone to factors that may make him or her unhealthy for ethical reasons. So researchers typically must rely on correlational studies to learn about factors that influence one's health. The knowledge they gain from such studies can often indicate the likelihood of certain conditions occurring with other factors. Strong positive correlations between age and incidence of Alzheimer's disease have been found such that by the time a person reaches the age of 85, the person has a 50% chance of developing Alzheimer's disease (Alzheimer's Association, 2011). However, few researchers would argue that age, in and of itself, causes the disease. Instead, it is likely that factors that also are related to age cause the disease. Another correlational study showed that men who had one or more servings of tomatoes a week were 60% less likely to develop prostate cancer (Park, 2007). Again, this does not mean that tomatoes cause the reduction in cancer rates. It could simply be a relationship that co-occurs with another factor (e.g., overall healthy eating) that directly affects cancer rates. Thus, important information can be gained from correlational studies about the likelihood of an event based on the relationship with another event, but this relationship may or may not be causal.

Descriptive Research Question: a research question that asks about the presence of behavior, how frequently it is exhibited, or whether there is a relationship between different behaviors

Predictive Research Question: a research question that asks if one behavior can be predicted from another behavior to allow predictions of future behavior

RESEARCH QUESTIONS IN CORRELATIONAL STUDIES

Correlational studies are designed to address descriptive and predictive research questions. In other words, the researcher of a correlational study may be attempting to answer one type of descriptive research question regarding simple relationships between variables to determine if behaviors co-occur (see Chapter 2 for examples of other types of descriptive research questions).

❧

Predictor Variable: the dependent variable in a correlational study that is used to predict the score on another variable

Outcome Variable: the dependent variable in a correlational study that is being predicted by the predictor variable

---

Alternatively, a researcher may conduct a correlational study with the ultimate goal of predicting one behavior from another behavior (e.g., predicting grades from the number of hours of TV a person watches per week). Whenever a strong relationship exists between variables, prediction of one variable from other variables is possible. For correlational studies with predictive research questions, the variable that is used for the prediction is called the predictor variable, and the variable being predicted is called the outcome variable. If you have already read Chapter 9 on survey research, these two types of research questions probably sound familiar. In fact, most survey research involves a correlational study, and many correlational studies use surveys to measure behavior. Surveys are a very common observational technique in correlational studies. However, correlational studies can also involve naturalistic observations or systematic observations.

Regardless of the type of observational technique used to measure behavior, the goal of any correlational study is to examine relationships between two or more measures of behavior. These relationships allow researchers to better describe the behaviors being studied or predict one behavior from another behavior. Hypothesized relationships are typically tested using correlational analyses (e.g., Pearson *r*) or regression analyses that allow predictions. See Chapter 15 for more discussion of these types of tests. A correlational study cannot, however, provide causal information about the relationship between the measures; it can only describe the relationship between the behaviors. As described in Chapter 4, this is due to the lack of manipulation of an independent variable in correlational studies and subsequent lack of control of other extraneous variables. Only an experimental study has these features, which allow a causal relationship to be tested.

❧

Pearson *r* Test: a significance test used to determine whether a linear relationship exists between two variables measured on interval or ratio scales

---

Despite the lack of causal information, correlational studies do provide important information about relationships between variables in cases where manipulation is not possible. For example, to determine the link between certain behaviors (e.g., smoking) and poor health, correlational studies are often conducted, because manipulation of the behaviors that may cause poor health is unethical. An experiment that examines this relationship might involve a researcher randomly assigning some participants to smoke and others not to smoke. This study would be unethical if the researcher believes that smoking may be detrimental to health (e.g., animal studies have shown smoking to be harmful). It is unethical to conduct a study where some participants are assigned to a condition that may be harmful to them. Thus, most of the research showing a link between smoking and long-term health in humans involves correlational studies. Experimental studies providing evidence of a causal relationship between smoking and health have been conducted with animal subjects, illustrating how important animal studies can be in understanding certain kinds of everyday problems that humans face.

The key to understanding correlational studies is remembering that *correlation does not equal causation*. The direction of the cause and effect relationship cannot be determined from a correlational study because none of the variables is manipulated in the study. For example, suppose researchers find a negative relationship between two dependent (i.e., measured) variables: number of hours of TV watched per week and grades in school for children. They cannot conclude from this result that watching more TV causes lower grades. It is possible that this causal relationship exists between these measures, but it is also possible that having lower grades causes children to watch more TV because they are not spending that time doing homework or studying. In addition, Chapter 4 introduced the third-variable

Third-Variable Problem: the presence of extraneous factors in a study that affect the dependent variable and can decrease the internal validity of the study

problem as an issue for correlational studies. Because correlational studies cannot control for extraneous variables in the way that experiments can, it is always possible that a third variable (i.e., the third-variable problem discussed in Chapters 4 and 11) is responsible for the relationship between the measures. It is possible that parental influences have a causal relationship with both the number of hours of TV their children watch and their grades. Children with parents who force them to study for a certain amount of time per week and who reinforce good grades may also restrict the number of hours of TV their children watch. Conversely, some parents may encourage their children to watch TV with them and not encourage them to spend time studying or doing homework.

Figure 10.2 presents the three possible causal relationships that might exist for the example above. Consider what a researcher needs to do in order to tease apart these possible causal relationships to find out which one is accurate. To test Relationship A in Figure 10.2, the number of hours of TV the children watched per week has to be manipulated (i.e., an experiment would need to be done) to determine its effect on their grades. In other words, some children are assigned to watch no TV for a month and others are assigned to watch a set number of hours of TV per week for that month, depending on how many groups the researcher wanted to compare. Then the TV watching groups are compared on their average grades to determine if they differ. To test Relationship B in Figure 10.2, the children's grades would need to be manipulated (or at least the grades they are told they are earning), and then the grade groups be compared for how much TV they watch per week. Testing Relationship C might be difficult; however, a researcher can assign parents to groups, where the groups are asked to encourage their children either to spend their time on academic tasks (such as doing homework and studying) or to spend their time watching TV. The researcher then measures the children's grades and how much TV they watch after a period of time. Notice, though, that each of these tests of the different possible relationships requires an experiment to be conducted because a correlational study of these variables reveals whether a relationship between them exists but does not reveal the type of causal relationship that might be present.

However, if the study described above found a relationship between the number of hours of TV watched per week and the child's grades, this relationship can be used to predict one behavior from the other for other individuals. The researcher's goal in conducting this study may have been to use the number of hours of TV watched that is measured for children entering elementary school to predict their future grades (i.e., there was a predictive research question) and, thus, evenly distribute children of different academic abilities across different classrooms. In this case, the number of hours of TV watched variable is a predictor variable, and the grades variable is an outcome variable. This relationship can also be used to screen children entering elementary school for gifted programs. In reality, the relationship between TV watching and grades is probably not as strong as is the relationship between grades and scores on certain types of standardized tests (e.g., intelligence questionnaires). Thus, school psychologists are more likely to use these tests to predict future grades for children.

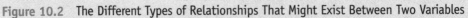

Figure 10.2   The Different Types of Relationships That Might Exist Between Two Variables

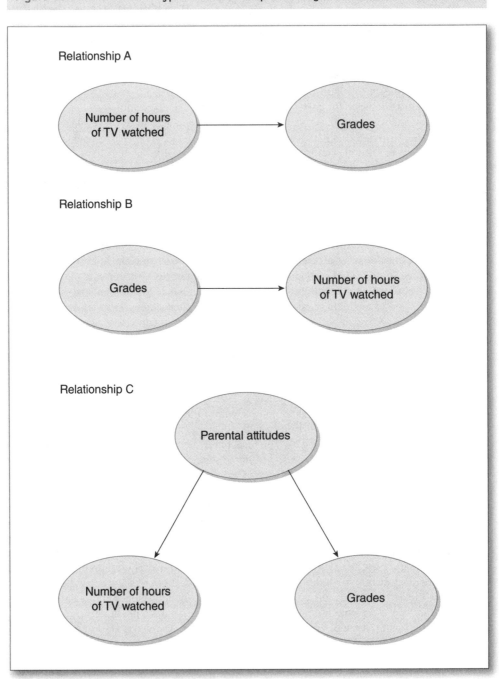

(10.1)   Explain why a correlational study does not provide an answer to causal research questions.

(10.2)   For each study described below, identify the predictor and outcome variables:

- A researcher examined the relationship between students' ACT/SAT score when they entered college and their graduation GPA.
- Researchers were interested in whether students who get less sleep are more anxious.
- A study tested whether higher test scores were earned by students who exercised regularly.

CORRELATIONAL STUDY EXAMPLES

Correlational studies occur most frequently in personality, clinical and counseling, industrial-organizational, and social areas of psychology, but they can be used in any area of psychology where manipulation of a variable of interest is difficult or impossible. Thus, as described above, correlational studies are used to answer descriptive and predictive research questions. The examples below highlight each of these types of questions.

Descriptive Studies

An example of a correlational study designed to describe the relationship between weather, mood, and cognitive abilities (e.g., ability to remember a short list of digits for a short period of time) was conducted by Keller et al. (2005, Study 1). Based on inconsistent findings in previous studies, their goal was to determine whether a relationship existed in their study for these dependent variables, and if one was found, what type of relationship was present. The participants in this study completed a mood questionnaire and cognitive tasks at a single session. The weather was determined based on the temperature and barometric pressure (as a measure related to how much sunlight is present) reported by the National Climatic Data Center. In addition, activity level and time spent outside that day were considered in the data analysis. Keller et al.'s results indicated that there was no direct relationship between weather and mood. Instead, the relationship between weather and mood was *moderated* or changed by the amount of time the participants spent outside. In other words, a positive relationship was shown for people who spent more time outside that day (i.e., 30 min or more), meaning that as temperature increased, so did mood for these participants. However, a

Positive Relationship: the variables change together in the same direction (both increasing together or decreasing together)

Negative Relationship: a relationship between variables characterized by an increase in one variable that occurs with a decrease in the other variable

negative relationship was shown for people who spent less time outside that day, meaning that as temperature increased, mood decreased for these participants. See Figure 10.3 for a graph showing these relationships. Similar results were shown for the relationship between weather and cognitive abilities: A positive relationship was seen between the variables only for individuals who spent the most time outside that day. The researchers concluded that positive relationships do exist between weather and mood and weather and cognitive abilities but only when people spend a reasonable amount of time outside (more than 30 min a day).

Campbell, Bosson, Goheen, Lakey, and Kernis (2007) also conducted a correlational study to examine the relationship between narcissism (having an inflated self-image) and self-esteem because of suggestions that narcissists show high explicit self-esteem but actually have low self-esteem at an implicit level. Participants in the study completed a narcissism survey, an explicit self-esteem survey, and the Implicit Association Test (IAT) to measure implicit self-esteem (the IAT is a cognitive test that measures implicit attitudes based on the time it takes to respond to associated items—see Chapter 4 for more discussion of the IAT). Despite suggestions about the relationship between narcissism and implicit self-esteem, scores on the narcissism survey and the IAT were not related in the study. However, narcissism scores and explicit self-esteem scores were positively correlated. Thus, the researchers suggest that the idea that narcissists actually have implicit low self-esteem may not be accurate.

Predictive Studies

An example of a correlational study that was conducted to examine a predictive relationship between variables comes from Boger, Tompson, Briggs-Gowan, Pavlis, and Carter (2008).

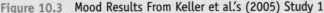

Figure 10.3   Mood Results From Keller et al.'s (2005) Study 1

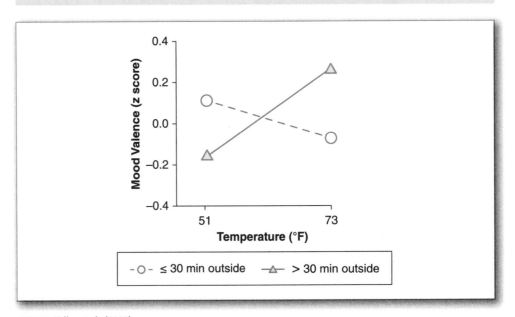

SOURCE: Keller et al. (2005)

These researchers were interested in *predicting* expressed emotion in families from specific family characteristics to allow predictions of family dynamics from family characteristics. Expressed emotion is a measure that indicates how family members feel about one another and has been shown in past studies to be linked to the course of mental disorders in children and adults. The current study addressed whether expressed emotion can be predicted from family stress and functioning. Such a prediction might ultimately be useful in counseling situations to determine what types of treatments can be beneficial for different types of families. The study participants were mothers who completed surveys at different points in time. The measures of family stress and functioning included a survey regarding the quality of the parents' marital relationship, a report of stressful life events in the family, a survey regarding parenting stress, and a survey that assessed family expressiveness and conflict. The mothers also completed a survey that measured expressed emotion. Results indicated that of these measures of family stress, only family expressiveness (i.e., communication among family members) predicted expressed emotion (family members' attitudes toward each other). Outside stressors (such as stressful life events) did not predict expressed emotion. Thus, the study provided information about what factors do and do not predict positive and negative attitudes among family members.

Another study that examined factors that can predict a behavior focused on working alliance, which indicates how well clients and therapists are able to work together during therapy (Patterson, Uhlin, & Anderson, 2008). Previous studies have shown that working alliance is related to positive therapy outcomes. From these different studies, a prediction of working alliance in therapy can be made based on several measures previously found to be related to this behavior. Thus, Patterson et al. examined whether clients' preexisting expectations of counseling can predict their working alliance in a therapeutic relationship with a therapist. The participants were clients receiving therapy at a university counseling center. The participants completed a survey regarding their expectations about counseling before they started therapy. They then completed a survey regarding working alliance after their third therapy session. The results indicated that positive therapy expectations predicted good working alliance among the clients in the study. Thus the researchers concluded that therapists can use information about client expectations to tailor their therapeutic style so as to maximize working alliance in the therapeutic relationships with their clients.

Summary

The correlational study examples described above illustrate an important issue regarding this research design type: Despite similar methodologies (i.e., use of surveys or other dependent measures) and general goals (i.e., examining relationships), the specific research question being asked in the study determines what is learned about the relationships among the variables. In some cases, the research question is descriptive in nature, such that the goal of the study is to examine if a relationship exists and, if one does exist, what form of relationship (e.g., positive or negative) exists between the variables. In other cases, the research question is predictive in nature, such that the goal of the study is to examine whether certain measures can be used to predict a behavior of interest. With knowledge about prediction, measures can be used in situations outside the study to predict behavior, as is done by colleges and universities to predict which applicants are most likely to succeed in college based on high school grades and entrance exam scores (e.g., the SAT [Scholastic Aptitude Test] or ACT [American College Test]).

Stop and Think

(10.3)   For each description below, indicate whether a positive, negative, or no relationship is described.

- People who exercise more show fewer cognitive problems in older adulthood.
- Students who read more earn higher scores on the Verbal portion of the Graduate Record Exam (GRE).
- In areas where the temperature is lower in winter, people tend to score higher on depression surveys.
- Kids who watch a lot of TV can have both high and low grades.

CHAPTER SUMMARY

Reconsider the questions from the beginning of the chapter:

- What types of research questions can be answered with correlational studies? Correlational studies can answer descriptive or predictive research questions.
- What is the difference between correlational and causal hypotheses? Hypotheses tested in correlational studies are about describing or predicting behavior. Causal hypotheses predict a specific cause of a behavior.
- What aspects of correlational studies prohibit testing causal hypotheses? Correlational studies do not contain independent variables that are manipulated by the researcher. Thus, the third-variable problem exists in correlational studies due to a lack of sufficient control of extraneous factors.
- How do correlational studies allow us to predict behavior? Regression analysis of the relationship between factors in a correlational study can test predictive relationships between variables (see Chapter 15 for more information on regression analyses).

THINKING ABOUT RESEARCH

A summary of a research study in psychology is given below. As you read the summary, think about the following questions:

1. The sample in this study is described as "representative." What do you think this means based on the type of sample collected?

2. Explain why the research question asked in this study is predictive instead of merely descriptive.

3. List the dependent variables included in this study and indicate which are predictor and outcome variables.

4. In what ways did the researchers use correlations to answer their research question?

5. Describe a study that would test whether one's spouse's personality causes higher job satisfaction. How feasible would it be to ethically conduct your study?

Research Study. Solomon, B. C., & Jackson, J. J. (2014). The long reach of one's spouse: Spouse's personality influences occupational success. *Psychological Science, 25*, 2189–2198.

Purpose of the Study. The purpose of this study was to examine relationships between married couples' home and work life. Using archival survey data, they tested the relationships between spouse's personality characteristics and job satisfaction, income, and likelihood of promotion at work. They predicted cross-over effects between work and home life such that spouse's personality would predict work outcomes.

Method of the Study. Data were analyzed from the Household Income and Labour Dynamics in Australia (HILDA) survey collected annually since 2000. The data collected for the years 2005–2009 were analyzed. These data included representative married heterosexual couples with 4,544 participants. Personality traits were measured with a survey assessing extraversion, agreeableness, openness, and neuroticism with seven to eight items per characteristic. Job satisfaction was measured with a rating from 0 (totally dissatisfied) to 10 (totally satisfied) for a 4-year period. Income was measured from self-reported weekly gross wages. Job promotion was measured with an item asking if the person had been promoted during the previous 12 months (yes or no).

Results of the Study. Regression analyses were used to test whether spouse's personality traits predicted job outcome measures. Significant relationships were found for all variables. Higher conscientiousness in spouses predicted high job satisfaction, income, and likelihood of promotion.

Conclusions of the Study. The authors concluded from this study that cross-over effects between work and home life occur such that one's spouse's personality affects job outcomes and satisfaction. These results are likely due to the more satisfying home life in married couples with conscientious spouses, which allows them to focus more on work.

COMMON PITFALLS AND HOW TO AVOID THEM

Problem: Confusing correlation and causation—when correlations are presented between two factors, people often interpret the relationship as causal without a causal test.

Solution: As the story at the beginning of the chapter illustrates, reports of treatments should be carefully interpreted. This is particularly true for reports read in the media. Carefully consider the type of relationship that was tested in a study that is reported. If two factors simply co-occur, this does not indicate a causal relationship. To determine if a relationship between factors is causal, an independent variable must be manipulated in a study. A correlational study does not test a causal relationship; however, it can provide evidence of some type of relationship that researchers can further explore to determine the relationship's nature.

Problem: Confusion of different types of variables—it can be difficult to distinguish between independent and dependent variables.

Solution: Remember that for a variable to be an independent variable, it must be manipulated by the researcher. This means that unless a researcher has randomly assigned participants to the different conditions of the variable or each participant is completing all conditions of the variable, it is not an independent variable. (See Chapter 11 for more discussion.) However, dependent variables can be used as predictor variables to predict the score of another dependent variable, as described in this chapter.

TEST YOURSELF

1. Suppose you read a news report that a study was conducted where people who reported drinking green tea each day as part of their diet were less likely to be diagnosed with cancer over the 5 years in which the study took place. Why can't we conclude that drinking green tea makes one less likely to develop cancer? Describe two possible explanations for the results reported from the study.

2. For the study described in (1), explain how the researchers could have done a study to test the causal relationship between drinking green tea and incidence of cancer.

3. Explain the difference between a descriptive research question and a predictive research question. Provide an example of each type of research question.

4. Identify the dependent variables included in the studies described in the Correlational Study Examples section of the chapter that are listed below. In addition, in the last two studies (c and d) indicate which of these variables are predictor variables and which are outcome variables.

    (a)   Keller et al. (2005)
    (b)   Campbell et al. (2007)
    (c)   Boger et al. (2008)
    (d)   Patterson et al. (2008)

5. Suppose a study was conducted to examine the relationship between how often people exercise and how happy they are with their lives. Participants in this study were asked to report how many times a week they exercise for 30 min or more at a time and to complete a questionnaire with items that measure their quality of life (e.g., How many times in the past week do you remember feeling happy?). A positive relationship is found between the number of times per week people exercise and their quality of life score. Answer the questions below about this study.

    (a)   What are the dependent variables in this study?
    (b)   Describe the three different types of causal relationships that could exist between the dependent variables you described in (a).
    (c)   Explain why this study does not provide evidence for any of the causal relationships you described in (b).

6. When two measures are related such that as the value of one measure increases, the value of the other measure also increases, this is called a _____ relationship.

7. If you are attempting to determine the value of one measure based on its relationship with another measure, you are testing a _____ research question.

8. How are correlational studies different from quasi-experiments?

Answers can be found at edge.sagepub/mcbride3e.

STOP AND THINK ANSWERS

(10.1)   Because there are always extraneous factors that can affect the results in a correlational study, correlational studies can only answer descriptive and predictive research questions.

(10.2)   Predictor: ACT/SAT score, outcome: graduation GPA

Predictor: amount of sleep, outcome: anxiety level

Predictor: amount of exercise (or frequency of exercise), outcome: test scores

(10.3)   Negative, positive, none

⑤SAGE edge™

Visit edge.sagepub.com/mcbride3e for the tools you need to sharpen your study skills:

- Web Quizzes
- eFlashcards
- Thinking About Research

- SAGE Journal Articles
- Web and Multimedia Resources

Chapter 11

The Nuts and Bolts of One-Factor Experiments

Consider the following questions as you read Chapter 11

- What aspects of an experiment make it different from other research designs?
- What aspects of experiments allow for greater internal validity than other research designs?
- What are the different ways that independent variables can be manipulated to allow comparisons of conditions?
- What are the limitations of testing a single factor in an experiment?

When our dog Daphne (see Figure 11.1) became a member of our family, she did not like to be left in the house without us. Whenever we went out, even for short periods of time, she would have "accidents" on the rug and engage in destructive chewing behaviors. She ruined a few small items of furniture and more than a few pairs of my husband's shoes. In an attempt to improve her behavior, we researched the issue and found several suggested "treatments" for this sort of behavior. We bought her a toy that held treats, accessed by chewing, that we could give her while we were away from home. We gave her some objects that we had used recently and smelled like us (e.g., an old T-shirt) to help her feel that we were nearby. We confined her to one room in the house to help her feel less anxious by being in a smaller space. Because we did not know which of these would best improve her behavior, we decided to try these treatments one at a time, five times each to make sure that the treatments were tested under different conditions (different days of the week, different times of day, etc.). After each trip away from home where one of these treatments was applied, we counted the number of "bad" behaviors there was evidence of in the house. We operationally defined (see Chapter 4 for more discussion of operational definitions) bad behaviors as soiling the floor or rug and chewing anything in the house that she was not supposed to chew. In other words, we used our knowledge of research methods to conduct an experiment to determine which treatment was most effective at stopping Daphne's bad behaviors while we were away from home. In most cases, an experiment involves several individuals being tested (e.g., several dogs in a study), but as we were only interested in how the treatments affected Daphne, we used a small-*n* experiment to test the treatments (see Chapter 14 for more discussion of small-*n* designs). In this experiment, Daphne experienced all the treatments, each at different times. We controlled for other possible explanations of her behavior by keeping her environment the same other than the changing of the treatment. We tested the treatments each time we went out until we had tested each treatment 5 times, but we randomly chose a treatment each time to make sure we did not accidentally test one treatment in several days that she was feeling less anxious about being on her own.

Figure 11.1 An Experiment on Daphne

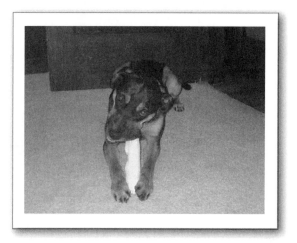

NOTE: This experiment helped determine the best treatment to stop her bad behaviors.

Finally, we tested each treatment condition five times to make sure that extreme behaviors that occurred during any single trip away from home would not bias the results. We wished to learn which treatment for Daphne would be most effective by comparing the treatments in terms of their effect on the dependent variable, her bad behavior. Through this experiment, we determined that the chew toy was the most effective in reducing Daphne's undesirable behaviors.

If the example above sounds like something you have tried in your life for yourself or a pet, then you may already be familiar with the concept of an experiment. Perhaps you ran an experiment to determine which study techniques work best in improving your exam scores. The experiments conducted by psychologists in their research follow the same principles as the example above. Different treatments or conditions of an independent variable are compared to determine whether those treatments or conditions differ in their effects on behavior and which of those treatments or conditions has the greatest effect on the behavior of interest.

In this chapter, we discuss the "nuts and bolts" of experiments (Figure 11.2): how an experiment can increase the internal validity of a study, issues to consider for different types of independent variable manipulations, and what we can learn from simple experiments that manipulate just one independent variable. In the next chapter, we will consider more complex experiments that contain more than one independent variable. The discussion in this chapter relies on your knowledge of concepts covered in Chapter 4; thus, you may wish to review the section on experiments in Chapter 4 before you read the rest of this chapter.

Experiment: a type of research design that involves manipulation of an independent variable, allowing control of extraneous variables that could affect the results

Small-*n* Design: an experiment conducted with one or a few participants to better understand the behavior of those individuals

Figure 11.2   Steps in the Research Process: Designing the Study

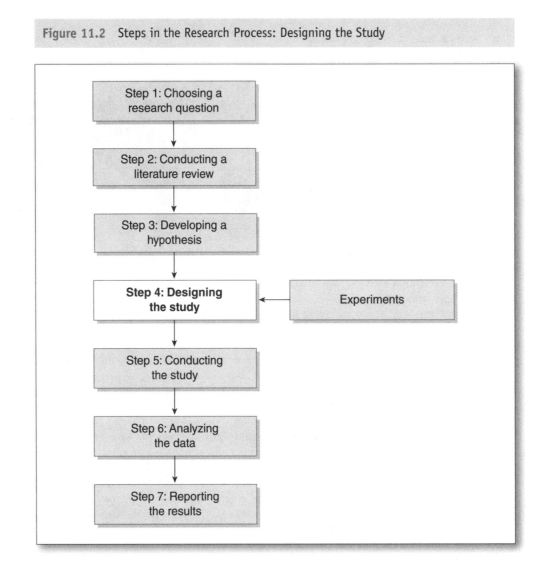

LEARNING ABOUT CAUSATION
THROUGH MANIPULATION AND CONTROL

Remember from Chapter 4 that the experimental research design is the only type of research design that contains a true independent variable that is manipulated by the researcher. One aspect of an experiment that can seem confusing is the concept of manipulation. What does it mean to *manipulate* an independent variable? Generally, a manipulation of an independent variable involves researcher control of the administration of the levels of the variable to the participants. In other words, an independent variable is manipulated such that participants are randomly assigned to levels; the assignment is not based on any characteristic of the participants themselves.

For example, a participant's gender, personality, and smoking status cannot be independent variables because these characteristics are not randomly assigned for a participant by the researcher. Instead, the participant comes to the study with these factors already determined.

The manipulation of an independent variable in an experiment allows the researcher to learn about the causal relationship between the independent and dependent variables. In other words, manipulation of an independent variable in a study increases the internal validity of the study. Recall from Chapters 4 and 5 that a study with good internal validity is one that provides a good test of a causal hypothesis. Without the manipulation of an independent variable, it is very difficult to rule out other possible factors as causes of a change in the dependent variable. This is called the third-variable problem and must be considered in all studies. When researchers design an experiment, they already are controlling for extraneous factors that can affect the results of the study through the use of a manipulated independent variable. However, there are other ways that extraneous factors can affect the results of an experiment, and a researcher must identify these factors and design the experiment to control for these factors as best as possible. For example, even when an independent variable is manipulated, it is still possible that an extraneous factor (i.e., a confounding variable—see Chapters 4 and 5 for more discussion of confounding variables) changes systematically with the levels of the variable (time of day experiments are run, slight alteration in instructions given by different experimenters, etc.). Thus, the researcher must design an experiment to control for the confounding variables as they may affect the results. Some specific types of confounding variables are discussed in Chapter 5.

The manipulation of the independent variable can occur in two ways: the variable can be manipulated between subjects or within subjects. In between-subjects manipulations, each participant receives only one level of the independent variable. Participants are typically randomly assigned to the different levels of between-subjects variables. For example, a researcher interested in the effects of text format on learning can manipulate text format as a between-subjects variable by randomly assigning different students in a class to a hard

---

Independent Variable: a variable in an experiment that is manipulated by the researcher such that the levels of the variable change across or within subjects in the experiment

Third-Variable Problem: the presence of extraneous factors in a study that affect the dependent variable and can decrease the internal validity of the study

Confounding Variable: an extraneous factor present in a study that may affect the results

Between-Subjects Variable: each participant experiences only one level of the independent variable

Within-Subjects Variable: each participant experiences all levels of the independent variable

Random Assignment: participants are randomly assigned to levels of the independent variable in an experiment to control for individual differences as an extraneous variable

---

copy version of the text and an online version of the text. Random assignment of participants to levels allows random distribution of participant differences (study habits, academic achievement, etc.) across the levels, making it less likely that the participants' differences cause a difference across groups for the dependent variable being measured. This also means the researcher can be more certain that when a difference across conditions is found, it is due to the independent variable and not some other factor. In other words, random assignment means that subjects are

---
❧

Order Effects: occur when the order in which the participants experience conditions in an experiment affects the results of the study

Testing Effects: occur when participants are tested more than once in a study, with early testing affecting later testing

---

assigned to groups according to chance, not according to any characteristic they possess or any choice made by the researcher. Each subject has an equal chance of being in any of the conditions in the experiment. Random assignment is accomplished by chance; chance factors determine which participants will be in the different groups in the study. In this way, random assignment is a means of controlling for participant differences across groups and increases the internal validity of the experiment.

In within-subjects manipulations, each participant receives all levels of the independent variable. Thus, each subject serves as his or her own comparison, and this even better controls individual differences because it removes subject differences from the comparison across conditions. Subjects' scores in one condition are compared with their scores in the other condition. The researcher in the preceding example, who is interested in the effects of text format on learning, could manipulate text format within subjects by having each participant use each type of text for different chapters in the text. Random assignment is important for within-subjects variables in terms of the order in which participants receive the levels of the variable to control for possible order effects of the different levels of the variable. As in the example on the effects of text format, learning can be different depending on whether the participants receive the hard copy version or the online version of the text first. Order effects are a particular form of testing effects, with bias occurring because of multiple testings of a participant in a study. Thus, order effects are a disadvantage of using within-subjects designs.

CONTROL IN WITHIN-SUBJECTS AND BETWEEN-SUBJECTS EXPERIMENTS

As described above, random assignment is an important means of control in an experiment for both between-subjects and within-subjects variables. However, each type of manipulation uses random assignment in different ways to control for different extraneous factors. There are also cases where random assignment may not be sufficient to control for these extraneous factors and additional controls may be needed. Thus, researchers must consider the types of extraneous factors that may be present in an experiment when they decide whether to use a between-subjects or within-subjects independent variable. These issues are discussed here as they apply to each type of manipulation.

Between-Subjects Experiments

As described above, in a between-subjects manipulation randomly assigning participants to different groups controls for individual differences across the groups that might affect the data in addition to or instead of the independent variable. For example, suppose you wanted to examine the effects of background music on memory for course material. You might design an experiment in a course to compare test scores on an exam for three groups of students: one group that studies for 5 hr with classical music in the background, one group that studies for 5 hr with pop music in the background, and one group that studies for 5 hr with no music. To attempt to equate the groups, you might randomly assign the students to one of these groups, such that all students have an equal chance of being in any of the groups (i.e., they do not get to choose which group they are in based on their preference). This experiment involves the between-subjects independent variable of type of background music (classical, pop, none), because different students are randomly assigned to the groups (the students completed the study with only one type of the three background conditions).

However, the random assignment might not be sufficient. If you have mostly good students in your sample and the few poor students all end up in the pop music group, it may appear as if this condition has the worst effect on memory due to the inclusion of the poor students in this group. This would result in a source of bias in the study due to this individual difference across the groups that is not part of the independent variable.

In fact, the presence of individual differences across groups is the greatest concern for between-subjects experiments. In experiments where individual differences are likely to be present (such as the example about background music) and a small sample size is used, random assignment may not be sufficient to control for these differences. In this case, the researcher has two additional means of controlling for individual differences. The first is to manipulate the independent variable as a within-subjects variable. This allows participants to serve as their own controls so that individual differences across groups are no longer of concern. However, for some variables, order effects may be more problematic and make between-subjects manipulation preferable. Thus, the second means of control is to use a matched design for between-subjects experiments. In a matched design, participants are matched on a characteristic that may contribute to group differences. Then each participant within a matched set is randomly assigned to different groups. See Figure 11.3 for an illustration of this design.

For example, consider a study conducted by O'Hanlon and Roberson (2006). They completed a series of experiments to investigate causes of the difficulties young children encounter when learning color words. Different groups of children were taught color words under different feedback conditions to compare effects of feedback type on learning of the color words. However, the researchers were concerned about the effects of children's age and current vocabulary abilities on the learning of the color words. Thus, they created matched sets of participants who were matched on age and vocabulary abilities, and randomly assigned one member of each matched set to a different feedback condition. The matched sets allowed the researchers to control for the extraneous factors of age and vocabulary abilities that otherwise may have differed across groups and caused differences in the learning scores for the condition groups—effects that were not caused by the feedback conditions themselves. Due to this control for group differences, the researchers were able to conclude that feedback that corrects the child's errors in using color words allows the child to learn the color words faster than other forms of feedback.

Another way to ensure that participants in the groups are matched on some characteristic is to measure that characteristic (e.g., years of education, socioeconomic status, language abilities) during the experiment and then compare the groups in an additional analysis. This comparison indicates whether

Matched Design: a between-subjects experiment that involves sets of participants matched on a specific characteristic with each member of the set randomly assigned to a different level of the independent variable

Figure 11.3   Illustration of Matched Design, Counterbalancing, and Latin Square Design

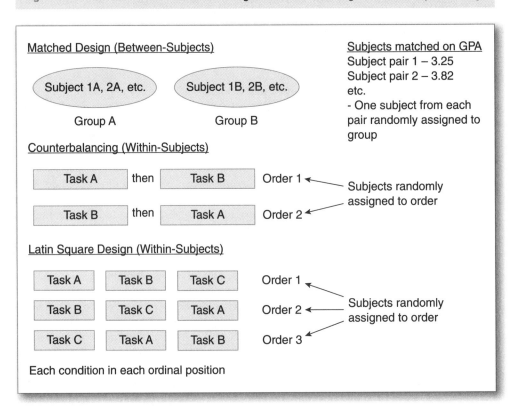

the groups are similar or different on that characteristic. However, if the groups are different, you are then left with the possibility that this difference affected your results. Thus, if you are concerned that a group difference is likely to affect your results, it is best to either use a within-subjects manipulation or to match your participants before you assign them to the groups. Alternatively, if a between-subjects design is preferred, statistical tools can be used to account for group differences in the analysis of the data (e.g., covariate analysis).

Within-Subjects Experiments

The primary concern with within-subjects variables is the order in which the participants receive the different levels of the independent variable. Because the participants receive all levels of the independent variable, it is possible that the order of the levels can affect the dependent variable measure. For example, suppose that a within-subjects variable in an experiment involves a task difficulty manipulation such that all participants receive both an easy task and a difficult task. The order in which they receive these tasks can certainly affect the outcome of the study. If participants receive an easy task first and then a difficult task, they are likely to view the difficult task as more difficult than they would if they had received it before the easy task. The opposite situation likely occurs for how they view the easy task, depending on whether the easy task is first or second (i.e., they may view it as "easier" if they complete the difficult task first than if they complete the difficult task second).

To solve the problem of order effects for within-subjects manipulations, a researcher typically uses counterbalancing of the order of the levels within the study. This means that different groups of participants receive different orders of the levels of the independent variable. For example, in the experiment described earlier, half of the participants would receive the easy task first, and half would receive the difficult task first with participants assigned in equal numbers to the two different orders. Random assignment to orders should be used. See Figure 11.3 for an illustration of counterbalancing. Using different orders of the levels counterbalances the order effects across the participants. The different orders can also be compared to determine if order effects exist, which is likely for this example. This can help a researcher determine if the effect of the independent variable depends on the order of the conditions the subjects receives. This type of alteration of the effect will be discussed further in Chapter 12.

Counterbalancing is relatively easy when there are only two conditions that participants experience in an experiment. However, many experimental designs involve more than two conditions, making counterbalancing a little more difficult for within-subjects manipulations because all the orders must be included in a full counterbalancing. To illustrate this issue, consider a within-subjects experiment with three conditions: A, B, and C. There are six possible orders in which participants can experience these three conditions: ABC, BCA, ACB, CBA, CAB, and BAC. To fully counterbalance these three conditions, you would need six different orders of the conditions and numbers of participants in multiples of six in order to make an equal number of participants randomly assigned to each of the six possible orders of conditions. Already, the counterbalancing is becoming rather complicated. What happens when you have four conditions in the experiment? The counterbalancing of four conditions is even more complicated. To simplify the counterbalancing in such a case, a partial counterbalancing technique, called a Latin square, can be used instead. In a Latin square, the number of orders used in the experiment is equal to the number of conditions in the design, and each condition is in each ordinal position (i.e., first, second, third, fourth) exactly once. See Figure 11.3 for an illustration of this design. Latin squares can be useful for within-subjects designs where independent variables have a number of levels.

For example, an experiment with four conditions (A, B, C, and D) can use a Latin square to include four different orders of the conditions. Each of these conditions is positioned first once, second once, and so on, within the order structure. Thus, the order for a Latin square would be ABDC, BCAD, CDBA, and DACB (see Grant, 1948, for the procedure to create a Latin square for a design with any number of conditions). In this order structure, you can see that each condition serves in each ordinal position once. The researcher then randomly assigns each participant to one of these orders, requiring fewer orders of conditions in the experiment and fewer multiples of participants to run in the experiment.

Counterbalancing: a control used in within-subjects experiments where equal numbers of participants are randomly assigned to different orders of the conditions

Latin Square: partial counterbalancing technique where the number of orders of conditions used is equal to the number of conditions in the study

---

Stop and Think

(11.1)　Describe one advantage and one disadvantage of a between-subjects design.

(11.2)　Describe one advantage and one disadvantage of a within-subjects design.

(11.3)　For each research description below, decide if you think a within-subjects or between-subjects design is better. Explain your choice in each case.

- Effect of teaching technique (comparing three different techniques) on exam scores
- Effect of social inclusion/exclusion on reading comprehension
- Effect of face familiarity on brain activity

EXPERIMENT EXAMPLES

Although any area of psychological research may include experiments, there are areas of psychology where experiments are used more often than in others. In cognitive, biological, social, and (in some cases) developmental research, one is most likely to encounter the experimental research design. Other areas of psychological research do include experiments, but manipulation can be difficult or impossible for some factors of interest (e.g., clinical conditions or personality types). Thus, the following examples come from areas where experiments are more likely to be used and illustrate how experiments are used in different areas of psychology as well as some of the experimental concepts (e.g., control) that are described in this chapter.

Cognitive Example

Cognitive psychology includes the study of basic processing of information from the world around us. Cognitive psychologists study memory, perception, language processes, and decision making. Much of the research in these areas is focused on understanding factors that influence these processes and how they operate. Thus, experiments are a very common research design for cognitive psychologists.

Storm and Stone (2015) conducted a simple cognitive experiment to investigate the effects of saving studied information in a computer file on one's ability to learn new information. They suggested that because a saved file can be accessed later for further study, saving a file of studied words (as compared with not saving the file) would free up cognitive resources to learn new information. On each trial of the experiments, subjects in the study were asked to study two PDF files of words on a flashdrive. Subjects were told that they would study the first file, then study the second file, and then be tested on the second file and the first file, in that order. For half of the trials, subjects were asked to save the first PDF list file before closing it and were told that whenever they saved the file, they would be able to go back to it later to study it before testing. On the other trials, subjects were instructed to simply close the first PDF file without saving it. Thus, the independent variable was whether the first list was saved or not. The variable was manipulated within-subjects because all the subjects received three "save" and three "no save" trials. The "save" or "no save" instruction appeared after the subjects had studied the first list. Then after a short delay, the subjects were tested on the second word list. If the first word list had been saved on that trial, they were able to restudy it before the test on that list. If it was not saved, they were tested on the first list right after the test on the second list (see Figure 11.4 for a diagram of the procedure of the experiment). Lists were counterbalanced across "save" and "no save" conditions to remove any bias that might be caused by the difficulty of the lists. The researchers then compared recall on the second list (the one that was never saved) for trials in which the first list was saved and trials in which the first list was not saved. The results of the experiment supported the researchers' hypothesis: Subjects recalled more words from the second list when the first list had been saved than when the first list had not been saved. They concluded that saving a file that can be accessed later frees up cognitive resources for other tasks, showing benefits of reliable technology on cognition.

Biological Example

Biological psychology (also called neuropsychology if it involves brain function) investigates the role of biological factors in behavior. Thus, experiments are often employed in this area of psychology to determine causal relationships between biology and behavior. In many cases, participants are asked to perform different tasks while brain function that corresponds to these tasks is recorded to better understand where brain activity occurs for different behaviors. Or stimulation of a biological system (e.g., the brain) may occur and resultant behaviors recorded. In other types of studies, brain function in animals is manipulated to observe the causal effect of the manipulation on a behavior of interest. In other words, the brain (or other biological) activity can be either the dependent variable or the independent variable in the experiment.

Ferrè, Lopez, and Haggard (2014) conducted an experiment to examine the link between the vestibular system (the system that controls our sense of balance) and one's perspective (i.e., first-person vs. another person's perspective). In their study, stimulation electrodes were placed

Figure 11.4   Diagram of the Procedure Used in Storm and Stone's (2015) Experiment 1

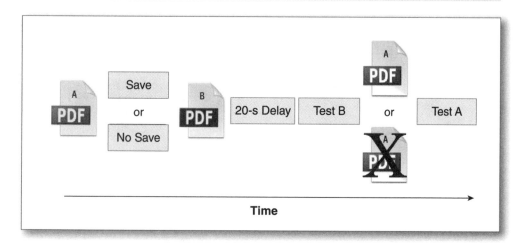

Figure 11.5   Diagram of the Procedure Used in Ferrè et al.'s (2014) Experiment

on the subjects' head below the ears (experimental trials) or neck (control trials). For the experimental trials subjects received the stimulation and during the control trials subjects did not receive stimulation. One second after stimulation began (for experimental trials), a reversible letter (e.g., b or d) was traced by the experimenter on the subject's forehead (see Figure 11.5). After 4 s of stimulation, a tone sounded and the subject was asked to name the letter. If the subject named the letter traced (e.g., b) it showed the experimenter's perspective. If the subject named the letter reversed (e.g., d), it showed the subject's perspective.

Figure 11.6 shows the results for the percentage of trials the subjects showed their own perspective. The percentage was higher for experimental trials (for both left and right stimulation) than for the control trials (labeled "sham," because they had fake electrodes attached for these trials). These results show that stimulation of the vestibular system increases first-person perspective, suggesting that this system is involved in our sense of self.

Figure 11.6   Results From Ferrè et al.'s (2015) Experiment

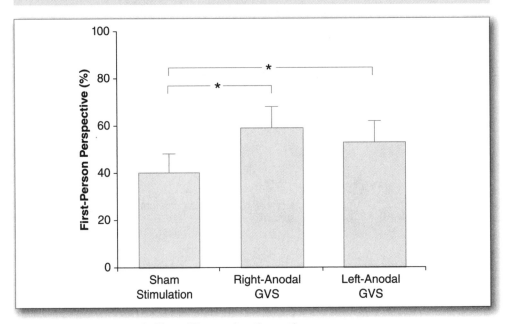

NOTE: The asterisks represent significant differences (see Chapter 7).

Social Example

Social psychologists examine the effects of social factors on different types of behaviors. In one study from this field, Bastian, Jetten, and Ferris (2014) tested the effects of experiencing pain on social bonding. In one of their experiments, subjects were randomly assigned to "pain" and "no pain" groups. The subjects in the "pain" group were asked to submerge their hand in icy water for as long as possible to complete a task sorting metal balls from the bowl of water into containers and then to hold a squat position against the wall for as long as possible. The subjects in the "no pain" group completed the ball sorting task from a bowl of room temperature water and were asked to balance on one leg for 60 s and to switch legs when one leg got tired. Thus, both groups performed the same types of tasks, but these tasks were painful for the subjects in the "pain" group. All subjects completed the experiment with other subjects (between 1 and 4 other people). After the tasks, subjects completed a survey measuring their feelings of bonding toward the other participants in the study. Figure 11.7 shows the mean bonding scores for the two groups. Subjects in the "pain" group rated their bonding higher than the subjects in the "no pain" group.

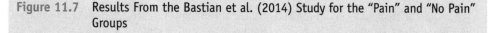

Figure 11.7   Results From the Bastian et al. (2014) Study for the "Pain" and "No Pain" Groups

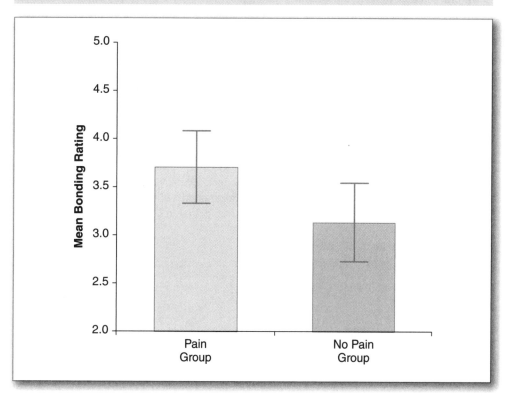

Stop and Think

(11.4)   For the experiments described in the Biological Example and Social Example sections above, identify the independent and dependent variables.

(11.5)   For each of the experimental examples in this chapter (Bastian et al., 2014; Ferrè et al., 2014; Storm & Stone, 2015) identify one possible source of bias in the study.

(11.6)   In the Bastian et al. (2014) experiment described in the Social Example section, why do you think the researchers made sure the "no pain" group did similar tasks to the "pain" group instead of just having that group talk to the subjects they were tested with?

CHAPTER SUMMARY

Reconsider the questions from the beginning of the chapter:

- What aspects of an experiment make it different from other research designs? Experiments contain an independent variable that is manipulated and allows for control of alternative explanations of the results. Thus, experiments are the best research design for testing causal relationships.
- What aspects of experiments allow for greater internal validity than other research designs? The manipulation of a variable (independent variable) and the additional controls for confounding variables allow for greater internal validity in experiments than other types of research designs.
- What are the different ways that independent variables can be manipulated to allow comparisons of conditions? Independent variables can be manipulated by type of something, amount of something, or the presence/absence of something (see Chapter 4 for more discussion of this aspect of independent variables). They can also be manipulated between subjects, where each participant receives only one level of the independent variable, or within subjects, where each participant receives all levels of the independent variable.
- What are the limitations of testing a single factor in an experiment? With a single independent variable (IV) in an experiment, you can examine only the effects of that one IV on the dependent variable in your study. In addition, you cannot examine the combined effects of the independent variables on the dependent variable. This issue will be further discussed in Chapter 12.

THINKING ABOUT RESEARCH

A summary of a research study in psychology is given below. As you read the summary, think about the following questions:

1. What aspects of this study allow us to define it as an experiment?

2. What is the independent variable? What are the levels of the independent variable? What is the dependent variable?

3. Was the independent variable in this experiment manipulated between-subjects or within-subjects? How do you know?

4. Do you think this study could have been conducted as the other type of design (i.e., the opposite of your answer to 3)? Why or why not?

5. What possible sources of bias can you identify in this study?

Research Study. Brown-Iannuzzi, J. L., Lundberg, K. B., Kay, A. C., & Payne, B. K. (2015). Subjective status shapes political preferences. *Psychological Science, 26*, 15–26.

Note: Study 2 of this article is described below.

Purpose of the Study. How does a person's perception of his or her wealth in reference to others' wealth influence his or her ideas about the redistribution of wealth as a political concept? The authors conducted four studies to answer this question. We will examine Study 2 here. In this experiment, the effect of subjective wealth status on wealth redistribution agreement was tested. The authors hypothesized that subjects who believed they were wealthier than their peers would more strongly oppose the redistribution of wealth as measured by survey score.

Method of the Study. There were 153 participants in the experiment. They were recruited through the Amazon site MechanicalTurk. Participants were first given false feedback to a questionnaire about their subjective wealth status. They were randomly assigned to either the high status group (where they were given a positive score on a false "Composite Discretionary Index" scale) or the low status group (where they were given a negative score on the false "Composite Discretionary Index" scale). Participants were told to interpret positive scores as their having more discretionary (i.e., extra) income than their peers and negative scores as their having less discretionary income than their peers. Thus, participants' actual income did not change, but their perception of their comparison in wealth to others was manipulated. An 11-item survey about the redistribution of wealth (e.g., "In general, the wealthy should be taxed to provide benefits to the poor.") was used to measure their attitude about redistribution of wealth from the total score on the survey.

Results of the Study. The results indicated a difference between the high and low status groups in redistribution attitudes. The low status group had a higher mean score on the survey, indicating that they were more strongly in favor of redistribution of wealth.

Conclusions of the Study. The results from the study indicate that one's subjective sense of wealth compared with others influences one's political attitude toward redistribution of wealth independent of actual wealth.

COMMON PITFALLS AND HOW TO AVOID THEM

Problem: Interpretation of causal results—not considering other possible explanations of results.

Solution: Even in experiments where independent variables are manipulated, one must consider other possible explanations for the results, as it can be difficult to rule out all possible confounding variables in a single experiment.

Problem: Identifying true independent variables—the difference between true independent variables and subject variables can be confusing.

Solution: If the design is a between-subjects design, determine whether the participants were randomly assigned to groups. If they were not, then the variable is probably a subject variable. Consider if the variable can be manipulated. Subject variables are often variables that cannot be manipulated. If the design is a within-subjects design, the variable is likely a true independent variable.

Problem: Identifying the design of an experiment—independent and dependent variables can be difficult to identify.

Solution: It is often helpful to examine graphs or tables within a journal article to identify the design of an experiment. The dependent variable is typically identified from table captions or labels along the *y*-axis. The independent variables are typically identified from table captions, legends in a figure, or labels along the *x*-axis.

TEST YOURSELF

1. What aspects of an experiment allow tests of causal relationships?

2. What is the advantage of using a Latin square over full counterbalancing when counterbalancing the order of conditions in a within-subjects design? How many orders are used in a Latin square?

3. Reread the sample experiment about our dog Daphne presented at the beginning of the chapter to answer the following questions:

   (a) What is the independent variable, and what are the levels of this variable in the experiment?

   (b) Was the independent variable manipulated between-subjects or within-subjects?

   (c) What controls for confounding variables are described for this experiment?

   (d) If you were interested in testing the effectiveness of the "treatments" for the population of all dogs, how would you conduct such an experiment?

4. A researcher conducted a study to investigate the effects of smiling on helping behavior. Participants completed a survey that they thought was the purpose of the study, but in reality, the experiment took place after they completed the survey. At the end of the survey session, half of the subjects were thanked with a smile and half were thanked without a smile. Whether the subject received a smile or not was randomly determined. The subjects then passed a confederate in the hallway on their way out of the lab who had just dropped a large stack of books. The number of subjects who helped the confederate pick up his books for the smile and no smile groups was compared.

   (a) What is the independent variable in this experiment? Is the independent variable manipulated between-subjects or within-subjects?

   (b) Can you think of an important ethical issue for this experiment and how to handle it in the procedure of the experiment?

Answers can be found at edge.sagepub/mcbride3e.

STOP AND THINK ANSWERS

(11.1)   Advantages: No carry-over effects from one condition to another, subjects' participation is short, Disadvantages: group differences may be present, need more subjects

(11.2)   Advantages: No group differences will be present, don't need as many subjects, Disadvantages: carry-over effects from one condition to another may occur, need subjects for longer period of time

(11.3)   Answers will vary

(11.4)   Biological—Type of trial (right stimulation, left stimulation, sham)

Social—Pain group (pain, no pain)

(11.5)   Answers will vary

(11.6)   This reduced the possible bias due to the type of tasks used (e.g., arm in water regardless of temperature, physical activity regardless of pain).

⑤SAGE edge™

Visit **edge.sagepub.com/mcbride3e** for the tools you need to sharpen your study skills:

- Web Quizzes
- eFlashcards
- Thinking About Research

- SAGE Journal Articles
- Web and Multimedia Resources

Chapter 12

The Nuts and Bolts of Multi-Factor Experiments

Consider the following questions as you read Chapter 12

- How do factorial experiments differ from single factor experiments?
- What are the advantages of conducting experiments with more than one independent variable?
- What is an interaction and what can we learn from testing interactions?

Recall the story at the beginning of Chapter 11 about our dog Daphne and her "bad behavior." We conducted a single factor experiment in that situation to compare different "treatments" to help Daphne's separation anxiety. Now suppose that the chew toys that contained treats had only helped reduce her bad behaviors on some occasions—sometimes she stopped these behaviors with the chew toy and sometimes she did not. In addition, suppose that giving her our worn clothes had also helped reduce her bad behaviors on some occasions, but not others. It may be that different situations called for different treatments—one treatment did not help in every case.

If this had happened, we may have considered what factors went along with the differences in the effectiveness of the treatments and conducted a second, more complex, experiment. For example, suppose that we noticed that some of the times we tried the treatments, we were gone all day at work and school, whereas other trials with the treatments were with shorter trips (to the grocery store, etc.). We might hypothesize that the effectiveness of the different treatments *depends* on the length of our outing. To test this hypothesis, we might conduct an experiment with a factorial design to examine both the effects of the two treatments (our worn clothing and the chew toy) and the length of outing (1–2 hr and all day) on the reduction of bad behavior. Figure 12.1 illustrates the design of this experiment. This more

---
❧

Factorial Design: an experiment or quasi-experiment that includes more than one independent variable

complex experiment with two independent variables would allow us to learn whether the worn clothing works best for one of the outing lengths and the chew toy works best for the other outing length. We can also test overall effects of the treatments (does one treatment work better than the other regardless of outing length?) and the outing length (are more bad behaviors exhibited on longer outings overall regardless of the treatment we try?). This is the main advantage of factorial designs: You can examine the effects of each independent variable on its own as well as the combined effects of the independent variables and answer the question "Does the effect of one independent variable depend on the level of the other independent variable?"

Figure 12.2 shows a possible outcome of our experiment with Daphne. In this case, our hypothesis that different treatments are effective for different outing lengths is supported. The graph shows that when we leave for short outings, the chew toy is better at reducing her bad behaviors, but when we are gone all day for a long outing, the worn clothing is better at reducing her bad behaviors.

FACTORIAL DESIGNS

Many of the experimental examples we discuss in this and other chapters of the text involve a single independent variable, where the goal of the experiment is to compare the observations for the different levels of the independent variable. However, many experiments conducted by researchers are factorial designs, meaning they contain more than one independent variable. The primary advantages of a factorial design over simpler experiments are that a researcher can be more efficient in testing the effects of multiple independent variables in a single experiment

Figure 12.1   Design of the Factorial Experiment With Daphne

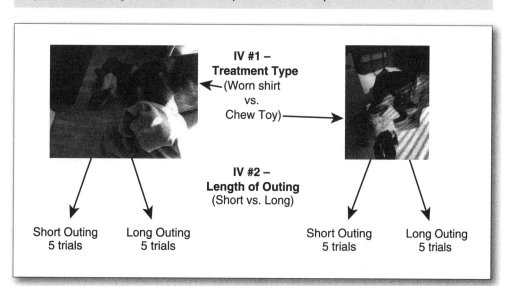

Figure 12.2   Results From the Experiment With Daphne

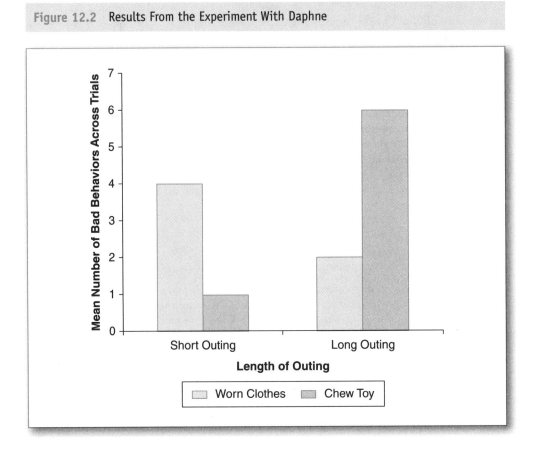

and can also examine the combined effects of those independent variables on the dependent variable. Thus, many experiments conducted by psychologists are factorial designs because of these benefits of factorial designs.

Testing the combined effects of the independent variables is the unique feature of factorial designs. Without including multiple independent variables in a single experiment, we would not be able to detect the different effects a factor might have on behavior in different situations. For example, if we compare the outcomes of the two experiments with Daphne, we would come to different conclusions about the best treatment for her bad behaviors. In the single factor experiment described in Chapter 11, we decided that the chew toy was the best treatment. But what if we had more short outing trials in that experiment than long outing trials? This would lead us to believe that the chew toy was best when, in reality, it was best only for short outings. By including the length of outing as a second independent variable in our factorial experiment, we are able to determine that, overall, the chew toy and the worn clothes are both effective, but for different outing lengths. If we're gone all day, the worn clothing is actually better at keeping her on her best behavior. When the effect of one independent variable (e.g., treatment type) depends on the levels of another independent variable (e.g., short or long outing), this is called an interaction effect.

In factorial designs, the comparison of the mean scores for the levels of one independent variable is the test of the main effect of that independent variable. Remember from Chapter 4 that the levels of the independent variable are the different conditions that are part of the independent variable. For example, the chew toy and the worn clothes are the levels of the independent variable of treatment type in our experiment with Daphne. The main effects provide a test of the separate effect of each independent variable on the dependent variable in a factorial design. The main effect is one type of effect tested in an analysis of variance (ANOVA), which is the type of statistical analysis used most often for a factorial experiment (see Chapter 15 for further discussion of ANOVA). The other type of effect tested in an ANOVA is an interaction effect. The interaction effect tests the effect of one independent variable for each level of another independent variable to determine how the independent variables *interact* to affect the dependent variable. Thus, a test for an interaction effect compares the differences between the levels of one independent variable across the levels of another independent variable. This will determine whether the effects of one independent variable *depend* on the level of the other independent variable the scores were measured under.

Interaction Effect: tests the effect of one independent variable at each level of another independent variable in an ANOVA

Levels of the Independent Variable: different situations or conditions that participants experience in an experiment because of the manipulation of the independent variable

Main Effect: test of the differences between all means for each level of an independent variable in an ANOVA

Analysis of Variance (ANOVA): inferential test used for designs with three or more sample means

To make the concept of an interaction more concrete, consider the factorial design in Figure 12.3. This design contains two independent variables, IVA and IVB, each with two levels. The columns indicate levels of IVA, and the rows indicate levels of IVB. The cells indicate the conditions created by combining the levels of the two independent variables. To determine the overall means for a level of an independent variable (i.e., the means compared in a main effect), the researcher averages the means for the cells in the columns and the rows. Main effects are determined by comparing the level means for each independent variable (i.e., comparing means for the rows and comparing means for the columns). To examine the interaction effect, the researcher must consider the differences between rows or columns. For example, one way to look at an interaction effect would be to consider the difference between $A1B1$ and $A1B2$ and compare it with the difference between $A2B1$ and $A2B2$. If those differences are not the same, then there is an interaction effect. In other words, the effect of IVB depends on whether you are looking at the $A1$ level or the $A2$ level of IVA.

It may take some time to understand interactions, so let's consider an example to further illustrate the concept. Suppose that the design illustrated in Figure 12.3 corresponds to independent variables of mode of study presentation (IVA) and mode of test (IVB) in a memory experiment. Figure 12.4 presents the variables and the levels of each variable, as well as the conditions created by the combination of these levels. In addition, means for each level of the independent variables and conditions are included. To determine main effects for study presentation mode, the condition means for each of the conditions that involve visual study are averaged and compared with the average of the condition means that involve auditory study (i.e., column averages). In other words, the main effect of study mode involves a comparison

Figure 12.3   Diagram of a General Factorial Design With Two Independent Variables (IV), Each With Two Levels

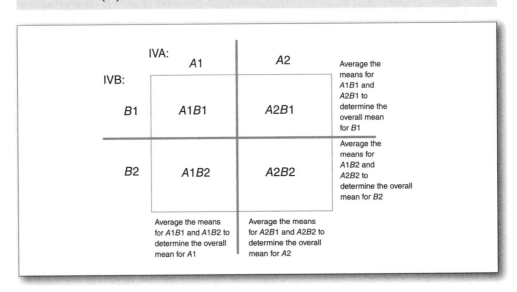

of 62.5 (for visual) and 67.5 (for auditory). This procedure is similarly followed to determine if there is a main effect of mode of test by averaging the means for the conditions in each row. The main effect for test mode involves a comparison of 67.5 (visual) and 62.5 (for auditory).

There are several ways by which the means for the conditions may create an interaction between mode of study presentation and mode of test. Often, creating a graph of the condition means illustrates an interaction best. If the lines in a line graph are not parallel, this can indicate an interaction between the independent variables (the effect also needs to be confirmed by inferential statistics—see Chapters 7 and 15 for more information about ANOVAs). The most likely scenario for this experiment is that when study mode and test mode match, memory is best. Thus, the independent variables are most likely to interact according to Panel 1 in Figure 12.5, and this graph illustrates the interaction shown in the condition means in Figure 12.4. You can see in this graph that the mean memory score is highest for the visual study and visual test condition and for the auditory study and auditory test condition. Memory scores are lower when the study and test modes do not match.

MORE ABOUT INTERACTIONS

Another way these independent variables might interact is with similar memory scores for visual study regardless of test mode but different memory scores for auditory study depending on test mode. Panel 2 in Figure 12.5 illustrates this scenario. The reverse scenario can also occur with similar scores for auditory study conditions but different scores for visual study conditions depending on test mode. Finally, these independent variables can interact such that the memory scores are different for the two test modes at both levels of study mode. Panel 3 in

Figure 12.4   Diagram of a Specific Factorial Design With Two Independent Variables, Each With Two Levels

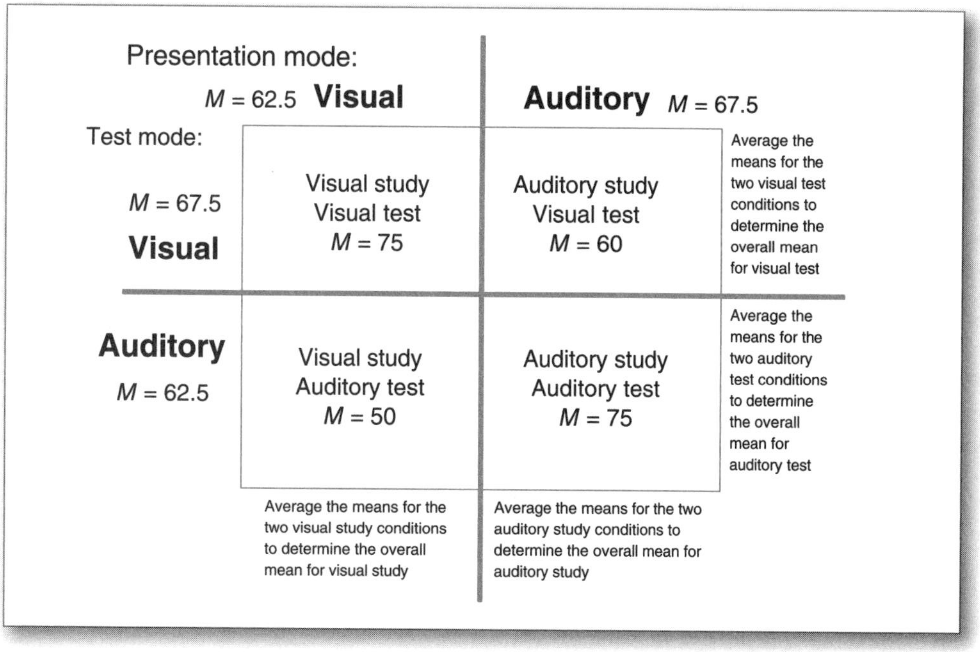

Presentation mode:

$M = 62.5$ **Visual**   **Auditory** $M = 67.5$

Test mode:

$M = 67.5$ **Visual**

| Visual study Visual test $M = 75$ | Auditory study Visual test $M = 60$ | Average the means for the two visual test conditions to determine the overall mean for visual test |

Auditory $M = 62.5$

| Visual study Auditory test $M = 50$ | Auditory study Auditory test $M = 75$ | Average the means for the two auditory test conditions to determine the overall mean for auditory test |

Average the means for the two visual study conditions to determine the overall mean for visual study

Average the means for the two auditory study conditions to determine the overall mean for auditory study

NOTE: *M* stands for mean.

Figure 12.5 illustrates this possibility. Each of these outcomes represents an interaction effect between study and test mode variables. Graphs are useful in determining the type of interaction that occurred and should be followed up with additional statistical tests to determine exactly where the differences between the conditions in the interaction are in order to best describe the interaction effect. The follow-up statistical tests are called simple effects tests. These tests are described further in Chapter 15.

Simple Effects Tests: statistical tests conducted to characterize an interaction effect when one is found in an ANOVA

Interactions between independent variables can reveal interesting effects of the variables beyond what is seen in the main effects of each variable. For example, in the results shown in Panel 1 of Figure 12.5, there would be no main effects of the independent variables (if you average the two means for visual study and for auditory study, you get similar values; if you average the two means for visual test and for auditory test, you get similar values), but there is a clear interaction of these variables. If study mode had been the only independent variable included in the experiment with a visual test, the results might have led the researchers to conclude that presenting study information visually provides for better memory of the information later. However, this would be an incomplete picture of how memory works.

Figure 12.5   Examples of Different Types of Interaction Effects

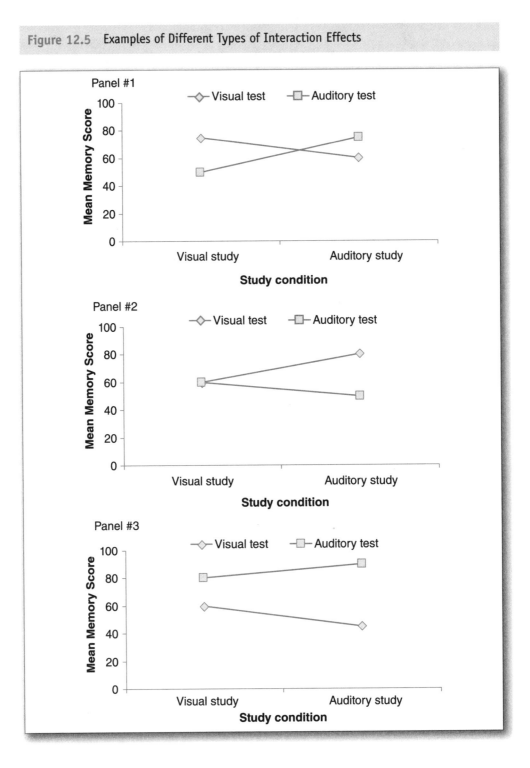

The addition of the test mode independent variable to the experiment provides a lot more information than either the study mode or test mode variables provide in a single factor experiment. Thus, factorial experiments can provide researchers with much more information about behavior.

Another example may help further illustrate the concept of an interaction. Suppose that you work for a company that makes ice cream. Your boss has tasked you with the job of finding out if two proposed changes affect ice cream sales by conducting an experiment to test the effects of these changes on consumer preferences. One proposal is to add more chocolate chips to the chocolate chip flavor of the ice cream. The other proposal is to use real vanilla in all the ice cream flavors (currently, the company uses artificial vanilla flavoring). Both proposals cost the company money, so they want you to determine if either proposal increases consumer preference for the ice cream to decide if these additions are worthwhile. Thus, your experiment includes two independent variables: Chocolate chip ice cream with (1) type of vanilla (artificial or real) manipulated and (2) amount of chips manipulated (current amount or 30% more chips). Figure 12.6 illustrates this design. You collect ratings of the ice cream from a group of 100 consumers, each of whom rates each type of ice cream on a scale of 1 to 7 for desire to purchase the ice cream. In other words, your design is a within-subjects design, as all participants rate all the ice cream conditions (in different counterbalanced orders).

Figure 12.6   Diagram of the Ice Cream Experiment Design

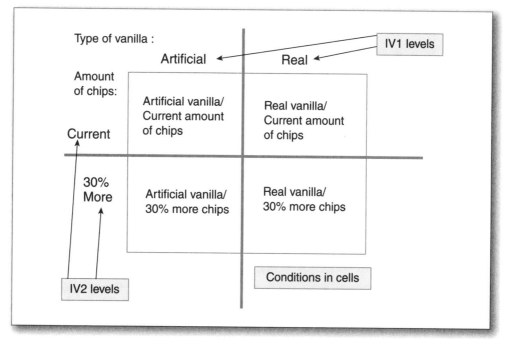

NOTE: IV stands for independent variable.

Figure 12.7 includes hypothetical mean ratings for each ice cream condition. Marginal means are also included for each level of the two independent variables. Looking at the marginal means, it appears as though the two independent variables each independently affected the participants' ratings. For type of vanilla, the real vanilla received a mean rating of 4.5, whereas the artificial vanilla received a rating of only 3. The amount of chips variable shows similar results: Participants gave higher ratings to the ice cream with 30% more chips ($M = 4.5$, where M is the mean) than with the current level of chips ($M = 3.0$). Thus, if you just looked at the main effects, you might be tempted to recommend that your company implement both an increase in chocolate chips and using real vanilla in all their ice cream flavors. However, looking at the condition means indicates something different. All the condition means show a rating of 3.0 for the ice cream, except in the real vanilla/30% more chips condition, where the mean rating was much higher than the other conditions ($M = 6.0$). In other words, the two variables interacted in such a way that this single condition seemed to result in the most preferred type of ice cream. Changing from artificial to real vanilla did not affect the ratings if the amount of chips stayed the same. Likewise, adding 30% more chips did not affect ratings if artificial vanilla was used. Only the combination of real vanilla and 30% more chips resulted in high ratings for the ice cream. This description of the interaction of the two independent variables provides the clearest picture of the results. Based on the interaction shown in the conditions means, your recommendation should be to implement both proposals together only for the chocolate chip ice cream (at least until more flavors can be tested to determine how these factors affect other flavors). This example illustrates the importance of interactions in factorial designs.

Figure 12.7 Hypothetical Means for the Ice Cream Experiment

Amount of chips: / Type of vanilla:	Artificial	Real	
Current	3	3	3
30% More	3	6	4.5
	3	4.5	

Stop and Think

(12.1)   Imagine that the results of the ice cream experiment had been different. Suppose instead that ratings for the ice cream were higher whenever more chocolate chips were used regardless of whether real or artificial vanilla was used. Would this represent an interaction? Why or why not?

(12.2)   Now imagine that the results from the ice cream experiment showed that ratings were higher when real vanilla was used regardless of the proportion of chocolate chips. Would this represent an interaction? Why or why not?

EXPERIMENT EXAMPLES

As in Chapter 11, some experiment examples from different areas of psychology follow. In each case, a factorial design was used. The descriptions will focus on the aspects of factorial designs focused on this chapter: main effects and interactions.

Cognitive Example

Experiments are very common in cognitive research. The Thinking About Research section at the end of the chapter describes one cognitive experiment focused on motor perception and object recognition. The study example that follows here tested effects of suggestive retrieval techniques on false memories for having committed a crime. In this study by Shaw and Porter (2015), subjects were recruited who had not had previous contact with police, had not committed the crimes used in the study, and had experienced an emotional event between the ages of 11 and 14 (based on reports from caregivers). Subjects were interviewed three times with about 1 week between interviews. At the interviews, subjects were told about one real event that had occurred (an emotional event reported by the caregivers) and one false event. For half of the subjects, the false event was of them committing a crime. For the other half, the false event was a noncriminal emotional event. After the events were described to the subjects, they were asked to recall as much as they could about each event. During the first interview, none of the subjects could recall anything about the false event, as expected. Subjects were encouraged to try to remember what they could when they reported no memory for the events. Subjects were told to imagine themselves in the scenario and were guided through an imagining of the event. They were encouraged to imagine themselves in the event and to try to remember the details each night before bed. At the two additional interviews, subjects were asked to try to remember the events. Their recall was videotaped. They were also asked to rate their anxiety level during the event, their confidence in their memories, and the vividness of their memories. During debriefing, subjects were asked if they had believed the false event had actually occurred.

Results showed that 83.3% of the subjects reported they believed the false event had actually happened. For just the criminal false event, 70% reported that they believed the event had occurred, showing that false memories for having committed a crime can be induced using imagination techniques. Figure 12.8 shows the ratings for anxiety during the event, vividness of memories, and confidence in memories for the subjects who believed the false event had

Figure 12.8   Results From Shaw and Porter's (2015) Experiment

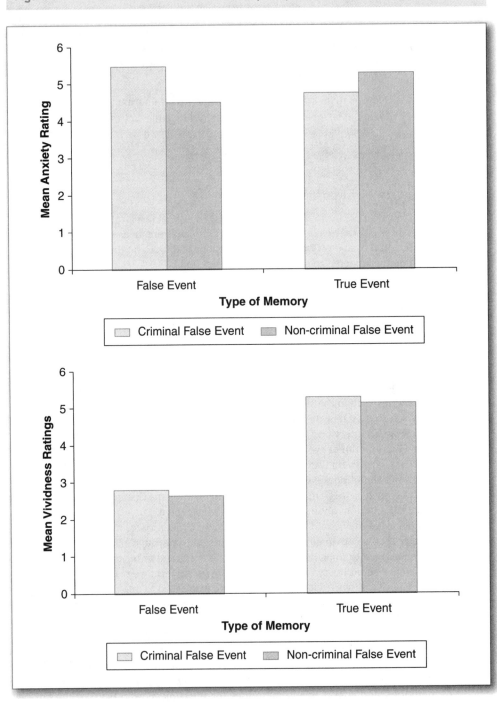

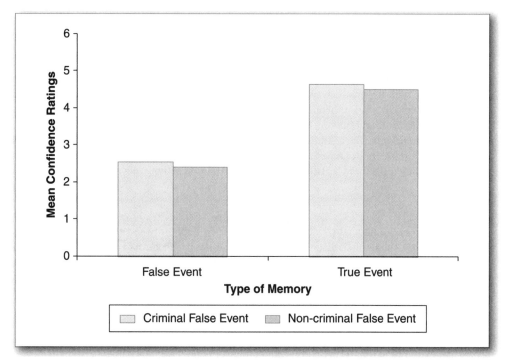

SOURCE: Shaw and Porter (2015).

occurred (i.e., had a false memory for the event). Main effects of memory type (true or false) are evident for the vividness and confidence ratings (higher ratings for true than false memories); however, an interaction may be present for the anxiety ratings. Based on the reported mean ratings, for those who received a criminal false event, anxiety seems to be higher for the false event than the true event (which was a noncriminal event), but for those who received a noncriminal (but emotional) false event, anxiety seems to be higher for the true event than for the false event. Thus, the anxiety rating difference between true and false events depended on whether the subject received a false criminal or false noncriminal event.

Biological Example

Studies in neuropsychology also sometimes involve experiments comparing brain activity for different conditions. In one such study, researchers (Silvers et al., 2014) were interested in comparing the brain activity and behavioral responses to appetizing food for children and adults. They tested the hypothesis that food craving (as measured by participants' ratings and activity in an area of the brain known as the ventral striatum) differs as a function of age. Participants were asked to consider the food shown in two conditions, a "close" condition or a "far" condition. In the "close" condition, subjects were asked to imagine the food in front of them and to think about the taste and smell of the food. In the "far" condition, subjects were asked to focus on the color and shape of the food rather than its appetitive qualities. Subjects were then shown appetizing foods (half were sweet and half were salty to reduce bias due to type of food) and to think about the foods according to the instruction ("close" or "far") on that trial. Then they were asked to rate how much they wanted to eat the food on a 5-point scale. Figure 12.9 shows the sequence of events in the task. Brain activity in the ventral striatum was measured using functional magnetic imaging (fMRI) while subjects completed the task.

Results showed that adults reported lower craving ratings than children. In addition, lower craving ratings were seen on "far" than "close" trials. There was no interaction of age and trial type on craving ratings. For the brain activity measure, adults showed lower activity in the ventral striatum than children, indicating there was less brain activity in adults related to craving than in children. Older adults also showed more activity than children in the prefrontal cortex where inhibition is controlled. This study shows that not only is there an age effect on craving of appetizing food, there is also an age effect on the brain activity that accompanies craving of food.

Social Example

Experiments in social psychology have been described in the other chapters of this text. In Chapter 4, the implicit association test (IAT) was described as an example of systematic observation where word associations are manipulated and the participants' speed at reacting to the words is measured (see Figure 4.2). In Chapter 3, the Zimbardo (1973) experiment, where a randomly assigned role as a prisoner or guard in a mock prison affected participants' behavior, was described as an example of a study that may have violated ethical standards. Thus, if you have read these chapters, you have already encountered some examples of the use of experiments in social psychology. The example presented in this chapter elaborates on the IAT procedure with an experiment that used this procedure to test the unconscious biases of participants.

Recall from Chapter 4 (see Figure 4.2) that the IAT procedure measures reaction times of participants when they make judgments about combinations of concepts with the same key press (e.g., press the right key when you see items that are female and items that a firefighter might use; press the left key when you see items that are male and items that a teacher might use). Longer reaction times to uncommon associations (e.g., female and firefighter) indicate implicit biases (e.g., against female firefighters) that the participant may have.

Ahern and Hetherington (2006) used the IAT to evaluate implicit attitudes toward the concepts of "thin" and "fat." Pictures of individuals were presented to represent thin and fat

Figure 12.9   Task Used in the Silvers et al. (2014) Experiment

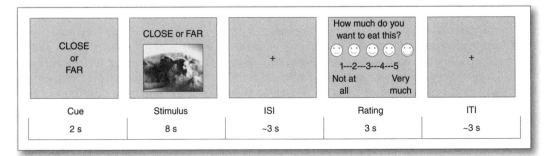

SOURCE: Silvers et al. (2014).

concepts. Words were presented to represent positive and negative concepts. Participants first completed trials associating a specific key with a concept (e.g., thin—right key, fat—left key; positive—right key, negative—left key). After the key association trials, the participants were given blocks of test association trials, where each concept pair (i.e., thin-positive, fat-negative or thin-negative, fat-positive) was presented with the same key. Thus, the independent variable was the concept pairing (match with stereotype, such as thin-positive, or mismatch with stereotype, such as fat-positive). A comparison of the different test association trial reaction times indicated the implicit bias of the participants. For example, if participants are faster for the thin-positive/fat-negative block than the other concept pairing block, then this indicates that they have an implicit bias toward thin as positive and fat as negative.

The blocks of test association trials for each concept pairing were counterbalanced in this within-subjects experiment to control for order effects of the presentation of the concept pairings. In other words, half of the participants completed the thin-positive/fat-negative pairing blocks first, and the other half of the participants completed the thin-negative/fat-positive pairing block first. This shows the counterbalancing of the order of the conditions for the independent variable in the experiment: concept pairing block. The researchers then compared the effect of concept pairing block on the reaction times of the participants. In addition, the pictures used were as similar as possible for pose of the individual pictured, clothing worn by the individual pictured, activity being performed in the photo by the individual pictured, and emotional expression of the individual pictured.

Figure 12.10 illustrates the IAT results of the experiment. The analyses indicated that reaction time was faster for the thin-positive/fat-negative concept pairing than for the reverse pairing. This result indicates that overall, the participants showed a negative bias toward the concept

Figure 12.10   Results of the Ahern and Hetherington (2006) Implicit Association Test (IAT) Experiment

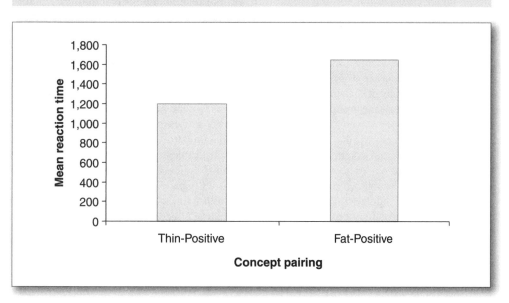

of fat and a positive bias toward the concept of thin, with a large majority of the participants having this bias (86%). The researchers did not find any evidence that the IAT scores correlated with any explicit measure they collected, including body dissatisfaction and body mass index, which is "a measure of body fat that is the ratio of the weight of the body in kilograms to the square of its height in meters" ("Body Mass Index," 2014). Thus, the researchers concluded that the positive bias toward thin and the negative bias toward fat is very strong in the population the sample was drawn from.

Developmental Example

Whereas many studies in developmental psychology are quasi-experiments because of the inclusion of age as a subject variable (see Chapters 13 and 14 for further discussion), some developmental psychologists are also interested in exploring how causal relationships change across age groups. Thus, some researchers conduct experiments that contain a true independent variable and age as a subject variable, making them factorial in design.

An example of this type of study was conducted by Hund and Plumert (2003). These researchers were interested in how memory for the location of objects is influenced by the similarity of objects and whether this relationship is the same for different age groups. They tested 7-, 9-, and 11-year-olds and adults in an experiment that manipulated the similarity of target objects. The participants in the experiment were asked to learn the location of objects in a model house. The objects were placed on dots in different sections of the house to help the participants learn the locations. Then the dots were removed, and the participants were asked to place the objects in the locations they remembered the experimenter placing them during the learning phase of the experiment. Half of the participants in each age group were shown objects in the same category (e.g., vehicles) placed in the same section of the house (i.e., location was related to object similarity). The other half of the participants in each age group were shown objects that were randomly placed in different sections of the house (i.e., location was not related to object similarity). Location errors (i.e., how far the participant placed the objects from their original positions) were recorded for the two object-type groups.

The researchers randomly assigned the participants to object-type groups to control possible group differences. The objects were also placed in the house in a random order to control for possible order effects in the placement of the objects.

The results of the study indicated that although older participants made fewer errors, participants in all age groups placed related objects closer together (i.e., had greater location error) than unrelated objects. This difference across object-type groups was present for all age groups, indicating that location memory relies on the similarity of objects for individuals from age 7 years through adulthood. In other words, "Information about what objects are influences memory for where objects are located" (Hund & Plumert, 2003, p. 946). However, remember that age is a subject (or quasi-independent—see Chapter 13 for more discussion) variable that was not manipulated. Thus, any differences found for age groups (e.g., fewer errors for older participants) cannot be fully interpreted as a causal effect because of the absence of a manipulation for this variable. This limitation exists for all developmental designs that compare age groups as a subject variable, even if another manipulated variable is included in the design, as in the Hund and Plumert experiment.

> ### Stop and Think
>
> (12.3)   What is a source of bias that might be present in the Shaw and Porter (2015) experiment?
>
> (12.4)   What is a source of bias that might be present in the Silvers et al. (2014) experiment?

CHAPTER SUMMARY

Reconsider the questions from the beginning of the chapter:

- How do factorial experiments differ from single factor experiments? In factorial experiments, more than one independent variable (IV) is included in the design. This means the crossing of the levels of these IVs creates four or more conditions to consider in the experiment. The separate effects of each IV are seen by comparing the overall means for each level of an IV while ignoring the levels of the other IV(s). These are the main effects. There is also the interaction of the IVs in a factorial experiment that can be tested.
- What are the advantages of conducting experiments with more than one independent variable? One advantage is that it is more efficient than a single-factor design. You only need one sample to collect data about multiple factors. The other main advantage is the testing of the interactions between variables. This allows you to determine whether the effects of one IV depend on the levels of another IV in your design. Single-factor designs do not allow for testing of interaction effects.
- What is an interaction and what can we learn from testing interactions? An interaction can occur between independent variables such that the effect of one independent variable depends on which level of the other independent variable one is looking at. For example, an independent variable can show a difference between levels for the first level of another independent variable but show no difference between levels for the second level of the other independent variable. We can learn about the combined effects of multiple independent variables on the dependent variable by testing multiple independent variables in factorial designs.

THINKING ABOUT RESEARCH

A summary of a research study in psychology is given below. As you read the summary, think about the following questions:

1. What are the independent variables in this experiment? Identify the levels of each IV.

2. What are the dependent variables (hint: look at Figure 12.13)?

3. From what you see in Figure 12.13, did the results indicate an interaction effect between the IVs? If so, describe the interaction.

4. Does the graph in Figure 12.13 show main effects of either IV?

Figure 12.11 Stimuli Used in Bub et al.'s (2013) Experiment

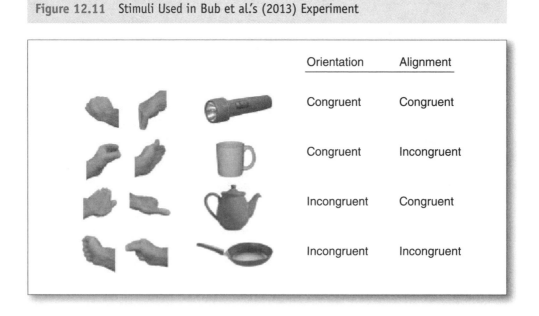

Research Study. Bub, D. N., Masson, M. E. J., & Lin, T. (2013). Features of planned hand actions influence identification of graspable objects. *Psychological Science, 24,* 1269–1276.

Purpose of the Study. These researchers investigated how action plans (e.g., moving your hand and arm to pick up an object) influences object identification. One might think that object identification

Figure 12.12 Trial Sequence Used in Bub et al.'s (2013) Experiment

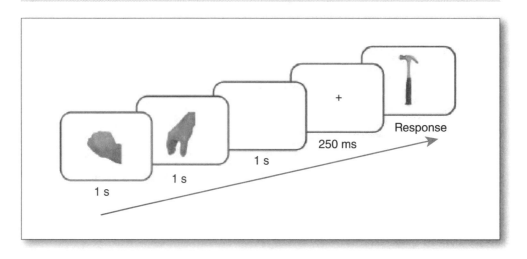

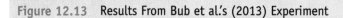

Figure 12.13 Results From Bub et al.'s (2013) Experiment

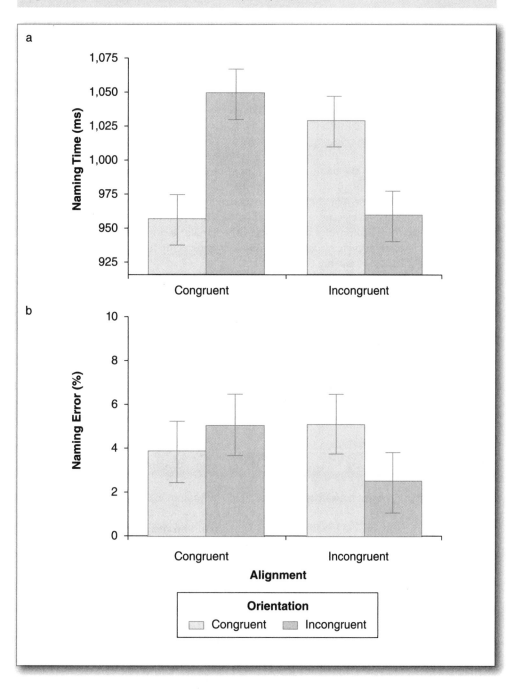

would affect action plans (e.g., you would plan your movements differently to pick up a mug versus a frying pan). However, these researchers suggested that the causal relationship can also go the other way, that the action plan made can influence how well you identify an object. After familiarization trials, they gave subjects an action plan for their hand and then asked them to identify an object that could be held in the hand as quickly and accurately as possible. They hypothesized that when the action plan matched the way the object would be held, subjects would be faster at naming the objects.

Method of the Study. There were 20 undergraduate students in the experiment. The subjects first received familiarization trials with the action plans. They were shown pictures of hands and asked to mimic the hand posture (see Figure 12.11 for hand pictures). Subjects then received familiarization trials with the objects. Each object (see Figure 12.11 for pictures of the objects) was presented with its name and the subject read the name out loud. Then the critical trials were presented. On each trial, a hand action plan in two hand pictures (see Figure 12.12 for the sequence of events in a trial) was shown to the subjects one at a time. Then, after a 250 ms fixation cross was shown, the object appeared and subjects were to name the object as quickly as possible. Their response was recorded by the computer's microphone with their naming time for each trial. Thus, trials were either congruent or incongruent in terms of the hand orientation (vertical or horizontal) for picking up the objects and the hand alignment (left hand or right hand) for picking up the objects.

Results of the Study. Figure 12.13 presents the results for naming time and naming errors according to the congruency of the orientation and alignment of the action plans shown before the pictures. These results show that naming time was fastest when both features (i.e., orientation and alignment) either matched or did not match the object shown for picking it up. Thus, if only one feature matched and the other feature did not, subjects were slower to name the object than when they both matched or both did not match.

Conclusions of the Study. The results of the study showed that action plans affected object identification as the authors predicted. Having one motor feature in mind that can be used to pick up the object and one motor feature that cannot be used to pick up the object interfered with naming of the objects.

COMMON PITFALLS AND HOW TO AVOID THEM

Problem: Identifying interactions—interactions can be difficult to identify and describe.

Solution: It is often helpful to create a graph of the condition means of a factorial design to determine whether an interaction is present. If a line graph is created, an interaction can be seen in nonparallel lines.

Problem: Understanding the difference between main effects and interactions—it can be difficult to understand how these are different.

Solution: Main effects test the separate effects of an IV on a dependent variable. Thus, one must ignore (i.e., average across) the other IVs in a design in order to consider main effects. These can be hard to see in graphs of all the condition means. A separate graph or averaging the mean values across levels of other

IVs can help you see these effects. To examine interactions, you must consider the condition means, though, so a graph is often best to examine whether the effects of an IV depend on the levels of other IVs.

TEST YOURSELF

Figure 12.A

Therapy type:

	Talk	Drug
Therapy length: 4 weeks	60	75
12 weeks	90	75

1. For the table of condition means above (means are mood scores), indicate which effects (main effect of type of therapy, main effect of length of therapy, interaction between type and length of therapy) are likely to be present. If an effect is present, indicate which levels or conditions were higher.

2. Create a graph of the results in (1). Be sure to correctly label the axes of your graph.

3. Reread the sample factorial experiment about our dog Daphne presented at the beginning of the chapter to answer the following questions:

   (a) What are the independent variables, and what are the levels of these variables in the experiment?

   (b) Were the independent variables manipulated between subjects or within subjects?

   (c) Was an interaction effect found in this experiment? If so, describe it.

4. Identify the independent and dependent variables included in the studies described in the Experiment Examples section and listed below. For any independent variable(s), also state the levels of the independent variable.

   (a) Shaw and Porter (2015)

(b) Silvers et al. (2014)

(c) Ahern and Hetherington (2006)

(d) Hund and Plumert (2003)

5. A researcher conducted a study to investigate the effects of smiling on helping behavior. Participants completed a survey that they thought was the purpose of the study, but in reality, the experiment took place after they completed the survey. At the end of the survey session, half of the subjects were thanked with a smile and half were thanked without a smile. Whether the subject received a smile or not was randomly determined. The gender of the person giving the smile also varied by participant: some subjects received the smile from a female researcher and some subjects received the smile from a male researcher. The subjects then passed a confederate in the hallway on their way out of the lab who had just dropped a large stack of books. The number of subjects who helped the confederate pick up his books was measured. The results showed that the subjects who were thanked by a male researcher showed similar helping behaviors across smile and no smile conditions. However, subjects who were thanked by a female researcher showed more helping behaviors when they received a smile than when they did not.

(a) What are the independent variables in this experiment? Identify how each independent variable was manipulated (i.e., between-subjects or within-subjects).

(b) From the description of the results, was an interaction present? Explain your answer.

Answers can be found at edge.sagepub/mcbride3e.

STOP AND THINK ANSWERS

(12.1) No, this would be a main effect of amount of chips.

(12.2) No, this would be a main effect of type of vanilla.

(12.3) Answers will vary.

(12.4) Answers will vary.

ⓈSAGE edge™

Visit edge.sagepub.com/mcbride3e for the tools you need to sharpen your study skills:

- Web Quizzes
- eFlashcards
- Thinking About Research

- SAGE Journal Articles
- Web and Multimedia Resources

Chapter 13

The Nuts and Bolts of Quasi-Experiments

Consider the following questions as you read Chapter 13

- What aspects of a quasi-experiment make it different from other research designs?
- What is required to test causal relationships between variables?
- What is a pretest-posttest design? In what way is it a quasi-experiment?
- What is a time series design? In what way is it a quasi-experiment?

Consider a study that examined the claim that females are more social than males. The study, conducted by Benenson et al. (2009, Study 1), examined roommate satisfaction among 30 male and 30 female college students. All of the students in the study reported having one roommate at the time of the study. Half of the participants of each gender were having a current conflict with their roommate, and the other half for each gender reported planning to live with their current roommate for the rest of the current school year. All participants completed a questionnaire about their roommate. The authors reasoned that same-sex tolerance (e.g., being satisfied with a roommate who was the same gender as the participant) was related to the level of sociability of the participants. In other words, if females are more sociable, then they should show higher ratings of their roommate than males, indicating greater tolerance of same-sex, nonfamilial relationships. Contrary to the idea that females are more sociable and tolerant of same-sex friendships, results indicated that in both groups (conflict-with-roommate group and planning-to-continue-living-with-roommate group), more than twice as many males were satisfied with their roommate than females. See Figure 13.1 for a graph of the results. From these results, the researchers concluded that males are more tolerant of same-sex friends than females. However, the researchers could not conclude that the sex of the participants caused them to be more tolerant. This conclusion would have required that the researchers randomly assign participants to be male or female, and this is obviously not possible, as it would require the researcher choosing by chance

Figure 13.1   Males Were More Satisfied Overall With Their Roommates Than Females

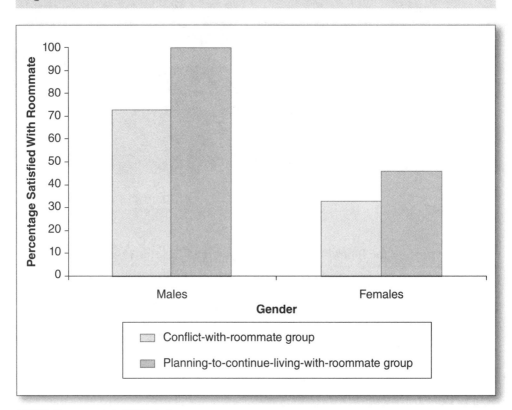

SOURCE: Benenson et al. (2009) study.

Quasi-Experiment: a type of research design where a comparison is made, as in an experiment, but no random assignment of participants to groups occurs

Quasi-Independent/Subject Variable: variable that allows comparison of groups of participants without manipulation (i.e., no random assignment)

who would be male and who would be female. Thus, the researchers are limited in the causal information they can gain from this study, because the study is a quasi-experiment that does not contain a manipulated independent variable (see Chapters 5, 11, and 12 for more discussion of independent variables and tests of causal relationships). Instead, gender is examined as a subject or quasi-independent/subject variable.

In other chapters of this text, many examples of quasi-experiments are described, because this research design type allows for the comparison of groups that are typically of interest to psychologists. For example, gender, age, whether one smokes or not, handedness, and years in school are all quasi-independent variables that cannot be manipulated as true independent variables. Other variables, such as whether someone has experienced a divorce, an illness, or abuse, cannot ethically be manipulated. Thus, to investigate these variables, a researcher often conducts a

quasi-experiment, where groups of participants are compared on a behavior of interest,
as in an experiment, but the quasi-independent variable is not manipulated, which leaves
the study open to other possible explanations
of the results. In other words, groups that have
not been randomly assigned can be compared
in a quasi-experiment, but one cannot gain
strong causal information, because of the lack of random assignment.

Random Assignment: participants are randomly assigned to levels of the independent variable in an experiment to control for individual differences as an extraneous variable

Another example of a quasi-experiment illustrates some of the issues in this research design type. Benenson and Koulnazarian (2008) conducted a quasi-experiment to investigate at what age gender differences appear in help-seeking behaviors. Previous studies with adults and adolescents showed that women tend to seek help from others more often than men. However, it is unclear how these gender differences develop. These researchers sought to determine if girls ask for help more often than boys at young ages (3 years and 6 years of age). In addition, children were grouped by socioeconomic status to examine differences between children with a low and an upper-middle socioeconomic status. The children in the study were asked to complete a series of tasks (e.g., drawing objects), and the time they spent on the task before they asked for help was recorded. Overall, girls asked for help after a shorter time with the task than boys. In addition, younger children requested help faster than older children. Finally, children from the low socioeconomic status group requested help faster than the children from the upper-middle socioeconomic status group. Benenson and Koulnazarian concluded that gender differences in helping behavior may not be due to learned gender roles, because in children as young as 3 years old, girls requested help more quickly than boys. This study illustrates a basic quasi-experimental research design with three factors compared in the study: age, gender, and socioeconomic status. Each of these factors was used to group participants according to characteristics they had at the start of the study. None of these factors can be manipulated as independent variables (e.g., a researcher cannot randomly assign participants to different age groups). Thus, the researchers cannot conclude that any of these factors *caused* the group differences found. It is possible that additional variables that change with these factors (e.g., quality of education may differ with socioeconomic status, different parental attitudes may depend on socioeconomic status) contributed to the observed relationship between the factor and the help-seeking behavior measured. Figure 13.2 shows where in the research process the researcher must consider whether to implement a quasi-experiment.

TYPES OF QUASI-EXPERIMENTS

The type of quasi-experiment illustrated by the preceding example is the simplest form of a quasi-experiment. It is in all other ways like an experiment, but the random assignment of participants to groups is lacking. In fact, Shadish, Cook, and Campbell (2002) propose that a lack of random assignment in an experiment is the definition of a quasi-experiment. While this definition holds for the designs that psychologists consider quasi-experiments, there are some specific types of quasi-experiments that are used in psychological research. In this chapter, we consider two general types of quasi-experiments and the more specific forms of each design type that are dependent on the researcher's goals and the restrictions of the situation or behaviors to be studied. It

Figure 13.2 Steps in the Research Process: Designing the Study

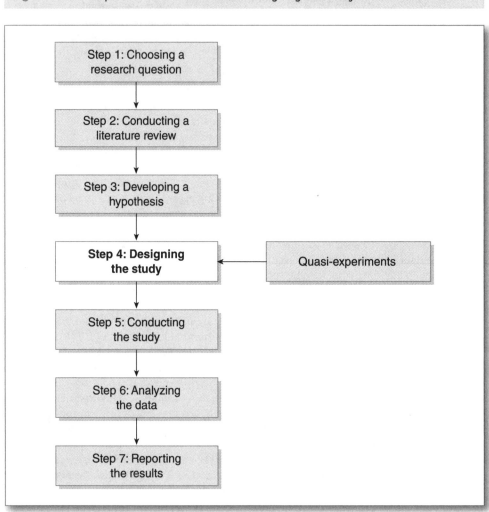

should be noted that many applied studies that examine realistic behaviors use quasi-experiments because random assignment would be difficult, impossible, or unethical. For example, research done in educational settings often involves a quasi-experiment, because the researcher cannot affect either the students' teacher or classroom setting. Thus, due to the inability to randomly assign groups, the researcher may test the hypotheses by comparing different factors as they change across different classes of students.

Pretest-Posttest Designs

In the simplest type of pretest-posttest design, a behavior is measured twice: once before a treatment or condition is implemented (the pretest) and once after it has been implemented (the posttest). This design is a quasi-experiment because there is no random assignment of participants to the treatment. In this case, all the participants get the treatment. The researcher compares the scores from the pretest and the posttest, looking for a change based on the treatment or condition occurring in the time between the two measurements. However, if a change occurs in this design, the researcher cannot automatically conclude that the treatment or condition caused the change because other factors (besides the treatment or condition) may have occurred as well between the two measurements. Consider a hypothetical study testing the effectiveness of a smoking-cessation program. It would be unethical to randomly assign some participants to smoke in order to conduct an experiment for this study because this would force participants to endure something harmful. Thus, a pretest-posttest quasi-experiment is a more appropriate design for test-

Figure 13.3   Pretest-Posttest Designs Can Help Evaluate the Effectiveness of Smoking Cessation Programs, But Without Random Assignment to the Program and a Control Group to Compare It With, It Is Difficult to Conclude That the Program Caused a Change in Smoking Habits

SOURCE: © iStockphoto.com/tomeng.

ing the program's effectiveness. The study can be designed such that at pretest, participants report the number of cigarettes they smoked that week. They then take part in the program. After the program concludes, each participant again reports the number of cigarettes he or she smoked that week (see Figure 13.3).

Suppose the number of cigarettes smoked goes down from pretest to posttest. Can the researcher conclude that the smoking-cessation program worked? Why not? What other possible explanations are there for the decline in smoking? There are several possible alternative explanations in this case. For example, suppose a study was reported in the media during the time between measurements that concluded that smoking has extremely harmful effects (i.e., a history effect biased the results—see below for more discussion of history effects as a source of bias). That may have caused the participants to be more motivated to quit, and they reduced the number of cigarettes smoked due to their new motivation. Another possibility is that a new law was passed to ban smoking in public places (another history effect). This is becoming more frequent

Pretest-Posttest Design: a type of research design (often a quasi-experiment) where behavior is measured both before and after a treatment or condition is implemented

History Effect: events that occur during the course of a study to all participants or to individual participants that can result in bias

as cities and states in the United States and cities and countries in Europe are passing such bans. The smoking rates may have declined because of the ban. There are many other possibilities for the results in this study that are plausible alternatives to the conclusion that the smoking-cessation program is the cause of the smoking decline.

Researchers can attempt to deal with some of the alternative explanations in pretest-posttest designs by including a control group. If participants are randomly assigned to the control group and the treatment group, the study becomes an experiment. However, in many situations random assignment to groups may not be possible. Without random assignment, the study is still a quasi-experiment, where it is difficult to rule out alternative explanations of the results. This design is a pretest-posttest design with nonequivalent groups, because group differences that might account for the results are not controlled by random assignment to groups. In this design, the researcher considers the difference between the pretest and posttest scores across the control and experimental groups. Was there a difference for the experimental group than the treatment group? If so, the treatment or condition received by the experimental group may have caused this difference. However, group differences can also have caused this difference. Without random assignment to groups, it can be difficult to determine the cause. However, this research design can be useful when random assignment is not possible.

Doherty and Hilberg (2007) conducted a pretest-posttest design with nonequivalent groups to examine the results of an effective teaching standards model (e.g., discussion of topics being learned between students and teachers) on student achievement in primarily low-income elementary school students. Two elementary schools were compared: one school at which the standards for effective instruction developed by Tharp, Estrada, Dalton, and Yamauchi (2000) were being practiced and one school at which the standards were not being practiced. Standardized test scores for the children at the two schools were collected and compared at the beginning of the school year (pretest) and the end of the school year (posttest). The results showed that as teachers at the standards school used the standards to a greater extent in their teaching, language arts scores showed a greater difference between the schools, with the "standards school" showing higher scores. The study involved students at two schools, where a difference in teaching technique existed between the schools and between individual instructors at the start of the study. In other words, children were not randomly assigned to teachers using the standards and teachers not using the standards. Thus, this study used a quasi-experimental design with a pretest-posttest method with nonequivalent groups.

One issue to consider for this type of study is that schools with low-scoring students are more likely to receive funding for standards studies such as the one described here. Thus, the standardized test scores that increased for students at the standards school may show regression toward the mean (see Chapter 5 for more discussion of this and other sources of bias relevant to quasi-experiments). In other words, a high score achieved at posttest may be an extreme score in some cases, and with additional testing, these students may score closer to their original mean (which is typically lower than the norm). Pretest-posttest designs are susceptible to bias due to regression toward the mean because one extreme score (high or low) can skew the change in scores between the pretests and posttests. This source of bias should be considered when results from these types of studies are interpreted.

Nonequivalent Groups: groups compared in a study where participants are not randomly assigned

Regression Toward the Mean: can occur when participants score higher or lower than their personal average—the next time they are tested, they are more likely to score near their personal average, making scores unreliable

Shadish et al. (2002) recommend several variations to the pretest-posttest design with non-equivalent groups to allow researchers to rule out some possible alternative explanations of group differences. For example, one way to reduce the likelihood of extraneous effects on the pretest-posttest score difference is to include two pretests. If results show a similar pretest-posttest difference across the control and experimental groups, it will be unclear why this result occurred. The treatment may have caused the difference in the experimental group, whereas another factor (e.g., group characteristics that are different from the experimental group) caused the effect in the control group. Using two pretests helps the researcher understand these results. If both groups take Pretest 1 and Pretest 2 with a time delay between them, the researcher can compare the groups for baseline differences across the groups. Then Pretest 2 scores can be compared with Posttest scores (with the same time delay used as was used for the delay between Pretest 1 and Pretest 2) to see if the difference for each group is similar to the Pretest 1 and Pretest 2 score difference. This clarifies the control and experimental comparison.

Another suggestion by Shadish et al. (2002) is to allow both groups to be the experimental and control groups in alternating order. In other words, there are two posttests used: one after Group 1 has the treatment and Group 2 is the control, and one after Group 2 has the treatment and Group 1 is the control. This design allows group differences to be controlled such that each group serves once in each condition (experimental and control). Figure 13.4 illustrates this type of pretest-posttest design. However, not all designs allow this alternation of treatment and control across participant groups. In some cases, for example, the control condition cannot be given after the treatment without the treatment affecting the behavior in the control condition. Consider a memory study where participants are asked to remember to look for and to respond to an animal word while performing another task. The control condition involves performing the task without the instruction to look for the animal word. If participants first complete the task looking for the animal word, it may be difficult for them to stop looking for the animal word during the control condition that follows. Thus, this suggestion may not apply to all types of studies.

One major drawback to the pretest-posttest design is that the participants are tested twice on the same behavior. This can cause a source of bias known as testing effects. Testing effects occur when participants are tested multiple times and each subsequent test is affected by the previous tests. For example, participants may get better on the tests over time with practice. Alternatively, they may become fatigued or bored with the test after taking it once. Testing effects can occur in many types of designs (see Chapters 5, 9, and 11 for more discussion of testing effects in other contexts). In pretest-posttest designs, they can occur as the experience of the pretest changes how participants experience the posttest. One method of evaluating testing effects in pretest-posttest studies is the use of the Solomon four-group design (Shadish et al., 2002). In the Solomon four-group design, the pretest-posttest design with nonequivalent groups is used. However, two sets of each group type are included: one set that takes the pretest and posttest as illustrated in Figure 13.4 and one set that takes only the posttest to allow comparison of the two sets of groups. See Figure 13.5 for the

Testing Effects: occur when participants are tested more than once in a study, with early testing affecting later testing

Solomon Four-Group Design: pretest-posttest design with two sets of nonequivalent groups, one set that takes the pretest and posttest and one set that takes only the posttest

Figure 13.4   Illustration of Different Types of Pretest-Posttest Designs

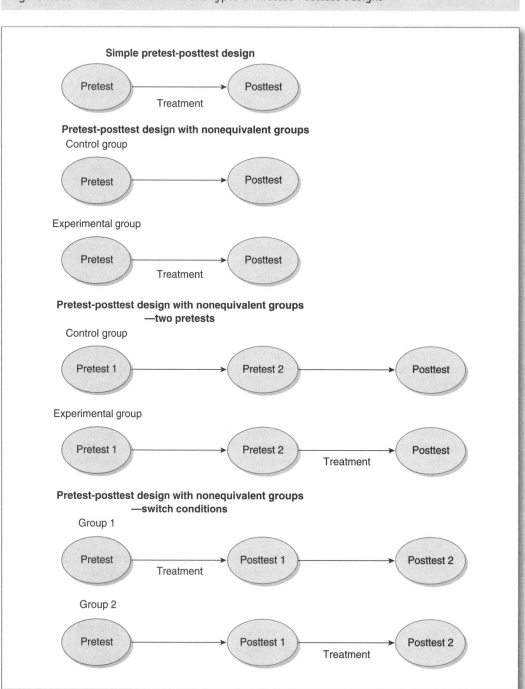

Figure 13.5   Solomon Four-Group Design

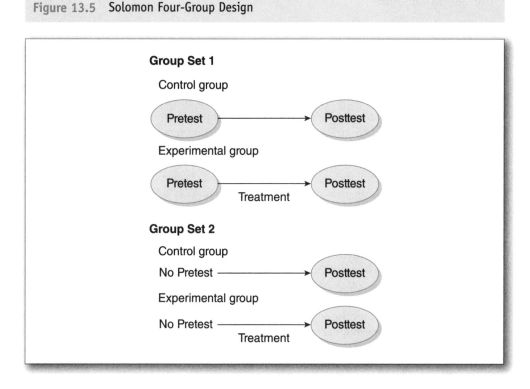

full Solomon four-group design. Comparison across the group sets indicates whether testing effects occur. For example, comparing posttest scores for the groups that take the pretest and posttest and the groups that take only the posttest allows the researcher to determine if testing effects have occurred in the posttest scores. If no testing effects have occurred, the scores should be similar for the two control groups and for the two experimental groups, as the only difference between each set is whether they have taken the pretest or not.

Stop and Think

(13.1)   Suppose that you wanted to try out a new study technique that a friend suggested to you (e.g., taking quizzes on the material). Describe a pretest-posttest study you might conduct on your own learning to evaluate the new technique.

(13.2)   Explain why testing effects are especially problematic in pretest-posttest designs.

(13.3)   A researcher wants to evaluate a new treatment for obsessive-compulsive disorder. Describe how she might evaluate the effectiveness of the treatment using a quasi-experiment. Explain how she could change the study you describe into an experiment.

Time Series Designs

For some measures of behavior or attitudes, the measures may fluctuate a good deal from week to week or month to month. In these cases, a single pretest and a single posttest are unlikely to capture the true nature of the behavior. The pretest can occur at a time when scores happen to be particularly high or particularly low, which can bias the change in scores from pretest to posttest. Time series designs are special pretest-posttest designs that account for these fluctuations by measuring the behavior or attitude multiple times before the treatment and multiple times after the treatment for the same length of time. Then the patterns of scores before and after the treatment are compared to determine if a difference has occurred over time. The patterns of scores are compared in a time series design, rather than two scores as in the simple pretest-posttest design shown at the top of Figure 13.4. For example, a researcher may wish to determine if Americans were more depressed during the war in Iraq than before it. To study this question, the researchers may use a time series design, in which they recruit individuals from counseling centers who have been receiving counseling and have been taking a depression questionnaire each month during their treatment. With permission from the clients, the researchers can look at the pattern of depression for the year before the war started and for the year after the war started and compare the two patterns of scores. It is likely that over a year, a client's depression scores fluctuate from month to month as holidays and seasons come and go. Thus, if there is no difference in scores before and after the war in Iraq, the two patterns of depression scores for the year (averaged across clients) should be similar. It is the pattern of depression scores over the course of a year (or other time period) that is compared both before and after treatment in order to determine the treatment's effects—the pattern of scores both before and after contain the monthly fluctuations in depression, but if the treatment has an effect, the pattern is higher or lower overall.

The time series design described above is called an interrupted time series design because the treatment is an independent event that the researchers have no control over. Events such as a war, passage of a new law, or other historical events are considered "treatments" in an interrupted time series design in that patterns of scores are compared before and after the event occurs. In many cases, the researchers are unable to predict the occurrence of the event. This limits them to measures that are collected periodically by other agencies. In other words, archival data are used as observations in the study (see Chapter 4 for a discussion of archival data observations). For example, specific agencies periodically collect information regarding the confidence people in different countries have in the economy (e.g., the Consumer Confidence Index; see www.conference-board.org/ for information about this measure). It is determined from responses to a survey of the spending and savings activities of the people in a particular country. In weaker economic times in a country, the scores are lower on this measure. Because the Consumer Confidence Index is continually measured, researchers can use this measure to determine if people's optimism about the economy is affected by various events, such as wars, laws, and other historical events. Thus, patterns of scores can be compared before and after historical events to determine if a change has occurred. A time series design is appropriate for this measure because people's confidence in the economy tends to fluctuate naturally from month to month in different parts of the year.

A recent example of a study using an interrupted time series design was conducted by Libby et al. (2007). These researchers conducted an investigation of antidepressant prescription rates in children before and after the U.S. Food and Drug Administration (FDA) issued a warning regarding the link between antidepressants and suicidal behavior in children. The warning was issued in October 2003. Thus, the researchers obtained archival data regarding antidepressant and alternative treatments of depression in children for each month for the 60 months before the FDA warning and for 24 months after the warning. The patterns of antidepressant prescriptions and alternative treatments were compared for the period before and the period after the warning. See Figure 13.6 for a graph of these patterns. The results indicated that in the 24 months following the warning, prescriptions for antidepressants to children with depression declined, whereas alternative treatment methods increased. In other words, Libby et al. found a relationship between the FDA warning and a change in the treatments prescribed for children with depression.

Time Series Design: a research design where patterns of scores over time are compared from before a treatment is implemented and after a treatment is implemented

Interrupted Time Series Design: a time series design where the "treatment" is an independent event, such as a historical event

Noninterrupted Time Series Design: a time series design where the "treatment" is implemented by the researcher

Figure 13.6   Time Series Data for Treatment Rates of Children's Depression From Libby et al.'s (2007) Study

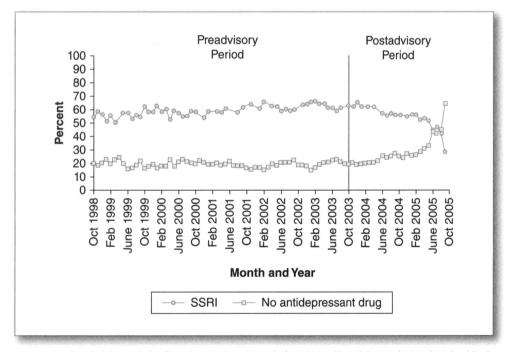

SOURCE: Reprinted with permission from the *American Journal of Psychiatry* (Copyright 2007). American Psychiatric Association.

Similar designs with a researcher-implemented treatment are called noninterrupted time series designs. (I use this term to distinguish it from an interrupted time series design. This design is also referred to as a nonequivalent control group design [Bordens & Abbott, 1999].) The behavior of interest is measured over time both before and after a treatment has been introduced. For example, suppose a researcher is interested in the effect of a new therapy on depression. The researcher can choose to conduct an interrupted time series design study because depressive symptoms may change throughout the year (e.g., be worse around holidays, get better when spring begins). Thus in this case, in a noninterrupted time series design, the participants' depression symptoms are measured over a period of time before they began the new therapy (e.g., for 6 months or 1 year before). Then the new therapy is given to the participants, and their depressive symptoms are measured for the same period of time with the new therapy. As in the examples above, the pattern of depressive symptoms is compared for the period before the new therapy and after the new therapy is implemented.

As with pretest-posttest designs, limitations of time series designs exist due to possible extraneous factors that can affect a score pattern change other than the treatment or event of interest. Thus, as with all quasi-experiments, researchers must be cautious in interpreting relationships found between the treatment or event and the results. However, if a control group is included with random assignment of participants to the treatment or the control group, the study becomes an experiment, and more information regarding a causal relationship between the factors can be obtained. Random assignment of participants is more likely in studies using time series designs with a researcher-implemented treatment than in a study with an independent event examined in an interrupted time series design.

One final issue regarding time series designs should be considered. Due to the focus on patterns of scores over time, traditional data analysis techniques (such as those described in Chapter 14) are typically inadequate to test hypotheses for these types of designs. Specialized statistical techniques are available, but they are too advanced for the scope of an introductory methods text and course.

SOURCES OF BIAS IN QUASI-EXPERIMENTS

History. In studies that take place over a period of time, a few different sources of bias can occur during that time period. For example, suppose a researcher is conducting a study to compare different treatments for depression. The treatments typically take time to implement. During this time period, the effects of the treatments (if there are any) occur. However, effects of other factors may also arise. One example is the effects of historical events (i.e., history effect). These historical events can be experienced by a large group of individuals or personally experienced by individuals. For example, suppose that during the time the depression study was being conducted, the economy took a turn for the worse and many people were losing their jobs and having difficulty paying bills. In this case, the historical event (the economy declining) can affect the depression levels of participants in the study, making it difficult to detect positive effects of the treatments being tested. Alternatively, individual participants in the study can experience personal events that affect their level of depression (loss of a loved one, a promotion at work, etc.). Thus, history of the participants (either shared or personal) can affect the data in the study and reduce the internal validity.

Effects of history (and other sources of bias that occur over time) are most likely to occur in pretest-posttest designs. In Chapter 4, pretest-posttest designs were described as designs where participants are tested both before (pretest) and after (posttest) the implementation of a treatment or other type of variable. The best way to minimize effects that occur over time in a pretest-posttest design is to include a control group that takes the pretest and posttest at the same time as the experimental group but does not receive the treatment given to the experimental group. On average, effects of history (and other sources of bias) occur equally for the experimental and control groups, which allows the researcher based on a comparison of the groups to see the effects of the treatment in the experimental group.

Maturation. Another factor that can affect a study conducted over a period of time is maturation. Maturation occurs when participants exhibit natural changes over the course of a study. This can include actual maturation, as in developmental studies where individuals are observed at different ages, or other types of changes that occur to individuals over a period of time. For example, in the study described above to test several treatments for depression, suppose there are two groups of depressed participants: one group receives a drug therapy for 12 weeks, whereas the other group receives a talk therapy for 12 weeks. Suppose also that both groups showed the same amount of improvement over the 12-week period in their symptoms of depression. One possible interpretation of these data is that both

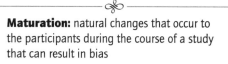

Maturation: natural changes that occur to the participants during the course of a study that can result in bias

Attrition/Mortality: occurs when participants choose not to complete a study

treatments are equally effective in improving symptoms of depression. However, another possible interpretation of these data is that symptoms of depression improve on their own without treatment (e.g., participants may become more hopeful about their lives if they know they are being treated) and that neither treatment is actually effective. In other words, maturation affected the data such that the participants improved as a natural consequence of factors that occurred during the 12 weeks in which the study was done.

As described above, the best way to minimize effects of maturation is to include a control group that does not receive the treatment to allow a comparison of groups that have similar experiences except for the treatment. In the treatment of depression study, this means adding a third group that has depression tested at the start of the 12 weeks and at the end of the 12 weeks but does not receive any treatment for their depression. (They should also be told that they are on the waiting list for receiving therapy so that any effects of knowing they will be receiving treatment can occur for the control group as well.) If the control group shows the same improvement as the two treatment groups, then maturation has likely occurred and participants have improved on their own and not as a result of the treatments. However, if the treatment groups show improvement above and beyond any improvement shown by the control group, then these improvements can more confidently be interpreted as due to the treatment the participants received.

Attrition. Attrition (also called mortality) occurs when participants drop out of a study after completing only part of the study. This is more likely to occur in long-term studies that are conducted over a period of time. Attrition results in data being deleted from a study (or a portion of a study). The particular problem with participants dropping out during a study is that it is possible that the participants who drop out of a study may have different characteristics from the participants who remain to complete a study, thus biasing the full set of data toward participants with the characteristics required for completing the study. For example, in the depression treatment study, suppose that some of the participants in the study drop out during the 12-week period and do not return for the posttest. It is possible that these participants who have chosen not to complete the study did so because they have worse depression symptoms than the participants who remained in the study (i.e., someone who is highly depressed may be less likely than someone who is not as highly depressed to return to the study to take the posttest). In this case, the data obtained in the study tell the researcher about the effects of treatment for individuals who are moderately depressed and not for individuals who are severely depressed because the severely depressed participants dropped out. It is also possible that participants drop out of this study because their depression symptoms improve and they feel they no longer need to continue treatment. Without knowing the cause of the attrition, the results of the study are even more difficult to interpret. Thus, attrition reduces the validity of the data by making it generalizable to only moderately depressed individuals.

As with the other sources of bias described above that occur over a time period, attrition is best handled by the inclusion of a control group. This spreads the attrition (on average) across the groups, and allows the researcher to make group comparisons to test the effect of the independent variable. However, the problem of generalizing the data to the larger population of interest (e.g., all individuals with depression symptoms) still remains. This is a problem with external validity (do the results generalize outside the study?), rather than one of internal validity that would occur if different numbers of individuals dropped out from the different groups, making the groups more unequal. We consider issues of external validity in the next chapter.

Stop and Think

(13.4) A researcher wants to evaluate the effect of a new set of teaching standards on 5th grade math scores. Explain how each of the sources of bias listed below could affect his results:

- testing effects
- history effects
- maturation
- attrition

CHAPTER SUMMARY

Reconsider the questions from the beginning of the chapter:

- What aspects of a quasi-experiment make it different from other research designs? A quasi-experiment can be similar in design to an experiment, but no true independent variable is manipulated in the study.
- What is required to test a causal relationship between variables? To test a causal relationship between variables, an independent variable must be manipulated such that the participants are assigned to levels of the independent variable by the researcher.

- What is a pretest-posttest design? In what way is it a quasi-experiment? A pretest-posttest design is a design in which the dependent variable is measured both before and after a treatment is implemented. It is a quasi-experiment because other factors may affect a change in scores besides the treatment (i.e., the third-variable problem). However, if a control group that does not receive the treatment is included with participants randomly assigned to the treatment or control group, the design becomes an experiment.
- What is a time series design? In what way is it a quasi-experiment? A time series design is similar to a pretest-posttest design in that the dependent variable is measured more than once. However, in a time series design, the dependent variable is measured many times over a period of time, which may or may not include a treatment. As with the pretest-posttest design, the pattern of scores examined in a time series design may be affected by factors other than the treatment.

THINKING ABOUT RESEARCH

A summary of a research study in psychology is given below. As you read the summary, think about the following questions:

1. What types of quasi-experimental designs were used in this study?

2. Can the researchers conclude that reading the books caused the higher sexual desire scores in the "Read" group? Why or why not? What about the decrease in sexual behavior scores shown by the women who read the books in the study?

3. What other factors do you think might contribute to the results of this study besides the reading of the books?

4. Why is this study considered a quasi-experiment instead of an experiment? How could the design be changed to create an experiment?

5. What are some of the disadvantages of comparing scores before and after a treatment, as was done for the "Not Read" group in this study?

Research Study. Reese-Weber, M., & McBride, D. M. (in press). The effects of sexually-explicit literature on sexual behaviors and desires of women. *Psychology of Popular Media Culture.* doi:10.1037/ppm0000044

Purpose of the Study. The researchers of this study investigated media claims that reading romantic fiction novels (e.g., *Fifty Shades of Grey*) increased women's sexual desires and behaviors. College women who had and had not read the *Fifty Shades of Grey* books were compared on self-reported sexual self-esteem, behaviors, and desires. Following media claims, it was hypothesized that those who had read the books would show higher scores on all sexual measures. In a second part of the study, the women who had not read the books were asked to do so. Their sexual self-esteem, behaviors, and desires were then measured again after reading the books to determine whether those scores increased after they read them.

Method of the Study. College women (*N* = 258) were recruited for the study. Each subject completed surveys asking about their sexual self-esteem (e.g., experience, skill), sexual behaviors (specific sexual behaviors they had previously engaged in), and sexual desires (willingness to engage in the sexual behaviors). Based on a question at the end of the survey about whether they had read the *Fifty*

Shades of Grey books, the women were separated into "Read" and "Not Read" groups. The "Not Read" subjects who agreed to continue the study (n = 49) were then asked to read the first two books in the trilogy. The three sexual measures were then repeated to examine a change in scores before and after reading the books.

Results of the Study. Results showed that only sexual desire scores were different between the groups. The "Read" group showed higher sexual desire scores than the "Not Read" group. However, sexual self-esteem and sexual behaviors did not differ between groups. For the "Not Read" group, no difference from pretest to posttest was found for sexual self-esteem or desire. Sexual behavior scores decreased from pre- to posttest.

Conclusions of the Study. The conclusions from this study were that no evidence was found to support media claims that women who read the *Fifty Shades of Grey* novels showed increased sexual desires or behaviors. In fact, the women in the "Not Read" group who read the books showed a decrease in sexual behaviors and no change in sexual self-esteem or desires after reading the books.

COMMON PITFALLS AND HOW TO AVOID THEM

Problem: Confusing experiments and quasi-experiments.

Solution: Carefully consider the design of a study. Are groups compared without random assignment to the groups? If so, the study is likely a quasi-experiment.

Problem: Difference between pretest-posttest designs and within-subjects designs—this distinction can be confusing.

Solution: A within-subjects design is any design with an independent variable manipulated such that all participants received all levels of the variable. A pretest-posttest design specifically involves measurement of the dependent variable both before and after a treatment has been implemented. A special case of the pretest-posttest design can involve randomly assigned treatment and control groups in an experiment. In this type of design, the time of test (pre- and post-) can be considered a within-subjects independent variable. However, this is only the case if both the treatment and control groups are included and participants are randomly assigned to the groups.

Problem: Confusing correlational studies and quasi-experiments.

Solution: The goals of these two types of research design are very different. In correlational studies, two or more dependent variables are measured with the goal of testing the relationship between the variables. In a quasi-experiment, the goal is typically to compare groups that are not randomly assigned or to examine the change in the dependent variable after a treatment has been implemented. Thus, an examination of the goal of the study and the types of results that are reported for the study helps you to distinguish these types of designs.

TEST YOURSELF

1. What aspects of a study allow tests of causal relationships?

2. In what way does a time series design differ from a simple pretest-posttest design that includes only one pretest and one posttest measure?

3. Choosing a research question of interest to you, design a quasi-experiment that uses the pretest-posttest with nonequivalent groups design. Describe how your study is to be conducted.

4. Describe a time series design that a researcher might conduct to investigate whether a change occurred in approval ratings of U.S. President Barrack Obama before and after the U.S. government's credit rating was downgraded in August 2011.

5. Describe three main sources of bias that can affect results in a quasi-experiment.

Answers can be found at edge.sagepub/mcbride3e.

STOP AND THINK ANSWERS

(13.1)   Answers will vary, but should involve testing before and after you try the technique.

(13.2)   In these designs, testing is always done multiple times. Thus, giving the same or a similar test more than once can result in fatigue or practice testing effects.

(13.3)   Answers will vary, but the quasi-experiment will involve either pre-existing groups or pretest-posttest without a control group and the experiment will involve random assignment to treatment groups.

(13.4)   Answers will vary.

⑤SAGE edge™

Visit edge.sagepub.com/mcbride3e for the tools you need to sharpen your study skills:

- Web Quizzes
- eFlashcards
- Thinking About Research
- SAGE Journal Articles
- Web and Multimedia Resources

Chapter 14

The Nuts and Bolts of Other Specialized Designs

Consider the following questions as you read Chapter 14

- Why do developmental psychologists need specialized designs?
- What are the differences between longitudinal, cross-sectional, and cohort-sequential designs?
- What role do small-*n* designs play in psychological research?

For many of the designs discussed elsewhere in this text, some context is provided to illustrate which areas of psychology are most likely to employ those design types. In this chapter, we consider two additional types of designs that were developed in specific areas of psychology to gain particular information about behavior. One set of specialized designs is used commonly by developmental psychologists to examine the differences in behavior across different-aged participants. The other type of design discussed in this chapter is the small-*n* design (this design was mentioned in Chapter 11 when we discussed the experiment with my dog, Daphne), one of the earliest designs employed by psychologists as they began to investigate basic processes involved in behavior. Small-*n* designs are now also commonly used in studies testing behavioral interventions. Each of these design types is introduced in this chapter.

DEVELOPMENTAL DESIGNS

There are three main types of developmental designs (see Figure 14.1 for where developmental designs fit into the steps in the research process) that treat the factor of age in a different way: longitudinal designs, cross-sectional designs, and cohort-sequential designs. Longitudinal designs treat age as a within-subjects variable (see Chapter 11 for more discussion of within-subjects variables). In a longitudinal design, participants are tested at different ages in their lives. For example, a single

Figure 14.1   Steps in the Research Process: Designing the Study

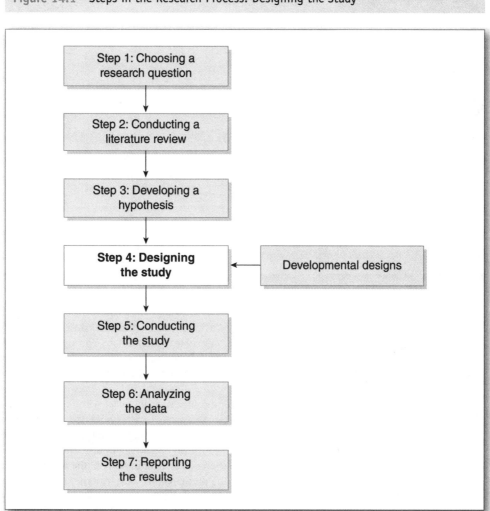

sample of participants may be tested at age 5, at age 10, at age 15, and at age 20. In other words, each participant provides observations at each of the ages tested in the study. Figure 14.2 illustrates the longitudinal design. This is how age is considered a within-subjects variable in the longitudinal design, although age is not an independent variable in this case because age cannot be manipulated.

Longitudinal Design: a developmental design where a single sample of participants is followed over time and tested at different ages

Within-Subjects Variable: each participant experiences all levels of the independent variable

Booth-LaForce and Oxford (2008) conducted a study that provides an example of a longitudinal design. Their study was designed to examine social withdrawal of children over time. Social withdrawal was measured by teacher reports of the students in the study each

Figure 14.2   Longitudinal Design: Same Sample Is Tested at Different Ages

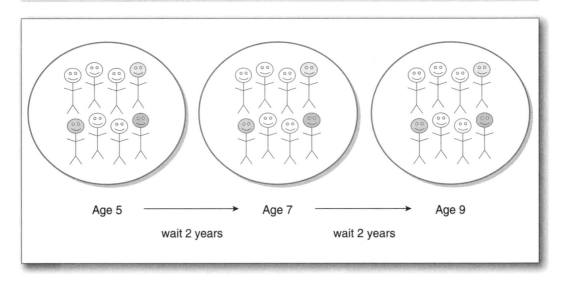

Attrition/Mortality: occurs when participants choose not to complete a study

Testing Effects: occur when participants are tested more than once in a study, with early testing affecting later testing

year while the students were in Grades 1 through 6. By tracking social withdrawal over time, the researchers were able to identify three groups of children: those not socially withdrawn, those who showed early social withdrawal and a decrease in social withdrawal over time, and those who did not show early withdrawal but showed increases in social withdrawal over time. The latter two groups each contained a small percentage of the sample. These researchers began recruiting the children for the study in 1991 at the time they were born but did not publish their study until 2008. Data collection in elementary schools took 6 years. This illustrates one of the disadvantages of the longitudinal design: It takes time to wait for the participants to age. Another disadvantage is that attrition/mortality (i.e., some participants do not complete the study) may occur over time as the study is conducted. Attrition can be a source of bias in the study if the participants who drop out are different from the participants who remain. Attrition can occur in longitudinal studies for various reasons. For example, participants may get tired of being in the study, or they may move and lose contact with the researchers. A third disadvantage is that testing effects can occur with multiple testings of the same participants. In other words, being tested on the measures early in the study can affect the later testings, as participants' scores can show effects of practice or of fatigue.

An alternative to treating age as a within-subjects variable, as in the longitudinal design, is to treat age as a between-subjects variable by testing different groups of participants of different ages with each participant tested only once for his or her age at the time of the study. Developmental designs that treat age as a between-subjects variable (see Chapter 11 for more discussion of between-subjects variables) are called cross-sectional designs. These designs compare different age groups of participants, where each participant contributes data for only one age group. Figure 14.3 illustrates the cross-sectional design.

Figure 14.3   Cross-Sectional Design: Different Samples Are Tested at Different Ages

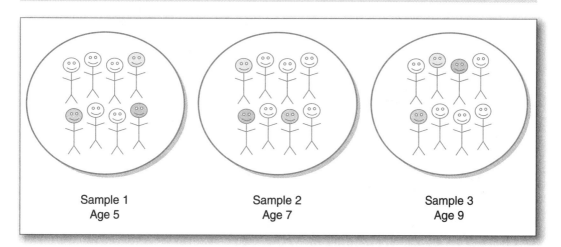

Sample 1   Sample 2   Sample 3
Age 5   Age 7   Age 9

Zimmerman, Gerson, Monroe, and Kearney (2007, Experiment 1) provide an example of a cross-sectional design in their study that investigated the development of students' understanding of their own knowledge of a topic area and how well their perceived knowledge matched their actual knowledge in that area. Junior high school, high school, and college students were tested on their comprehension in several topic areas: psychology, biology, chemistry, and physics. Students also provided a measure of their perceived knowledge in each topic area. The difference between the students' perceived and actual knowledge was calculated for each topic area and age group. Zimmerman et al. found that the difference between perceived and actual knowledge differed by age group. Whereas junior and high school students were fairly accurate at judging their knowledge in the topic areas, the college students underestimated their knowledge in physics and chemistry. In addition, all age groups overestimated their knowledge in psychology. In other words, the college students knew more about physics and chemistry than they thought they did, and all students knew less about psychology than they thought they did. This study showed that the accuracy of perceived knowledge may decrease with age and depends on topic area.

As you might imagine, the cross-sectional design solves many of the problems that can occur with longitudinal designs. Each participant is tested only once, which reduces the chance of attrition. In addition, because the researcher collects data from all age groups at the same time, the study can be completed more quickly with a cross-sectional design. However, there are some drawbacks to the cross-sectional design that are more problematic than in longitudinal designs. For example, if the age groups being tested contain participants from different generations, generation effects (also called cohort effects) might affect the results. These effects occur when the experiences of one generation (e.g., growing up with or without computers) are very different from those of another generation and affect the way the participants complete the task or

Between-Subjects Variable: each participant experiences only one level of the independent variable

Cross-Sectional Design: a developmental design where multiple samples of participants of different ages are tested once

Generation/Cohort Effects: a confound that can occur in cross-sectional designs due to different experiences that different generations have

Cohort-Sequential Design: a developmental design where multiple samples of participants of different ages are followed over time and tested at different ages

measure in the study. For example, if younger and older adults are tested with a survey presented on a computer, it is possible that the older adults may have more difficulty completing the survey because some may lack experience with computers. In other words, the older participants can exhibit lower scores than the younger participants that are not due to the difference in age between the groups.

The third type of developmental design combines elements of the longitudinal and cross-sectional designs. In a cohort-sequential design, age is treated as both a between-subjects and within-subjects factor. Cohort-sequential designs begin with separate samples of different age groups, as in a cross-sectional design. Then these age groups are tested multiple times as they develop to allow participants to be tested at multiple ages, as in a longitudinal design. Figure 14.4 illustrates the cohort-sequential design.

Chouinard and Roy (2008) conducted a cohort-sequential study to investigate the decline in motivation in math studies in high school students. A sample of 704 students in 7th grade and 625 students in 9th grade completed a scale that measured competency in math skills. All students were attending high schools in the Canadian area of Montreal, Quebec, at the time of the study. Repeated administration of the competency scale occurred twice a year for 3 years. Thus, when the study was completed, the students who were first tested in 7th grade had completed 9th grade, and the students who were first tested in 9th grade had completed 11th grade.

Results showed that math motivation declined over the 3-year period for the students, confirming the researchers' prediction that math motivation declines during high school years. In addition, although boys scored higher than girls initially, they showed a faster decline in motivation scores than girls. Thus, the decline in motivation appeared to affect boys more than it affected girls.

Whereas a cohort-sequential study takes time to complete because researchers must wait for the participants to age (e.g., it took 3 years to collect the data in the study described above), it allows researchers to compare ages quickly with the first testing of the different-aged samples. In addition, generation effects may be less problematic, because participants are also tested at multiple ages. Thus, in some cases, this design is preferable to either a longitudinal or a cross-sectional design.

Stop and Think

(14.1) For each description below, identify the type of developmental design used:

- A researcher tests groups of 1st graders, 5th graders, and 8th graders on their ability to correctly identify another person's intentions in a story.
- A group of 6-month-olds is tested every 6 months for 5 years on their fine motor skills.
- Groups of 3-year-olds and 10-year-olds are tested each year over 10 years on their ability to pay attention to a task.

(14.2) For each study described above, identify a source of bias that the researcher should consider.

Figure 14.4   Cohort-Sequential Design: Different Samples Are Tested at Multiple Times as They Age

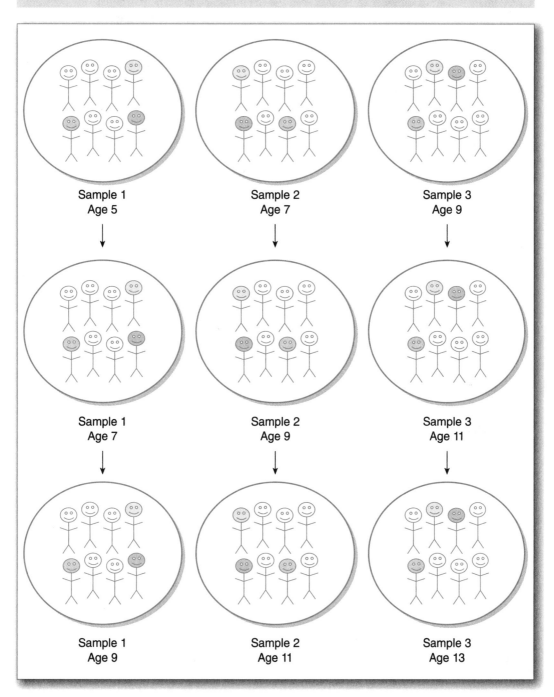

SMALL-*n* DESIGNS

Imagine a situation where a teacher identifies a child in a class who has behavioral problems. The child is disruptive in class during the lessons, and the teacher is frustrated. In an attempt to solve this problem, the teacher consults with a school psychologist, who conducts an experiment with a small-*n* design (see Figure 14.5) to determine if a treatment can be found that will change the disruptive student's behavior. The psychologist measures the student's disruptive behavior (e.g., number of times in a day the student talks in class without raising his or her hand) to determine the behavior rate that currently exists. This is called the baseline measurement. A treatment is then implemented (e.g., the student receives a sticker for each 15-min period that he or she stays quiet during the lesson), and the disruptive behavior is measured again. The school psychologist finds that the disruptive behavior decreases with the treatment. However, to be certain that it was the treatment that caused the behavior to change (and not some other extraneous factor), the treatment is then ended and disruptive behavior is measured again to take another baseline measurement. If the disruptive behavior returns without the treatment, then the psychologist can be fairly confident that the treatment works. The psychologist can then recommend the teacher use this methodology to change the student's behavior or the psychologist may elect to try the treatment one more time to make certain that the behavior is still affected by the treatment.

—————— ✤ ——————

Small-*n* Design: an experiment conducted with one or a few participants to better understand the behavior of those individuals

Baseline Measurement: measurement of behavior without a treatment used as a comparison

The example described above illustrates a current use of a small-*n* design. These designs are sometimes called single-subject or single-case designs, but they often include more than one participant; thus, small *n* is a better descriptor of this design type. The goal of a small-*n* study is to understand an individual's behavior, either to better describe the behavior as it occurs for many individuals or in order to change that behavior. Remember that in Chapter 3 we discussed a case study; this design is different from a case study in that the goal of a case study is to explore an individual's behavior when little is known about the behavior. In a small-*n* design, a researcher is typically testing a theory about how a behavior works for most individuals or testing a treatment for a problematic behavior of an individual or group of individuals. In a small-*n* design, this is accomplished through repeated measurement of behavior (Barlow & Hersen, 1984). The repeated measurement of behavior takes two forms: (1) discrete trials designs, where one or a few participants complete a large number of trials of a task to describe how performance on the task operates, and (2) baseline designs, where the repeated measurement of the baseline behavior of one or a few participants is compared with their behavior during the implementation of a treatment.

—————— ✤ ——————

Discrete Trials Design: a small-*n* design that involves a large number of trials completed by one or a few individuals and conducted to describe basic behaviors

Baseline Design: a small-*n* design that involves baseline measurements of behavior as compared with measures of behavior during the implementation of a treatment

The primary advantage of small-*n* designs comes from the large number of observations collected from one or a few participants. Using a large number of observations reduces the error in the data (seen in the low variability of the scores) and makes it easier for a researcher to detect an effect of an independent variable. Using a small number of participants also makes it easier for a researcher to control for

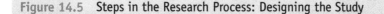

Figure 14.5   Steps in the Research Process: Designing the Study

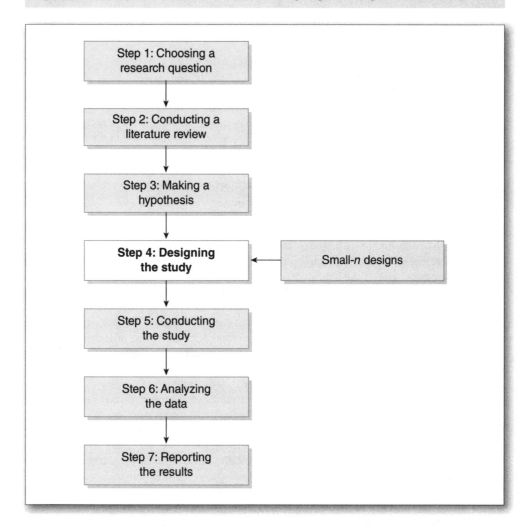

extraneous factors that may bias the data. This control increases the internal validity of the study. The main disadvantage to small-*n* designs is that the results cannot always be generalized to people outside the study. This is why they are typically used to study very basic behaviors (e.g., sensory processes, learning processes), where the behaviors being measured should be very similar from person to person, and for studies where the goal is to tailor a treatment to a specific person. In addition, small-*n* designs cannot be used to measure many types of behavior. Due to the large number of observations collected, carryover effects can occur for tasks that may affect future

Carryover Effects: occur when participants' experience in one condition affects their behavior in another condition of a study

performance over time. In other words, participants' experiences in the treatment condition can affect their later behavior in a second baseline condition that follows the treatment condition. Thus, researchers must consider these issues when choosing a small-n design.

Discrete Trials Designs

Some of the earliest studies in psychology used the discrete trials type of small-n design. Early psychologists, such as Weber, Fechner, Ebbinghaus, and Skinner, were interested in describing basic behaviors such as sensory stimulation, memory, and conditioning (Barlow & Hersen, 1984). They accomplished this through repeated measurement of these behaviors over an enormous number of trials with a small number of participants. Ebbinghaus, for example, conducted his studies of basic memory processes using himself as his subject. He repeatedly memorized nonsense syllables (FAL, JIV, etc.) to perfection and then measured his memory for these syllables after a period of time had passed. From his work, researchers learned that most of the forgetting that occurs for information is rapid, tapering off with longer delays (Neath & Surprenant, 2003).

Discrete trials designs help researchers describe basic behavioral processes, such as the way that information is forgotten in memory. This can be done with just a few participants who complete a very large number of trials because this method reduces the variability in the measurement of the behavior. Lower variability across trials (either within or across individual participants) increases the validity and reliability of the measurement of a behavior (see Chapters 6 and 7 for more discussion of the role of variability in the internal validity of a study). With the controls used in an experiment and the large amount of data collected under these conditions, discrete trials designs allow for good tests of causal relationships for behaviors where there are few individual differences. Thus, discrete trials designs tend to achieve stable measures of behavior with high internal validity.

In current psychological research, discrete trials designs are typically used by researchers who study the basic processes of psychophysics and learning, also called the *experimental analysis of behavior* (Barlow & Hersen, 1984). For example, Magoon and Critchfield (2008) conducted a small-n design to better understand the consequences of positive and negative reinforcement with consistent (all positive or all negative reinforcement) or inconsistent (a mix of positive and negative reinforcement) schedules. They tested a general prediction supported by past studies that avoiding aversive events (negative reinforcement) has a stronger effect on behavior than positive reinforcement. These researchers reported data from three participants who completed approximately 45 hr of a task involving mouse clicks with different positive and negative reinforcement schedules. Different mouse clicks earned participants money (positive reinforcement) or kept participants from losing money (negative reinforcement), depending on the session and reinforcement schedule.

Participants completed trials in short sessions, several days a week for a number of weeks. Thus, each participant completed a large number of trials to collect stable measurements of his or her behavior in a series of reinforcement conditions. With this large number of measurements of the participants' behavior for the different reinforcement conditions, the researchers were able to provide a mathematical description of behavior. In other words, they described the data with a mathematical function based on the prediction that negative reinforcement should affect behavior more than positive reinforcement. This type of data analysis allows better understanding of the processes involved in the behavior and better prediction of a change in behavior as a function of one of the variables. Mathematical description of behavior is often a common goal of discrete trials designs, which is possible with the large number of measurements collected of basic behaviors. By analyzing the individual participant data in this manner, Magoon and Critchfield (2008) showed that the positive and negative reinforcements affected task behavior in a similar way, indicating that the hypothesis described earlier was not supported.

Baseline Designs

As described above, baseline designs involve experimental comparison of baseline behavior and behavior with a treatment. The goal is to determine whether a treatment creates a desired change in the behavior of interest (often an undesirable behavior), a technique also called *behavior modification* (Barlow & Hersen, 1984). There are several ways that baseline designs can be conducted. In what is

> **A-B-A/Reversal Design:** a small-*n*, baseline design where the baseline behavior is measured, followed by implementation of a treatment, followed by another baseline measure after the treatment has ended

known as an A-B-A design or reversal design (Barlow & Hersen, 1984), the baseline measure of behavior (designated as Condition A) is first taken. Then the treatment (designated as Condition B) is implemented, and behavior is measured again, this time with the treatment. Finally, a baseline measure (A) is made again after the treatment has been stopped to determine if the baseline behavior appears once again after the treatment has been stopped. However, it is common in such designs for behavior to approach baseline levels but not fully achieve initial baseline levels after a treatment has been implemented (Barlow & Hersen, 1984). In other words, the effect of the treatment may carry over into the second baseline measure. A common variant of this procedure is the A-B-A-B design, where the treatment is then implemented a second time to determine if the behavior still changes with implementation of the treatment.

Tasky, Rudrud, Schulze, and Rapp (2008) conducted a study using a variant of the A-B-A design. They were interested in testing a treatment to improve task behavior for individuals who had suffered a brain injury. Three participants receiving inpatient rehabilitation after suffering brain trauma due to a car accident participated in the study. The goal of the study was to increase completion of tasks by the participants through a treatment that allowed the participants to choose which tasks they wished to complete during the session. Time on task was compared for the choice treatment and the baseline conditions, where tasks were assigned by the experimenter. An A-B-A-B design was used, with a modified baseline condition for the second baseline measurement. The second baseline was modified to assign tasks to the participants that they had chosen during the first treatment session. Figure 14.6 illustrates the results for each condition by participant. The graphs show that for each participant, the choice sessions increased time on task compared with the two baseline conditions. Thus, the researchers reported results supporting the idea that the treatment they tested was effective in improving the time all patients spent on the tasks they were given.

Data Analysis in Small-*n* Designs

Because there are no group means to present in small-*n* designs, data are often presented for the individual participants in the study (with no identifying information to protect their confidentiality). In fact, the graph seen in Figure 14.6 is a common method of reporting results from small-*n* designs,

Figure 14.6   On-Task Results for the Participants in Tasky et al.'s (2008) Study

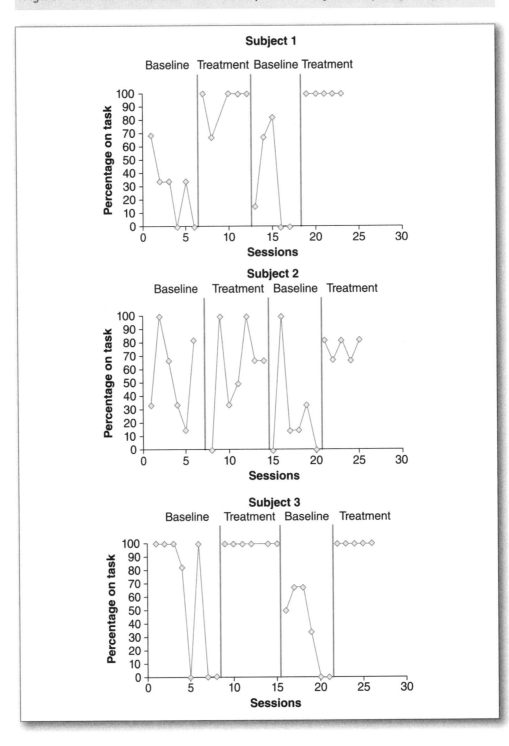

especially for baseline designs (Rosenthal & Rosnow, 2008). Inferential statistics can only be used in baseline designs if a large number of observations are collected for each individual. Inferential statistics are sometimes reported for discrete trials designs for within-subjects variables that are manipulated in these types of designs. It is common, though, for researchers to report mathematical descriptions of behavior in discrete trials designs, as in the example presented above by Magoon and Critchfield (2008).

> ### Stop and Think
>
> (14.3)   Explain why small-*n* designs are also experiments.
>
> (14.4)   Describe the difference between discrete trials designs and baseline designs. What is the primary purpose of each of these designs?

CHAPTER SUMMARY

Reconsider the questions from the beginning of the chapter:

- Why do developmental psychologists need specialized designs? Developmental psychologists use specialized designs to allow them to examine different types of age effects in a study. Because age cannot be manipulated as a true independent variable, many of these designs are quasi-experiments that compare age across participant groups or within participant groups longitudinally.
- What are the differences between longitudinal, cross-sectional, and cohort-sequential designs? The primary difference in these designs is in how age is treated as a variable. In longitudinal designs, behavior is compared at different ages for a single group of participants over time. In a cross-sectional design, behavior is compared for different groups of participants of different ages. In cohort-sequential designs, different groups of participants of different ages (cohorts) are tested over time to see a change in behavior for each group as they age.
- What role do small-*n* designs play in psychological research? Small-*n* designs allow psychologists to test laws of behavior (often in mathematical form) and to test treatments that might be effective for a single participant or a small group of participants. These two goals are met in discrete trials and baseline designs, respectively.

THINKING ABOUT RESEARCH

A summary of a research study in psychology is given below. As you read the summary, think about the following questions:

1. What type of developmental design was used in this study? Explain your answer.

2. What are the advantages of the developmental design type used in this study? What are the disadvantages?

3. Was the study an experiment (see Chapter 11) or quasi-experiment (see Chapter 13)? How do you know?

4. What types of extraneous factors can affect the results in this study? Explain how each factor may have caused the results found by the researchers.

Research Study. Peña, M., Arias, D., & Dehaene-Lambertz, G. (2014). Gaze following is accelerated in healthy preterm infants. *Psychological Science, 25,* 1884–1892. (NOTE: Experiment 1 of this study is described below.)

Purpose of the Study. The researchers conducted a study to investigate whether preterm infants (i.e., those born before the full 9 months) show advanced abilities to follow another person's gaze. They point out that gaze following is an important communication tool in humans; thus, developing this ability is important in infants trying to connect with the people in their environment. They suggest that because preterm infants have additional time to interact with other humans than full-term infants, by the age of 7 months they should show more sensitivity to others' gaze.

Method of the Study. Four groups of healthy infants were included in the study. Infants were grouped as full-term 4-month-olds (FT4), preterm 7-month-olds (PT4), full-term 7-month-olds (FT7), or preterm 10-month-olds (PT7). The age in parentheses represents their developmental age from conception. Thus, the FT4 and PT4 groups both experienced the same length of time for development, but the PT4 infants had been exposed to human eye gaze for an additional 3 months as compared to the FT4 infants. If this exposure made a difference, the PT4 infants should show better gaze following abilities than the FT4 infants. If time for development is all that matters, these groups should show similar abilities.

Each group included between 19 and 23 infants. Infants were shown videos of adult women. The women first directed their gaze at the infant. Then the woman in the video looked at a blank white square on either the left or the right of the screen. Figure 14.7 shows the trial sequence seen by the infants. Toys then moved across both of the white squares to capture the infant's attention. Infants completed 20 of these trials. Their gaze was recorded by an eye-tracking device. The direction the infant first gazed in when the toys appeared was recorded to determine if it was the same direction as the woman's gaze.

Results of the Study. Figure 14.8 displays the proportion of correct gaze direction results for each age group. As the graph shows, the FT4 infants who had 3 months less exposure to humans than the PT4 group (but the same development time since conception) showed lower correct gaze direction than the other groups.

Figure 14.7   Trial Sequence Used in the Study

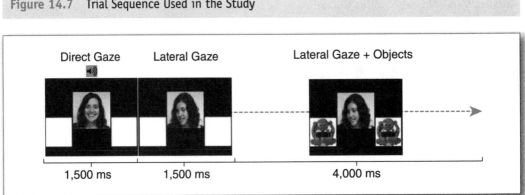

SOURCE: From Peña et al. (2014).

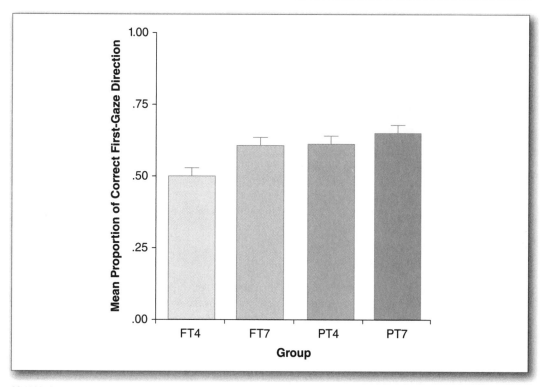

Figure 14.8   Mean Proportion Correct Gazes by Group

SOURCE: From Peña et al. (2014).

Conclusions of the Study. From these results, the researchers concluded that the additional experience that preterm infants have with humans provides a benefit in development of gaze following abilities. They note that longitudinal studies are needed to examine the influence of the early development of this ability on social communication.

COMMON PITFALLS AND HOW TO AVOID THEM

Problem: Distinguishing experiments and quasi-experiments—developmental designs can be experiments or quasi-experiments.

Solution: In a developmental design, age is included as a subject or quasi-experimental variable. Thus, if there is no manipulated variable, the design is a quasi-experiment. However, in some cases, researchers are interested in how the effects of a manipulated independent variable change for different ages. In these cases, the design is an experiment, because a true independent variable is included along with the age variable.

Problem: Assuming causal effects of age—it can be tempting to conclude that age effects on behavior are causal.

Solution: Remember that age cannot be manipulated as an independent variable. Thus, the third-variable problem (see Chapters 3, 10, and 11) is always possible for effects of age on behavior. There are alternative explanations for a change in behavior with age.

TEST YOURSELF

Match the descriptions below with the correct design type:

(a) longitudinal, (b) cross-sectional, (c) cohort-sequential, (d) discrete trials small-n design, (e) baseline small-n design.

1. Two participants each complete 5,000 trials of a cognitive task to mathematically describe performance on the task.

2. Separate groups of 9-year-olds, 20-year-olds, and 50-year-olds complete a personality survey to determine if scores change with age.

3. Three-year-olds are recruited for a study that measures social skills as the participants age. Each participant is tested at age 3, 16, 25, and 35 to determine how social skills develop over time.

4. A schoolchild who displays anxiety during math lessons participates in a study to test the effectiveness of an anxiety-reducing treatment. The anxious behaviors are measured before the treatment is implemented, while the treatment is being implemented, and then again without the treatment to compare anxious behaviors in the different conditions.

5. Participants born in the years 1960, 1980, and 2000 are tested initially on their vocabulary and spelling abilities. Then, each group is tested every 10 years to determine whether the participants' initial abilities change as they age.

Answers can be found at edge.sagepub/mcbride3e.

STOP AND THINK ANSWERS

(14.1)   Cross-sectional, longitudinal, cohort-sequential

(14.2)   Answers will vary, but cross-sectional designs may have generational/cohort effects and longitudinal designs may have attrition and testing effects.

(14.3)   Small-n designs are typically conducted with within-subjects independent variables, making them experiments.

(14.4)   Discrete trials designs typically examine fundamental processes of behavior that operate similarly across individuals (i.e., few or no individual differences). Baseline designs are typically used to examine the effectiveness of an intervention on an individual's behavior.

⑨SAGE edge™

Visit edge.sagepub.com/mcbride3e for the tools you need to sharpen your study skills:

- Web Quizzes
- eFlashcards
- Thinking About Research

- SAGE Journal Articles
- Web and Multimedia Resources

Chapter 15

The Nuts and Bolts of Using Statistics

Consider the following questions as you read Chapter 15

- Which statistical tests are best for different research designs?
- How do we choose an appropriate statistical test?
- How do we use SPSS to run statistical tests?
- What information is provided in an SPSS output?

Every time I teach statistics and research methods courses, one of the most difficult things for students to master is knowing how to choose an appropriate statistical test for a particular research design. There are many research designs to keep track of and several different common statistical tests used to understand data from these designs, so this process can sometimes seem confusing and overwhelming. The goal of this chapter is to simplify this process, to help you understand what kinds of tests are appropriate for different types of research designs and measurement scales, to help you choose an appropriate statistical test for a study, and to instruct you in using SPSS software to analyze data (Figure 15.1). In Chapter 7, the conceptual logic of inferential statistics was described generally for hypothesis tests. In this chapter, the discussion focuses on specific tests and how they are calculated. However, the current discussion builds on concepts covered in Chapter 7; thus, you should review Chapter 7 before reading this chapter.

❧

Null Hypothesis: the hypothesis that an effect or relationship does not exist (or exists in the opposite direction of the alternative hypothesis) in the population

Recall from Chapter 7 that depending on what type of research question a study is intended to answer, hypothesis tests are designed to look for evidence against the null hypothesis that predicts no difference between conditions or no relationship between variables. This evidence comes in the form of extreme scores in the distribution of the statistic for scores

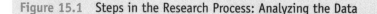

Figure 15.1   Steps in the Research Process: Analyzing the Data

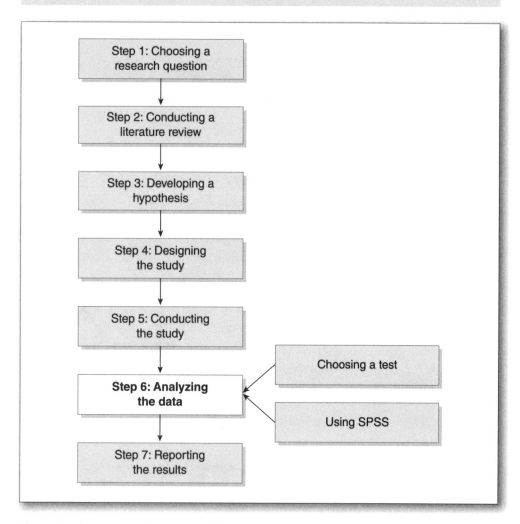

obtained when the null hypothesis is true. When we conduct the statistical test based on the data from our study, our calculated statistic is compared with this distribution to determine whether our value is extreme or uncommon when the null hypothesis is true. If our calculated statistic falls in the most extreme portion of this distribution, called the critical region, we have enough evidence to reject the null hypothesis and accept the scientific/alternative hypothesis that there

---

Critical Region: the most extreme portion of a distribution of statistical values for the null hypothesis, determined by the alpha level (typically 5%)

Scientific/Alternative Hypothesis: the hypothesis that an effect or relationship exists (or exists in a specific direction) in the population

Figure 15.2   Statistical Test Decision Flow Chart

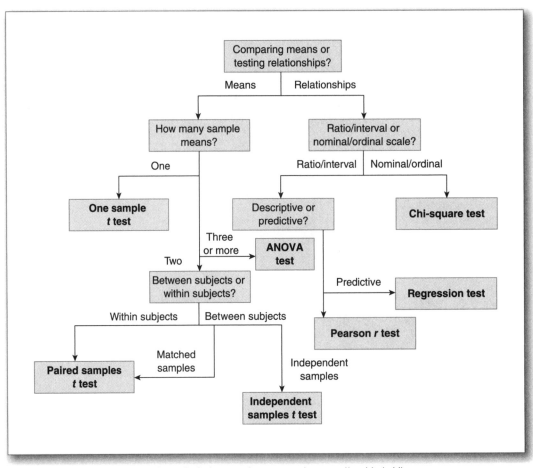

NOTE: Answer each question about the study design to arrive at a test (tests are listed in bold).

Significant Test: the *p* value is less than or equal to alpha in an inferential test, and the null hypothesis can be rejected

---

is a difference or relationship. In other words, our test is significant because we have rejected the null hypothesis. We now turn our discussion to the specific statistics that are used for some of the research designs we have discussed, including how those statistics are calculated. The type of statistical test chosen depends on the type of hypothesis researchers make for a study. Certain tests are used to test hypotheses regarding group differences and other tests are used to test hypotheses regarding relationships. See Chapter 7 for a discussion of how to state these types of hypotheses. Figure 15.2 provides a flow chart to help you choose the appropriate statistic for your study. This figure is referenced as we discuss the different tests highlighted in the chart. Also note that all data examples in this chapter can be found as SPSS files on the student website. Additional practice data files are also available on this site.

COMPARING GROUPS OR CONDITIONS

In experiments and quasi-experiments, hypotheses about effects are often tested by comparing groups (e.g., men and women) or conditions (e.g., visual presentation and auditory presentation). A significant difference between groups or conditions allows researchers to conclude that an effect exists in the population because they are able to reject the null hypothesis in a significant test. Sample mean differences can be caused by the effect, by sampling error, or both. Thus, statistical tests for effects are based on a ratio of the size of the difference in the sample means (that may contain both the treatment effect and sampling error) and sampling error to allow us to determine what part of the mean difference is

---

Power: ability of a significance test to detect an effect or relationship when one exists (equal to 1—the probability of a Type II error)

---

due to the effect and what part is due to sampling error. The size of the statistic calculated is determined by the treatment effect because the sampling error in the denominator of the equation is reduced by the numerator of the equation according to how much error is in the data. In other words, a larger statistical value indicates a larger treatment effect because it represents the sample mean difference due just to the effect (i.e., sampling error has been removed in the ratio). Larger statistical values also lead to more power to detect effects with the test (see Chapter 7 for more discussion of power). Thus, reducing error can help increase power in a design. In equation form, the statistical value is expressed as follows:

$$\text{Statistic} = \text{Sample mean difference}$$

$$\text{Sampling error}$$

As described above, the chance of obtaining this statistical value when the null hypothesis is true is then determined by looking for evidence against the null hypothesis (i.e., a very low probability of obtaining this statistical value when the null hypothesis is true). The distribution of statistical values when the null hypothesis is true is used to determine the p value for the value calculated in the test. If the p value for the statistic is less than or equal to the alpha level, the null hypothesis is rejected, and the researchers conclude that there is an effect. When researchers reject the null hypothesis, this means they have evidence for the alternative hypothesis and can conclude that it is supported by their study. If the p value is greater than the alpha level, the researchers cannot reject the null hypothesis and must conclude that there is no evidence of an effect. Remember, though, that you cannot conclude that there is no effect—the test does not provide evidence *for* the null hypothesis.

In inferential tests, sampling error is estimated from measures of variability in the sample. Variability of the sample indicates the amount of sampling error present because samples with high variability are less likely to be good representations of the population. The more the scores differ from one another, the less they resemble the population mean. Thus, samples with high variability typically have a larger margin of error in the population mean estimate (i.e., larger sampling error). This occurs because samples with high variability often contain extreme scores that can affect the sample mean, producing a sample mean that is dissimilar to the population mean. However, samples with low variability contain scores that are similar to one another and are more likely to represent the population mean. Thus, if variability in a sample is high, there is likely to be more sampling error. This is why measures of variability are used for estimates of sampling error in inferential statistics. To view details of the calculations of the tests, see the Appendix.

Stop and Think

(15.1)   Explain what power is in the context of a statistical test.

(15.2)   How is sampling error estimated in an inferential statistical test?

Comparing Two Means With *t* Tests

The appropriate significance test to use to compare two means is a *t* test. There are three types of *t* tests used to compare means: the one-sample *t* test, the independent samples *t* test, and the repeated measures (or paired samples) *t* test (see Table 15.1 for a comparison of some of the commonly used inferential significance tests and the left portion of Figure 15.2 for the decisions leading to the use of the different *t* tests). A one-sample *t* test is often used when the population mean without a treatment is known and is being compared with a sample mean that represents the population with a treatment. Population means are known for certain types of variables, such as standardized tests that were given to samples in the past or were designed to have a specific population mean. For example, IQ (Intelligent Quotient) tests have a population mean of 100. Thus, if a researcher wants to determine if a treatment (e.g., a new drug) has an effect on IQ scores, he or she can collect IQ scores for a sample with that treatment and compare the sample mean with the known population mean of 100. The one-sample *t* test is designed for this situation. Another use of this test is when chance performance is the comparison value. Suppose participants complete an experiment where objects are presented subliminally during a task (e.g., Coke ads are flashed at very fast rates during movie ads). Participants are then given a recognition test for images of the ads, where two images are presented and participants must choose which one of the two was presented. If participants are able to process the subliminal ads, then their performance should be above chance (50 %). If the ads were not processed and the participants are only guessing, then their performance should be similar to chance. Thus, the one-sample *t* test can be used to compare the mean recognition rate for the subliminal ads to the chance level of 50 %.

The independent samples *t* test is used when two samples of different individuals are compared. Each sample represents the population for that group or condition. Thus, there are two sample means that are compared in the test. For example, if researchers are interested in differences in depression scores between men and women, they would collect a sample of men and a sample of women and compare the two sample means for depression scores. Each sample represents the population for that group. The independent samples *t* test determines whether the sample means are significantly different in this case.

If two related samples (e.g., each individual in one sample is matched with one individual in the other sample on some characteristic) or two sets of scores from the same individual (i.e., the

---

— ✌ —

***t* Test:** significance test used to compare means

Table 15.1   Some Common Inferential Statistics and Their Uses

Statistical Test	What It Tests	When to Use It
One-sample t test	An effect	When the population mean without the treatment is known and is compared with a single sample
Independent samples t test	An effect	When two samples of different individuals are compared
Repeated measures/paired samples t test	An effect	When two related samples or two sets of scores from the same individual are compared
ANOVA	An effect	When more than two samples or sets of scores from the same individual are compared
Pearson r test	A relationship	When the relationship between two sets of scores is being tested
Regression	A relationship	When you want to predict an individual's score on one variable from the score on a second, related variable

individual provides scores in more than one condition) are compared, a repeated measures (also called a paired samples) t test is used. If two sample means are related from matched individuals or the same individual, the variability is likely to be lower, and an effect is more likely to be detected (i.e., the test has more power) than if the samples are independent. In other words, these designs produce less error in the data than comparable between-subjects designs and, thus, have more power to detect effects that exist. In t tests, the standard deviation of the samples is used in the calculation of the sampling error for the denominator of the statistics equation.

Using SPSS® to Conduct t Tests

When researchers conduct inferential statistics tests, they rarely conduct the tests with hand calculations (however, see the Appendix for how to hand-calculate the tests so that you will understand how these tests are conducted). Instead, most researchers use a statistical software package, such as SPSS, to conduct the tests. The software package takes the raw data the researcher inputs, calculates descriptive statistics, and conducts significance tests that the researcher specifies. In other words, to use the software package to conduct inferential statistics tests, the researcher needs to know which tests are appropriate for the study, choose these tests in the software, and interpret the output that the software package generates for the tests. The output typically includes descriptive values (e.g., means, standard deviations), the value of the test statistic calculated (e.g., t, F, r), and the p value associated with the statistical value calculated. Researchers still need to compare the p value in the output to their chosen alpha level (usually .05) in order to determine whether a test is significant so that they are able to make a decision

> **Alpha Level:** the probability level used by researchers to indicate the cutoff probability level (highest value) that allows them to reject the null hypothesis

about the null hypothesis. In most cases, the software package does not indicate if a test is significant in the output for the test. Thus, even though the software package completes the calculations, researchers still need to have a good working knowledge of statistics and how to use them in order to ensure that they use the software and interpret their data correctly.

SPSS is a software package commonly used by psychologists to conduct statistical tests. Accordingly, we focus on some of the basics of using this software. Different versions of SPSS may have a slightly different look, but the basic operations discussed in this chapter of typing in data and running the tests are very similar from version to version.

When you first open the SPSS program, you see a window that allows you to choose to open saved data files or type in data into the Data Window. For the examples in this chapter, choose the *type in data* option to follow along. The Data Window looks like a large spreadsheet when it opens. There are tabs at the top that can be defined for different variables and cells for typing in data. Data can be typed in as numbers or strings of letters. The most important thing to remember about typing in data to the Data Window is that data from each individual participant (or matched set of participants) should be typed in across the rows. In other words, all the data from one participant or set of matched participants are contained in a single row. Thus, you need to be familiar with your design before you type in your data. We begin with a single group design that compares the sample mean with a known population mean to use the one-sample *t* test (see chart in Example 1).

One-Sample *t* Test

Example 1. Suppose that the example described above to determine if participants process and remember subliminal ads was conducted with 10 participants. Percentage correct recognition scores for each participant are as given below:

Participant 1	56
Participant 2	60
Participant 3	49
Participant 4	35
Participant 5	51
Participant 6	65
Participant 7	70
Participant 8	44
Participant 9	58
Participant 10	47

The sample mean is compared with the chance value of 50% that is expected if the participants are merely guessing in the recognition test. Looking at the chart in Figure 15.2, you can see that the one-sample *t* test is appropriate for this example, because there is one sample mean to be compared with a known population mean.

In the first column of the Data Window, begin by typing in the data above, one score per row. Although different versions of SPSS differ in appearance, your Data Window should look similar to this:

	VAR0001
1	56.00
2	60.00
3	49.00
4	35.00
5	51.00
6	65.00
7	70.00
8	44.00
9	58.00
10	47.00

It is a good idea to label the column as the dependent variable, so choose the Variable View tab at the bottom of the Data Window. You will see a space to name the variable for each column in the Data Window. Then simply type in a name for the variable in the first cell (e.g., "recog" for recognition scores). You can also include longer descriptions in the Label cell for that variable.

	Name	Type	Width	Decimals
1	recog	Numeric	8	2

To conduct the one-sample *t* test for these data, choose "Compare Means" from the "Analyze" menu at the top. The "Analyze" menu contains the options for the different tests and descriptive statistics a researcher may want to calculate for his or her design. Select the "One-sample *t*-test" option in the menu of tests. The window that opens allows you to click the data column into the "Test Variable" position on the right to indicate that this column contains the dependent variable to be analyzed. You also need to indicate the known mean for comparison in the "Test Value" box. For Example 1, the test value is 50 (for the chance value of 50%). When you click the "OK" button, the analysis begins automatically, and the output appears in a separate Output Window. A view of the output window can be seen in Figure 15.3.

The output from the test contains several important values. The sample mean can be seen in the first box along with the standard deviation. These are the standard descriptive statistics

Figure 15.3   Output Window From the One-Sample *t* Test in Example 1

t Test

One-Sample Statistics

	N	Mean	Std. Deviation	Std. Error Mean
Recognition Scores	10	53.5000	10.40566	3.29056

One-Sample Test

	Test Value = 50					
					95% Confidence Interval of the Difference	
	t	*df*	Sig. (two-tailed)	Mean Difference	Lower	Upper
Recognition Scores	1.064	9	.315	3.50000	–3.9438	10.9438

---❦---

Degrees of Freedom: number of scores that can vary in the calculation of a statistic

included in the output for a *t* test. The *t* test values are included in the second box in the output. The *t* value (1.064 for Example 1), the degrees of freedom (abbreviated *df,* calculated from the sample size), and the *p* value listed in the Sig. column of the box. The default test is a two-tailed test in SPSS for *t* tests, but you can convert the value to a one-tailed test by dividing the *p* value in half if the means differ in the predicted direction (the one-tailed test has a critical region at one end of the *t* distribution that is twice the size of the critical region for a two-tailed test—thus, the one-tailed test has a *p* value that is half the *p* value for the two-tailed test). The *p* value in the output for Example 1 is .315. In Example 1, if there is an effect, we expect the mean recognition score to be higher than 50%. In other words, a one-tailed test is warranted. Thus, we must divide the given *p* value in half to obtain a *p* = .1575 for this one-tailed *t* test. As this value is *not* equal to or lower than alpha of .05 (the standard alpha level used in psychological research), the null hypothesis cannot be rejected and must be retained. In other words, there is no evidence that participants in the sample experiment remembered the subliminal ads because their performance was not better than what is expected by chance. If you need to report the outcome of this test in APA style, you might include a statement such as "The mean recognition score for subliminal ads (*M* = 53.50) was not significantly higher than the chance value of 50%, *t*(9) = 1.06, *p* = .16, one-tailed." The statistical values (rounded here to two significant digits) are stated as support for a statement about the results of the study. If a two-tailed hypothesis had been made for this study, then the result would be reported as "not significantly different."

Independent Samples *t* Test

The other two *t* tests are conducted in a similar manner. As another example (see chart in Example 2), suppose that in the study in Example 1, the researcher predicted a differ-

Between-Subjects Variable: each participant experiences only one level of the independent variable

Quasi-Independent/Subject Variable: variable that allows comparison of groups of participants without manipulation (i.e., no random assignment)

ence between men and women in how well subliminal ads are remembered. Thus, in Example 2, samples of each gender are compared. An examination of the chart in Figure 15.2 indicates that the independent samples *t* test is appropriate for this design. There are two sample means, and the design is considered between-subjects, because the samples are from different, unrelated participants. However, in this case gender is a quasi-independent or subject variable rather than a manipulated independent variable. The data for this study are given below.

Men		Women	
Participant 1	56	Participant 11	70
Participant 2	60	Participant 12	68
Participant 3	49	Participant 13	41
Participant 4	35	Participant 14	50
Participant 5	51	Participant 15	32
Participant 6	65	Participant 16	72
Participant 7	70	Participant 17	41
Participant 8	44	Participant 18	61
Participant 9	58	Participant 19	39
Participant 10	47	Participant 20	55

Example 2. Independent Samples t *Test.* The data for the men in the example are the same as data for the sample in Example 1. To add the data for the women to the SPSS Data Window, type them in the same column as the men in Rows 11 through 20. In Column 2, you need to indicate which sample the data belong to. You can code Rows 1 through 10 in the second column with a "1" for men and Rows 11 through 20 with a "2" for women. In the Variable View, you can define these groups by indicating labels for each number in the Values column for this variable. Select the values cell for this variable and click on the gray box to open the definition window. You should also name this variable (e.g., gender).

To conduct the independent samples *t* test for these data, go back to the "Compare Means" tab in the "Analyze" menu and choose the "Independent-samples *t*-test" option. The test window allows you to click on the recognition score column as the Test Variable and the gender

---

Homogeneity of Variances: assumption of between-subjects *t* tests and ANOVAs that the variance in the scores in the population is equal across groups

Within-Subjects Variable: each participant experiences all levels of the independent variable

---

codes as the Grouping Variable. You must then choose "Define Groups" to indicate that the values in this column range from 1 to 2. When you click "OK," the test automatically runs and the output appears in the Output Window (see Figure 15.4). The first box in the output provides descriptive statistics for each group. The second box contains the test statistic and *p* value. For Example 2, the *t* value is .107 and the *p* value (see in the Sig. column) is .916. This is a two-tailed test (it is possible that either men or women could have higher recognition scores) so the *p* value given can be directly compared with alpha. Once again, the *p* value is not equal to or lower than the alpha of .05, and the null hypothesis cannot be rejected. Thus, there is no evidence in these data that men and women differ in their memories for subliminal ads.

Notice that there are two rows of values for the *t* statistic for the independent samples test. The first row is labeled "Equal variances assumed," and the second row is labeled "Equal variances not assumed." These statements refer to the homogeneity of variances, which is an assumption of between-subjects tests (*t* tests and ANOVAs). The assumption is that the variance of the scores in the population is equal across the groups. If this assumption is violated, the *t* test may be inaccurate. Thus, Levene's test for this assumption is provided in the output (left side of the second box). If this test is significant (comparing *p* to alpha), then the statistical values need to be adjusted, and the second row of values in this box should be used. The two rows in this box are given to allow for both possibilities.

Paired Samples *t* Test

To illustrate the paired samples *t* test, suppose that in Example 1 the researcher was interested in comparing memory for two types of subliminal material: standard ads (e.g., Coke ads) and emotional ads (e.g., ads with a sexy model). Thus, in Example 3, one sample of participants is tested for their recognition of both standard ads and emotional ads. The chart in Figure 15.2 leads us to the paired samples *t* test for this example because the two sample means are from the same participants, making this study type a within-subjects variable. The data for Example 3 are at the left.

Example 3. Paired Samples t *Test.* To set up the Data Window, you need two columns of data, one for each condition. Remember that each row in the Data Window represents one participant; thus the pair of scores for an individual participant appears in the same row. Define the variables according to the conditions (e.g., standard ads and emotional ads). To run the test, choose the "Paired-samples *t* test" in the "Compare Means" portion of the "Analyze" menu. To compare the two conditions, click the first one to add it as "Variable 1" and then the second condition as "Variable 2." Then, click the arrow to add them as a "Paired Variable." When you click "OK," the test runs, and the output appears in the Output Window.

Participant No.	Standard Ads	Emotional Ads
1	56	71
2	60	59
3	49	66
4	35	78
5	51	49
6	65	82
7	70	77
8	44	52
9	58	51
10	47	78

t Test

Independent Samples Test

		Levene's Test for Equality of Variances		*t*-test for Equality of Means						95% Confidence Interval of the Difference	
		F	Sig.	t	df	Sig (2-tailed)	Mean Difference	Std.Error Difference		Lower	Upper
Recognition Scores	Equal variances assumed	2.217	.154	.107	18	.916	.6000	5.62870		−11.225	12.4255
	Equal variances not assumed			.107	16.361	.916	.60000	5.62870		−11.311	12.5109

Group Statistics

	Gender	N	Mean	Std. Deviation	Std. Error Mean
Recognition Scores	Men	10	53.5000	10.40566	3.29056
	Women	10	52.9000	14.44107	4.56667

The output indicates descriptive statistics in the first box and the test statistic and p value in the third box (see Figure 15.5). For Example 3, the t value is -2.624 with a p value of .028. For this example, the p value is lower than alpha of .05. Thus, the null hypothesis (that there is no difference between the ad types) can be rejected and the alternative hypothesis (that there is a difference between the ad types) can be accepted. The means indicate which ad type was remembered better: In this case, the emotional ads ($M = 66.3$) were remembered better than the standard ads ($M = 53.5$), $t(9) = -2.62$, $p = .03$. The second box of the output provides a test of the relationship between the two sets of scores (see below for more information about tests for relationships).

Stop and Think

(15.3) For each description below, indicate which t test would be most appropriate for analyzing the data:

- A researcher matches two groups of subjects on their average GPA. Then the groups are compared on their memory scores after studying a list of words. Group 1 sleeps for 8 hours after study, and Group 2 stays awake for 8 hours after study.
- Subjects are randomly assigned to either a treatment group or a control group. Their scores on a depression questionnaire are then compared.
- An ACT practice class compares the mean scores on the test for students who took the class with the known mean of 18 on the test for all students who took the test that year.
- Subjects are tested on time to complete a Sudoku puzzle both with and without caffeine.

Multivalent Variable: an independent variable that includes three or more levels—a design is considered multivalent if there is only one independent variable that contains three or more levels

Factorial Design: an experiment or quasi-experiment that includes more than one independent variable

Analysis of Variance (ANOVA): inferential test used for designs with three or more sample means

Comparing More Than Two Means With ANOVA

When more than two means are being compared, such as with multivalent variables or factorial designs (see Chapters 5, 11, and 12 for more discussion of these design types), the difference between the means becomes a bit more complicated to calculate (see the Appendix for calculations). Analysis of variance (ANOVA) is used to test an effect when more than two groups or conditions are being considered. The average variance is used in the calculation of mean differences and sampling error, which is why the test is called *analysis of variance*. An F statistic is calculated for each effect tested based on the ratio of average variance between the condition means and the average variance within the conditions. The calculated F statistic is compared with the distribution of F values when the null hypothesis is true to determine the corresponding p value

Figure 15.5 Output Window From the Paired-Samples *t* Test in Example 3

t Test

Paired Samples Statistics

		Mean	N	Std. Deviation	Std. Error Mean
Pair 1	Standard Ads	53.5000	10	10.40566	3.29056
	Emotional Ads	66.3000	10	12.68464	4.01123

Paired Samples Correlations

		N	Correlation	Sig.
Pair 1	Standard Ads and Emotional Ads	10	.118	.745

Paired Samples Test

		Paired Differences					*t*	*df*	Sig. (2-tailed)
		Mean	Std. Deviation	Std. Error Mean	95% Confidence Interval of the Difference				
					Lower	Upper			
Pair 1	Standard Ads and Emotional Ads	−12.800	15.42581	4.87807	−23.835	−1.7650	−2.624	9	.028

❦

Main Effect: test of the differences between all means for each level of an independent variable in an ANOVA

Post Hoc Tests: additional significance tests conducted to determine which means are significantly different for a main effect

Interaction Effect: tests the effect of one independent variable at each level of another independent variable in an ANOVA

---

based on the critical region of the distribution set by the alpha level. In the chart in Figure 15.2, you can see that ANOVA is recommended for designs with three or more sample or condition means.

The comparison of means for each level of an independent (or quasi-independent) variable is called the main effect. Thus, an ANOVA tests main effects for each independent variable separately in the analysis. If a main effect is significant in an ANOVA, it indicates that there is a mean difference somewhere among the means tested. But the main effect does not tell you which means are different from one another. You must conduct additional tests, called post hoc tests, to determine which means are different. An interaction effect is also tested in an ANOVA for all combinations of independent variables. The interaction effect tests the effect of one independent variable at each level of the other variable. In other words, does the independent variable effect depend on the levels of another independent variable? The interaction effect is tested by comparing the difference in condition means across levels of one independent variable for each level of the other independent variable(s). Main effects and interactions are also discussed in Chapter 11. In this chapter, we focus on how to calculate main effects and interactions in an ANOVA using SPSS (but see the Appendix for hand calculations of these effects).

Using SPSS to Conduct ANOVAs

Both the main effects and interaction effects for each combination of variables are run simultaneously in a single ANOVA for the entire design. However, the test options (and calculations—see the Appendix) differ for between-subjects and within-subjects variables. Thus, an example to test the main effect of each type of variable is discussed along with an example of a factorial design.

Between-Subjects Design

Consider a study in which a researcher tests the effect of study modality on learning. Participants are randomly assigned to a modality condition: paper text, computer text, or computer with voice text. Participants are presented with text material on three different topics during a study phase. The material on each topic is presented in a manner consistent with the condition to which the participant is assigned. All participants then perform a word puzzle to distract them from the material for 10 minutes. After the puzzle task, all the participants complete a multiple-choice test for the material they studied. Percentage correct on the test is calculated for the participants in each condition. These data are presented in Example 4.

Example 4. Between-Subjects ANOVA. To input the data into the Data Window in SPSS, you enter the scores in one column, as with the data from Example 2, because both designs contain only between-subjects variables. The second column is used to code the conditions with a different code number for each condition (e.g., (1) for paper text, (2) for computer text, and (3) for computer with voice text). Remember to name the variables and define the code values in the Variable View.

Participant No.	Paper Text	Participant No.	Computer Text	Participant No.	Computer With Voice Text
1	74	11	88	21	72
2	62	12	90	22	86
3	59	13	54	23	93
4	78	14	79	24	91
5	65	15	85	25	80
6	90	16	78	26	79
7	45	17	92	27	84
8	51	18	74	28	75
9	67	19	89	29	78
10	71	20	77	30	92

To run an ANOVA with a single between-subjects variable, you also choose the "Compare Means" option in the "Analyze" menu. Then, select the "One-way ANOVA" test (one-way means one independent or subject variable). The variable definition window appears. Click the Test Score column into the Dependent List window to define the dependent variable. Then click the text condition code column into the Factor window to define it as the independent variable. You must also choose the "Options" button and select "Descriptives" if you want to view descriptive statistics for the samples. The post hoc button allows you to run post hoc tests along with the ANOVA. These tests are useful if the text condition main effect is significant, indicating a difference between at least two of the text groups. Selecting the post hoc button brings up a list of different post hoc tests. A comparison of these tests is beyond the scope of this text. However, you should be aware of common post hoc tests used in psychological studies (in order of conservativeness), such as the least significant difference (LSD), Bonferroni, and Tukey tests. Next, click "OK" to begin the ANOVA.

The output window contains a box with descriptive statistics (if you choose that option), a box with the F statistic and p value, and a box with the post hoc tests (if you choose that option). The between-groups row of the statistics box in Figure 15.6 indicates a significant effect of text condition with $F = 7.036$ and a p value of .003. The test is significant because the p value is lower than an alpha of .05. In other words, we can reject the null hypothesis that there is no difference between the condition means. This result might be reported as "The effect of text condition was significant, $F(2, 27) = 7.04, p = .003$." Although this test is significant, it does not tell us which conditions are different from each other.

The post hoc tests indicate which pairs of means are significantly different from one another. Post hoc tests are different from normal sets of t tests because they adjust for an inflated alpha level. Each time a pairwise comparison is made, it becomes more likely that a Type I error is made. In other words, the likelihood of making a Type I error is higher for multiple

Type I Error: error made in a significance test when the researcher rejects the null hypothesis when it is actually true

Figure 15.6 Output Window From the Between-Subjects ANOVA in Example 4

One way

Descriptives

Test Score - Percentage Correct

	N	Mean	Std. Deviation	Std. Error	95% Confidence Interval for Mean Lower Bound	95% Confidence Interval for Mean Upper Bound
Paper text	10	66.2000	13.08774	4.13871	56.8376	75.5624
Computer text	10	80.6000	11.23684	3.55340	72.5616	88.6384
Computer with voice text	10	83.0000	7.37865	2.33333	77.7216	88.2784
Total	30	76.6000	12.89106	2.35357	71.7864	81.4136

Descriptives

Test Score - Percentage Correct

	Minimum	Maximum
Paper text	45.00	90.00
Computer text	54.00	92.00
Computer with voice text	72.00	93.00
Total	45.00	93.00

ANOVA

Test Score - Percentage Correct

	Sum of Squares	df	Mean Square	F	Sig.
Between groups	1651.200	2	825.600	7.036	.003
Within groups	3168.000	27	117.333		
Total	4819.200	29			

Post Hoc Tests

Multiple Comparisons

Dependent Variable: Test Score - Percentage Correct

LSD (I) Text Condition	(J) Text Condition	Mean Difference (I – J)	Std. Error	Sig.	95% Confidence Interval	
					Lower Bound	Upper Bound
Paper text	Computer text	−14.4000*	4.84424	.006	−24.3396	−4.4604
	Computer with voice text	−16.8000*	4.84424	.002	−26.7396	−6.8604
Computer text	Paper text	14.40000*	4.84424	.006	4.4604	24.3396
	Computer with voice text	−2.40000	4.84424	.624	−12.3396	7.5396
Computer with voice text	Paper text	16.80000*	4.84424	.002	6.8604	26.7396
	Computer text	2.40000	4.84424	.624	−7.5396	12.3396

*The mean difference is significant at the .05 level.

t tests than for a single test. Thus, the post hoc tests keep alpha at .05 for each test by adjusting the alpha level for the set of tests based on the number of tests conducted. These tests are shown in the third box in Figure 15.6. The LSD test was chosen in this example. The box shows p values (in the Sig. column) lower than .05 for the paper text versus computer text and paper text versus computer with voice text tests but not for the computer text versus computer with voice text test. Thus, if we examine the means shown in the first box of Figure 16.5, we see that both of the computer conditions resulted in higher test scores than the paper text condition, but the two computer conditions do not significantly differ from each other.

Within-Subjects Design

For within-subjects designs, two things change in SPSS from the between-subjects example described above: (1) the data appear in separate columns for each condition in the Data Window (remember that each participant or set of matched participants has data in a single row), and (2) we use the "Repeated Measures" test in the "General Linear Model" option of the "Analyze" menu.

For Example 5, consider an alteration to Example 4. Suppose the researcher in this study asked each participant to study each one of the three topics in a different text condition (with different participants receiving different assignments of topic to text condition, a design feature called counterbalancing

✄

Counterbalancing: a control used in within-subjects experiments where equal numbers of participants are randomly assigned to different orders of the conditions

that is used to control bias—see Chapter 11 for more discussion of counterbalancing). Thus, Example 5 has the same data in each condition, but each set of scores comes from a single sample of participants instead of three separate samples. In other words, a within-subjects design is used. These data are presented in the table shown in Example 5.

Example 5. Within-Subjects ANOVA. As indicated above, each of these conditions is listed in a different column in the Data Window in SPSS with the column labeled by condition. In addition, the within-subjects ANOVA is run by choosing the "Repeated Measures" test in the "General Linear Model" portion of the "Analyze" menu. This test is used to conduct an ANOVA for any design that contains a within-subjects variable. The first window that appears for this test is the within-subjects variable definition window. In the top space, name the variable (e.g., textcond) and then indicate the number of conditions for this variable (e.g., 3) by typing the number into the Number of Levels space and adding this variable to the list. Then, click "Define" to choose the columns for each level on the right side of the next window that appears. If your design also contains a between-subjects variable, you can define that variable here as well, in the Between-Subjects factor box. To run post hoc tests for this design (in the case that the main effect of text condition is significant in the ANOVA), you must choose the "Options" button (the Post Hoc button is used only for between-subjects variables), click over the text condition variable into the Display Means box, and then check the Compare main effects box. You can then choose a post hoc test from the drop-down bar. You may also wish to choose the Display Descriptive Statistics option in this window. Click "Continue" and "OK" to run the test.

The output (see Figure 15.7) is more complex for the repeated measures test than for the other tests we have seen. However, the output still contains the information needed to determine whether the tests are significant. To evaluate the main effect of the text condition, look

Participant No.	Paper Text	Computer Text	Computer With Voice Text
1	74	88	72
2	62	90	86
3	59	54	93
4	78	79	91
5	65	85	80
6	90	78	79
7	45	92	84
8	51	74	75
9	67	89	78
10	71	77	92

Figure 15.7   Output From Output Window for the Within-Subjects ANOVA in Example 5

General Linear Model

Within-Subjects Factors

Measure: MEASURE_1

textcond	Dependent Variable
1	paper
2	comp
3	compvoice

Descriptive Statistics

	Mean	Std.Deviation	N
Paper text	66.2000	13.08774	10
Computer text	80.6000	11.23684	10
Computer with voice text	83.0000	7.37865	10

Multivariate Tests[a]

Effect		Value	F	Hypothesis df	Error df	Sig.
textcond	Pillai's Trace	.591	5.784[b]	2.000	8.000	.028
	Wilks' Lambda	.409	5.784[b]	2.000	8.000	.028
	Hotelling's Trace	1.446	5.784[b]	2.000	8.000	.028
	Roy's Largest Root	1.446	5.784[b]	2.000	8.000	.028

[a] Design: Intercept
  Within-Subjects Design: textcond

[b] Exact statistic

(Continued)

Figure 15.7   (Continued)

Mauchly's Test of Sphericity[a]

Measure: MEASURE_1

Within-Subjects Effect	Mauchly's W	Approx.Chi-Square	df	Sig.
textcond	.975	.205	2	.902

Tests the null hypothesis that the error covariance matrix of the orthonormalized transformed dependent variables is proportional to an identity matrix.

Mauchly's Test of Sphericity[a]

Measure: MEASURE_1

	Epsilon[b]		
Within-Subjects Effect	Greenhouse-Geisser	Huynh-Feldt	Lower bound
textcond	.975	1.000	.500

Tests the null hypothesis that the error covariance matrix of the orthonormalized transformed dependent variables is proportional to an identity matrix.

a. Design: Intercept
   Within-Subjects Design: textcond

b. May be used to adjust the degrees of freedom for the averaged tests of significance. Corrected tests are displayed in the Tests of Within-Subjects Effects table.

Tests of Within-Subjects Effects

Measure: MEASURE_1

Source		Type III Sum of Squares	df	Mean Square
textcond	Sphericity Assumed	1651.200	2	825.600
	Greenhouse-Geisser	1651.200	1.951	846.514
	Huynh-Feldt	1651.200	2.000	825.600
	Lower-bound	1651.200	1.000	1651.200
Error(textcond)	Sphericity Assumed	2379.467	18	132.193
	Greenhouse-Geisser	2379.467	17.555	135.541
	Huynh-Feldt	2379.467	18.000	132.193
	Lower-bound	2379.467	9.000	264.385

Tests of Within-Subjects Effects

Measure: MEASURE_1

Source		F	Sig.
textcond	Sphericity Assumed	6.245	.009
	Greenhouse-Geisser	6.245	.009
	Huynh-Feldt	6.245	.009
	Lower-bound	6.245	.034
Error(textcond)	Sphericity Assumed		
	Greenhouse-Geisser		
	Huynh-Feldt		
	Lower-bound		

Tests of Within-Subjects Contrasts

Measure: MEASURE_1

Source	textcond	Type III Sum of Squares	df	Mean Square	F	Sig.
textcond	Linear	1411.200	1	1411.200	12.168	.007
	Quadratic	240.000	1	240.000	1.617	.235
Error(textcond)	Linear	1043.800	9	115.978		
	Quadratic	1335.667	9	115.978		

Tests of Between-Subjects Effects

Measure: MEASURE_1

Transformed Variable: Average

Source	Type III Sum of Squares	df	Mean Square	F	Sig.
Intercept	176026.800	1	176026.800	2009.099	.000
Error	788.533	9	87.615		

(Continued)

Figure 15.7   (Continued)

Estimated Marginal Means

textcond

Estimates

Measure: MEASURE_1

textcond	Mean	Std. Error	95% Confidence Interval	
			Lower Bound	Upper Bound
1	66.200	4.139	56.838	75.562
2	80.600	3.553	72.562	88.638
3	83.000	2.333	77.722	88.278

Pairwise Comparisons

Measure: MEASURE_1

(I) textcond	(J) textcond	Mean Difference (I – J)	Std. Error	Sig.[a]	95% Confidence Interval for Difference[a]	
					Lower Bound	Upper Bound
1	2	−14.400*	5.512	.028	−26.869	−1.931
	3	−16.800*	4.816	.007	−27.695	−5.905
2	1	14.400*	5.512	.028	1.931	26.869
	3	−2.400	5.073	.647	−13.876	9.076
3	1	16.800*	4.816	.007	5.905	27.695
	2	2.400	5.073	.647	−9.076	13.876

Based on estimated marginal means

a. Adjustment for multiple comparisons: Least Significant Difference (equivalent to no adjustments).

*The mean difference is significant at the .05 level.

Multivariate Tests

	Value	F	Hypothesis df	Error df	Sig.
Pillai's trace	.591	5.784[a]	2.000	8.000	.028
Wilks' lambda	.409	5.784[a]	2.000	8.000	.028
Hotelling's trace	1.446	5.784[a]	2.000	8.000	.028
Roy's largest root	1.446	5.784[a]	2.000	8.000	.028

Each F tests the multivariate effect of textcond. These tests are based on the linearly independent pairwise comparisons among the estimated marginal means.

a. Exact statistic

Sphericity Assumption: assumption of the repeated measures (within-subjects) ANOVA that pairs of scores in the population have equal variance

---

for the "Tests of Within-Subjects Effects" box. The first column of this box shows the F and p values. For Example 5, the $F = 6.245$ and $p = .009$. Thus, we can reject the null hypothesis that there is no difference in condition means, because the main effect of text condition is significant. The post hoc tests are shown in the box of the output labeled "Pairwise Comparisons." The conditions are indicated by code value with p values listed in the Sig. column. As in Example 4, the post hoc tests indicate that learning for the paper text condition is lower than both of the computer conditions, but the two computer conditions do not significantly differ from each other.

You also see a box in the output for Mauchly's Test of Sphericity. Sphericity is an assumption of the repeated measures test. The assumption is that pairs of scores in the population have similar variability. If the sphericity test is significant in the repeated measures output, the F statistic needs to be adjusted in order to retain accuracy of the test. Thus, the "Tests of Within-Subjects Effects" box contains a few different corrections below the "Sphericity Assumed" row. The sphericity assumed values are used if the sphericity test is not significant. However, if the sphericity test is significant, a correction is used because violations of this assumption can increase the chance of a Type I error (Keppel & Wickens, 2004). A common correction used in psychological research is the Greenhouse-Geisser correction. A full discussion of the correction techniques is provided in Howell's (2009) statistics text.

Factorial ANOVA

To complete the discussion of ANOVA, let's consider a simple factorial ANOVA with two independent variables, each with two levels (i.e., a 2 × 2 design or two-way). As in the previous two ANOVA examples, we are interested in the main effects tested for each independent variable. In addition, an interaction effect is considered. The factorial ANOVA shown in Example 6 is of a between-subjects design (i.e., both independent variables are manipulated between subjects); however, as described in the previous example, if any of the independent variables in a factorial design are manipulated within subjects, the repeated measures test should be used.

Example 6. Factorial ANOVA. Consider a study where memory is compared for different types of items. In this experiment, two factors are manipulated: the type of item under study (either pictures or words) and the type of test a participant receives (recognition of items formatted as words or pictures). In this study, the researcher considers whether memory performance differs for studied pictures and words (i.e., the main effect of study format), differs for tested pictures and words (i.e., the main effect of test format), and whether format match (picture or word) across study and test is better than when the format mismatches (i.e., the interaction of these factors). Percentage correct recognition data are presented in the table in Example 6.

Participant No.	Picture Study Picture Test	Participant No.	Picture Study Word Test
1	92	11	68
2	88	12	50
3	87	13	54
4	78	14	80
5	95	15	85
6	90	16	78
7	71	17	92
8	89	18	74
9	93	19	79
10	89	20	77
Word Study Picture Test		Word Study Word Test	
21	56	31	88
22	62	32	90
23	59	33	67
24	70	34	79
25	65	35	85
26	67	36	78
27	45	37	90
28	51	38	74
29	67	39	89
30	71	40	77

Recall from the examples above that the data should all be entered into one column in the Data Window in SPSS because each score is from a different participant. You will need two columns of codes, one for the study format and one for the test format. Remember to label the columns with the variable names and to insert value labels for the codes.

To run the two-way, between-subjects ANOVA, choose the "Univariate" test option in the "General Linear Model" portion of the "Analyze" menu. A definition window appears where you can click over the dependent and independent (Fixed Factor box) variables. You do not need to select any post hoc tests for the main effects in this design because there are only two levels of each independent variable. An examination of the means indicates which level results in higher recognition for any significant main effects. If you select "Descriptives" in the Options window, these means appear in the output. Click "OK" to begin the analysis.

The output is similar to that for Example 4 above; however, three tests of interest appear in the "Tests of Between-Subjects Effects" box (see Figure 15.8). The two main effects are indicated in the rows with the variable labels ("study" and "test" for Example 6). The main effect of study format was significant, $F(1, 36) = 8.91, p = .005$; however, the main effect of test format was not significant, $F(1, 36) = 1.32, p = .257$. The means in the Descriptive Statistics box indicate that studied pictures ($M = 80.45$) were better remembered than studied words ($M = 71.50$), regardless of test format. This is a common finding in memory studies (Paivio, 2007). However, the interaction between study format and test format was also significant, $F(1, 36) = 31.96$, $p < .001$. Note that the p value in the output for the interaction is listed as .000. This value represents a value smaller than .0005 that has been rounded to three significant digits. In fact, p can never equal 0. The convention used in reporting such values is to indicate that the p was less than .001. The graph in Figure 15.9 illustrates this interaction. From the graph, one can see that the match in study and test format did affect recognition scores such that a match in format from study to test resulted in higher scores than the mismatch conditions.

Figure 15.8 Output From Output Window for the Factorial ANOVA in Example 6

Univariate Analysis of Variance

Between-Subjects Factors

		Value Label	N
Study format	1.00	Picture	20
	2.00	Word	20
Test format	1.00	Picture	20
	2.00	Word	20

(Continued)

Figure 15.8   (Continued)

Descriptive Statistics

Dependent Variable: Recognition Score

Study Format	Test Format	Mean	Std. Deviation	N
Picture	Picture	87.2000	7.29992	10
	Word	73.7000	13.08986	10
	Total	80.4500	12.42440	20
Word	Picture	61.3000	8.52513	10
	Word	81.7000	7.88881	10
	Total	71.5000	13.16894	20
Total	Picture	74.2500	15.36871	20
	Word	77.7000	11.29089	20
	Total	75.9750	13.42498	40

Tests of Between-Subjects Effects

Dependent Variable: Recognition Score

Source	Type III Sum of Squares	df	Mean Square	F	Sig.
Corrected model	3793.075[a]	3	1264.358	14.066	.000
Intercept	230888.025	1	230888.025	2568.673	.000
Study	801.025	1	801.025	8.912	.005
Test	119.025	1	119.025	1.324	.257
Study *test	2873.025	1	2873.025	31.963	.000
Error	3235.900	36	89.886		
Total	327917.000	40			
Corrected Total	7028.975	39			

a. $r^2 = .540$ (Adjusted $r^2 = .501$)

Figure 15.9   Line Graph of the Interaction Between Study Format and Test Format in Example 6

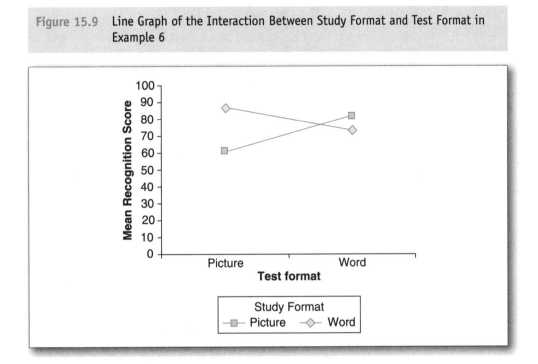

Stop and Think

(15.4)   For each description below, indicate which type of effect is being tested (main effect or interaction):

- In a multivalent design, three groups of subjects are exposed to three different types of stories to compare the effect of type of story on reading speed.
- In a factorial design, researchers examine whether the effect of note-taking method (by hand or on computer) on test score depends on the type of class a student is taking.
- A study tested the effects of both room color and presence/absence of plants on recovery time in a hospital. The individual effects of room color and presence/absence of plants were tested.

(15.5)   A researcher tested the effect of type of music (classical, country, and rock) on subjects' moods. An alpha level of .05 was used. The outcome of the ANOVA was $F(2,65) = 16.92$, $p < .001$. What can the researcher conclude from the outcome of this test?

Looking for Relationships With Pearson r and Regression Tests

Different inferential statistics are used when one is testing hypotheses about relationships across distributions of scores. To simply determine whether there is a relationship between two distributions, a chi-square or Pearson r test is conducted, depending on the type of scale used to measure the dependent variable (see Figure 15.2). The chi-square test is used for nominal and ordinal data, and the Pearson r test is used for interval and ratio data. Both tests indicate whether a significant relationship exists between variables in a data set.

Chi-Square Test: a significance test used to determine whether a relationship exists between two variables measured on nominal or ordinal scales

Pearson r Test: a significance test used to determine whether a linear relationship exists between two variables measured on interval or ratio scales

---

The Pearson r statistic tests linear relationships. The values of the statistic range from -1.0 to $+1.0$. A Pearson r of $+1.0$ represents a perfect positive relationship. A Pearson r of -1.0 represents a perfect negative relationship. A value of 0 indicates no relationship. The Pearson r statistic is used as a descriptive statistic to simply describe the type and degree of relationship for the sample distributions. Values closer to $+1.0$ and -1.0 are stronger relationships. Values closer to 0 represent weaker relationships (see Figure 15.10). Pearson r can also be used as an inferential statistic to determine if a significant relationship exists between two variables. The test relies on the same principles as the comparison tests described above. The Pearson r value calculated from the sample distributions (based on overlap in scores between the distributions with sampling error removed) is compared with the distribution of possible Pearson r values for samples of that size when there is no relationship in the population. If the sample Pearson r is an extreme score, in the most extreme 5% of the distribution, for example, there is evidence to reject the null hypothesis that there is no relationship (i.e., the test is significant) and accept the alternative hypothesis that there is a relationship (or a specific relationship if a one-tailed test is used).

Another way in which psychologists examine relationships between distributions is with regression. In a regression analysis, a researcher conducts a test to determine if a set of data can be described by a function. In linear regression, the test determines how well the data fit a straight line. If a function is found to fit the data well, the function is then used to predict the score of one variable from the score of another variable. Thus, a regression analysis provides information about how well the function describes the data and a function equation that can be used to make predictions of one variable from another variable. Figure 15.11 illustrates a linear regression analysis of an equation fit to specific data from Figure 15.10. The r^2 value given in the graph indicates how well the line fits the data. Higher r^2 values indicate a better fit with a maximum r^2 value of 1.0 for a perfect fit (i.e., the data perfectly follow a straight line). In the case of linear regression with two variables, r^2 is simply the square of the Pearson r value.

Linear Regression: a statistical technique that determines the best fit line to a set of data to allow prediction of the score on one variable from the score on another variable

---

The first scatterplot shows a strong positive relationship between amount of rain and height of a river. The second scatterplot shows a moderate negative relationship between GPA and hours of TV watched. The third scatterplot shows a very weak positive relationship between number of books returned to the library and height of river, two variables that are not directly related, but might be indirectly related with fewer people returning books on rainy days. However, the river might be high on non-rainy days so these variables show only a weak relationship.

Figure 15.10   Possible Relationships Between Distributions With Corresponding Pearson *r* Values

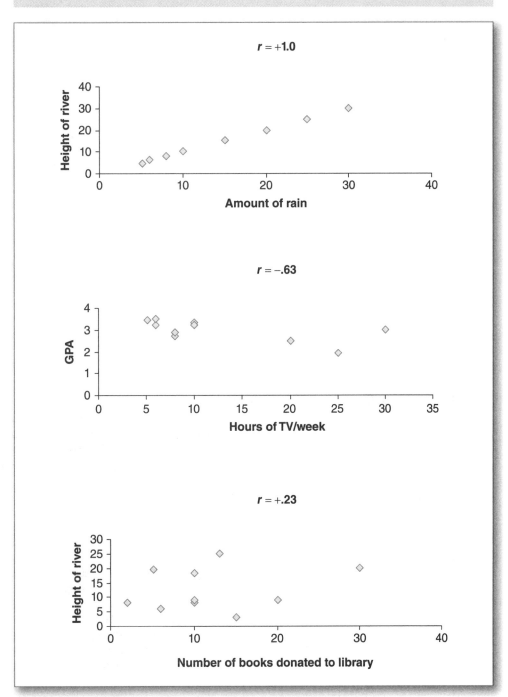

Figure 15.11   Linear Regression Equation for Two Distributions

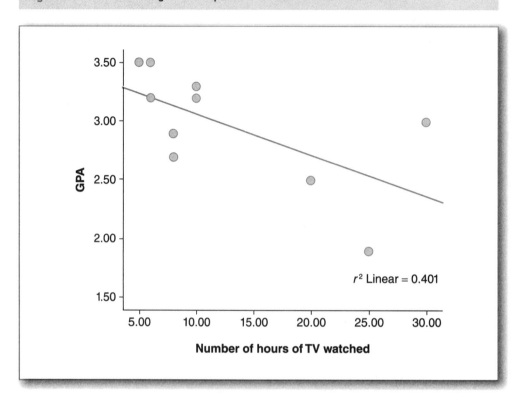

Using SPSS to Conduct Chi-Square Analyses

Consider a study where older and younger participants are compared on their ability to remember to perform a task (e.g., mail a postcard) at some point in the future. The data in this study are on a nominal scale: the participant either remembers to mail the card (a response of *yes*) or does not (a response of *no*). The data for the younger and older participants are presented in Example 7.

Example 7. Chi-Square. The Data Window for this data set contains two (or more) columns of the coded variables (e.g., "1" for yes response, "2" for no response in one column, and "1" for older participants, "2" for younger participants in another column). To run the chi-square analysis, choose the "Crosstabs" option in the "Descriptive Statistics" portion of the "Analyze" menu. Click one variable into the Row box and the other variable into the Column box. Choose the statistics tab to click the chi-square test from the list. Click "Continue" and "OK" to start the analysis.

The output from the chi-square is shown in Figure 15.12. The second box in the output shows the cross-tabulation with the number of participants in each condition (Younger/yes, etc.). The values for the chi-square test are shown in the box labeled "Chi-square tests." The Pearson chi-square value of 3.333 is shown in the first row with its p value of .068. For this example, the relationship is not significant because the p value is greater than the alpha level of .05. In other words, the type of response ("yes" or "no") is not significantly related to the age group of the participants.

Figure 15.12   Output From Output Window for the Chi-Square Test in Example 7

Crosstabs

Case Processing Summary

	Cases					
	Valid		Missing		Total	
	N	Percentage	N	Percentage	N	Percentage
Age* Response	20	100.0%	0	.0%	20	100.0%

Age* Response Crosstabulation

Count

		Response		Total
		Yes	No	
Age	Older	8	2	10
	Younger	4	6	10
Total		12	8	20

Chi-square Tests

	Value	df	Asymp. Sig. (2-sided)	Exact Sig. (2-sided)	Exact Sig. (1-sided)
Pearson chi-square	3.333[a]	1	.068		
Continuity correction[b]	1.875	1	.171		
Likelihood ratio	3.452	1	.063		
Fisher's exact test				.170	.085
N of valid cases	20				

a. 2 cells (50.0%) have expected count less than 5. The minimum expected count is 4.00
b. Computed only for a 2x2 table

Participant 1	Older	Yes	Participant 11	Younger	No
Participant 2	Older	Yes	Participant 12	Younger	No
Participant 3	Older	No	Participant 13	Younger	Yes
Participant 4	Older	Yes	Participant 14	Younger	Yes
Participant 5	Older	Yes	Participant 15	Younger	No
Participant 6	Older	No	Participant 16	Younger	No
Participant 7	Older	Yes	Participant 17	Younger	No
Participant 8	Older	Yes	Participant 18	Younger	Yes
Participant 9	Older	Yes	Participant 19	Younger	No
Participant 10	Older	Yes	Participant 20	Younger	Yes

Using SPSS to Conduct a Pearson r Test

The Pearson r test can be used to test relationships when the variables are measured on interval or ratio scales. For example, suppose that in the study described in Example 7, the exact ages of the participants were measured as well as the number of days that passed before the participant remembered to perform the task of mailing the postcard. In this case, a Pearson r test can be used to determine if age is related to the number of days needed to remember the task. These data are given in the table in Example 8.

Example 8. Pearson r Test. The Data Window should contain two columns of data: the age and the number of days. To run the Pearson r test, choose the "Bivariate" test in the "Correlate" option in the "Analyze" menu. Click the two variables into the Variables box. The Pearson test box should be clicked. You can also choose to conduct a two-tailed test (either a positive or negative relationship is predicted) or a one-tailed test if the prediction is for a specific type (positive or negative) of relationship. Click "OK" to run the test. The Correlations box in the output (see Figure 15.13) indicates the Pearson r value (including the direction of relationship) in the first row and the p value in the second row. For Example 8, the variables are significantly related (negatively) with $r = -.90$ and $p < .001$. In other words, in this study as age increased, the number of days it took participants to remember to mail the card decreased.

Participant No.	Age	Number of Days	Participant No.	Age	Number of Days
1	81	1	5	89	0
2	77	0	6	67	1
3	69	0	7	65	1
4	73	2	8	70	0

(Continued)

(Continued)

9	78	2	15	20	5
10	75	0	16	21	8
11	21	3	17	22	7
12	18	10	18	18	6
13	19	8	19	19	7
14	24	7	20	20	9

Figure 15.13   Output From Output Window for the Pearson *r* Test in Example 8

Correlations

		Age	Days
Age	Pearson correlation	1	−.900**
	Sig. (2-tailed)		.00
	N	20	20
Days	Pearson correlation	−.900**	1
	Sig. (2-tailed)	.000	
	N	20	20

**Correlation is significant at the 0.01 level.

Using SPSS to Conduct a Simple Linear Regression

An alternate method of analyzing the data in Example 8 is to conduct a simple linear regression analysis to examine the relationship between age and the number of days it took participants to mail the card. The simple linear regression produces a linear function that allows researchers to predict one variable from another. In the case of this example, the researcher may wish to predict from their age the number of days it takes participants to mail the card.

Example 9. Simple Linear Regression. The simple linear regression for the data in Example 8 begins with the data set up in the Data Window the same way: Each variable is typed into a separate, labeled column in the Data Window. To conduct the analysis, choose the "Linear" option in the "Regression" portion of the "Analyze" menu. For this analysis, you must decide ahead of time which variable you are trying to predict (designated the dependent variable for the analysis) from the other (the predictor variable in this analysis). The dependent variable is

Figure 15.14   Output From Output Window for the Simple Linear Regression Test in Example 9

Regression

Variables Entered/Removed[a]

Model	Variables Entered	Variables Removed	Method
1	age[b]	.	Enter

a. Dependent Variable: days

b. All requested variables entered

Model Summary

Model	r	r^2	Adjusted r^2	Std. Error of the Estimate
1	.900[a]	.811	.800	1.59066

a. Predictors: (Constant), age

ANOVA[a]

Model		Sum of Squares	df	Mean Square	F	Sig.
1	Regression	195.006	1	195.006	77.071	.000[b]
	Residual	45.544	18	2.530		
	Total	240.550	19			

a. Dependent Variable: days

b. Predictors: (Constant), age

Coefficients[a]

Model		Unstandardized Coefficients		Standardized Coefficients	t	Sig.
		B	Std. Error	Beta		
1	(Constant)	9.209	.707		13.035	.000
	Age	−.113	.013	−.900	−8.779	.000

a. Dependent Variable: days

clicked into the Dependent box, and the predictor variable is clicked into the Independent box. For Example 9, age is the predictor, and number of days is the dependent variable.

Figure 15.14 illustrates the output from the linear regression. The last box contains the output information needed to determine the regression equation and whether age significantly predicts number of days. The t test in the bottom row provides the significance test. In this case, the test is significant, $t(18) = -8.78, p < .001$. Thus, age significantly predicts number of days to mail the card. The prediction can be made from the following equation:

$$\text{Number of days} = -0.11 \text{ Age} + 9.21$$

The slope of the regression line is -0.11, and it is given in the Age row of the Coefficients box. The intercept of the equation is 9.21, and it is given in the Constant row of the box. Thus, for a participant of 50 years of age, the predicted number of days to mail the card is as follows:

$$\text{Number of days} = -0.11(50) + 9.21 = 3.71$$

Stop and Think

(15.6) Describe the different situations where a chi square and a correlation analysis are appropriate.

(15.7) A researcher believes that there is a relationship between gender and satisfaction with roommate (yes/no). The results from the chi square test were $\chi^2(4, n = 90) = 10.51, p = .03$. What can the researcher conclude from these results?

CHAPTER SUMMARY

Reconsider the questions from the beginning of the chapter:

- Which statistical tests are best for different research designs? As described in this chapter, different designs and measurement scales call for different types of statistical tests. The chart in Figure 15.2 can help you decide which test is appropriate for different designs and measurement scales.
- How do we choose an appropriate statistical test? As seen in Figure 15.2, a test is chosen based on (1) whether you are comparing means or looking for relationships, (2) what type of measurement scale is used to collect the data, and (3) the design of the study (the number of independent variables, the number of levels of the independent variables, etc.).
- How do we use SPSS to run statistical tests? SPSS is a software package that allows researchers to compute descriptive and inferential statistics. Different inferential statistics require different types of tests to be run within the SPSS program. Descriptions of several of these tests are included in this chapter.
- What information is provided in an SPSS output? SPSS output differs a bit from test to test, but the output for all tests described in this chapter includes sample means and standard deviations, the statistical value (t, F, r, etc.), and the p value that corresponds to the statistic calculated.

THINKING ABOUT RESEARCH

A summary of a research study in psychology is given below. As you read the summary, think about the following questions:

1. Is the goal of this study to test an effect or a relationship? Given your answer and the design of the study, what is the appropriate statistical test for this study (see Figure 14.2)?

2. The description of the results indicates three significant differences and one nonsignificant difference. How should the p values compare with alpha for the significant differences? What is the lowest p value that can be obtained for the nonsignificant difference (assume $\alpha = .05$)?

3. Suppose the same participants participate in both the synchronous and control groups (i.e., they had done the walk twice with different groups in different conditions). How does that change the design of the study? What is the correct statistical test for the changed design?

4. Suppose that in reality, shared activities do not affect cooperation, trust, or connectedness. In this case, what type of error have the researchers made in this study?

Research Study. Wiltermuth, S. S., & Heath, C. (2009). Synchrony and cooperation. *Psychological Science, 20,* 1–5.

Purpose of the Study. The researchers were interested in the effects of joint activities (e.g., synchronous marching in the military) on the subsequent behavior of group members. They asked several research questions regarding this effect: (1) Do joint activities result in similar coordinated behavior across group members? (2) Do joint activities result in a feeling of connectedness with group members? (3) Do joint activities result in trust among group members? (4) Do joint activities result in feelings of happiness among group members?

Method of the Study. Thirty individuals participated in the study. They followed an experimenter in groups of three on a walk around campus. Walks took place in one of two conditions: the synchronous condition and the control condition. For the synchronous condition, groups walked together in step. For the control condition, groups walked normally. The participants were then asked to complete an exercise with their group that was presented as a separate and unrelated experiment. In the exercise, group members had to choose numbers between 1 and 7, such that higher numbers and smaller differences between numbers chosen by group members earned the group members higher amounts of money. Group members could not communicate during the game. Thus, group members who cooperated with each other were more likely to choose higher numbers. After the exercise, participants completed a survey asking them to rate how connected they felt with group members during the walk, how much they trusted other group members after the walk, and how happy they felt on a 1 to 7 scale.

Results of the Study. The synchronous and control groups were compared on the measures. Synchronous groups chose higher numbers ($M = 5.40$) in the first round of the exercise than the control groups ($M = 3.60$), indicating that group members coordinated more in the synchronous groups. Synchronous groups also indicated that they felt more connected ($M = 4.50$) than the control groups ($M = 2.90$) and that they trusted their group members more ($M = 5.60$) than the control groups ($M = 4.10$). However, no difference in happiness was found between the two group types ($M = 4.70$ for synchronous groups, $M = 4.80$ for control groups).

Conclusions of the Study. Wiltermuth and Heath (2009) concluded from their results that shared activities among group members lead to greater cooperation across group members, greater trust among group members, and a greater feeling of connectedness among group members. However, their hypothesis that shared activities lead to greater happiness of group members was not supported by the results of this study.

COMMON PITFALLS AND HOW TO AVOID THEM

Problem: Confusing independent and related samples tests—a common error made by students learning to conduct statistical tests is choosing the wrong type of *t* test for a study's design or entering data into the SPSS Data Window incorrectly for the design.

Solution: Remember that independent samples tests are for studies with groups made up of different, unrelated participants, and scores are entered into a single column in the Data Window with a second column for the group codes. Related samples tests are for studies with participants receiving all the conditions or groups of participants who are matched in some way. For related samples tests, scores for different conditions go in separate columns; no group codes are needed.

Problem: Confusing levels and conditions—with a factorial design, the difference between levels and conditions can be confusing.

Solution: Remember that levels are specific to an independent variable and conditions represent the combinations of levels of different variables in a factorial design. Thus, means for each level that are compared in main effects tests are different from the means for conditions that are considered in an interaction effect.

TEST YOURSELF

Reconsider the studies described in the Test Yourself section of Chapter 7 (assume α = .05 for all tests).

1. Suppose you conducted a study to test the hypothesis that social pressure affects memory accuracy. You set up a study where participants view a video of a person robbing a convenience store. Then, half of the participants watch a video of other "participants" discussing the crime. In reality, the "participants" in the video are part of the experiment, and some of the details of the crime that are discussed are inaccurate. The actual participants are told that they should consider other people's perspectives on the crime because it is difficult for any one person to accurately remember all the details. The other half of the participants do not view the video discussion of the crime but are also told that it is difficult for any one person to accurately remember all the details of the crime. Thirty minutes after viewing the original crime video, all participants are given a recognition memory test about details of the crime. For this study, answer the following questions:

   (a) Using the chart in Figure 15.2 and what you know about the design of this study, what is the correct statistical test that should be used to analyze the data?

   (b) What is the null hypothesis that will be tested in the statistical test you described in (a)?

(c)   Suppose that 10 participants participated in each group in the study. For the recognition accuracy data provided below, use SPSS to conduct the correct statistical test to analyze these data.

- *Video Discussion Group:* 67, 80, 69, 72, 75, 79, 66, 71, 69, 79
- *No Video Discussion Group:* 78, 65, 79, 84, 88, 79, 89, 90, 85, 87

(d)   From the SPSS output you obtained, what can be concluded about the null hypothesis you stated in (b) above?

2.   Suppose you conducted a study to determine if some people have the ability to predict which of two cards a poker player has been dealt for a poker hand. The study involves a single sample of people who claim to be "better than average poker players." In the study, all participants are asked to view a poker player being given a card by the dealer. They are asked to judge from the player's reaction whether the card dealt to the player is a card that will "complete a four of a kind hand" or "not complete a four of a kind hand." They complete 100 judgment trials, and their overall percentage accuracy is calculated. In other words, across all trials, the participants have a 50% chance of being correct if they have no ability to interpret the player's "poker face" (i.e., they are guessing). If they are able to interpret the player's poker face, the participants should perform better than chance (50%) in correctly choosing which type of card the player has been dealt.

(a)   Using the chart in Figure 15.2 and what you know about the design of this study, what is the correct statistical test that should be used to analyze the data?

(b)   What is the null hypothesis that will be tested in the statistical test you described in (a)?

(c)   Suppose that 10 participants participated in the study. For the accuracy data provided below, use SPSS to conduct the correct statistical test to analyze these data.

- *Sample Accuracy Data:* 50, 44, 51, 45, 52, 53, 52, 50, 56, 51

(d)   From the SPSS output you obtained, what can be concluded about the null hypothesis you stated in (b) above?

Now, consider a new study.

3.   A social psychologist is interested in how ad types affect desire to purchase different types of products. She asks 20 participants to participate in an experiment where video ads are shown to the participants for either a new car model or a new energy drink. The video ads either highlight that the product promotes a feeling of youthfulness (i.e., young, active people are featured in the ad) or a feeling of attractiveness (i.e., attractive people are featured in the ad). Participants are randomly assigned to view one of the four videos. After viewing the video, each participant is asked to rate his or her desire to purchase the product on a 1 to 7 scale, where higher numbers indicate more desire to buy.

(a)   What are the independent variables in this experiment? Describe the levels for each independent variable.

(b)   Based on this design, what is the appropriate statistical test for analysis of the data? What effects are tested in this analysis?

(c)   For data listed below, conduct the statistical test you described in (b) above. Which effects are significant?

- Youthfulness Car Ad: 5, 4, 5, 6, 3
- Youthfulness Energy Drink Ad: 7, 6, 7, 7, 6
- Attractiveness Car Ad: 3, 4, 3, 4, 5
- Attractiveness Energy Drink Ad: 5, 6, 6, 5, 6

(d)   From the outcome of the tests, what can be concluded about the effects of ad type and product type on desire to buy a product?

Answers can be found at edge.sagepub/mcbride3e.

STOP AND THINK ANSWERS

(15.1)   Power is the ability of a test to detect an effect of a factor when one exists.

(15.2)   Sampling error is estimated from the variability in the data.

(15.3)   Paired-samples t test, independent-samples t test, one-sample t test, paired-samples t test

(15.4)   Main effect, interaction, main effects (but this is a factorial design so an interaction, which is not described, would be tested as well)

(15.5)   That type of music affects mood, but they cannot determine which type of music showed better mood without follow-up tests.

(15.6)   Chi-square tests are used with nominal/ordinal scales. Correlational analyses are more appropriate for continuous scales (e.g., interval/ratio).

(15.7)   That there is a relationship between these factors. The test was significant.

⑤SAGE edge™

Visit edge.sagepub.com/mcbride3e for the tools you need to sharpen your study skills:

- Web Quizzes
- eFlashcards
- Thinking About Research

- SAGE Journal Articles
- Web and Multimedia Resources

Appendix

Statistical Calculations

Calculation formulas and examples are provided below for descriptive and inferential statistics discussed in Chapters 7 and 15.

DESCRIPTIVE STATISTICS

These examples use the data set (X values): 4, 3, 5, 3, 2, 4, 5, 3, 2, 1.

Statistic	Formula/Definition	Calculations
Mean (M)	$M = \dfrac{\sum X}{n}$	$M = \dfrac{(4+3+5+3+2+4+5+3+2+1)}{10} = \dfrac{32}{10} = 3.2$
Median	Middle score or average of middle scores	Order scores from lowest to highest: 1, 2, 2, 3, 3, 3, 4, 4, 5, 5 Average middle scores: (3 + 3)/2 = 3
Mode	Most common score or scores	3
Range	Difference between highest and lowest scores	Range = (5–1) = 4
Variance	$\text{Variance} = \dfrac{\sum (X - M)^2}{n-1}$	$\text{Variance} = \dfrac{\begin{array}{l}[(4-3.2)^2 + (3-3.2)^2 + (5-3.2)^2 + \\ (3-3.2)^2 + (2-3.2)^2 + (4-3.2)^2 + \\ (5-3.2)^2 + (3-3.2)^2 + (2-3.2)^2 + (1-3.2)^2]\end{array}}{(10-1)} = 1.73$

Standard deviation (SD)	$SD = \sqrt{\dfrac{\Sigma(X-M)^2}{n-1}}$	$SD = \sqrt{\dfrac{\begin{array}{l}[(4-3.2)^2 + (3-3.2)^2 + (5-3.2)^2 + \\ (3-3.2)^2 + (2-3.2)^2 + (4-3.2)^2 + \\ (5-3.2)^2 + (3-3.2)^2 + (2-3.2)^2 + (1-3.2)^2]\end{array}}{(10-1)}} = 1.32$

NOTE: Σ= *sum all values after this symbol, n = number of scores.*

INFERENTIAL STATISTICS

Test	Example
One-sample t test	Sample values (X values): 4, 3, 5, 3, 2, 4, 5, 3, 2, 1 Population mean (μ) = 3.0, n is the number of scores in the sample $$t = \frac{(M - \mu)^2}{SD / \sqrt{n}} = \frac{(3.2 - 3.0)}{1.32 / \sqrt{10}} = \frac{.2}{.42} = .48$$ This calculated t value is then compared with the appropriate t critical value (based on alpha and df of [$n - 1$]) to determine significance. See www.psychology.ilstu.edu/psy138/resources/tables.html
Independent samples t test	Sample 1 values (X_1 values): 4, 3, 5, 3, 2, 4, 5, 3, 2, 1 Sample 2 values (X_2 values): 2, 3, 2, 3, 2, 2, 4, 3, 2, 2 $$t = \frac{(M_1 - M_2)}{\sqrt{s_p^2 / n_1 + s_p^2 / n_2}}$$ s_p^2 (pooled variance)—based on variance of each sample and n for each sample $$s_p^2 = \frac{(n_1 - 1)(SD_1^2) + (n_2 - 1)(SD_2^2)}{(n_1 - 1) + (n_2 - 1)}$$ $SD_1^2 = 1.73$ (from descriptive statistics section above) $$M_2 = \frac{2 + 3 + 2 + 3 + 2 + 2 + 4 + 3 + 2 + 2}{10} = 2.5$$ $$SD_2^2 = \frac{\begin{array}{c}[(2\text{-}2.5)^2 + (3\text{-}2.5)^2 + (2\text{-}2.5)^2 + (3\text{-}2.5)^2 + \\ (2\text{-}2.5)^2 + (2\text{-}2.5)^2 + (4\text{-}2.5)^2 + (3\text{-}2.5)^2 + (2\text{-}2.5)^2]\end{array}}{(10 - 1)} = .5$$ $$s_p^2 = \frac{(10 - 1)(1.73) + (10 - 1)(.5)}{(10 - 1) + (10 - 1)} = \frac{15.57 + 4.5}{18} = 1.12$$ $$t = \frac{(3.2 - 2.5)}{\sqrt{1.12 / 10 + 1.12 / 10}} = \frac{.7}{.47} = 1.43$$ This calculated t value is then compared with the appropriate t critical value (based on alpha and df of [$n_1 + n_2 - 2$]) to determine significance. See www.psychology.ilstu.edu/psy138/resources/tables.html

Test	Example
Related/Paired samples t *test*	Condition 1 values: 4, 3, 5, 3, 2, 4, 5, 3, 2, 1

Condition 2 values from same or matched subjects: 2, 3, 2, 3, 2, 2, 4, 3, 2, 2

t is calculated in this test based on difference scores for each participant or across matched pairs. Thus, difference scores are first calculated by subtracting the score in Condition 2 from the score for Condition 1 for each participant (e.g., 4 – 2 for Participant 1).

Difference scores (*D values*): 2, 0, 3, 0, 0, 2, 1, 0, 0, 1

$$\text{Mean of } D \text{ scores } (M_D) = \frac{(2+0+3+0+0+2+1+0+0-1)}{10} = .7$$

$$SD \text{ of } D\,(SD_D) = \sqrt{\frac{\Sigma(D-M_D)^2}{n-1}} =$$

$$\sqrt{\frac{\begin{array}{l}[(2-.7)^2+(0-.7)^2+(3-.7)^2+(0-.7)^2+ \\ (0-.7)^2+(2-.7)^2+(1-.7)^2+(0-.7)^2+ \\ (0-.7)^2+(-1-.7)^2]\end{array}}{(10-1)}} = \sqrt{\frac{14.1}{9}} = 1.25$$

$$t = \frac{M_D}{SD_D / \sqrt{n}} = \frac{.7}{1.25 / \sqrt{10}} = .\frac{7}{.4} = 1.75$$

This calculated *t* value is then compared with the appropriate *t* critical value (based on alpha and *df* of [*n* – 1]) to determine significance. See www.psychology.ilstu.edu/psy138/resources/tables.html

One-way, between-subjects ANOVA	Sample 1 (*X*₁ values): 10, 15, 20, 13 (*M*₁ = 14.50)

Sample 1 (X_1 values): 10, 15, 20, 13 ($M_1 = 14.50$)

Sample 2 (X_2 values): 15, 25, 30, 25 ($M_2 = 23.75$)

Sample 3 (X_3 values): 20, 17, 25, 20 ($M_3 = 20.50$)

Overall mean for all samples (M_T) = 19.58

$$F = \frac{SS_A / a - 1}{SS_{error} / a(n-1)}$$

$SS_A = n\Sigma(M_A - M_T)^2$ Sum of squared deviations for Factor A term (SS_A): *n* = number of scores per sample, M_A indicates each sample mean

$$SS_A = 4[(14.5 - 19.58)^2)\,(23.75 - 19.58)^2)\,(20.5 - 19.58)^2]$$
$$= 4[25.81 + 17.89 + .85] = 4(44.55) = 178.20$$

a – 1 = 3 – 1 = 2 *a* = number of groups in Factor A (*df* for Factor A term)

Test	Example
	Sum of squared deviations for error term (SS_{error}): X is an individual score, M_A is the sample mean for that score
	$SS_{error} = [(10 - 14.5)^2 + (15 - 14.5)^2 + (20 - 14.5)^2 + (13 - 14.5)^2 + (15 - 23.75)^2 + (25 - 23.75)^2 + (30 - 23.75)^2 + (25 - 23.75)^2 + (20 - 20.5)^2 + (17 - 20.5)^2 + (25 - 20.5)^2 + (20 - 20.5)^2]$
	$= [20.25 + .25 + 30.25 + 2.25 + 76.56 + 1.56 + 39.06 + 1.56 + .25 + 12.25 + 20.25 + .25]$
	$= 204.74$
	$a\ (n - 1) = 3\ (4 - 1) = 9$ (df for error term)
	$$F = \frac{178.2 / 2}{204.74 / 9} = \frac{89.1}{22.75} = 3.92$$
	This calculated F value is then compared with the appropriate F critical value (based on alpha and df values) to determine significance. See www.psychology.ilstu.edu/psy138/resources/tables.html
Factorial, between-subjects ANOVA	Samples for two factors (A and B), each with two levels (1 and 2)
	Sample A1, B1 ($X_{A1,\ B1}$ values): 67, 80, 75, 77, 78
	($M_{A1,\ B1} = 75.40$)
	Sample A2, B1 ($X_{A2,\ B1}$ values): 65, 59, 70, 62, 60
	($M_{A2,\ B1} = 63.20$)
	Sample A1, B2 ($X_{A1,\ B2}$ values): 59, 60, 67, 52, 60
	($M_{A1,\ B2} = 59.60$)
	Sample A2, B2 ($X_{A2,\ B2}$ values): 87, 90, 82, 86, 85
	($M_{A2,\ B2} = 86.00$)
	Overall means for Factor A: $M_{A1} = 67.50$, $M_{A2} = 74.6$
	Overall means for Factor B: $M_{B1} = 69.30$, $M_{B2} = 72.80$
	Overall mean for all scores: $M_T = 71.05$
	$a = 2$ (number of levels for Factor A)
	$b = 2$ (number of levels for Factor B)
	$n = 5$ (number of scores per group)
	Three effects tested: Main effect of Factor A (F_A), Main effect of Factor B (F_B), and Interaction of A and B ($F_{A \times B}$)
	$$F_A = \frac{SS_A / a - 1}{SS_{error} / ab(n - 1)}$$
	$(a - 1)$ is df for Factor A term, $ab(n - 1)$ is df for error term
	$$F_B = \frac{SS_B / b - 1}{SS_{error} / ab(n - 1)}$$
	$(b - 1)$ is df for Factor B term

Test	Example
	$F_{A \times B} = \dfrac{SS_{A \times B} / (a-1)(b-1)}{SS_{error} / ab(n-1)}$

$(a - 1)(b - 1)$ is df for interaction $A \times B$ term

$SS_A = 5(2)\ S\ [(67.5 - 71.05)^2 + (74.6 - 71.05)^2] = 252$

$SSs/AB = \Sigma\ [(67 - 75.4)^2 + (80 - 75.4)^2 + (75 - 75.4)^2 + (77 - 75.4)^2 + (78 - 75.4)^2 +$
$(65 - 63.2)^2 + (59 - 63.2)^2 + (70 - 63.2)^2 + (62 - 63.2)^2 + (60 - 63.2)^2 + (50 - 59.6)^2 +$
$(60 - 59.6)^2 + (67 - 59.6)^2 + (52 - 59.6)^2 + (60 - 59.6)^2 + (87 - 86)^2 + (90 - 86)^2 +$
$(82 - 86)^2 + (86 - 86)^2 + (85 - 86)^2] = 327.2$

$F_A = \dfrac{252 / (2-1)}{327.2 / [2(2)(5-1)]} = \dfrac{252}{20.45} = 12.33$

$SS_B = 5(2)\ S\ [(69.3 - 71.05)^2 + (72.8 - 71.05)^2] = 61.25$

$F_B = \dfrac{61.25 / 2 - 1}{327.2 / [2(2)(5-1)]} = \dfrac{61.25}{20.45} = 3.00$

$SS_{A \times B} = n\ S\ (M_{AB} - M_A - M_B + M_T)^2$, where M_{AB} is the AB condition mean, M_A is the mean for that level of Factor A, and M_B is the mean for that level of Factor B

$SS_{A \times B} = 5\ S\ [(75.4 - 67.5 - 69.3 + 71.05)^2 + (86 - 74.6 - 72.8 + 71.05)^2] = 1862.45$

$F_{A \times B} = \dfrac{1862.45 / [(2-1)(2-1)]}{327.2 / [2(2)(5-1)]} = \dfrac{1862.45}{20.45} = 91.07$

Each of these calculated F values is then compared with the appropriate F critical value (based on alpha and df values) to determine significance. See www.psychology.ilstu.edu/psy138/resources/tables.html

Test	Example
Pearson r correlation	Measure 1 values (X values): 4, 3, 5, 3, 2, 4, 5, 3, 2, 1 ($M_X = 3.2$ from above) Measure 2 values (Y values): 2, 3, 2, 3, 2, 2, 4, 3, 2, 2 ($M_Y = 2.5$ from above)

$$r = \dfrac{\Sigma[(X - M_X)(Y - M_Y)]}{\sqrt{\Sigma[(X - M_X)^2 (Y - M_Y)^2]}}$$

$$= \dfrac{\begin{aligned}&[(4 - 3.2)(2 - 2.5) + (3 - 3.2)(3 - 3.5) + (5 - 3.2)(2 - 2.5) +\\ &(3 - 3.2)(3 - 2.5) + (2 - 3.2)(2 - 2.5) + (4 - 3.2)(2 - 2.5) +\\ &(5 - 3.2)(4 - 2.5) + (3 - 3.2)(3 - 3.2) + (2 - 3.2)(2 - 2.5) +\\ &(1 - 3.2)(2 - 2.5)]\end{aligned}}{\sqrt{\begin{aligned}&[(4 - 3.2)^2 + (3 - 3.2)^2 + (5 - 3.2)^2 + (3 - 3.2)^2 + (2 - 3.2)^2 +\\ &((4 - 3.2)^2 + (5 - 3.2)^2 + (3 - 3.2)^2 + (2 - 3.2)^2 + (1 - 3.2)^2]\\ &[(2 - 2.5)^2 + (3 - 2.5)^2 + (2 - 2.5)^2 + (3 - 2.5)^2 + (2 - 2.5)^2 +\\ &(2 - 2.5)^2 + (4 - 2.5)^2 + (3 - 2.5)^2 + (2 - 2.5)^2 + (2 - 2.5)^2\end{aligned}}}$$

Test	Example
	$$= \frac{[-.4 + -.1 + -.9 + -.1 + .6 + -.4 + 2.7 + -.1 + .6 + 1.1]}{\sqrt{[0.64 + 0.04 + 3.24 + 0.04 + 1.44 + 0.64 + 3.24 + 0.04 + 1.44 + 4.84]} \sqrt{[0.25 + 0.25 + 0.25 + 0.25 + 0.25 + 0.25 + 2.25 + 0.25 + 0.25 + 0.25]}}$$ $$= \frac{3}{\sqrt{[15.6][4.5]}} = \frac{3}{8.38} = .36$$ This calculated r value is then compared with the appropriate r critical value (based on alpha and df of $[n - 2]$) to determine significance. See www.psychology.ilstu.edu/psy138/resources/tables.html.
Linear regression	Predictor variable values (X values): 4, 3, 5, 3, 2, 4, 5, 3, 2, 1 (M_X = 3.2 from above) Outcome variable values (Y values): 2, 3, 2, 3, 2, 2, 4, 3, 2, 2 (M_Y = 2.5 from above) $\hat{Y}$ = b X + a: regression line to predict Y value ($\hat{Y}$) from the value of X, must calculate b (slope of the line) and a (the intercept of the line—the value of Y when X = 0) $$b = \frac{\Sigma(X - M_X)(Y - M_Y)}{\Sigma(X - M_X)^2}$$ the numerator of this equation is equivalent to the numerator of the Pearson r calculation done above (3.00); the denominator is the sum of squared deviations for the predictor variable X(SS_X) $$SS_X = [(4 - 3.2)^2 + (3 - 3.2)^2 + (5 - 3.2)^2 + (3 - 3.2)^2$$ $$+ (2 - 3.2)^2 + (4 - 3.2)^2 + (5 - 3.2)^2 + (3 - 3.2)^2$$ $$+ (2 - 3.2)^2 + (1 - 3.2)^2] = 15.6$$ $$b = \frac{3}{15.6} = .19. \text{ This is the slope of the "best fit" line}$$ $a = M_Y - b(M_X) = 2.5 - .19(3.2) = 1.89$. This is the intercept for the "best fit" line Thus, the regression equation is $\hat{Y}$ = .19X + 1.89 This equation can be used to predict a value of the outcome variable Y from the predictor variable X.
Pearson chi-square test	Frequency data from Example in Chapter 15: 		Older	Younger	Total	|---|---|---|---|	Yes	8	4	12		No	2	6	8		Total	10	10		

Test	Example
	The first step is to calculate expected frequencies for each combination of factors above if there is no relationship between these factors:

$$f_e = \frac{f_{column}(f_{row})}{n}$$

Expected older (yes): $f_e = \dfrac{10(12)}{20} = 6$

Expected older (no): $f_e = \dfrac{10(8)}{20} = 4$

Expected younger (yes): $f_e = \dfrac{10(12)}{20} = 6$

Expected younger (no): $f_e = \dfrac{10(8)}{20} = 4$

Expected frequencies:

	Older	Younger
Yes	6	6
No	4	4

The chi-square statistic is calculated from the difference between the observed and expected frequencies:

$$\chi^2 = \Sigma \frac{(f_{observed} - f_{expected})^2}{f_{expected}} = \frac{(8-6)^2}{6} + \frac{(4-6)^2}{6} + \frac{(2-4)^2}{4} + \frac{(6-4)^2}{4}$$

$$= .67 + .67 + 1 + 1 = 3.34$$

This calculated χ^2 value is then compared with the appropriate χ^2 critical value (based on alpha and *df* of number of columns × number of rows) to determine significance. See www.psychology.ilstu.edu/psy138/resources/tables.html.

STATISTICAL TABLES

The tables below provide critical statistical values for the inferential statistics calculated above.

Critical t Values

	One-tailed Test					
	0.25	0.10	0.05	0.025	0.01	0.005
	Two-tailed Test					
df	0.50	0.20	0.10	0.05	0.02	0.01
1	1.000	3.078	6.314	12.706	31.821	63.657
2	0.816	1.886	2.920	4.303	6.965	9.925
3	0.765	1.638	2.353	3.182	4.541	5.841
4	0.741	1.533	2.132	2.776	3.747	4.604
5	0.727	1.476	2.015	2.571	3.365	4.032
6	0.718	1.440	1.943	2.447	3.143	3.707
7	0.711	1.415	1.895	2.365	2.998	3.499
8	0.706	1.397	1.860	2.306	2.896	3.355
9	0.703	1.383	1.833	2.262	2.821	3.250
10	0.700	1.372	1.812	2.228	2.764	3.169
11	0.697	1.363	1.796	2.201	2.718	3.106
12	0.695	1.356	1.782	2.179	2.681	3.055
13	0.694	1.350	1.771	2.160	2.650	3.012
14	0.692	1.345	1.761	2.145	2.624	2.977
15	0.691	1.341	1.753	2.131	2.602	2.947
16	0.690	1.337	1.746	2.120	2.583	2.921
17	0.689	1.333	1.740	2.110	2.567	2.898
18	0.688	1.330	1.734	2.101	2.552	2.878
19	0.688	1.328	1.729	2.093	2.539	2.861
20	0.687	1.325	1.725	2.086	2.528	2.845
21	0.686	1.323	1.721	2.080	2.518	2.831
22	0.686	1.321	1.717	2.074	2.508	2.819

	One-tailed Test					
	0.25	0.10	0.05	0.025	0.01	0.005
	Two-tailed Test					
df	0.50	0.20	0.10	0.05	0.02	0.01
23	0.685	1.319	1.714	2.069	2.500	2.807
24	0.685	1.318	1.711	2.064	2.492	2.797
25	0.684	1.316	1.708	2.060	2.485	2.787
26	0.684	1.315	1.706	2.056	2.479	2.779
27	0.684	1.314	1.703	2.052	2.473	2.771
28	0.683	1.313	1.701	2.048	2.467	2.763
29	0.683	1.311	1.699	2.045	2.462	2.756
30	0.683	1.310	1.697	2.042	2.457	2.750
40	0.681	1.303	1.684	2.021	2.423	2.704
60	0.679	1.296	1.671	2.000	2.390	2.660
120	0.677	1.289	1.658	1.980	2.358	2.617
∞	0.674	1.282	1.645	1.960	2.326	2.576

Critical F Values

p = .05 in bold

p = .01 in italics

Degrees of freedom for numerator

Degrees of freedom for denominator	1	2	3	4	5	6	7	8	9	10
1	**161.4**	**199.5**	**215.7**	**224.6**	**230.2**	**234.0**	**236.8**	**240.5**	**241.9**	**243.9**
	4052	*5000*	*5403*	*5625*	*5764*	*5859*	*5928*	*5981*	*6022*	*6056*
2	**18.51**	**19.00**	**19.16**	**19.25**	**19.30**	**19.33**	**19.35**	**19.37**	**19.38**	**19.40**
	98.5	*99.0*	*99.2*	*99.2*	*99.3*	*99.3*	*99.4*	*99.4*	*99.4*	*99.4*
3	**10.3**	**9.55**	**9.28**	**9.12**	**9.01**	**8.94**	**8.89**	**8.85**	**8.81**	**8.79**
	34.1	*30.8*	*29.5*	*28.7*	*28.2*	*27.9*	*27.7*	*27.5*	*27.3*	*27.2*

Degrees of freedom for denominator	1	2	3	4	5	6	7	8	9	10
4	**7.71**	**6.94**	**6.59**	**6.39**	**6.26**	**6.16**	**6.09**	**6.04**	**6.00**	**5.96**
	21.2	*18.0*	*16.7*	*16.0*	*15.5*	*15.2*	*15.0*	*14.8*	*14.7*	*14.5*
5	**6.61**	**5.79**	**5.41**	**5.19**	**5.05**	**4.95**	**4.88**	**4.82**	**4.77**	**4.74**
	16.3	*13.3*	*12.1*	*11.4*	*11.0*	*10.7*	*10.5*	*10.3*	*10.2*	*10.1*
6	5.99	5.14	4.76	4.53	4.39	4.28	4.21	4.15	4.10	4.06
	13.7	*10.9*	*9.78*	*9.15*	*8.75*	*8.47*	*8.26*	*8.10*	*7.98*	*7.87*
7	**5.59**	**4.74**	**4.35**	**4.12**	**3.97**	**3.87**	**3.79**	**3.73**	**3.68**	**3.64**
	12.2	*9.55*	*8.45*	*7.85*	*7.46*	*7.19*	*6.99*	*6.84*	*6.72*	*6.62*
8	**5.32**	**4.46**	**4.07**	**3.84**	**3.69**	**3.58**	**3.50**	**3.44**	**3.39**	**3.35**
	11.3	*8.65*	*7.59*	*7.01*	*6.63*	*6.37*	*6.18*	*6.03*	*5.91*	*5.81*
9	**5.12**	**4.26**	**3.86**	**3.63**	**3.48**	**3.37**	**3.29**	**3.23**	**3.18**	**3.14**
	10.6	*8.02*	*6.99*	*6.42*	*6.06*	*5.80*	*5.61*	*5.47*	*5.35*	*5.26*
10	**4.96**	**4.10**	**3.71**	**3.48**	**3.33**	**3.22**	**3.14**	**3.07**	**3.02**	**2.98**
	10.0	*7.56*	*6.55*	*5.99*	*5.64*	*5.39*	*5.20*	*5.06*	*4.94*	*4.85*
11	4.84	3.98	3.59	3.36	3.20	3.09	3.01	2.95	2.90	2.85
	9.65	*7.21*	*6.22*	*5.67*	*5.32*	*5.07*	*4.89*	*4.74*	*4.63*	*4.54*
12	**4.75**	**3.89**	**3.49**	**3.26**	**3.11**	**3.00**	**2.91**	**2.85**	**2.80**	**2.75**
	9.33	*6.93*	*5.95*	*5.41*	*5.06*	*4.82*	*4.64*	*4.50*	*4.39*	*4.30*
13	**4.67**	**3.81**	**3.41**	**3.18**	**3.03**	**2.92**	**2.83**	**2.77**	**2.71**	**2.67**
	9.07	*6.70*	*5.74*	*5.21*	*4.86*	*4.62*	*4.44*	*4.30*	*4.19*	*4.10*
14	**4.60**	**3.74**	**3.34**	**3.11**	**2.96**	**2.85**	**2.76**	**2.70**	**2.65**	**2.60**
	8.86	*6.51*	*5.56*	*5.04*	*4.69*	*4.46*	*4.28*	*4.14*	*4.03*	*3.94*
15	**4.54**	**3.68**	**3.29**	**3.06**	**2.90**	**2.79**	**2.71**	**2.64**	**2.59**	**2.54**
	8.68	*6.36*	*5.42*	*4.89*	*4.56*	*4.32*	*4.14*	*4.00*	*3.89*	*3.80*
16	**4.49**	**3.63**	**3.24**	**3.01**	**2.85**	**2.74**	**2.66**	**2.59**	**2.54**	**2.49**
	8.53	*6.23*	*5.29*	*4.77*	*4.44*	*4.20*	*4.03*	*3.89*	*3.78*	*3.69*

Degrees of freedom for denominator	1	2	3	4	5	6	7	8	9	10
17	**4.45**	**3.59**	**3.20**	**2.96**	**2.81**	**2.70**	**2.61**	**2.55**	**2.49**	**2.45**
	8.40	6.11	5.18	4.67	4.34	4.10	3.93	3.79	3.68	3.59
18	**4.41**	**3.55**	**3.16**	**2.93**	**2.77**	**2.66**	**2.58**	**2.51**	**2.46**	**2.41**
	8.29	6.01	5.09	4.58	4.25	4.01	3.84	3.71	3.60	3.51
19	**4.38**	**3.52**	**3.13**	**2.90**	**2.74**	**2.63**	**2.54**	**2.48**	**2.42**	**2.38**
	8.18	5.93	5.01	4.50	4.17	3.94	3.77	3.63	3.52	3.43
20	**4.35**	**3.49**	**3.10**	**2.87**	**2.71**	**2.60**	**2.51**	**2.45**	**2.39**	**2.35**
	8.10	5.85	4.94	4.43	4.10	3.87	3.70	3.56	3.46	3.37
22	**4.30**	**3.44**	**3.05**	**2.82**	**2.66**	**2.55**	**2.46**	**2.40**	**2.34**	**2.30**
	7.95	5.72	4.82	4.31	3.99	3.76	3.59	3.45	3.35	3.26
30	**4.17**	**3.32**	**2.92**	**2.69**	**2.53**	**2.42**	**2.33**	**2.27**	**2.21**	**2.16**
	7.56	5.39	4.51	4.02	3.70	3.47	3.30	3.17	3.07	2.98
40	**4.08**	**3.23**	**2.84**	**2.61**	**2.45**	**2.34**	**2.25**	**2.18**	**2.12**	**2.08**
	7.31	5.18	4.31	3.83	3.51	3.29	3.12	2.99	2.89	2.80
60	**4.00**	**3.15**	**2.76**	**2.53**	**2.37**	**2.25**	**2.17**	**2.10**	**2.04**	**1.99**
	7.08	4.98	4.13	3.65	3.34	3.12	2.95	2.82	2.72	2.63
120	**3.92**	**3.07**	**2.68**	**2.45**	**2.29**	**2.17**	**2.09**	**2.02**	**1.96**	**1.91**
	6.85	4.79	3.95	3.48	3.17	2.96	2.79	2.66	2.56	2.47
∞	**3.84**	**3.00**	**2.60**	**2.37**	**2.21**	**2.10**	**2.00**	**1.94**	**1.88**	**1.83**
	6.63	4.61	3.78	3.32	3.02	2.80	2.64	2.51	2.41	2.32

Critical *r* Values

	One-tailed Test			
	0.05	0.025	0.01	0.005
	Two-tailed Test			
df	0.10	0.05	0.02	0.01
1	.988	.997	.9995	.9999
2	.900	.950	.980	.990
3	.805	.878	.934	.959
4	.729	.811	.882	.917
5	.669	.754	.833	.874
6	.622	.707	.789	.834
7	.582	.666	.750	.798
8	.549	.632	.716	.765
9	.521	.602	.685	.735
10	.497	.576	.658	.708
11	.476	.553	.634	.684
12	.458	.532	.612	.661
13	.441	.514	.592	.641
14	.426	.497	.574	.623
15	.412	.482	.558	.606
16	.400	.468	.542	.590
17	.389	.456	.528	.575
18	.378	.444	.516	.561
19	.369	.433	.503	.549
20	.360	.423	.492	.537
21	.352	.413	.482	.526
22	.344	.404	.472	.515
23	.337	.396	.462	.505

	One-tailed Test			
	0.05	0.025	0.01	0.005
	Two-tailed Test			
df	0.10	0.05	0.02	0.01
24	.330	.388	.453	.496
25	.323	.381	.445	.487
26	.317	.374	.437	.479
27	.311	.367	.430	.471
28	.306	.361	.423	.463
29	.301	.355	.416	.456
30	.296	.349	.409	.449
35	.275	.325	.381	.418
40	.257	.304	.358	.393
45	.243	.288	.338	.372
50	.231	.273	.322	.354
60	.211	.250	.295	.325
70	.195	.232	.274	.302
80	.183	.217	.256	.283
90	.173	.205	.242	.267
100	.164	.195	.230	.254

Critical χ^2 Values

df	Level of Significance		
	0.05	0.025	0.01
1	3.84	5.02	6.64
2	5.99	7.38	9.21
3	7.81	9.35	11.34
4	9.49	11.14	13.28
5	11.07	12.83	15.09
6	12.59	14.45	16.81
7	14.07	16.01	18.48
8	15.51	17.53	20.09
9	16.92	19.02	21.67
10	18.31	20.48	23.21
11	19.68	21.92	24.72
12	21.03	23.34	26.22
13	22.36	24.74	27.69
14	23.68	26.11	29.14
15	25.00	27.49	30.58
16	26.30	28.85	32.00
17	27.59	30.19	33.41
18	28.87	31.53	34.80
19	30.14	32.85	36.19
20	31.41	34.17	37.57
21	32.67	35.48	38.93
22	33.92	36.78	40.29
23	35.17	38.08	41.64
24	36.42	39.36	42.98
25	37.65	40.65	44.31

Level of Significance			
df	0.05	0.025	0.01
26	38.88	41.92	45.64
27	40.11	43.19	46.96
28	41.34	44.46	48.28
29	42.56	45.72	49.59
30	43.77	46.98	50.89
40	55.76	59.34	63.69
50	67.50	71.42	76.15

Glossary

A-B-A/Reversal Design: a small-*n*, baseline design where the baseline behavior is measured, followed by implementation of a treatment, followed by another baseline measure after the treatment has ended

Abstract: a summary of an article that appears at the beginning of the article and in searchable databases of journal articles

Alpha Level: the probability level used by researchers to indicate the cutoff probability level (highest value) that allows them to reject the null hypothesis

Amount Variable: a variable that includes levels with a different amount of the treatment changing from level to level

Analysis of Variance (ANOVA): inferential test used for designs with three or more sample means

Applied Research: research conducted with the goal of solving everyday problems

Archival Data: a data collection technique that involves analysis of pre-existing data

Attrition/Mortality: occurs when participants choose not to complete a study

Authority: relying on a knowledgeable person or group as a means of knowing about the world

Bar Graph: a graph of the means for different conditions in a study where the bar height represents the size of the mean

Baseline Design: a small-*n* design that involves baseline measurements of behavior as compared with measures of behavior during the implementation of a treatment

Baseline Measurement: measurement of behavior without a treatment; used as a comparison

Basic Research: research conducted with the goal of understanding fundamental processes of phenomena

Between-Subjects Variable: each participant experiences only one level of the independent variable

Bivalent Independent Variable: an independent variable with two levels—a design is considered bivalent if it contains only one bivalent independent variable

Carryover Effects: occur when participants' experience in one condition affects their behavior in another condition of a study

Case Study: a research design that involves intensive study of particular individuals and their behaviors

Causal Hypothesis: a prediction about the results of a study that includes the causes of a behavior

Causal Research Question: a research question that asks what causes specific behaviors to occur

Central Tendency: representation of a typical score in a distribution

Chi-Square Test: a significance test used to determine whether a relationship exists between two variables measured on nominal or ordinal scales

Closed-Ended Response Scale: participants respond to survey questions according to the response options provided by the researcher

Cluster Sample: sample chosen randomly from clusters identified in the population

Coercion: forcing participants to participate in research without their consent

Cohort-Sequential Design: a developmental design where multiple samples of participants of different ages are followed over time and tested at different ages

Confederate: a person who is part of a research study, but acts as though he or she is not, to deceive the participant about the study's purpose

Confidence Interval: a range of values that the population mean likely falls in with a specific level of certainty

Confidentiality: it is the researcher's responsibility to protect the participants' identity and right to privacy (including participant responses) during and after the research study

Confirmation Bias: seeking only evidence that supports our beliefs and ignoring evidence that contradicts those beliefs

Confounding Variable: an extraneous factor present in a study that may affect the results

Consent Form: a form provided to the participants at the beginning of a research study to obtain their consent for the study and to explain the study's purpose and risks and the participants' rights as participants

Construct Validity: indicates that a survey measures the behavior it is designed to measure

Content Analysis: an archival data collection technique that involves analysis of the content of an individual's spoken or written record

Control Group: the group of participants in an experiment who do not experience the treatment level of the independent variable

Convenience/Purposive Sample: sample chosen such that the probability of an individual being chosen cannot be determined

Correlational Study: a type of research design that examines the relationships between multiple dependent variables, without manipulating any of the variables

Counterbalancing: a control used in within-subjects experiments where equal numbers of participants are randomly assigned to different orders of the conditions

Coverage Error: a sampling error that occurs when the sample chosen to complete a survey does not provide a good representation of the population

Criterion-Related Validity: determining the validity of the scores of a survey by examining the relationship between the survey scores and other established measures of the behavior of interest

Critical Region: the most extreme portion of a distribution of statistical values for the null hypothesis determined by the alpha level (typically 5%)

Cronbach's Alpha (α): method of testing scores' internal consistency that indicates the average correlation between scores on all pairs of items on a survey

Cross-Sectional Design: a developmental design where multiple samples of participants of different ages are tested once

Data-Driven Hypothesis: hypothesis for a study that is based on the results of previous, related studies

Debriefing: discussing the purpose and benefits of a research study with participants, often done at the end of the study

Deception: misleading participants about the purpose or procedures of a research study

Deduction: using logical reasoning and current knowledge as a means of knowing about the world

Deductive Reasoning: using general information to make a specific prediction

Degrees of Freedom: number of scores that can vary in the calculation of a statistic

Demand Characteristics: a source of bias that can occur in a study due to participants' changing their behavior based on their perception of the study and its purpose

Dependent/Response Variable: a variable that is measured or observed from an individual

Descriptive Hypothesis: a prediction about the results of a study that describes the behavior or the relationship between behaviors

Descriptive Research Question: a research question that asks about the presence of behavior, how frequently it is exhibited, or whether there is a relationship between different behaviors

Descriptive Statistics: measures that help us summarize data sets

Determinism: the assumption that phenomena have identifiable causes

Discrete Trials Design: a small-n design that involves a large number of trials completed by one or a few individuals and conducted to describe basic behaviors

Discussion: section of an APA-style article that compares the results of a study to the predictions and the results of previous studies

Distribution: a set of scores

Distribution of Sample Means: the distribution of all possible sample means for all possible samples from a population

Double-Blind Design: procedure used to control for experimenter bias by keeping the knowledge of the group assignments from both the participants and the researchers who interact with the participants

Empiricism: gaining knowledge through systematic observation of the world

Ex Post Facto Design: a quasi-experiment where subjects are grouped based on a characteristic they already possess (e.g., age or gender)

Experiment: a type of research design that involves manipulation of an independent variable, allowing control of extraneous variables that could affect the results

Experimental Group: the group of participants in an experiment who experience the treatment level of the independent variable

Experimenter Bias: a source of bias in a study created when a researcher treats groups differently (often unknowingly) based on knowledge of the hypothesis

External Validity: the degree to which the results of a study apply to individuals and realistic behaviors outside the study

Face Validity: on the surface, a study or scale appears to be intuitively valid

Factor Analysis: a set of statistical techniques used to analyze responses from a survey or questionnaire to group items together by concept

Factorial Design: an experiment or quasi-experiment that includes more than one independent variable

Field Experiment: an experiment conducted in the participants' natural environment

Frequency Distribution: a graph of a distribution showing the frequency of each response in the distribution

Generation/Cohort Effects: a confound that can occur in cross-sectional designs due to different experiences that different generations have

Hawthorne Effect: a source of bias that can occur in a study due to participants' changing their behavior because they are aware that they are being observed

History Effect: events that occur during the course of a study to all participants or to individual participants that can result in bias

Homogeneity of Variances: assumption of between-subjects t tests and ANOVAs that the variance in the scores in the population is equal across groups

Hypothesis: prediction regarding the results of a research study

Independent Variable: a variable in an experiment that is manipulated by the researcher such that the levels of the variable change across or within subjects in the experiment

Inductive Reasoning: using specific information to make a more general prediction

Inferential Statistics: a set of statistical procedures used by researchers to test hypotheses about populations

Informed Consent: consent obtained from participants for participation in research after the participants have been informed about the purpose, procedure, and risks of the research

Institutional Animal Care and Use Committee (IACUC): committee of knowledgeable individuals that oversees the ethics of research with non-human animal subjects at an institution

Institutional Review Board (IRB): a committee of knowledgeable individuals who oversee the ethics of research with human participants conducted at an institution

Interaction Effect: tests the effect of one independent variable at each level of another independent variable in an ANOVA

Internal Consistency: a form of reliability that tests relationships between scores on different items of a survey

Internal Validity: the degree to which a study provides causal information about behavior

Internet Sample: sample chosen from the population by recruiting on the Internet

Inter-observer/Inter-rater Reliability: a measure of the degree to which different observers observe or code behaviors in similar ways

Interrupted Time Series Design: a time series design where the "treatment" is an independent event, such as a historical event

Interval Scale: a scale of data measurement that involves numerical responses that are equally spaced, but scores are not ratios of each other

Interviews: a data collection technique that involves direct questioning of individuals about their behaviors and attitudes

Introduction: a section of an APA-style article that introduces the topic of the study, reviews relevant background studies, and presents predictions for the data

Intuition: relying on common sense as a means of knowing about the world

Latin Square: partial counterbalancing technique where the number of orders of conditions used is equal to the number of conditions in the study

Levels of the Independent Variable: different situations or conditions that participants experience in an experiment because of the manipulation of the independent variable

Likert Scale: a scale of responses that measures a participant's agreement or disagreement with different types of statements, often with a rating from 1 to 5 or 1 to 7

Line Graph: a graph of the means for different conditions in a study where each mean is graphed as a point and the points are connected in a line to show differences between mean scores

Linear Regression: a statistical technique that determines the best fit line to a set of data to allow prediction of the score on one variable from the score on another variable

Literature Review: a process of searching for and reviewing previous studies related to a study being developed to add to the knowledge in an area and make appropriate predictions about the data

Longitudinal Design: a developmental design where a single sample of participants is followed over time and tested at different ages

Main Effect: test of the differences between all means for each level of an independent variable in an ANOVA

Matched Design: a between-subjects experiment that involves sets of participants matched on a specific characteristic with each member of the set randomly assigned to a different level of the independent variable

Maturation: natural changes that occur to the participants during the course of a study that can result in bias

Mean: the calculated average of the scores in a distribution

Median: the middle score in a distribution, such that half of the scores are above and half are below that value

Method: section of an APA-style article that describes the participants, design, stimuli, apparatus, and procedure used in the study

Mode: the most common score in a distribution

Multivalent Variable: an independent variable that includes three or more levels—a design is considered multivalent if there is only one independent variable that contains three or more levels

Naturalistic Observation: a data collection technique involving noninvasive observation of individuals in their natural environments

Negative Relationship: a relationship between variables characterized by an increase in one variable that occurs with a decrease in the other variable

Nominal Scale: a scale of data measurement that involves nonordered categorical responses

Nonequivalent Groups: groups compared in a study where participants are not randomly assigned

Noninterrupted Time Series Design: a time series design where the "treatment" is implemented by the researcher

Nonresponse Error: a sampling error that occurs when individuals chosen for the sample do not respond to the survey, biasing the sample

Nonverbal Scale: survey response scale that involves pictorial response categories for participants with low verbal skills (e.g., children)

Null Hypothesis: the hypothesis that an effect or relationship does not exist (or exists in the opposite direction of the alternative hypothesis) in the population

Nuremberg Code: set of ethical guidelines developed for research with human participants based on information gained during the Nuremberg trials after World War II

Observation: relying on what one observes as a means of knowing about the world

One-Tailed Hypothesis: only one direction of an effect or relationship is predicted in the alternative hypothesis of the test

Open-Ended Response Scale: participants respond to survey questions in any manner they feel is appropriate for the question

Operational Definition: the definition of an abstract concept used by a researcher to measure or manipulate the concept in a research study

Order Effects: occur when the order in which the participants experience conditions in an experiment affects the results of the study

Ordinal Scale: a scale of data measurement that involves ordered categorical responses

Outcome Variable: the dependent variable in a correlational study that is being predicted by the predictor variable

Outliers: extreme high or low scores in a distribution

p Value: probability value associated with an inferential test that indicates the likelihood of obtaining the data in a study when the null hypothesis is true

Parsimony: the assumption that the simplest explanation of a phenomenon is most likely to be correct

Pearson *r* Test: a significance test used to determine whether a linear relationship exists between two variables measured on interval or ratio scales

Peer Review: a process that takes place prior to publication of an article in many journals where experts make suggestions for improving an article and make a recommendation about whether an article should be published in a journal

Placebo: a sugar pill given to the control group in a drug study to allow all groups to believe that they are receiving a treatment

Plagiarism: claiming another's work or ideas as one's own

Population: a group of individuals a researcher seeks to learn about from a research study

Positive Relationship: the variables change together in the same direction (both increasing together or decreasing together)

Post Hoc Tests: additional significance tests conducted to determine which means are significantly different for a main effect

Power: ability of a significance test to detect an effect or relationship when one exists (equal to 1—the probability of a Type II error)

Predictive Research Question: a research question that asks if one behavior can be predicted from another behavior to allow predictions of future behavior

Predictor Variable: the dependent variable in a correlational study that is used to predict the score on another variable

Presence/Absence Variable: a variable that involves a manipulation with a level that involves the treatment and a level that does not involve the treatment

Pretest-Posttest Design: a type of research design (often a quasi-experiment) where behavior is measured both before and after a treatment or condition is implemented

Probability Sample: sample chosen such that individuals are chosen with a specific probability

Psychometrics: area of psychological research that involves the development, validation, and refinement of surveys and tests to measure psychological constructs

Qualitative Data: nonnumerical participant responses

Quantitative Data: numerical data

Quasi-Experiment: a type of research design where a comparison is made, as in an experiment, but no random assignment of subjects to groups occurs

Quasi-Independent/Subject Variable: variable that allows comparison of groups of participants without manipulation (i.e., no random assignment)

Quota Sample: sample chosen from the population such that available individuals are chosen with equivalent proportions of individuals for a specific characteristic in the population and sample

Random Assignment: participants are randomly assigned to levels of the independent variable in an experiment to control for individual differences as an extraneous variable

Range: the difference between the highest and lowest scores in a distribution

Ratio Scale: a scale of data measurement that involves numerical responses, where scores are ratios of each other

Reaction Time: measurement of the length of time to complete a task

Regression Toward the Mean: can occur when participants score higher or lower than their personal average—the next time they are tested, they are more likely to score near their personal average, making scores unreliable

Reliability: the degree to which the results of a study can be replicated under similar conditions

Response Rate: the percentage of people out of the total number available who respond to a survey

Results: section of an APA-style article that presents a summary of the results and the statistical tests of the predictions

Risk-Benefit Analysis: weighing the risks against the benefits of a research study to ensure that the benefits outweigh the risks

Sample: the group of individuals chosen from the population to represent it in a research study

Sampling Error: the difference between the observations in a population and in the sample that represents that population in a study

Scatterplot: a graph showing the relationship between two dependent variables for a group of individuals

Scientific/Alternative Hypothesis: the hypothesis that an effect or relationship exists (or exists in a specific direction) in the population

Significant Test: the p value is less than or equal to alpha in an inferential test, and the null hypothesis can be rejected

Simple Effects Tests: statistical tests conducted to characterize an interaction effect when one is found in an ANOVA

Simple Random Sample: sample chosen randomly from the population such that each individual has an equal chance of being selected

Single-Blind Design: procedure used to hide the group assignment from the participants in a study to prevent their beliefs about the effectiveness of a treatment from affecting the results

Small-n Design: an experiment conducted with one or a few participants to better understand the behavior of those individuals

Social Desirability Bias: bias created in survey responses from respondents' desire to be viewed more favorably by others, typically resulting in overreporting of "positive" behaviors and underreporting of "negative" behaviors

Solomon Four-Group Design: pretest-posttest design with two sets of nonequivalent groups, in which one set takes the pretest and posttest and one set takes only the posttest

Sphericity Assumption: assumption of the repeated measures (within-subjects) ANOVA that pairs of scores in the population have equal variance

Split-Half Reliability: method of testing scores' internal consistency that indicates if the scores are similar on different sets of questions on a survey that address similar topics

Standard Deviation: a measure representing the average difference between the scores and the mean of a distribution

Stratified Random Sample: sample chosen from the population such that the proportion of individuals with a particular characteristic is equivalent in the population and the sample

Survey Research: a research study that uses the survey observational technique to measure behavior

Systematic Observation: data collection technique where control is exerted over the conditions under which the behavior is observed

t Test: significance test used to compare means

Testability: the assumption that explanations of behavior can be tested and falsified through observation

Testing Effects: occur when participants are tested more than once in a study, with early testing affecting later testing

Test-Retest Reliability: indicates that the scores on a survey will be similar when participants complete the survey more than once

Theory: an explanation of behavior that can be tested through research studies

Theory-Driven Hypothesis: hypothesis for a study that is based on a theory about the behavior of interest

Third-Variable Problem: the presence of extraneous factors in a study that affect the dependent variable and can decrease the internal validity of the study

Time Series Design: a research design where patterns of scores over time are compared from before a treatment is implemented and after a treatment is implemented

Two-Tailed Hypothesis: both directions of an effect or relationship are considered in the alternative hypothesis of the test

Type I Error: error made in a significance test when the researcher rejects the null hypothesis when it is actually true

Type II Error: error made in a significance test when the researcher fails to reject the null hypothesis when it is actually false

Type Variable: a variable that involves a manipulation of types of a treatment

Variability: the spread of scores in a distribution

Variable: an attribute that can vary across individuals

Variance: the standard deviation of a distribution squared

Volunteer Sample: sample chosen from the population such that available individuals are chosen based on who volunteers to participate

Within-Subjects Variable: each participant experiences all levels of the independent variable

References

Abramson, P. R. (1984). *Sarah: A sexual biography*. Albany: State University of New York Press.

Adair, J. G. (1984). The Hawthorne effect: A reconsideration of the methodological artifact. *Journal of Applied Psychology, 69*, 334–345.

Ahern, A. L., & Hetherington, M. M. (2006). The thin ideal and body image: An experimental study of implicit attitudes. *Psychology of Addictive Behaviors, 20*, 338–342.

Alzheimer's Association. (2011). *Risk factors*. Retrieved July 22, 2011, from http://www.alz .org/alzheimers_disease_causes_risk_factors.asp

American Psychological Association. (2002). *Ethical principles of psychologists and code of conduct*. Retrieved June 15, 2008, from http://www.apa .org/ethics/code2002.pdf

American Psychological Association. (2003). *1999 Doctorate Employment Survey*. Retrieved January 11, 2008, from http://research.apa.org/des-99report.html#patterms

American Psychological Association. (2010). *Publication manual of the American Psychological Association* (6th ed.). Washington, DC: Author.

American Psychological Association. (n.d.). *Research with animals in psychology*. Retrieved June 15, 2008, from http://www.apa.org/science/animal2.html

Anderson, B., & Harvey, T. (1996). Alterations in cortical thickness and neuronal density in the frontal cortex of Albert Einstein. *Neuroscience Letters, 21*, 161–164.

Ashe, S. E. (1955). Opinions and social pressure. *Scientific American, 193*, 31–35.

Baker, J. C., Hanley, G. P., & Mathews, R. M. (2006). Staff-administered functional analysis and treatment of aggression by an elder with dementia. *Journal of Applied Behavior Analysis, 39*, 469–474.

Ban, S. W., Lee, M., & Yang, H. S. (2004). A face detection using biologically motivated bottom-up saliency map model and top-down perception model. *Neurocomputing: An International Journal, 56*, 475–480.

Barlow, D. H., & Durand, V. M. (2008). *Abnormal psychology: An integrative approach* (5th ed.). Belmont, CA: Wadsworth.

Barlow, D. H., & Hersen, M. (1984). *Single case experimental designs: Strategies for studying behavior change*. New York, NY: Pergamon Press.

Barnett, R. C., Marshall, N. L., & Singer, J. D. (1992). Job experiences over time, multiple roles, and women's mental health: A longitudinal study. *Journal of Personality and Social Psychology, 62*, 634–644.

Bartecchi, C., Aldever, R. N., Nevin-Woods, C., Thomas, W. M., Estacio, R. M., Bartelson, B. B., & Krantz, M. J. (2006). Reduction in the incidence of acute myocardial infarction associated with a citywide smoking ordinance. *Circulation, 114*, 1490–1496.

Bastian, B., Jetten, J., & Ferris, L. J. (2014). Pain as social glue: Shared pain increases cooperation. *Psychological Science, 25*, 2079–2085.

Beck, A. T., & Steer, R. A. (1993). *Beck Anxiety Inventory manual*. San Antonio, TX: PsychCorp.

Beck, A. T., Steer, R. A., & Brown, G. K. (1996). *Manual for the Beck Depression Inventory–II*. San Antonio, TX: PsychCorp.

Benenson, J. F., & Koulnazarian, M. (2008). Sex differences in help-seeking appear in early childhood. *British Journal of Developmental Psychology, 26*, 163–169.

Benenson, J. F., Markovits, H., Fitzgerald, C., Geoffroy, D., Flemming, J., Kahlenberg, S. M., & Wrangham, R. W. (2009). Males' greater tolerance of same-sex peers. *Psychological Science, 20*, 184–190.

Birnbaum, M. H. (2001). *Introduction to behavioral research on the Internet.* Upper Saddle River, NJ: Prentice Hall.

Body mass index. (2014). *Merriam-Webster's Collegiate Dictionary* (11th ed.). Springfield, MA: Merriam-Webster.

Boezeman, E. J., & Ellemers, N. (2008). Volunteer recruitment: The role of organizational support and anticipated respect in non-volunteer's attraction to charitable volunteer organizations. *Journal of Applied Psychology, 93,* 1013–1026.

Boger, K. D., Tompson, M. C., Briggs-Gowan, M. J., Pavlis, L. E., & Carter, A. S. (2008). Parental expressed emotion toward children: Prediction from early family functioning. *Journal of Family Psychology, 22,* 784–788.

Bohbot, V. D., & Corkin, S. (2007). Posterior parahippocampal place learning in H.M. *Hippocampus, 17,* 863–872.

Boothby, E. J., Clark, M. S., & Bargh, J. A. (2014). Shared experiences are amplified. *Psychological Science, 25,* 2209–2216.

Booth-LaForce, C., & Oxford, M. L. (2008). Trajectories of social withdrawal from grades 1 to 6: Prediction from early parenting, attachment, and temperament. *Developmental Psychology, 44,* 1298–1313.

Bordens, K. S., & Abbott, B. B. (1999). *Research design and methods: A process approach.* Mountain View, CA: Mayfield.

Bramel, D., & Friend, R. (1981). Hawthorne, the myth of the docile worker, and class bias in psychology. *American Psychologist, 36,* 867–868.

Brandt, A. (2000). Racism and research: The case of the Tuskegee syphilis experiment. In S. M. Reverby (Ed.), *Tuskegee's truths: Rethinking the Tuskegee syphilis study* (pp. 15–33). Chapel Hill: University of North Carolina Press.

Brody, J. E. (1996). Good habits outweigh genes as key to a healthy old age. *The New York Times.* Retrieved June 3, 2009, from http://www.nytimes.com/1996/02/28/us/good-habits-outweigh-genes-as-key-to-a-healthy-old-age.html?scp = 1&sq = alzheimers %20 cognitive&st = cse

Brown-Iannuzzi, J. L., Lundberg, K. B., Kay, A. C., & Payne, B. K. (2015). Subjective status shapes political preferences. *Psychological Science, 26,* 15–26.

Broyles, L. M., Tate, J. A., & Happ, M. B. (2008). Videorecording in clinical research. *Nursing Research, 57,* 59–63.

Bub, D. N., Masson, M. E. J., & Lin, T. (2013). Features of planned hand actions influence identification of graspable objects. *Psychological Science, 24,* 1269–1276.

Burger, J. M. (2009). Replicating Milgram: Would people still obey today? *American Psychologist, 64,* 1–11.

Campbell, W. K., Bosson, J. K., Goheen, T. W., Lakey, C. E., & Kernis, M. H. (2007). Do narcissists dislike themselves "deep down inside"? *Psychological Science, 18,* 227–229.

Centers for Disease Control and Prevention. (2011). *FastStats.* Retrieved June 9, 2015, from http://www.cdc.gov/nchs/fastats/heart.htm

Cheung, F. M., Leung, K., Fan, R., Song, W., Zhang, J.-X., & Zhang, J.-P. (1996). Development of the Chinese Personality Assessment Inventory (CPAI). *Journal of Cross-Cultural Psychology, 27,* 181–199.

Chiang, H. (2008). Communicative spontaneity of children with autism: A preliminary analysis. *Autism, 12,* 9–21.

Chouinard, R., & Roy, N. (2008). Changes in high school students' competence beliefs, utility value, and achievement goals in mathematics. *British Journal of Educational Psychology, 78,* 31–50.

Coane, J. H., & McBride, D. M. (2006). The role of test structure in creating false memories. *Memory & Cognition, 34,* 1026–1036.

Cohen, J. (1988). *Statistical power analysis for the behavioral sciences* (2nd ed.). Hillsdale, NJ: Lawrence Erlbaum.

Cohen, J. (1990). Things I have learned (so far). *American Psychologist, 45,* 1304–1312.

Cohen, J. (1994). The earth is round ($p < .05$). *American Psychologist, 49,* 997–1003.

Compton, M. T., Goulding, S. M., & Walker, E. F. (2007). Cannabis use, first-episode psychosis, and schizotypy: A summary and synthesis of recent literature. *Current Psychiatry Review, 3,* 161–171.

Corneille, O., Monin, B., & Pleyers, G. (2005). Is positivity a cue or a response option? Warm glow vs evaluative matching in the familiarity for attractive and not-so-attractive face. *Journal of Experimental Social Psychology, 41,* 431–437.

Coyle, T. R., & Pillow, D. R. (2008). SAT and ACT predict college GPA after removing g. *Intelligence, 36,* 719–729.

Creasey, G., & Ladd, A. (2005). Negative mood regulation expectancies and conflict behaviors in late adolescent college student romantic relationships: The moderating role of generalized attachment representations. *Journal of Research on Adolescence, 14,* 235–255.

Crowne, D. P., & Marlowe, D. (1960). A new scale of social desirability independent of psychopathology. *Journal of Consulting Psychology, 24,* 349–354.

DeSouza, E., & Fansler, A. G. (2003). Contrapower sexual harassment: A survey of students and faculty members. *Sex Roles, 48,* 519–542.

Dillman, D. A. (2000). *Mail and Internet surveys: The tailored design method.* New York, NY: Wiley.

Doherty, R. W., & Hilberg, R. S. (2007). Standards for effective pedagogy, classroom organization, English proficiency, student achievement. *Journal of Educational Research, 101,* 24–34.

Egan, L. C., Santos, L. R., & Bloom, P. (2007). The origins of cognitive dissonance: Evidence from children and monkeys. *Psychological Science, 18,* 978–983.

Einstein, G. O., & McDaniel, M. A. (2005). Prospective memory: Multiple retrieval processes. *Current Directions in Psychological Science, 14,* 286–290.

Ferrè, E. R., Lopez, C., & Haggard, P. (2014). Anchoring the self to the body: Vestibular contribution to the sense of self. *Psychological Science, 25,* 2106–2108.

Fowers, B. J., & Olson, D. H. (1993). ENRICH Marital Satisfaction Scale: A brief research clinical tool. *Journal of Family Psychology, 7,* 176–185.

Fromkin, V., Krashen, S., Curtiss, S., Rigler, D., & Rigler, M. (1974). The development of language in Genie: A case of language acquisition beyond the "critical period." *Brain and Language, 1,* 81–107.

Gardner, H. (1999). *Intelligence reframed: Multiple intelligences for the 21st century.* New York, NY: Basic Books.

Geraerts, E., Bernstein, D. M., Merekelbach, H., Linders, C., Raymaekers, L., & Loftus, E. F. (2008). Lasting false beliefs and their behavioral consequences. *Psychological Science, 19,* 749–753.

Gino, F., & Schweitzer, M. E. (2008). Blinded by anger or feeling the love: How emotions influence advice taking. *Journal of Applied Psychology, 93,* 1165–1173.

Goleman, D. (1995). *Emotional intelligence.* New York, NY: Bantam Books.

Grant, D. A. (1948). The Latin square principle in the design and analysis of psychological experiments. *Psychological Bulletin, 45,* 427–442.

Green, S. B., & Salkind, N. J. (2007). *Using SPSS for Windows and Macintosh: Analyzing and understanding data* (5th ed.). Upper Saddle River, NJ: Pearson/Prentice Hall.

Green, S. M., Hadjistavropoulos, T., & Sharpe, D. (2008). Client personality characteristics predict satisfaction with cognitive behavior therapy. *Journal of Clinical Psychology, 64,* 40–51.

Greenwald, A. G. (1975). Consequences of prejudice against the null hypothesis. *Psychological Bulletin, 82,* 1–20.

Greenwald, A. G., McGhee, D. E., & Schwartz, J. L. K. (1998). Measuring individual differences in implicit cognition: The Implicit Association Test. *Journal of Personality and Social Psychology, 74,* 1464–1480.

Haun, D. B. M., Rekers, Y., & Tomasello, M. (2014). Children conform to the behavior of peers; Other great apes stick with what they know. *Psychological Science, 25,* 2160–2167.

Heidenreich, B. A. (1993). Investigations into the effects of repeated amphetamine administration and crus cerebri lesions on the electrophysiology of midbrain dopamine neurons in the rat. *Dissertation Abstracts International, 53,* 4522.

Henrich, J., Heine, S. J., & Norenzayan, A. (2010). The weirdest people in the world? *Behavioral and Brain Sciences, 33,* 61–135.

Hilts, P. J. (1996). *Memory's ghost: The nature of memory and the strange tale of Mr. M.* New York, NY: Touchstone.

Hite, S. (1987). *Women and love: A cultural revolution in progress.* New York, NY: St. Martin's Press.

Howell, D. C. (2009). *Statistical methods for psychology*. Belmont, CA: Wadsworth.

Hund, A. M., & Plumert, J. M. (2003). Does information about what things are influence children's memory for where things are? *Developmental Psychology, 39*, 939–948.

Jalonick, M. C. (2011, July 8). Mississippi tips scale as nation's fattest state. *The Pantagraph*, A7.

Kahn, J. H., & Hessling, R. M. (2001). Measuring the tendency to conceal versus disclose psychological distress. *Journal of Social and Clinical Psychology, 20*, 41–65.

Kahn, J. H., & Schlosser, L. Z. (2010). The graduate research training environment in professional psychology: A multilevel investigation. *Training and Education in Professional Psychology, 4*, 183–193.

Kardash, C. M. (2000). Evaluation of undergraduate research experience: Perceptions of undergraduate interns and their faculty mentors. *Journal of Educational Research, 92*, 191–201.

Keller, M. C., Fredrickson, B. L., Ybarra, O., Côté, S., Johnson, K., Mikels, J., ... Wager, T. (2005). A warm heart and a clear head: The contingent effects of weather on mood and cognition. *Psychological Science, 16*, 724–731.

Keppel, G., & Wickens, T. D. (2004). *Design and analysis: A researcher's handbook*. Upper Saddle River, NJ: Pearson.

Killingsworth, M. A., & Gilbert, D. T. (2010). A wandering mind is an unhappy mind. *Science, 330*, 932.

Krantz, J. H., & Dalal, R. (2000). Validity of web-based psychological research. In M. H. Birnbaum (Ed.), *Psychological experiments on the Internet* (pp. 35–60). San Diego, CA: Academic Press.

Kumar, A., Killingsworth, M. A., & Gilovich, T. (2014). Waiting for Merlot: Anticipatory consumption of experiential and material purchases. *Psychological Science, 25*, 1924–1931.

Lakin, J. L., Chartrand, T. L., & Arkin, R. M. (2008). I am too just like you: Nonconscious mimicry as an automatic behavioral response to social exclusion. *Psychological Science, 19*, 816–822.

Laland, K. N., & Galef, B. G. (2009). *The question of animal culture*. Cambridge, MA: Harvard University Press.

Landrum, R. E., & Nelson, L. R. (2002). The undergraduate research assistantship: An analysis of the benefits. *Teaching of Psychology, 29*, 15–19.

Landsberger, H. (1955). Interaction process analysis of professional behavior: A study of labor mediators in twelve labor-management disputes. *American Sociological Review, 20*, 566–575.

Lee, L., Frederick, S., & Ariely, D. (2006). Try it, you'll like it: The influence of expectation, consumption, and revelation on preferences for beer. *Psychological Science, 17*, 1054–1058.

Lester, D. (2006). Understanding suicide through studies of diaries: The case of Cesare Pavese. *Archives of Suicide Research, 10*, 295–302.

Levine, L. J., Burgess, S. L., & Laney, C. (2008). Effects of discrete emotions on young children's suggestibility. *Developmental Psychology, 44*, 681–694.

Libby, A. M., Brent, D. A., Morrato, E. H., Orton, H. D., Allen, R., & Valuck, R. J. (2007). Decline in treatment of pediatric depression after FDA advisory on risk of suicidality with SSRIs. *American Journal of Psychiatry, 164*, 884–891.

Lipman, P. D., & Caplan, L. J. (1992). Adult age differences in memory for routes: Effects of instruction and spatial diagram. *Psychology and Aging, 7*, 435–442.

Loftus, E. F. (1993). Psychologists in the eyewitness world. *American Psychologist, 48*, 550–552.

Loftus, E. F. (2005). Planting misinformation in the human mind: A 30-year investigation of the malleability of memory. *Learning and Memory, 12*, 361–366.

Loftus, G. R. (1993). A picture is worth a thousand *p* values: On the irrelevance of hypothesis testing in the microcomputer age. *Behavior Research Methods, Instruments, & Computers, 25*, 250–256.

Luo, S., Chen, H., Yue, G., Zhang, G., Zhaoyang, R., & Xu, D. (2008). Predicting marital satisfaction from self, partner, and couple characteristics: Is it me, you, or us? *Journal of Personality, 76*, 1231–1265.

Lyness, K. S., & Judiesch, M. K. (2008). Can a manager have a life and a career? International and multisource perspectives on work-life balance and career advancement potential. *Journal of Applied Psychology, 93*, 789–805.

Magen, E., Dweck, C. S., & Gross, J. J. (2008). The hidden zero effect: Representing a single choice as an extended sequence reduces impulsive choice. *Psychological Science, 19*, 648–649.

Magoon, M. A., & Critchfield, T. S. (2008). Concurrent schedules of positive and negative reinforcement: Differential-impact and differential-outcomes hypotheses. *Journal of the Experimental Analysis of Behavior, 90*, 1–22.

McBride, D. M., Coane, J. H., & Raulerson, B. (2006). An investigation of false memory in perceptual implicit tasks. *Acta Psychologica, 123*, 240–260.

McNally, R. J. (2003). Recovering memories of trauma: A view from the laboratory. *Current Directions in Psychological Science, 12*, 32–35.

Messick, S. (1995). Validity of psychological assessment: Validation of inferences from persons' responses and performances as scientific inquiry into score meaning. *American Psychologist, 50*, 741–749.

Meyers, D. G. (2007). *Psychology* (8th ed.). New York, NY: Worth.

Middlemist, D. R., Knowles, E. S., & Matter, C. F. (1976). Personal space invasions in the lavatory: Suggestive evidence for arousal. *Journal of Personality and Social Psychology, 33*, 541–546.

Mihai, A., Damsa, C., Allen, M., Baleydier, B., Lazignac, C., & Heinz, A. (2006). Viewing videotape of themselves while experiencing delirium tremens could reduce the relapse rate in alcohol-dependent patients. *Addiction, 102*, 226–231.

Milgram, S. (1963). Behavioral study of obedience. *Journal of Abnormal and Social Psychology, 67*, 371–378.

Mook, D. G. (1983). The state of the art and the fate of the earth. *Journal of the Experimental Analysis of Behavior, 40*, 343–350.

Moore, D. S., & Johnson, S. P. (2008). Mental rotation in human infants: A sex difference. *Psychological Science, 19*, 1063–1066.

Moore, D. W. (2004). *Sweet dreams go with a good night's sleep*. Retrieved January 11, 2008, from http://www.gallup.com/poll/14380/Sweet-Dreams-Good-Nights-Sleep.aspx

Morales, L. (2008). *Most Americans consider smoking very harmful*. Retrieved August 5, 2008, from http://www.gallup.com/poll/109129/Most-Americans-Consider-Smoking-Very-Harmful.aspx

Morin, C. M., Belanger, L., & Fortier-Brochu, E. (2006). Sleep, insomnia, and psychopathology. *Canadian Psychology/Pschologie Canadienne, 47*, 245–262.

Morphy, H., Dunn, K. M., Lewis, M., Boardman, H. F., & Croft, P. R. (2007). Epidemiology of insomnia: A longitudinal study in a UK population. *Sleep: Journal of Sleep and Sleep Disorders Research, 30*, 274–280.

Mueller, C. M., & Dweck, C. S. (1998). Praise for intelligence can undermine children's motivation and performance. *Journal of Personality and Social Psychology, 75*, 33–52.

Nairne, J. S. (2009). *Psychology*. Belmont, CA: Thompson Wadsworth.

Nairne, J. S., VanArsdall, J. E., Pandeirada, J. N. S., Cogdill, M., & LeBreton, J. M. (2013). Adaptive memory: The mnemonic value of animacy. *Psychological Science, 24*, 2099–2105.

National Commission for the Protection of Human Subjects of Biomedical and Behavioral Research. (1979). *Belmont report*. Washington, DC: Department of Health and Human Services.

National Institutes for Health. (2011). *Medline Plus*. Retrieved June 29, 2011, from http://www.nlm.nih.gov/medlineplus/druginfo/natural/993.html

Nauta, M. M. (2007). Assessing college students' satisfaction with their academic majors. *Journal of Career Assessment, 15*, 446–462.

Neath, I., & Surprenant, A. (2003). *Human memory*. Belmont, CA: Wadsworth.

Nuseir, K., Heidenreich, B. A., & Proudfit, H. K. (1999). The antinociception produced by microinjection of a cholinergic agonist in the ventromedial medulla is mediated by noradrenergic neurons in the A7 catecholamine cell group. *Brain Research, 822*, 1–7.

Oakes, W. (1972). External validity and the use of real people as subjects. *American Psychologist, 27*, 959–962.

O'Hanlon, C. G., & Roberson, D. (2006). Learning in context: Linguistic and attentional constraints on children's color term learning. *Journal of Experimental Child Psychology, 94*, 275–300.

Olson, K. R., Banaji, M. R., Dweck, C. S., & Spelke, E. S. (2006). Children's biased evaluations of lucky versus unlucky people and their social groups. *Psychological Science, 17*, 845–846.

Olzmann, J. A. (2007). Pathogenic mechanisms of DJ-1 in Parkinson's disease. *Dissertation Abstracts International: Section B: The Sciences and Engineering, 68*, 2857.

Paivio, A. (2007). *Mind and its evolution: A dual coding theoretical approach.* London, UK: Psychology Press.

Pal, S., & Saksvik, P. O. (2008). Work-family conflict and psychosocial work environment stressors as predictors of job stress in a cross-cultural study. *International Journal of Stress Management, 15*, 22–42.

Park, A. (2007, July 11). When tomatoes fight cancer. *Time.* Retrieved July 22, 2011, from http://www.time.com/time/health/article/0,8599,1642152,00.html

Patterson, C. L., Uhlin, B., & Anderson, T. (2008). Clients' pretreatment counseling expectations as predictors of the working alliance. *Journal of Counseling Psychology, 55*, 528–534.

Peña, M., Arias, D., & Dehaene-Lambertz, G. (2014). Gaze following is accelerated in healthy preterm infants. *Psychological Science, 25*, 1884–1892.

Perilloux, C., & Kuzban, R. (2015). Do men overperceive women's sexual interest? *Psychological Science, 26*, 70–77.

Platt, J. R. (1964). Strong inference. *Science, 146*, 347–353.

Reese-Weber, M., & McBride, D. M. (in press). The effects of sexually-explicit literature on sexual behaviors and desires of women. *Psychology of Popular Media Culture.* doi:10.1037/ppm0000044

Regia-Corte, T., & Wagman, J. B. (2008). Perception of affordances for standing on an inclined surface depends on height of center of mass. *Experimental Brain Research, 191*, 25–35.

Reiniger, H. (Producer). (2001). *Discovering psychology* (Updated ed.) [Television series]. Burlington, VT: Annenberg.

Retrospection: Social sciences' problematic interfaces with the social order. (2008). *PsycCRITIQUES, 53*. Retrieved June 9, 2009, from http://psych.hanover.edu/research/exponnet.html

Robert Wood Johnson Foundation. (2013). *F as in fat: How obesity threatens America's future 2013.* Retrieved July 12, 2015, from http://www.rwjf.org/en/library/research/2013/08/f-as-in-fat--how-obesity-threatens-america-s-future-2013.html

Roediger, H. L., III, & McDermott, K. B. (1993). Implicit memory in normal human subjects. In F. Boller & J. Grafman (Eds.), *Handbook of neuropsychology* (Vol. 8, pp. 63–131). Amsterdam, the Netherlands: Elsevier.

Rosenthal, R., & Rosnow, R. L. (2008). *Essentials of behavioral research: Methods and data analysis* (3rd ed.). New York, NY: McGraw-Hill.

Rosnow, R. L., Rosenthal, R., McConochie, R. M., & Arms, R. L. (1969). Volunteer effects on experimental outcomes. *Educational and Psychological Measurement, 29*, 825–846.

Rubin, D. C., & Friendly, M. (1986). Predicting which words get recalled: Measures of free recall, availability, goodness, emotionality, and pronunciability for 925 nouns. *Memory & Cognition, 14*, 79–94.

Sackett, P. R., Kuncel, N. R., Arneson, J. J., Cooper, S. R., & Waters, S. D. (2009). Does socioeconomic status explain the relationship between admissions tests and post-secondary academic performance? *Psychological Bulletin, 135*, 1–22.

Sanders, M. A., Shirk, S. D., Burgin, C. J., & Martin, L. L. (2012). The gargle effect: Rinsing the mouth with glucose enhances self-control. *Psychological Science, 23*, 1470–1472.

Schnall, S., Benton, J., & Harvey, S. (2008). With a clean conscience: Cleanliness reduces the severity of moral judgments. *Psychological Science, 19*, 1219–1222.

Schnall, S., Haidt, J., Clore, G. L., & Jordan, A. H. (2008). Disgust as embodied moral judgment. *Personality and Social Psychology Bulletin, 34*, 1096–1109.

Schuler, H. (1982). *Ethical problems in psychological research.* New York, NY: Academic Press.

Sears, D. O. (1986). College sophomores in the laboratory: Influence of a narrow data base on social psychology's view of human nature. *Journal of Personality and Social Psychology, 51*, 515–530.

Shadish, W. R., Cook, T. D., & Campbell, D. T. (2002). *Experimental and quasi-experimental designs for generalized causal inference.* Boston, MA: Houghton Mifflin.

Sharratt, M. (1996). *Galileo: Decisive innovator*. London, UK: Cambridge University Press.

Shaw, J., & Porter, S. (2015). Constructing rich false memories of committing crime. *Psychological Science, 26*, 291–301.

Shea, C. (2011, November 13). Fraud scandal fuels debate over practices of social psychology. Chronicle of Higher Education. Retrieved July 12, 2015, from http://chronicle.com/article/As-Dutch-Research-Scandal/129746/

Silvers, J. A., Insel, C., Powers, A., Franz, P., Weber, J., Mischel, W., … Ochsner, K. N. (2014). Curbing craving: Behavioral and brain evidence that children regulate craving when instructed to do so but have higher baseline craving than adults. *Psychological Science, 25*, 1932–1942.

Smith, S. M., & Moynan, S. C. (2008). Forgetting and recovering the unforgettable. *Psychological Science, 19*, 462–468.

Sofer, C., Dotsch, R., Wigboldus, D. H. J., & Todorov, A. (2015). What is typical is good: The influence of face typicality on perceived trustworthiness. *Psychological Science, 26*, 39–47.

Solomon, B. C., & Jackson, J. J. (2014). The long reach of one's spouse: Spouse's personality influences occupational success. *Psychological Science, 25*, 2189–2198.

Storm, B. C., & Stone, S. M. (2015). Saving-enhanced memory: The benefits of saving on the learning and remembering of new information. *Psychological Science, 26*, 182–188.

Strayer, D. L., & Johnston, W. A. (2001). Driven to distraction: Dual-task studies of simulated driving and conversing on a cellular phone. *Psychological Science, 12*, 462–466.

Sue, S. (1999). Science, ethnicity, and bias: Where have we gone wrong? *American Psychologist, 54*, 1070–1077.

Szekely, C. A., Breitner, J. C. S., & Zandi, P. P. (2007). Prevention of Alzheimer's disease. *International Review of Psychiatry, 19*, 693–706.

Tasky, K. K., Rudrud, E. H., Schulze, K. A., & Rapp, J. T. (2008). Using choice to increase on-task behaviors in individuals with traumatic brain injury. *Journal of Applied Behavior Analysis, 41*, 261–265.

Tharp, R. G., Estrada, P., Dalton, S. S., & Yamauchi, L. A. (2000). *Teaching transformed: Achieving excellence, fairness, inclusion, and harmony*. Boulder, CO: Westview.

Tversky, A., & Kahneman, D. (1981). The framing of decisions and the psychology of choice. *Science, 211*, 453–458.

U.S. Department of Agriculture. (2007). *Animal Welfare Act*. Retrieved June 15, 2008, from http://www.aphis.usda.gov/animal_welfare/downloads/awa/awa.pdf

U.S. Department of Health and Human Services. (2005). *Code of federal regulations*. Retrieved June 15, 2008, from http://www.hhs.gov/ohrp/humansubjects/guidance/45cfr46.html

Van Bavel, J. J., Packer, D. J., & Cunningham, W. A. (2008). The neural substrates of in-group bias: A functional magnetic resonance imaging investigation. *Psychological Science, 19*, 1131–1139.

Verde, M. F. (2009). The list-strength effect in recall: Relative-strength competition and retrieval inhibition may both contribute to forgetting. *Journal of Experimental Psychology: Learning, Memory, and Cognition, 36*, 205–220.

Vogt, W. P. (2005). *Dictionary of statistics and methodology* (3rd ed.). Thousand Oaks, CA: Sage.

Vohs, K. D., & Schooler, J. W. (2008). The value of believing in free will: Encouraging a belief in determinism increases cheating. *Psychological Science, 19*, 49–54.

Wagman, J. B., & Taylor, K. R. (2005). Perceiving affordances for aperture crossing for the person-plus-object system. *Ecological Psychology, 17*, 105–130.

Wakefield, A. J., Murch, S. H., Anthony, A., Linnell, J., Casson, D. M., Mali, M., … Walker-Smith, J. A. (1998). Ileal-lymphoid-nodular hyperplasia, non-specific colitis, and pervasive developmental disorder in children. *The Lancet, 351*, 637–641.

Wallis, C. (1987, October 12). Back off, buddy. *Time, 130*, 68.

Wayment, H. A., & Dickson, K. L. (2008). Increasing student participation in undergraduate research benefits students, faculty, and department. *Teaching of Psychology, 35*, 194–197.

Wilson, R. S., Scherr, P. A., Schneider, J. A., Tang, Y., & Bennett, D. A. (2007). Relation of cognitive activity to risk of developing Alzheimer disease. *Neurology, 69*, 1911–1920.

Wiltermuth, S. S., & Heath, C. (2009). Synchrony and cooperation. *Psychological Science, 20,* 1–5.

Witelson, S., Kigar, D. L., & Harvey, T. (1999). The exceptional brain of Albert Einstein. *Lancet, 353,* 2149–2153.

Wynn, K. (1992). Addition and subtraction by human infants. *Nature, 358,* 749–750.

Xin, Z. (2001). *Values and behaviors in Chinese college students.* Unpublished doctoral dissertation.

Zimbardo, P. G. (1973). On the ethics of intervention in human psychological research: With special reference to the Stanford prison experiment. *Cognitions, 2,* 243–256.

Zimbardo, P. G. (1974). On "Obedience to authority." *American Psychologist, 29,* 566–567.

Zimmerman, C., Gerson, S., Monroe, A., & Kearney, A. M. (2007). Physics is harder than psychology (or is it?): Developmental differences in calibration of domain-specific texts. In D. S. McNamara & J. G. Trafton (Eds.), *Proceedings of the twenty-ninth annual Cognitive Science Society* (pp. 1683–1688). Austin, TX: Cognitive Science Society.

Index